HARDEN'S

UK Restaurants
2002

© Harden's Limited 2001

ISBN 1-873721-45-5 (paperback)
ISBN 1-873721-44-7 (bonded leather)

British Library Cataloguing-in-Publication data:
a catalogue record for this book is available from
the British Library.

Printed and bound in Finland by
WS Bookwell Ltd

Editorial Manager: Antonia Russell
Production Manager: Elizabeth Warman
Research assistant: Frances Gill

Harden's Limited
14 Buckingham Street
London WC2N 6DF

CONTENTS

HOW THIS BOOK IS ORGANISED

As response to the format of our London guide has generally been very favourable, we have tried, to the extent possible, to observe the same principles here.

London is covered first, and, in recognition of the scale and diversity of its restaurant scene, has an extensive introduction and indexes, as well as its own maps.
After the London section, the guide is organised strictly by place name – we could see no logic in separating England from Scotland, Wales and Northern Ireland, so Chester, Clachan and Cardiff alike appear under 'C'.

For *cities and larger towns*, you can therefore turn straight to the relevant section. In the major restaurant centres you will find a brief introduction before the reviews.

In *less densely populated areas*, you will generally find it easiest to start with the map of the relevant area at the back of the book, which will guide you to the appropriate place names.

HOW THIS BOOK IS RESEARCHED

This book is the result of a research effort involving some 10,000 people – our 'reporters'. This year, over 5,000 contributed to our eleventh annual survey of London restaurant-goers, and our fourth survey of restaurant-goers outside the capital similarly attracted over 5,000 participants.

The density of the feedback on London (where many of the top places attract several hundred reviews each) is such that the ratings for the restaurants in the capital included in this edition are almost exclusively statistical in derivation. We have, as it happens, visited all the restaurants in the London section, anonymously, and at our own expense, but we use our personal experiences only to inform the standpoint from which to interpret the consensus opinion.

In the case of the more commented-upon provincial restaurants, we have adopted an approach very similar to London. In the case of less-visited provincial establishments, however, the interpretation of survey results owes as much to art as it does to science.

In our experience, smaller establishments are – for better or worse – generally quite consistent, and we have therefore felt able to place a relatively high level of confidence in a lower level of commentary. Conservatism on our part, however, may have led to some smaller places being under-rated compared to their more visited peers.

RATINGS & PRICES

We see little point in traditional rating systems, which generally tell you nothing more than that expensive restaurants are 'better' than cheap ones because they use costlier ingredients and attempt more ambitious dishes. You probably knew that already. Our system assumes that, as prices rise, so do diners' expectations.

Prices and ratings are shown as follows:

£ Price

The cost of a three-course *dinner* for one person. We include half a bottle of house wine, coffee and service (or a 10% tip if there is no service charge).

Food

The following symbols indicate that, **in comparison with other restaurants in the same price-bracket**, the cooking at the establishment is:

★★   **Exceptional**
★   **Very good**

This year we have also introduced a new category for places which attract a notably high proportion of adverse comment:

✗   **Disappointing**

Ambience

Restaurants which provide a setting which is very charming, stylish or 'buzzy' are indicated as follows:

𝔸   **Particularly atmospheric**

Small print

Telephone number – All numbers in the London section are (020) numbers. Dublin numbers are shown for dialling within the Republic (the international code for which is + 353).

Sample dishes – these dishes exemplify the style of cooking at a particular establishment. They are merely samples – it is unlikely that these specific dishes will be available at the time of your visit.

Value tip – if we know of a particularly good-value set menu or some similar handy tip, we note this. Set lunch deals are for weekdays, unless stated. Details change, so always check ahead.

Details – the following information is given where relevant.

Directions – to help you find the establishment.

Website – if applicable.

Last orders time – at dinner (Sun may be up to 90 mins earlier).

Opening hours – unless otherwise stated, restaurants are open for lunch and dinner seven days a week.

Credit and debit cards – unless otherwise stated, Mastercard, Visa, Amex and Switch are accepted.

Dress – where appropriate, the management's preferences concerning patrons' dress are given.

Smoking – cigarette smoking restrictions are noted. Pipe or cigar smokers should always check ahead.

Children – if we know of a specified minimum age for children, we note this.

Accommodation – if an establishment has rooms, we list how many and the minimum price for a double.

FROM THE EDITORS

Although we have been in the business of publishing restaurant guides (to London) for the past eleven years, this is only the fourth edition of our guide to the UK as a whole.

In previous editions the books title was "Top UK Restaurants". This year we have dropped the 'Top', for fear that people might think our interest might be limited to expensive establishments. In fact, no other guide gives such a broad account of good and inexpensive pubs, cafés and chippies and we hope the new name reflects this better.

London restaurants have undergone a complete transformation during the period over which we have been writing guides about them. The period since we began publishing the UK guide has – no doubt coincidentally – seen the stirring of a similar revolution across the British Isles as a whole. It is exciting to play a part in recording what on any analysis is an important period of evolution and improvement of the British restaurant scene.

It would be a very arrogant – and, indeed, stupid – publisher who claimed any guide book as perfect, and we certainly make no such claim for this one. However, thanks largely to a high level of survey feedback, we have again been able to make this fourth edition of the guide bigger and, we believe, better balanced and more accurate than the previous editions. We hope that readers will think so too.

Our coverage in some areas is more patchy than we would like – especially in Ireland, and particularly in the Republic. Rather than cover it in an inconsistent and arbitrary manner, this year we have limited our reviewing to Dublin. Even in the heartland of England, however, there are surely deserving places which have been passed over. If you notice omissions, please remember that the solution lies partially in your own hands.

Assembling a large number of people interested to contribute their views on restaurants is no easy task, and we are most grateful to readers of the *Daily Telegraph* who completed survey forms distributed with the newspaper. We are no less grateful to the growing band of our "own" reporters who also took part.

All restaurant guides are the subject of continual revision. This is especially true when the restaurant scene is undergoing a period of rapid change, as at present. **Please help us to make the next edition even more comprehensive and accurate.** If you register for your free update (by returning the reply-paid card at the back of the book, by e-mail, or on the web at www.hardens.com) you will be invited, in the spring of 2002, to participate in our next survey. **If you take part you will, on publication, receive a complimentary copy of Harden's UK Restaurants 2003.**

Richard Harden   **Peter Harden**

LONDON
INTRODUCTION
& SURVEY RESULTS

LONDON INTRODUCTION

London today is incomparably a more interesting city to eat in than it was a decade ago. Not only are restaurants opening at a faster rate than ever, but this activity is being complemented by a diversity of cuisine, style, scale of operations and location without equal in the city's history. For quality *and* range, London now has only one serious competitor in the world, New York City. So great is the diversity that the choice can be rather daunting for the newcomer or occasional visitor, and this section is designed to be give you a few orientation points from which to navigate what follows.

A good starting point is the results from our London survey. On page 13 you will see which are the restaurants which Londoners themselves think are most worth talking about. Nowadays (it wasn't always so in recent years) it tends to be *quality* that gets a restaurant noticed, and if you're making a special dining visit to London you will probably want to include one or more of the places on that list.

If your ambitions are more local the area overviews (starting on page 56) will help you pick out the best places in any particular *quartier*. One of the joys of London nowadays is that there are few areas which do not have several restaurants well worth seeking out. We hope that the following answers to some Frequently Asked Questions will also assist.

Which is London's best restaurant?

'Best' in this sense still usually means 'grand French', and there are still relatively few truly world-class restaurants. Arguably, there are only two – *Gordon Ramsay* (modern) and *Le Gavroche* (traditional). *Pétrus,* however, might reasonably now be said to be beginning to establish itself in that class, and the *Capital Hotel* has an impressively consistent record over a long period, if perhaps one just short of the very first rank. As we go to press, Mr Ramsay is opening a second restaurant, at Claridges, which may well turn out to be a contender. Two restaurants which seldom make the gossip columns, but which score highly in our survey include *Pied à Terre* – a low key, foodie temple in Marylebone – and the City's *Tatsuso*, London's best Japanese.

Where would I go for old-fashioned grandeur?

Some of the top hotel dining rooms are worth seeking out for their stylish and comfortable settings and very good service. The *Connaught* is often held up as the benchmark of culinary consistency, and its less culinarily ambitious Mayfair competitor, the *Dorchester Grill,* offers a lot of spirited grandeur. At a slightly more modest cost, London's oldest restaurant, *Rules,* manages – remarkably – not to be a tourist trap.

Where is the culinary 'cutting-edge'?

'Fusion' between European and Eastern cuisines is the trendy culinary frontier of the moment. As a fashionable as well as culinary phenomenon, there's nowhere to beat *Nobu*. Among more established restaurants, the *Sugar Club* goes from strength to strength. *Mju*, *Nahm* and *The Providores* are newcomers with considerable ambitions.

Hang the food – where are the 'in' places?

The most perennially 'in' restaurants in London are the (always difficult to book) duo, *The Ivy* and *Le Caprice*. *Nobu* has become a major star venue. Oblivious, apparently, to such considerations as quality of cooking and service, the media and fashion worlds still seem besotted with the wacky creations of American design-hotelier Ian Schrager – *Asia de Cuba* and *Spoon+*. For what used to be called the jet-set, Knightsbridge's upmarket Italian restaurants retain a magnetic attraction.

Are there any key cuisines to seek out?

Two national cuisines currently account for a disproportionate number of the more interesting places.

Indian
London's pre-eminence as a city of Indian restaurants continues to grow, and it offers a range of outstanding places at all price-levels. At the grander end of the market London attempts 'haute' Indian cuisine in a way not really seen elsewhere, and the best names include the newly-opened *Cinnamon Club*, as well as *La Porte des Indes*, *Tamarind*, *Vama* and *Zaika* and, in a more traditional style, *Salloos*. In contrast, some of the best subcontinental food in London is incredibly cheap, and three of the names that have stood the test of time in recent years are *Kastoori, Rasa* and the *Lahore Kebab House*.

Italian
London's Italian cooking has in recent years emerged with a vengeance from the Anglicised torpor which has dominated since the '50s. Modern Italian establishments now offer some of the most exciting continental cuisine available. Notable followers of the new school include *Assaggi, Passione, Zafferano,* and the rising *Teca*. The famed *River Café* generates rather mixed feedback, largely on account of its punishing prices.

Suggestions for a good night out on a budget?

For top-quality food on a budget, ethnic restaurants are almost invariably the top choice – see the lists on page 14. Suggestions for a fun night out at relatively modest cost include *Pizza Metro, Sarastro, Souk* and *Andrew Edmunds*.

What about good pubs?

In the past decade, London has pioneered the concept of pub as a quality eating place where the cooking has nothing to do with traditional notions of pub grub. The original 'super-pub', Farringdon's *Eagle*, is still one of the best. Others worth seeking out include (to the west) the *Anglesea Arms* and the *Havelock Tavern*, and (to the north) the *Duke of Cambridge* and the *Engineer*.

Does London offer much choice for vegetarians?

Most London restaurants – the most notable exceptions being some of the classic French establishments – provide some vegetarian options, presumably explaining the existence of relatively few specialist veggies of any interest. *Blah!Blah!Blah!* and *The Gate* (which has a new north London offshoot) are notable exceptions. Some of the best vegetarian food is ethnic: Southern Indian, Greek, Turkish and Lebanese establishments almost invariably offer a good range of non-meat choices.

Are there any good rooms with views?

There seems to be an (almost) inexorable rule that London restaurants with views feel no particular obligation to provide food of particular interest – the egregious *Oxo Tower*, which has the best of the views, is a case in point. Two other places merit recommendation – *Twentyfour*, half-way up the former NatWest Tower, and *The Tenth*, a little-known hotel dining room which has an impressive view over Kensington Gardens.

Anything to avoid?

The West End – and in particular Covent Garden and many of the major thoroughfares – has many lacklustre restaurants so taking 'pot luck' is not really advisable. There *are* quality places, of course, and at all price levels – use the guide! Also, beware of concièrge recommendations to the huge brasseries which have opened over the past few years: it may be convenient for *him* to make you one of a block-booking of a dozen tables, but size is no guarantee of quality and our survey shows that discerning locals are fleeing these establishments in droves. If you insist on checking out these 'mega-brasseries', by far the best of them are *Bank* and *Le Palais du Jardin*.

SURVEY – MOST MENTIONED

These are the restaurants which were most frequently mentioned by reporters. (Last year's position is given in brackets.) An asterisk* indicates the first appearance in the list of a recently-opened restaurant.

1	The Ivy (1)
2	Oxo Tower (2)
3	Mirabelle (3)
4	Nobu (4)
5	Le Caprice (6)
6	J Sheekey (16)
7	Chez Bruce (13)
8	Gordon Ramsay (11)
9	Blue Elephant (7)
10	Pétrus (23)

11	Bank (12)
12	Zafferano (14)
13	Zaika (31)
14	The Square (9)
15	Club Gascon (21)
16	La Poule au Pot (17=)
17=	The River Café (10)
17=	Andrew Edmunds (27)
19	The Sugar Club (24)
20	Le Gavroche (19)

21=	Bluebird (5)
21=	The Criterion (17=)
23=	Moro (38)
23=	Coq d'Argent (25)
25	City Rhodes (22)
26	Smiths of Smithfield*
27	Bleeding Heart (-)
28	Bibendum (20)
29	Quaglino's (16)
30	Chutney Mary (29)

31	Mezzo (28)
32=	Le Palais du Jardin (30)
32=	Incognico (-)
34	Rules (39)
35	Joe Allen (40)
36	Tas*
37=	Vong (26)
37=	Asia de Cuba (-)
39=	1 Lombard Street (33)
39=	The Eagle (32)

LONDON – HIGHEST RATINGS

These are the restaurants which received the best average food ratings. All of the restaurants listed here are in the directory which starts on page 18.

We have divided the most represented restaurant cuisines (opposite) into two price-brackets – under and over £40.

Where the less represented cuisines (below) are concerned, just the best three performers in the survey are shown, regardless of price-bracket.

British, Traditional
1. Connaught
2. Dorchester Grill
3. Odin's

Vegetarian
1. The Gate W6, NW3
2. Blah! Blah! Blah!
3. Food for Thought

Burgers, etc
1. Gourmet Burger K'n
2. Hard Rock Café
3. Sticky Fingers

Pizza
1. Pizza Metro
2. Basilico
3. Pizzeria Castello

East/West
1. Nobu
2. Ubon
3. The Sugar Club

Thai
1. Thailand
2. Talad Thai
3. Chiang Mai

Fish & Chips
1. Faulkner's
2. Nautilus
3. Seashell

Fish & Seafood
1. Chez Liline
2. J Sheekey
3. Poissonnerie de l'Ave

Greek
1. The Real Greek
2. Vrisaki
3. Daphne

Spanish
1. Cambio de Tercio
2. Lomo
3. Gaudi

Turkish
1. Pasha
2. Ozer
3. Iznik

Lebanese
1. Ranoush
2. Phoenicia
3. Fairuz

Modern British

£40 and over
1 Chez Bruce
2 Clarke's
3 City Rhodes
4 Lindsay House
5 The Ivy

Under £40
1 The Glasshouse
2 Mesclun
3 The Stepping Stone
4 Parade
5 The Havelock Tavern

French

£40 and over
1 Gordon Ramsay
2 Pétrus
3 Le Gavroche
4 Monsieur Max
5 Capital Hotel

Under £40
1 Chinon
2 Les Associés
3 La Trompette
4 Soulard
5 Café du Marché

Italian/Mediterranean

£40 and over
1 Assaggi
2 Zafferano
3 Toto's
4 Passione
5 Teca

Under £40
1 Riva
2 Enoteca Turi
3 Alba
4 Il Bordello
5 Il Convivio

Indian

£40 and over
1 Zaika
2 Salloos
3 The Cinnamon Club
4 Tamarind
5 La Porte des Indes

Under £40
1 Kastoori
2 Rasa
3 Lahore Kebab House
4 Sarkhel's
5 Vama

Chinese

£40 and over
1 Kai
2 Ken Lo's Memories
3 Dorchester, Oriental
4 Mr Wing
5 Mr Chow

Under £40
1 Royal China
2 Hunan
3 Mandarin Kitchen
4 Mr Kong
5 Fung Shing

Japanese

£40 and over
1 Tatsuso
2 City Miyama
3 Shogun
4 Matsuri
5 Suntory

Under £40
1 K10
2 Café Japan
3 Sushi Say
4 Inaho
5 Abeno

SURVEY – NOMINATIONS

Ranked by the number of reporters' votes for:

Top gastronomic experience

1. Gordon Ramsay (1)
2. The Ivy (2)
3. Nobu (4)
4. Chez Bruce (5)
5. Pétrus (8)
6. Mirabelle (3)
7. Club Gascon (9)
8. The Square (6)
9. Le Gavroche (7)
10. Zafferano (-)

Favourite

1. The Ivy (1)
2. Le Caprice (3)
3. Chez Bruce (2)
4. Nobu (5)
5. Mirabelle (4)
6. Gordon Ramsay (6)
7. Moro (-)
8. Zafferano (8)
9. Andrew Edmunds (-)
10. Oxo Tower (9)

Best for business

1. City Rhodes (1)
2. Bank (4)
3. 1 Lombard Street (2)
4. Coq d'Argent (7)
5. Oxo Tower (9)
6. The Square (3)
7. Savoy Grill (8)
8. The Ivy (5)
9. Prism (10)
10. Bleeding Heart (-)

Best for romance

1. La Poule au Pot (1)
2. Andrew Edmunds (2)
3. The Ivy (3)
4. Julie's (6)
5. Oxo Tower (4)
6. Odette's (5)
7. Le Caprice (8)
8. Blue Elephant (7)
9. Bleeding Heart (-)
10. Launceston Place (9)

LONDON DIRECTORY

Abeno WC1 £ 28 ★
47 Museum St 7405 3211 1–1C
For "a different experience" and one that's "fun" and "very
reasonably priced", try the okonomi-yaki – a "delicious and filling
novelty", akin to an exotic omelette – served by notably "friendly"
and "attentive" staff at this simple Japanese café, near the British
Museum. / **Sample dishes:** Japanese fish salad; pancakes with pork, squid &
prawns; tropical fruit salad. **Details:** 10 pm; no smoking area.

Admiral Codrington SW3 £ 37
17 Mossop St 7581 0005 4–2C
"Improved loads", since its days as Sloane Central, this elegantly
revamped boozer serves "surprisingly good" food at prices that are
"reasonable" for Brompton Cross; outside tables and a retractable
roof add to its appeal. / **Sample dishes:** foie gras & chicken liver parfait;
baked marlin with artichokes & lime sauce; treacle tart. **Details:** 11 pm.

Alba EC1 £ 35 ★
107 Whitecross St 7588 1798 5–1B
The location is "unpromising" and the décor "dull", but this low-key
spot near the Barbican, is probably "the best Italian in the City";
the "first-rate thin and crispy pizzas" have a particular following.
/ **Sample dishes:** calamari with aubergine caponata; braised rabbit wth
olives & polenta; pannetone with chocolate mousse. **Details:** 11 pm; closed
Sat & Sun.

Andrew Edmunds W1 £ 31 A★
46 Lexington St 7437 5708 2–2D
It's "harder than ever to get a table" at this "cosy", "Bohemian"
Soho "treasure"; with its "great value", simple food,
its "attitude-free" service and its "excellent, reasonably-priced wine
list", it "just can't be beat" (especially "for a date"). / **Sample
dishes:** courgette & rocket pesto cake; gnocchi with bacon & sausage; tarte
Tatin. **Details:** 10.45 pm.

The Anglesea Arms W6 £ 27 ★★
35 Wingate Rd 8749 1291
"The odd celebrity fighting for space" can add lustre to a trip to
this "top-notch" boozer, near Ravenscourt Park, which offers the
"ne plus ultra of gastropub fare"; "getting the food is a challenge",
though, given the "mind-numbing waits" and the sometimes "surly"
or "hostile" service. / **Sample dishes:** goujons of sole & scampi; papardelle
with lamb's sweetbreads & lardons; Knickerbocker Glory. **Details:** 10.45 pm;
no Amex; no booking.

Arancia SE16 £ 24 A★★
52 Southwark Park Rd 7394 1751
"Why aren't there more restaurants like this?" – this cosy,
"crowded" local in an unlovely Bermondsey location delivers simple,
"authentic Italian" grub that shows "class", and it's "keenly priced"
too. / **Sample dishes:** minestrone soup; seared tuna with balsamic vinegar
dressing; chocolate semi-freddo. **Details:** 11 pm; closed Mon L & Tue L;
no Amex.

Archipelago W1 £ 56 A★
110 Whitfield St 7383 3346 1–1B
"The weirdness factor adds to the fun" at this "eclectic, surreal,
and intimate" Fitzrovia establishment, whose "amazing" menu
is certainly "refreshingly different" – in many respects the place
continues from where its predecessor, The Birdcage (RIP), left off.
/ **Sample dishes:** peacock & tropical fruit satay; smoked open lasagne; ginger
brûlée with nashi pears. **Value tip:** set £36(FP). **Details:** 10.30 pm; closed
Sat L & Sun; no smoking area.

Asia de Cuba WC2   £ 62   ✗
45 St Martin's Ln   7300 5500   3–4C
You do get "beautiful people" in the dining room of Ian Schrager's
Theatreland design-hotel, but the place "is really let down by its
wacky fusion menu" and by "disinterested staff who seem to be
*paid by the frown". / **Sample dishes:** calamari with bitter greens &*
cashews; chilli pork in red wine miso; 'Bay of Pigs' banana spilt.
***Details:** midnight, Sat 1 am.*

Assaggi W2   £ 44   🅐★★
39 Chepstow Pl   7792 5501
"It's so tough to get a table here that it feels really special when
you do" – the "stunning" cooking and "great" personal service at
this "basic" room above a Bayswater boozer make it reporters'
*"best Italian in town". / **Sample dishes:** pan-fried Pecorino with Parma*
*ham; rack of lamb with spring vegetables; fig & almond tart. **Details:** 11 pm;*
closed Sun.

Les Associés N8   £ 29   🅐★
172 Park Rd   8348 8944
"France comes to north London" at this "tiny and delightful"
Crouch End "gem", which offers "simple but delicious" cooking and
*"excellent" service. / **Sample dishes:** skate salad with caper sauce; quail*
*stuffed with pork; lemon tart. **Details:** 10 pm; D only, except Sun open L only;*
no Amex.

Aubergine SW10   £ 69   ★
11 Park Walk   7352 3449   4–3B
For some, the atmosphere "doesn't quite work", but William
Drabble's "impressive" modern French cooking generally "makes up
for it" at this "discreet" Chelsea establishment; for those who think
it "too expensive", the "great-value lunch" is worth bearing in mind.
*/ **Sample dishes:** crab & cauliflower salad with avocado purée; poached*
*turbot with red wine sauce; cherry beignet soufflé. **Value tip:** set weekday L*
*£43(FP). **Details:** 10.30 pm; closed Sun; jacket required.*

Aurora W1   £ 35   🅐★
49 Lexington St   7494 0514   2–2D
"It's a shame it's not BYO any more", but this "chilled" and "sweet"
little place still offers "a small but interesting" menu and "very
friendly" service, and its tiny garden "really is a hidden Soho gem".
*/ **Sample dishes:** yellow pepper soup; pork with spiced red cabbage &*
*caramelised pears; sticky toffee pudding. **Value tip:** set always available*
*£19(FP). **Details:** 10.30 pm; closed Sun; no Amex.*

L'Aventure NW8   £ 40   🅐★★
3 Blenheim Ter   7624 6232
"They take pride in their food, their ivy and their fairy lights" at this
"little bit of France" – a "great" St John's Wood "all-rounder" (and
a top "romantic" destination); it's "best in summer on the patio".
*/ **Sample dishes:** snail & oyster mushroom fricasée; rabbit confit with*
*lemon & dried tomatoes; apricot compote with creme anglaise. **Value tip:** set*
*weekday L £26(FP). **Details:** 11 pm; closed Sat L (& Sun in winter); no Switch.*

Babylon W8   £ 60   🅐✗
99 Kensington High St   7368 3993   4–1A
An August '01 visit found good vibes and great views at the
Sir Richard Branson's luxurious new bar/restaurant atop
Kensington's Roof Gardens; only a tycoon, though, would wish
to pay the exorbitant price charged for cooking of such limited
*ambition. / **Sample dishes:** chicken with black pudding & apple sauce;*
*pot-roasted lobster; plum tart with yoghurt ice-cream. **Details:** 11.15 pm;*
closed Sat L & Sun D; booking essential.

Back to Basics W1 £ 35 ★★

21a Foley St 7436 2181 1–1B

Is this "the best-value fish restaurant in London"? – its "friendly" Fitzrovia premises may be "cramped" and "plain", but its "creative" dishes are "huge" and "exciting". / Sample dishes: monkfish & spicy prawn couscous; deep-fried Dover sole with tartare sauce; bananas & rum baked in foil. Details: www.backtobasics.uk.com; 9.45 pm; closed Sat & Sun.

Balans £ 31

60 Old Compton St, W1 7437 5212
239 Brompton Rd, SW3 7584 0070
239 Old Brompton Rd, SW5 7244 8838
187 Kensington High St, W8 7376 0115

"Food seems secondary to cruising" nowadays at this increasingly "complacent" chain of gay-friendly diners; as "great places for weekend brunch", they still many fans. / Sample dishes: Serrano ham with tomato toast & caperberries; square-cut spaghetti with shrimps & chilli; lime tart with blueberry compote. Details: www.balans.co.uk; 1 am – W1 Mon-Sat 5 am, Sun 1 am; W1 no booking – SW5 Sat & Sun no booking.

Bank WC2 £ 44

1 Kingsway 7379 9797 1–2D

It's "noisy", "impersonal" and "quite expensive", but this huge Theatreland brasserie wins continued popularity – especially for business and for brunch – with its "slick" service and "consistent" cooking. / Sample dishes: tuna with miso dressing; calves liver with bubble & squeak; honey nougat with iced cherries. Value tip: set weekday L & pre-th. £25(FP). Details: www.bankrestaurants.com; 11 pm.

Bar Italia W1 £ 7 🅐

22 Frith St 7437 4520 3–2A

"Exceptional coffee any time of the day or night" fuels the buzz at this phenomenal, cramped Soho "rendezvous". / Sample dishes: ham & tomato panini; four cheese pizza; tiramisu. Details: open 24 hours Mon-Sat, Sun 4 am; no credit cards; no booking.

Basilico £ 27 ★★

690 Fulham Rd, SW6 0800 028 3531
175 Lavender Hill, SW11 0800 389 9770
178 Upper Richmond Rd, SW15 0800 096 8202

"Redefining perceptions of pizza", these "excellent" take-aways (with a few seats in some branches) are unanimously hailed for their "brilliant" cooking. / Sample dishes: Caesar salad; smoked haddock & spinach pizza; bittersweet chocolate tart. Details: www.basilico.co.uk; 11pm; no Amex; no booking.

Beirut Express W2 £ 15 ★★

112-114 Edgware Rd 7724 2700

"What a find!", say fans of "the best kebabs", "excellent fruit juices" and other "cheap and plentiful" grub at this "bland"-looking Lebanese, which is open till very late. / Sample dishes: mezze; chicken & lamb kebabs; baklava. Details: www.maroush.com; 1.45 am; no credit cards.

Belvedere W8 £ 55 🅐

Holland Park, off Abbotsbury Rd 7602 1238

With its "lovely Holland Park location" and its "beautiful" décor, this "revived" classic has so much going for it; what a shame, then, that the new régime has delivered "the usual MPW price inflation, with little improvement over the previous owner's indifferent standards". / Sample dishes: tarte Tatin of endive & foie gras; smoked haddock with poached egg & colcannon; caramel soufflé. Value tip: set Sun L £35(FP). Details: www.whitestarline.org.uk; 11 pm.

Bibendum SW3   **£ 62**

81 Fulham Rd   7581 5817   4–2C

*Some still feel "spoilt" on a visit to this "assured" establishment at Brompton Cross, but for too many reporters it's "a real let-down" nowadays – "haughty" service has always been a problem, and the modern Gallic cooking now often seems "bland", as well as "overpriced". / **Sample dishes:** sea bass tartare with dill crostini; steak with foie gras pithivier; tarte Tatin. **Details:** www.bibendum.co.uk; 11.30 pm.*

Bibendum Oyster Bar SW3   **£ 36**   A★★

81 Fulham Rd   7589 1480   4–2C

*"Oysters and champagne, what else do you need?" – this "sleek" bar, in the entrance of the Conran Shop, offers a range of "first-rate", "simple" seafood in "stylish" surroundings' "why oh why", though, "can't you make reservations?" / **Sample dishes:** rock oysters; Bibendum terrine with toast & salad; crème brûlée. **Details:** www.bibendum.co.uk; 10.30 pm; no booking.*

Blah! Blah! Blah! W12   **£ 23**   ★★

78 Goldhawk Rd   8746 1337

*"Don't be put off by the outside and the décor" – this Shepherd's Bush café doles out "fabulous vegetarian food loved even by committed carnivores"; oddly (especially for a BYO place), they "won't serve tap water". / **Sample dishes:** warm mushroom salad; pasta with asparagus; blueberry & amaretti tart. **Details:** 11 pm; closed Sun; no credit cards.*

Blakes Hotel SW7   **£ 82**   A

33 Roland Gdns   7370 6701   4–2B

*"You're paying for the seduction" when you visit this "sensual" South Kensington boutique-hotel basement; the eclectic cooking is "very, very expensive", especially "for what it is". / **Sample dishes:** ginger soup with prawn gyoza; rack of lamb with rosemary; tamarillo sorbet with biscuits. **Details:** 11.30 pm.*

Bleeding Heart EC1   **£ 40**   A★

Bleeding Heart Yd, Greville St   7242 8238   5–2A

*"Hard to find, but worth the effort", this "tucked-away" Gallic basement near Holborn is a "cosy" and "inviting" warren, which offers "first-class" food and a "very good wine list"; it has "much more character than most City restaurants", and can make a "romantic" evening destination. / **Sample dishes:** scallops with fennel & ginger; Welsh lamb with rosemary jus; blueberry & blackberry mousse. **Details:** 10.30 pm; closed Sat & Sun.*

Blue Elephant SW6   **£ 42**   A★

4-6 Fulham Broadway   7385 6595   4–4A

*"A total experience"; this vast and "almost dreamlike" Fulham Thai – famed for its "exotic", "jungle" décor and "romantic" atmosphere – defies cynics by consistently delivering cooking that's "not cheap, but worth it". / **Sample dishes:** citrus fruit, chicken & prawn salad; sweet & sour pork with mushrooms & baby corn; sour mango & roasted coconut. **Value tip:** set weekday L £22(FP). **Details:** www.blueelephant.com; midnight; closed Sat L.*

Blue Jade SW1   **£ 27**   A★

44 Hugh St   7828 0321   1–4B

*This is a "bad district for food", so it's a pleasant surprise to come across this backstreet Pimlico Thai, with its "elegant" décor and "honest", "reliable" cooking. / **Sample dishes:** prawn satay; green chicken curry with jasmine rice; banana & coconut milk ice cream. **Details:** 11 pm; closed Sat L & Sun.*

Bluebird SW3　　　　　　　£ 44　　　X
350 King's Rd　7559 1000　4–3C
Some find "compensation in the coolish décor", but Conran's "mechanical" and "overpriced" Chelsea landmark offers "luck-of-the-draw" service and "dull" food. / *Sample dishes:* spring pea soup; sautéed kidneys & bacon in mustard sauce; apricot clafoutis. **Details:** www.conran.com; 11 pm.

Boiled Egg & Soldiers SW11　　　£ 17
63 Northcote Rd　7223 4894　6–2C
"The kids can be overpowering", at this "upmarket greasy spoon" in Wandsworth's 'Nappy Valley' – you can "barely get in without tripping over a pram"; the breakfast, though, is "a great hangover cure". / *Sample dishes:* egg, ham & cheese muffin; vegetable pie; carrot cake. **Details:** L & afternoon tea only; only Switch; no booking.

Bombay Bicycle Club SW12　　　£ 32　　A★
95 Nightingale Ln　8673 6217　6–2C
"Delicious", "fresh" Indian cooking served in a "very European" environment makes this "old-favourite" Wandsworth subcontinental a key south London destination; for top value, however, many tip the take-aways – from Battersea (7720 0500), Putney (8785 1188) or Wimbledon (8540 9997). / **Details:** 11 pm; D only, closed Sun.

Bombay Brasserie SW7　　　　£ 40　　A★
Courtfield Clo, Gloucester Rd　7370 4040　4–2B
"The best all-rounder, and about as authentic as you can get" – this large, "tastefully decorated" South Kensington subcontinental (with an impressive conservatory) makes a "great but pricey" choice. / *Sample dishes:* pomegranate & chickpea salad; tandoori salmon with yoghurt & cinnamon; mango kulfi. **Value tip:** set always available £26(FP). **Details:** www.bombaybrasserielondon.com; midnight.

Il Bordello E1　　　　　　　£ 30　　A★
75-81 Wapping High St　7481 9950
"Huge wagon wheel pizzas" at "affordable prices" win rave reviews from most reporters for this Wapping Italian, which is "always full and buzzing"; we're with the minority who find it "safe, if a little dull". / *Sample dishes:* avocado & prawns wrapped in salmon; seafood pizza; tiramisu. **Details:** 11 pm; closed Sat L.

Brick Lane Beigel Bake E1　　£ 4　　★★
159 Brick Ln　7729 0616
"The best bagels in London" – "the one filled with salt beef is the best ever" – are "well worth queuing for" at this amazing "no-frills", 24-7 East End institution. / *Sample dishes:* cream cheese & tomato beigel; salt beef sandwich; no puddings. **Details:** open 24 hours; no credit cards; no smoking; no booking.

The Builder's Arms SW3　　　£ 29　　A★
13 Britten St　7349 9040　4–2C
Tucked away "in a charming part of Chelsea", this "excellent" boozer offers "good menu variety" and "large portions"; in the best gastropub tradition, however, service can be "grumpy" and "slow". / *Sample dishes:* goats cheese & grilled vegetable salad; Cumberland sausages & mash; lemon Mascarpone ice cream. **Details:** 9.45 pm; no Amex; no booking.

Café Bagatelle W1　　　　　£ 31　　A
Manchester Sq　7563 9505　2–1A
Potentially it's "a great place", but the Wallace Collection's impressively glazed atrium café is starting to look like "a wasted opportunity"; some do praise "interesting" food, but more find it "pretentious", and service is "poor". / *Sample dishes:* Dolcelatte with walnut bread crostini; lemon sole in ham with fennel gratin; vanilla & liquorice parfait. **Details:** www.wallace-collection.com; L only; no smoking.

Café du Marché EC1 £ 38 A★

22 Charterhouse Sq   7608 1609   5–1B
*"You feel at ease" at this "engaging" "slice of France", on the fringe
of Smithfield – a "bustling" place, which is equally at home for
a "good business lunch" or a "lovely" dinner. / **Sample dishes:** fish
soup; prawn & herb risotto; cherry sorbet. **Details:** 10 pm; closed Sat L & Sun;
no Amex.*

Café Japan NW11 £ 27 ★★

626 Finchley Rd   8455 6854
*"Outstanding sushi" and other "great, inexpensive food" is winning
an ever-wider audience for this "homely" and "crowded" fixture,
near Golders Green BR; it's usually "full of local Japanese families".
/ **Sample dishes:** salt-grilled mackerel; soup noodles with prawn & vegetable
tempura; azuki red bean ice cream. **Value tip:** set D £13(FP).
Details: 10.30 pm; closed Mon & Tue L; no Amex; no smoking area.*

Café Spice Namaste £ 32 A★

247 Lavender Hill, SW11   7738 1717
16 Prescot St, E1   7488 9242
*"Adventurous combinations" create "unusual, but vivid tastes" at
Cyrus Todiwala's large and colourful east-City Indian; feedback on
the Battersea offshoot is limited but positive. / **Sample dishes:** Parsee
lamb dhansak; tandoori salmon with green chutney; pistachio kulfi. **Value
tip:** set Sun L £17(FP). **Details:** 10.30 pm – SW11 Sat 11.30 pm; E1 closed
Sat L & Sun – SW11 closed Mon, Tue-Sat D only, Sun open for L & D.*

Cambio de Tercio SW5 £ 37 A★

163 Old Brompton Rd   7244 8970   4–2B
*"Authentic", "vibrant" and "different" – this "buzzy" Earl's Court
venture is emerging as a "great" destination, where "wonderful and
efficient" staff serve "some of the best Spanish food in London".
/ **Sample dishes:** octopus with paprika & olive oil; roast suckling pig; gin &
tonic sorbet. **Details:** 11.30 pm.*

Cantinetta Venegazzú SW11 £ 33 A★

31-32 Battersea Sq   7978 5395   4–4C
*"Service and portions can be erratic", but that may be part of the
"wonderful authenticity" that charms fans of this "hectic" Battersea
Venetian; it's "cramped", but "nice outside in the summer".
/ **Sample dishes:** deep-fried courgettes; spaghetti with seafood; tiramisu.
Value tip: set weekday L £16(FP). **Details:** 11 pm.*

Capital Hotel SW3 £ 72 ★

22-24 Basil St   7589 5171   4–1D
*Eric Chavot's "classically excellent" cooking makes this small dining
room near Harrods "a Gallic heaven" for many reporters; opinions
divide, though, on the "formal"-going-on-"sterile" décor. / **Sample
dishes:** veal sweetbreads & ham with truffle gnocchi; roast lamb with boudin
blanc & green peas; strawberry gratin with basil sorbet. **Value tip:** set
weekday L £44(FP). **Details:** www.capitalhotel.co.uk; 11 pm; jacket & tie
required at D.*

Le Caprice SW1 £ 46 A★

Arlington Hs, Arlington St   7629 2239   2–4C
*"Still lovely, even without Corbin and King" – this "slick", 'in'-crowd
brasserie near the Ritz seems to have taken its erstwhile owners'
departure in its stride, and praise for the "always superb" service
and the "predictable but enjoyable" cooking is as strong as ever.
/ **Sample dishes:** Chinese crispy duck; squid with chorizo & figs; Scandinavian
iced berries. **Details:** midnight.*

Caraffini SW1 £ 35 A★

61-63 Lower Sloane St 7259 0235 4–2D

Trattorias don't come much more "friendly" and "reliable" than this "all-time fab" spot, just south of Sloane Square; the chief drawback with this "energetic" joint is that it's "just too popular". / **Sample dishes:** antipasti; scallops with spinach & mushrooms; crème brûlée. **Details:** www.caraffini.co.uk; 11.30 pm; closed Sun.

Champor-Champor SE1 £ 28 A★★

62 Weston St 7403 4600 5–4C

"Odd décor, brilliant food" – it's certainly "an experience" to visit this tiny Borough newcomer, where a chef from The Birdcage (the restaurant now known as Archipelago) realises a madly eclectic (mainly Asian) menu surprisingly successfully. / **Sample dishes:** chicken satay with steamed Indian bread; smoked cobra dumplings in vermicelli broth; black rice pudding with durian ice cream . **Details:** www.champor-champor.com; 10.30 pm; closed Mon L, Sat L & Sun; booking: max 8.

Chez Bruce SW17 £ 43 A★★

2 Bellevue Rd 8672 0114 6–2C

Bruce Poole's "consistently ace" cooking helps guarantee "a fantastic meal" at this monumentally popular Wandsworth Common-sider – "friendly" and "knowledgeable" service and a "great" wine list help make it a "brilliant" "all-rounder". / **Sample dishes:** asparagus frittata with ham & Manchego; rabbit with stuffed cabbage & polenta; cherry & almond tart. **Details:** 10.30 pm; closed Sun D; booking: max 6.

Chez Liline N4 £ 30 ★★

101 Stroud Green Rd 7263 6550

Ignore appearances – this "dilapidated" Finsbury Park institution is "still going strong", and its Mauritian seafood cooking offers some "amazing" and "fresh" flavours. / **Sample dishes:** tuna & pesto with rocket salad; snapper in Creole sauce; coconut & passion fruit sorbet. **Details:** 11 pm; closed Mon L & Sun L.

Chez Lindsay TW10 £ 26 A★

11 Hill Rise 8948 7473

"Very good crêpes and cider" are highlights of the "authentic" Breton cuisine on offer at this "informal" and "very friendly" fixture, near Richmond Bridge. / **Sample dishes:** mussels; seafood pancake; crepes Suzette. **Details:** 11 pm; no Amex.

Chez Moi W11 £ 40 A★

1 Addison Ave 7603 8267

"Amusing service" enlivens this Holland Park "old favourite", which has "very romantic" décor and offers "predictable but good" Gallic food. / **Sample dishes:** borscht with cream & horseradish; roast venison with Parmesan gnocchi; pink grapefruit & Campari sorbet. **Value tip:** set weekday L £23(FP). **Details:** www.chezmoi-restaurant.co.uk; 10.30 pm; closed Mon L, Sat L & Sun; booking: max 8.

Chezmax SW10 £ 44 A★★

168 Ifield Rd 7835 0874 4–3A

"Terrific" French country cooking and a "theatrical" and "entertaining" maître d' feature largely in reports on this "intimate" and very "romantic" Earl's Court-fringe basement, which is widely noted for its "all-round excellence". / **Sample dishes:** shrimp, tomato & ginger brûlée; fish & saffron stew with baby vegetables; caramelised pear tarte Tatin. **Details:** 11 pm; closed Sun.

Chiang Mai W1 £ 32 ★★

48 Frith St 7437 7444 3–2A

"Unbeatable for Thai cooking" – this *"authentic"* Soho *"classic"* remains the best in the West End; the ambience is still pretty dreary but, amazingly, *"after all these years, the service is beginning to improve"*. / **Sample dishes:** chicken satay; deep-fried fish with tamarind & chilli sauce; green tea ice cream. **Details:** 11 pm; closed Sun L; no smoking area.

Chinon W14 £ 35 ★★

23 Richmond Way 7602 4082

"Outstanding" French food in *"huge portions"* offers *"amazing value-for-money"* at this *"remarkably consistent"*, if somewhat *"eccentric"*, hide-away, in a Shepherd's Bush backstreet; many find the *"intimate"* setting *"romantic"*. / **Sample dishes:** prawn tempura with lemon & raisin chutney; roast duck with apple sauce; crème brûlée with passionfruit sorbet. **Details:** 10.30 pm; D only, closed Sun.

Churchill Arms W8 £ 17 𝔸★

119 Kensington Church St 7792 1246

"It's hard to get a booking, but worth it" at this *"cheerful"* annexe to a Kensington boozer, where the *"freshly cooked Thai dishes for around a fiver"* are a *"bargain"*; service can be *"sloppy"*. / **Sample dishes:** pad Thai; Thai green chicken curry; apple pie. **Details:** 9.30 pm; closed Sun D; no Amex; no booking at L.

Chutney Mary SW10 £ 40 ★

535 King's Rd 7351 3113 4–4B

"A very different menu and approach" has made this *"consistent"* distant-Chelsea *"colonial Indian"* one of the most popular subcontinentals in town for many years; *"there's a lot more competition these days"*, however, and ratings slid slightly this year. / **Sample dishes:** mussel & coconut soup; Goan chicken curry; mango martini kulfi. **Value tip:** pre-th. £26(FP). **Details:** www.realindianfood.com; 11.30 pm; no smoking area.

Cicada EC1 £ 32 𝔸★

132-136 St John St 7608 1550 5–1B

"Always fun, and the food is good for such a trendy place" – this *"friendly"*, *"noisy"* and *"chaotic"* Clerkenwell bar/restaurant delivers an *"imaginative"* Pacific Rim menu with surprising consistency. / **Sample dishes:** spicy Chinese pork ribs; chilli-crusted tofu with yellow bean sauce; white chocolate & forest fruit dumplings. **Details:** www.cicada.nu; 10.45 pm; closed Sat L & Sun; no smoking area.

The Cinnamon Club SW1 £ 44 𝔸★★

Great Smith St 7222 2555 1–4C

Iqbal Wahhab's new Westminster subcontinental – two years in preparation – was *"worth the wait"*; *"beautifully presented, subtly flavoured"* Anglo-Indian cuisine is slickly served in a *"gentleman's club setting"* which most find *"stylish"* (but which some think *"lacking in atmosphere"*). / **Sample dishes:** smoked lamb kebabs; mustard tandoori prawns with saffron kedgeree; coconut cake with cumin yoghurt. **Value tip:** set brunch £21(FP). **Details:** www.cinnamonclub.com; 11 pm; closed Sat L & Sun D; no smoking area; booking: max 8.

City Miyama EC4 £ 55 ★★

17 Godliman St 7489 1937 5–3B

"Very formal" and rather *"dull"* it may be, but this City Japanese is *"one of the best in town"*, thanks to its *"sensational sushi"* and the *"great teppan-yaki bar"*. / **Sample dishes:** prawn dumplings; salted fish tempura; green tea ice cream. **Value tip:** set always available £35(FP). **Details:** 9.30 pm; closed Sat D & Sun.

City Rhodes EC4   **£ 59**   ★

New Street Sq   7583 1313   5–2A

Gary Rhodes's "slick", if rather "clinical", operation near Fleet Street is once again voted reporters' safest bet for a City lunch – "spot on" service is "efficient without being overbearing", and the "beautifully-presented" British cooking is often "excellent".
/ **Sample dishes:** *foie gras & pigeon terrine with quince jelly; halibut with shellfish linguine; raspberry shortbread pannacotta.* **Details:** *9 pm; closed Sat & Sun.*

Clarke's W8   **£ 55**   A★★

124 Kensington Church St   7221 9225

It's "Sally's choice" – ie none for diners – at Ms Clarke's long-established Kensington restaurant, but few seem to care, as her "fresh", deceptively "simple" Californian-style dishes "never fail", and service is "superb"; the atmosphere strikes most as "intimate", but it can also seem a touch "dull". / **Sample dishes:** *onion puff pastry with tomatoes & Mozzarella; salmon with courgette flower fritters; vanilla cream pot with lemon thyme shortbread.* **Details:** *www.sallyclarke.com; 10 pm; closed Sat & Sun; no smoking area at L, no smoking at D.*

Club Gascon EC1   **£ 40**   A★★

57 West Smithfield   7796 0600   5–2B

"Wine, foie gras, location, atmosphere…" – this "unique, and hugely enjoyable" Gascon tapas bar in Smithfield has it all, and its "superb and creative" cuisine has won a huge following. / **Sample dishes:** *foie gras consommé with oysters; steamed white fish with chorizo; French cheese selection.* **Details:** *10 pm, Fri & Sat 10.30 pm; closed Sat L & Sun.*

Connaught W1   **£ 81**   A

Carlos Pl   7499 7070   2–3B

Will the arrival of the sixth head chef in just over a century shake this "wonderfully old-fashioned" Mayfair dining room to the core? – 'new' boy Jerome Ponchelle has already worked here since 1988, so change at this "country house in the middle of London" seems a mercifully remote prospect. / **Sample dishes:** *foie gras in port jelly; sole meunière with puréed celery; chocolate truffle cake.* **Value tip:** *set weekday L £49(FP).* **Details:** *www.the-connaught.co.uk; 10.45 pm; Grill closed Sat L; jacket & tie required; appreciated if guests try to refrain from smoking.*

Conrad Gallagher W1   **£ 62**   A★

179 Shaftesbury Ave   7836 3111   3–2B

A groovy basement, on the outskirts of Covent Garden, provides an odd setting for the new London dining room of a top Irish chef; on an August '01 visit, we took to the 'vibe', and were impressed by first-rate cooking; it comes at a pretty price, though, and whether quality can be maintained on this scale is a moot point. / **Sample dishes:** *watercress risotto with rabbit & confit tomato; turbot with pea, bacon & foie gras casserole; strawberry & basil soup.* **Value tip:** *set weekday L & pre-th. £41(FP).* **Details:** *www.conradgallagher.co.uk; 11.30 pm.*

Il Convivio SW1   **£ 39**   A★

143 Ebury St   7730 4099   1–4A

"Real Italian cooking" that's "reasonably priced" by Belgravia standards, and staff who are "so professional" are winning increasing acclaim for this "friendly and stylish" yearling. / **Sample dishes:** *Jerusalem artichoke soup with Parmesan crisps; roast duck with fig sauce; candied lime cake.* **Details:** *www.etruscagroup.co.uk; 10.30 pm; closed Sun.*

Coq d'Argent EC3   **£ 50**   ✗

1 Poultry   7395 5000   5–2C

As "a great way to impress", this "slick" and "buzzy" sixth-floor Conran venue in the heart of the City is hard to beat, and, with its extensive terraces, it makes a "very attractive" sunny day destination; the "plain" and "unadventurous" cooking, though, is "really not worth the prices", and service is "slow". / *Sample dishes:* veal sweetbreads with pea purée; lamb with goat's cheese crust; peach gratin. *Details:* www.conran.com; 10 pm; closed Sat L & Sun D.

The Cow W2   **£ 39**   𝔸 ★

89 Westbourne Park Rd   7221 0021

Thanks to its "great simple food" and "good choice of beers", the "cosy" bar of Tom Conran's "reliable" Bayswater boozer is often "crowded"; upstairs, in the dining room, the more ambitious cooking is of a "high standard" – the setting is "poky and rickety, but that's half the charm". / *Sample dishes:* New England clam chowder; lamb chump with provençal vegetables; prune & almond tart. *Details:* 11 pm; D only, closed Sun (bar open Sun).

The Criterion W1   **£ 50**   𝔸

224 Piccadilly Circus   7930 0488   2–3D

Suffering the perennially "surly" service at this "beautiful" neo-Byzantine chamber was once a price worth paying for impressive, 'school-of-MPW' Gallic cuisine; these days, however, the food at "the most atmospheric dining room in town" is plain "boring", and the prices are "ridiculous". / *Sample dishes:* vichysoisse; roast pheasant with quince purée; lemon tart. *Value tip:* set weekday L & pre-th. £31(FP). *Details:* 11.30 pm; closed Sun L.

Dakota W11   **£ 41**

127 Ledbury Rd   7792 9191

"It's a fun place" that's "still good for brunch in the sun", say fans of this once-hip Notting Hill southwest American; service is often "snotty", though, and cooking standards are distinctly uneven. / *Sample dishes:* tortilla with scallops & avocado; tuna with seaweed; chocolate chip cookie sandwich. *Details:* www.dakotafood.co.uk; 11 pm.

Daphne NW1   **£ 21**

83 Bayham St   7267 7322

A "friendly family-run atmosphere" puts fans "in the right mood" to enjoy this "traditional" Camden Town Greek (with a roof terrace in summer); it serves "good, simple food" at "reasonable" prices. / *Sample dishes:* spinach & feta filo parcels; lamb baked with cumin; baklava. *Details:* 11.30 pm; closed Sun; no Amex.

De Cecco SW6   **£ 33**   𝔸 ★

189 New King's Rd   7736 1145   6–1B

"With this combination, you can never fail", say fans of this "always buzzing" Italian near Parson's Green – "affordable" grub and "fabulous" service are re-establishing it as the "local favourite". / *Sample dishes:* seared scallops; sea bass with polenta; tiramisu. *Details:* 11 pm; closed Sun.

Defune W1   **£ 55**   ★★

34 George St   7935 8311   1–1A

"The old place was a dump", but "the new location is vastly improved" – this long-established, "real Japanese" now has a "much nicer" Marylebone home (a couple of streets away from the original) in which to enjoy some of London's "best sushi at a reasonable price". / *Sample dishes:* salmon roe sushi; chicken teriyaki; green tea ice cream. *Value tip:* set weekday L £30(FP). *Details:* 11 pm; closed Sun L; no smoking.

The Don EC4 £ 44 A★

20 St Swithin's Ln 7626 2606 5–3C
"A wonderful surprise hidden in a City side street"; this charming "new sister to the Bleeding Heart" (similarly offering "a choice of bistro and restaurant") more than lives up to its sibling with its "good-value" Gallic cooking, its "original" wine list and its "excellent" service. / *Sample dishes:* scallops en croute with lime; venison with roasted figs & port mash; banana tarte Tatin. *Details:* 10.30 pm; closed Sat & Sun.

Dorchester Grill W1 £ 65 A

53 Park Ln 7629 8888 2–3A
With its "impressively impressive" Spanish Baronial setting, its "divine" service and its "reliable" British fare (not least "excellent roast beef"), this Mayfair dining room is one of the better options for a grand, traditional meal. / *Sample dishes:* smoked Norfolk duck with onion compote; Aberdeen beef with sautéed goose liver; flambéed peppered peaches. *Details:* www.dorchesterhotel.com; 11 pm.

Dorchester, Oriental W1 £ 80 ★

53 Park Ln 7629 8888 2–3A
"Zero atmosphere can ruin the meal" at London's grandest Chinese, whose décor is impressive but "dull"; the "succulent" cooking is of "excellent quality" (but "incredibly expensive"). / *Sample dishes:* spicy scallops, prawns & jellyfish; pork & bamboo shoots in sea spice sauce; sweet water chestnuts in lemon juice. *Value tip:* set weekday L £35(FP). *Details:* www.dorchesterhotel.com; 11 pm; closed Sat L & Sun; no jeans or trainers; booking: max 8.

The Duke of Cambridge N1 £ 31 A

30 St Peter's St 7359 3066
The organic food is "a touch pricey", but this "impressive" Islington gastropub makes "a good effort", and the place is usually "packed" and "full of atmosphere". / *Sample dishes:* white bean & chilli soup; pheasant with olive oil mash & prunes; plum & apple crumble. *Details:* www.singhboulton.co.uk; 10.30 pm; closed Mon L; no smoking.

The Eagle EC1 £ 22 A★

159 Farringdon Rd 7837 1353 5–1A
"Excellent, if you like a non-stop environment" – London's longest-established gastropub is "still the best", and still packs 'em in with its "wonderful", "rustic" Mediterranean fare; the service "can suffer", though, and some find the smokiness off-putting. / *Sample dishes:* halibut with Basque sauce; marinated lamb with ratatouille; Portugese custard tarts. *Details:* 10.30 pm; closed Sun D; only Switch; no booking.

Elistano SW3 £ 30 A★

25-27 Elystan St 7584 5248 4–2C
A "superb Italian stalwart" – it's the "brilliant, homely style" that makes this "fun and friendly" local hugely popular, despite its rather obscure Chelsea backstreet location. / *Sample dishes:* artichoke salad; pasta with aubergine & Mozzarella; tiramisu. *Details:* 10.45 pm.

The Engineer NW1 £ 35 A

65 Gloucester Ave 7722 0950
This "great" Primrose Hill gastropub draws a "glamorous" and "trendy" crowd, thanks to its "easy" and "relaxed" atmosphere and the quality of its "posh pub grub"; "arrive early for a seat in the garden". / *Sample dishes:* tequila-cured salmon with blinis; Thai peppered beef salad with green papaya; Stilton with quince paste & walnut bread. *Details:* www.the-engineer.com; 10.30 pm; no Amex.

Enoteca Turi SW15   £ 35   A ★

28 Putney High St   8785 4449   6–2B
*"Not your usual Italian", this "excellent" Putney fixture offers
"super regional cooking" and an "enormous" wine list, under the
all-seeing eyes of owners Mr and Mrs Giuseppe Turi. / Sample
dishes: Mozzarella with sardines & pine nuts; roast lamb; peach tart with lime
sorbet. Details: 11 pm; closed Sun.*

Esarn Kheaw W12   £ 26   ★ ★

314 Uxbridge Rd   8743 8930
*"You get very authentic Thai cooking", and it's "consistently
delicious", at this Shepherd's Bush oriental; all other aspects of the
place are eminently forgettable. / Sample dishes: spicy pork spare ribs;
squid in sweet basil & oyster sauce; sticky rice & mango. Details: 11 pm;
closed Sat L & Sun L.*

L'Escargot W1   £ 40   A ★

48 Greek St   7437 2679   3–2A
*"A quiet oasis in the heart of busy Soho", this "spacious" Gallic
"favourite" has lots of "old-style glamour" and is a "simply
outstanding" all-round performer that deserves greater recognition;
the Picasso (fine dining) Room upstairs is less of an attraction.
/ Sample dishes: foie gras & green peppercorn terrine; caramelised skate
wing with winkles; Grand Marnier soufflé. Details: www.whitestarline.org.uk;
11.30 pm; closed Sat L & Sun (Picasso Room also closed Mon).*

Fairuz W1   £ 27

3 Blandford St   7486 8108   1–1A
*"Good-quality Lebanese cooking", "friendly" service and a "relaxed"
atmosphere proves a simple but effective formula at this small
Marylebone spot. / Sample dishes: felafel with tahini sauce; spicy chicken
with cottage bread & salad; pistachio & honey pastries. Details: 11.30 pm.*

Faulkner's E8   £ 21   ★ ★

424-426 Kingsland Rd   7254 6152
*"You slum it, but with great haddock" at this long-established
Dalston stalwart – "the best chippy in London, if not the Universe!"
/ Sample dishes: fish soup; rock salmon & chips; pistachio ice cream.
Details: 10 pm; no Amex; no smoking area.*

Feng Shang NW1   £ 30   A ★

Opposite 15 Prince Albert Rd   7485 8137
*With its "very high standard of service" and its "attractive décor",
this "posh Chinese" – a barge moored by Regent's Park – offers
a "really special" night out, confounding the cynics with its very
enjoyable food. / Sample dishes: salt & pepper prawns; seafood medley
with noodles; toffee apples. Details: 11 pm; closed weekday L.*

Foliage SW1   £ 60   ★

66 Knightsbridge   7201 3723   4–1D
*David Nicholls's "interesting" and "beautifully presented" modern
French cooking aside, this dining room overlooking Hyde Park
strikes many as "pretentious" and "tiresome" – last year's
"anonymous" makeover by top American restaurant designer Adam
Tihany seems largely to blame. / Sample dishes: cauliflower & spiced
quail salad; roast bream with pumpkin ravioli; Cuban chocolate fondant. Value
tip: set weekday L £39(FP). Details: www.mandarinoriental.com; 10.30 pm;
closed Sat L & Sun; no smoking area; booking: max 6.*

Food for Thought WC2   £ 15   ★

31 Neal St   7836 0239   3–2C
*"Very cramped", it may be, but this "crowded" and "rushed"
Covent Garden "veggie delight" remains on cracking culinary form,
and offers "great value"; BYO. / Sample dishes: carrot & coriander
soup; Ethiopian vegetable wrap; strawberry crunch. Details: 8.15 pm; closed
Sun D; no credit cards; no smoking; no booking.*

Fox & Anchor EC1   **£ 23**   A

115 Charterhouse St   7253 5075   5–1B

"Awesomely big", "cholesterol-packed" early-morning fry-ups can (thanks to Smithfield Market's licensing laws) be supplemented by "a great pint of Guinness" at this famous institution. / **Sample dishes:** prawn cocktail; lamb shank with garlic mash; sticky toffee pudding. **Details:** breakfast & L only (bar open in evenings); closed Sat & Sun.

Frederick's N1   **£ 38**   A ★

106 Camden Pas   7359 2888

"Classy, without breaking the bank", this long-established Islington "all-rounder" is currently on top form, with "consistently good" ("but not 'wow'") Gallic cooking and "friendly", "discreet" service; as ever, though, it's the "lovely" conservatory which is the star attraction. / **Sample dishes:** smoked haddock & new potato salad; roast duck with French beans; fruit crudités with Greek yoghurt. **Value tip:** set weekday L & pre-th. £24(FP). **Details:** www.fredericks.co.uk; 11.30 pm; closed Sun; no smoking area.

Fung Shing WC2   **£ 34**   ★★

15 Lisle St   7437 1539   3–3A

Long hailed as "the best Chinese in Chinatown", this "fine" but "gloomy" Cantonese is "first-rate for fish and unusual dishes". / **Sample dishes:** quail with chilli & garlic; roast eel in honey sauce; sweet almond bean curd pudding. **Details:** www.fungshing.com; 11.15 pm.

The Gate   **£ 30**   A ★★

51 Queen Caroline St, W6   8748 6932

72 Belsize Ln, NW3   7435 7733

"They do exquisite things with vegetables" at London's best veggie, "tucked away in a Hammersmith courtyard"; it now has an equally exceptional, more prominently-situated Belsize Park offshoot, done out in similarly "plain" but "funky" style. / **Sample dishes:** courgette flower & feta salad; teriyaki aubergine with rice noodles; banana brûlée. **Details:** www.gateveg.co.uk; 10.45 pm; W6 closed Sun – NW3 closed Sun D; W6 booking: max 10.

Gaudi EC1   **£ 44**

63 Clerkenwell Rd   7608 3220   5–1A

Yet again, this controversial Clerkenwell Spaniard polarises debate; the 'ayes' say it serves "excellent Iberian dishes" (with puddings which are "works of art") in "interesting" surroundings – the 'nays' think it offers a "strange" experience that's "over-rated and overpriced". / **Sample dishes:** foie gras with four-onion salad; swordfish with piquillo peppers; deep-fried cream with walnut sauce. **Details:** www.turnmills.com; 10.30 pm; closed Sat L & Sun.

Le Gavroche W1   **£ 82**   ★★

43 Upper Brook St   7408 0881   2–2A

"A reminder of how food should be served and cooked"; it can seem "starchy" and "dated", but, for "old-fashioned quality", Michel Roux Jr's grand Mayfair basement – with its "brilliant" Gallic cooking and service that's "second to none" – is "still the best" for many reporters. / **Sample dishes:** artichoke heart with foie gras & chicken mousse; roast grouse with bread sauce; millefeuille with Mascarpone & mango. **Value tip:** set weekday L £43(FP). **Details:** www.le-gavroche.co.uk; 11 pm; closed Sat & Sun; jacket required.

Geeta NW6   **£ 15**   ★★

59 Willesden Ln   7624 1713

"It looks like a greasy spoon, but the food is excellent" – and as "cheap as it gets" – at this "super-friendly", if undeniably "gloomy", Kilburn spot; "terrific south Indian veggie dishes" are the top options. / **Sample dishes:** hot lentil curry; prawn curry with lemon rice; gulab jamon. **Details:** 10.30 pm, Fri & Sat 11.30 pm; no Switch.

Giraffe £ 26 A

6-8 Blandford St, W1   7935 2333
29-31 Essex Rd, N1   7359 5999
46 Rosslyn Hill, NW3   7435 0343

"We need more relaxed and child-friendly places" like these "cute",
"bright" and "cheerful" diners, whose "interesting" menus satisfy
"varied palates"; breakfasts – "a ray of sunshine, even on a grey
morning" – attract special praise. / *Sample dishes:* Balinese salmon
with beansprouts; firecracker sesame chicken with noodles; sticky toffee &
banana pudding. *Details:* 11.30 pm – W1 11 pm; no smoking; need 6+
to book.

The Glasshouse TW9 £ 38 A★★

14 Station Pde   8940 6777

"Superb food on every visit" and "enthusiastic", "individual" service
make it "worth the trek to Kew" for this "bubbly" two-year old
(sibling to Wandsworth's Chez Bruce) by the railway station;
it's "noisy" and "crowded", though. / *Sample dishes:* salt cod fishcake
with pickled cucumber; roast pork with black pudding & grainmustard;
rhubarb & yoghurt ice creams. *Details:* 10.30 pm.

Gordon Ramsay SW3 £ 83 A★★

68-69 Royal Hospital Rd   7352 4441   4–3D

"Really pretty faultless"; Mr Ramsay's other interests – Claridges,
Glasgow and Dubai, to name but three – are growing relentlessly,
but the "heavenly" modern French food at his "formal, but nicely
glamorous" Chelsea dining room just gets better and better; if there
is a gripe, it's of sometimes "sycophantic" or "patronising" service.
/ *Sample dishes:* hot foie gras with lentils; lobster & langoustine tortellini in
shellfish bisque; blood oranges in jelly. *Value tip:* set weekday L £50(FP).
Details: 11 pm; closed Sat & Sun; booking: max 6.

Gordon Ramsay at Claridges W1 £ 83

55 Brook St   7629 8860   2–2B

This illustrious Mayfair hotel has long offered a rather lacklustre
culinary experience, but its restaurant has now been put into the
hands of London's leading chef – on its re-opening in
September '01, this wonderful Art Deco chamber could quickly
become one of the capital's top dining rooms. / *Sample
dishes:* scallops with cauliflower purée & beetroot crisps; roast duck with
celeriac fondant & confit leeks; chocolate savarin with champagne granita.

Gordon's Wine Bar WC2 £ 22 A

47 Villiers St   7930 1408   3–4D

"Visitors can't believe there is such a place" – the wonderfully
gloomy cellars of this ancient "treasure" of a wine bar by
Embankment tube have a "unique" ambience (and, for the
summer, there are great outside tables); the "plain" fodder is
"expensive" for what it is. / *Sample dishes:* duck pâté & French bread;
sausages, mash & onion gravy; apple pie. *Details:* 9 pm; no Amex;
no booking.

Goring Hotel SW1 £ 52 A

15 Beeston Pl   7396 9000   1–4B

"Wonderful as ever" – for its (fairly mature) clientèle,
the "well-spaced" tables and "most courteous" service in the dining
room of this family-run Victoria hotel suit it to most occasions
(particularly business); the British cooking may be "unchallenging",
but it is very consistent. / *Sample dishes:* watercress soup; Norfolk duck
with caramelised apple; chocolate millefeuille with coffee ice cream.
Details: www.goringhotel.co.uk; 10 pm.

Gourmet Burger Kitchen SW11   £ 17   ★

44 Northcote Rd   7228 3309   6–2C

"Superb, juicy thick ones with all the trimmings" – including "excellent chips and scrummy dips" – have made an immediate success of this no-nonsense Battersea diner, which offers the eponymous dining experience in every flavour you could imagine. / **Sample dishes:** chunky chips with salsa; Jamaican burger with mango & ginger sauce; no puddings. **Details:** gbkinfo.co.uk; 10.45 pm; no smoking; no booking.

Greenhouse W1   £ 51

27a Hays Mews   7499 3331   2–3B

This comfortable and well-established restaurant in Mayfair was closed at press time for a major relaunch in September '01; the designer is the ubiquitous David Collins, so the characterful, if slightly cheesy, interior will presumably be rendered tasteful, but completely anonymous. / **Sample dishes:** duck confit, cranberry & truffle terrine; pan-fried sea bass with sag aloo & tomato pickle; chocolate fondant with peanut butter ice cream. **Details:** www.capitalgrp.co.uk; 11 pm; closed Sat L.

Gung-Ho NW6   £ 28   A★

328-332 West End Ln   7794 1444

West Hampstead's "first-class local Chinese" is "difficult to fault" as an all-round performer, and it "gets very busy". / **Sample dishes:** crispy duck; lamb with spring onions & rice; toffee apples. **Details:** 11.30 pm; no Amex.

Hakkasan W1   £ 46   A★

8 Hanway Pl   7927 7000   3–1A

"Sexy" design and "21st century" Chinese cooking have made this "expensive" oriental the smash 'beautiful people' hit of the year – despite its "dodgy" back-alley basement location, off Tottenham Court Road. / **Sample dishes:** steamed scallops with tobiko caviar; deep-fried Tienjing bun stuffed with chicken & prawn; mango spring roll. **Details:** 11 pm; no smoking area.

Hard Rock Café W1   £ 28   A

150 Old Park Ln   7629 0382   2–4B

Yes, it's for "tourists and out-of-towners", but this famously "noisy" Mayfair diner – the original of the worldwide chain (now celebrating its 30th birthday) – is still surprisingly "happening", and the faithful insist that it offers "the best burgers anywhere". / **Sample dishes:** cheese nachos; cheeseburger & chips; hot fudge brownie. **Details:** www.hardrock.com; midnight, Fri & Sat 1 am; no smoking area; no booking.

The Havelock Tavern W14   £ 28   ★★

57 Masbro Rd   7603 5374

"Get there early", if you want a seat at this "deafening", "no-frills" gastropub, behind Olympia – thanks to the "inspired" and "amazingly tasty" food it gets "ridiculously busy" (and "service suffers as a result"). / **Sample dishes:** pork & duck terrine; lamb shank with mash; sticky toffee pudding. **Details:** 10 pm; no credit cards; no booking.

Hunan SW1   £ 32   ★★

51 Pimlico Rd   7730 5712   4–2D

"Excitable but wise service" – "it's best to leave the menu choice to Mr Peng" – delivers "genuinely special" results at this "first-rate" Chinese of long standing, near Pimlico Green. / **Sample dishes:** garlic chilli beans; chicken in Hunan sauce; toffee-glazed bananas. **Details:** 11 pm; closed Sun; no smoking area.

Inaho W2 £ 31 ★★

4 Hereford Rd   7221 8495

"Cheap, but amazing sushi" – perhaps "the best in town" – and other "exceptional" cooking make it worth truffling out this "tiny" and "crammed" Japanese café in Bayswater; "shame it's so slow". / **Sample dishes:** *tuna sushi; salmon teriyaki; fresh fruit & ice cream.* **Value tip:** *set weekday L £17(FP).* **Details:** *11 pm; closed Sat L & Sun; no Amex or Switch.*

Incognico WC2 £ 43 ★

117 Shaftesbury Ave   7836 8866   3–2B

Nico Ladenis's "thoroughly slick" and "buzzy" brasserie yearling has "quickly established itself" as a major Theatreland destination thanks to its "proper" Gallic cooking and "reasonable" prices. / **Sample dishes:** *goat's cheese & roast pepper open ravioli; crispy salmon in ginger cream sauce; warm chocolate mousse.* **Value tip:** *set weekday L & pre-th. £25(FP).* **Details:** *midnight; closed Sun.*

Indigo WC2 £ 51 A★

1 Aldwych   7300 0400   1–2D

With its "amazing friendly service", its "really comfy" and "spacious" setting and its "good, sensible, tasty food", the "very urbane and well-placed" mezzanine restaurant of this swish Covent Garden hotel is something of "a hidden treasure". / **Sample dishes:** *monkfish carpaccio woth mango salsa; roast lamb with vegetable caviar; crunchy chocolate praline tart.* **Details:** *www.onealdwych.co.uk; 11.15 pm.*

The Ivy WC2 £ 47 A★

1 West St   7836 4751   3–3B

"London's best all-rounder" is still "top for celeb spotting" and – thanks to its "clever, but simple" food, its "spoiling" service and the "perfect" ambience of its Theatreland premises – you "still need to book three months ahead"; those who feared that the departure of Messrs Corbin and King would spell 'The End' may have a while to wait yet. / **Sample dishes:** *rock shrimp linguine; braised beef in Guinness with carrot mash; chocolate pudding soufflé.* **Value tip:** *set Sat L & Sun L £29(FP).* **Details:** *midnight.*

Iznik N5 £ 21 A

19 Highbury Park   7354 5697

The "jewel in Highbury's small crown" is not shining as brightly as it did; all reports acknowledge the "delightful" and "intimate" atmosphere, but whereas some still laud the Turkish cooking as "excellent and reasonably priced" others find it increasingly "variable". / **Sample dishes:** *courgette & feta fritters; lamb with stuffed aubergines; baklava.* **Details:** *11 pm; no Amex.*

Jin Kichi NW3 £ 30 ★★

73 Heath St   7794 6158

"Excellent" yakitori (grills on skewers) is the highlight at this "cosy", "small" and "friendly" Hampstead Japanese. / **Sample dishes:** *prawn & asparagus spring rolls; grilled chicken & pork skewers; green tea ice cream.* **Details:** *11 pm; closed Mon, Tue-Fri D only, Sat & Sun open L & D.*

Joe Allen WC2 £ 35 A

13 Exeter St   7836 0651   3–3D

For "good showbizzy fun" this "casual" Covent Garden basement is a celebrated late-night "old faithful" (book well ahead); the American cooking is "ordinary", though some claim the burgers (famously "off-menu") as "the best in town". / **Sample dishes:** *salmon & smoked haddock chowder; lamb & mint sausages with red lentil purée; banana cream pie.* **Details:** *www.joeallen.co.uk; 12.45 am; no smoking area.*

Julie's W11 £ 47 *A*
135 Portland Rd 7229 8331
An "exotic" subterranean Holland Park labyrinth which has long
offered one of London's most "seductive" dining experiences;
"it's a shame about the food", though, which is very "boring"
indeed. / *Sample dishes:* prosciutto & Parmesan summer salad; rack of
lamb with garlic bean mash; meringue with red berries.
Details: www.juliesrestaurant.com; 11.15 pm; closed Sat L.

K10 EC2 £ 20 *A*★★
20 Copthall Ave 7562 8510 5–2C
"The best conveyor-belt sushi in London" and an "interesting" hot
selection of Japanese-inspired dishes win rave reviews for this "cool"
but "friendly" yearling, near Liverpool Street. / *Sample
dishes:* courgette tempura; seared tuna with miso vinaigrette; ginger mousse.
Details: www.k10.net; 10 pm; closed Sat & Sun; no smoking; no booking.

Kai W1 £ 48 *A*★
65 South Audley Street 7493 8507 2–3A
This "smart" Mayfair Chinese lacks profile, but its "excellent"
(if "very pricey") cooking makes it one of the top orientals in town.
/ *Sample dishes:* deep-fried soft shell crab; Szechuan chicken with cashews &
crispy seaweed; green tea. *Details:* www.kaimayfair.co.uk; 10.45 pm.

Kastoori SW17 £ 19 ★★
188 Upper Tooting Rd 8767 7027 6–2C
"Don't let the exterior put you off" – there's "nothing
run-of-the-mill" about this "faultless" Tooting Indo-African, which
attracts regulars from far and wide with its "friendly" service and its
"outstanding" vegetarian cooking. / *Sample dishes:* samosas;
mushroom & spinach curry; Indian cheesecake. *Details:* 10.30 pm; closed
Mon L & Tue L; no Amex or Switch.

Ken Lo's Memories SW1 £ 45 ★★
67-69 Ebury St 7730 7734 1–4B
"It keeps standards up year after year", and this "civilised",
"top-class" Chinese near Victoria is 'on a roll' at present, offering
"memorable" cooking that's amongst the best in town; a major
refurbishment was under way at press time. / *Sample
dishes:* courgettes stuffed with prawns; stewed lamb with lemongrass; toffee
apple & banana. *Details:* 10.45 pm; closed Sun L.

Kennington Lane SE11 £ 32 *A*★
205-209 Kennington Ln 7793 8313
This understated yearling brings "West End" standards to an
unlovely corner of Kennington; virtues include "consistently
high-quality" cooking, "tirelessly helpful" service and a very
"agreeable" atmosphere (and the terrace is "a gem in summer").
/ *Sample dishes:* buffalo Mozzarella salad; sea bream with raspberry vinegar
sauce; almond tart. *Details:* 10.30 pm; closed Sat L.

The Ladbroke Arms W11 £ 31 ★
54 Ladbroke Rd 7727 6648
Some think this "nice" and "relaxed" Notting Hill boozer is
"too crowded" nowadays – blame the "reliable and original"
cooking, and also the sunny-day attractions of the "good outside
seating area". / *Sample dishes:* foccacia with Mozzarella & artichokes;
grilled squid with chili; chocolate fondue. *Details:* 9.45 pm; no Amex.

Lahore Kebab House E1 £ 16 ★★
2 Umberston St 7488 2551
It's a "back-to-basics" experience, but – for "stunning" and
"authentic" Pakistani fare – "it's worth the journey" to this
unpolished East End "gem". / *Sample dishes:* chicken tikka; lamb
Karahi; rice pudding. *Details:* midnight; no credit cards.

The Lanesborough SW1 £ 56 A

Hyde Park Corner 7259 5599 4–1D

"Beautifully-cooked breakfasts" and "very good teas" figure in many reports on the "fantastic", OTT conservatory dining room of this mega-swanky hotel; when it comes to 'proper' food, though, reporters tend to speak in terms of "average" cooking at "extortionate" prices. / *Sample dishes:* foie gras with apple & raisin Tatin; lamb shank with Swiss chard; plum tart with cinnamon ice cream. *Value tip:* set weekday L £28(FP). *Details:* www.lanesborough.com; midnight; jacket required at D.

Launceston Place W8 £ 45 A ★

1a Launceston Pl 7937 6912 4–1B

"An excellent stand-by for all seasons"; this "exemplary" Kensington townhouse is "still an English classic", offering consistently "good" food in a "very civilised" and "romantic" setting. / *Sample dishes:* deep-fried oysters with tartare sauce; Dover sole with parsley butter; apple soufflé. *Details:* 11.30 pm; closed Sat L & Sun D.

Lindsay House W1 £ 63 A

21 Romilly St 7439 0450 3–3A

This "lovely" Soho townhouse is hailed by some as the "ultimate romantic destination"; Irish chef Richard Corrigan's "indulgent" cooking has hit a more consistent beat of late, but it's still "not as good as it was a couple of years ago". / *Sample dishes:* crayfish gazpacho; stuffed guinea fowl with Madeira jus; banana soufflé. *Value tip:* set weekday L £40(FP). *Details:* www.lindsayhouse.co.uk; 11 pm; closed Sat L & Sun.

Lisboa Patisserie W10 £ 6 ★ ★

57 Golborne Rd 8968 5242

"Outstanding pasteis de nata" (custard tarts, to the uninitiated) are the highlight at this "essential" North Kensington Portuguese café – for many, it's "the best place in town for a coffee and a bun". / *Sample dishes:* cheese croissant; vegetable rissoles; custard tarts. *Details:* 8 pm; no credit cards; no booking.

Lomo SW10 £ 22 A

222-224 Fulham Rd 7349 8848 4–3B

"Fab" service and "fun and unusual" culinary combinations have made quite a name for this "buzzy" tapas bar, and its Chelsea 'Beach' location makes it "ideal for people-watching". / *Sample dishes:* Seville prawns; crispy chicken & garlic beans; Catalan cream. *Details:* www.lomo.co.uk; 11.30 pm; closed weekday L; no booking after 7.30 pm.

Lots Road SW10 £ 26 A ★

114 Lots Rd 7352 6645 4–4B

"Great burgers, chips and salads" are typical of the simple but "fresh" cooking at this "light", "airy" newcomer; thanks to its obscure distant-Chelsea location it "never gets overcrowded". / *Sample dishes:* frisée salad with soft poached eggs; mussels in lemongrass sauce; cinnamon brûlée. *Details:* 11 pm.

Lundum's SW7 £ 37 A ★

119 Old Brompton Rd 7373 7774 4–2B

"The owners are in charge, and it shows", at this "formal" but "comfortable" establishment on the fringe of South Kensington; its "authentic" and "beautifully-presented" Danish cooking, is beginning to develop a real following. / *Sample dishes:* marinated herrings; cured duck with radishes & honey sauce; crème brûlée. *Details:* 10.30 pm; closed Sun D.

Mandarin Kitchen W2   £ 28   ★★
14-16 Queensway   7727 9012
"Full of happy Chinese eating lobster" – *"superb"* seafood is the highlight at this *"chaotic"* and *"boring"*-looking Bayswater oriental. / **Sample dishes:** *razor clams with soft noodles; Cantonese-style roast chicken; lychees & ice cream.* **Value tip:** *set weekday L £17(FP).* **Details:** *11.15 pm.*

Mango Tree SW1   £ 45
46 Grosvenor Pl   7823 1888   1–4B
Pleasant and efficient service is a highlight at this airy new Belgravia Thai; its well-spaced tables and its rather tame cooking struck us, on our August '01 visit, as making it better suited to business than pleasure. / **Sample dishes:** *papaya salad; red monkfish curry with kaffir lime; mango cheesecake.* **Details:** www.mangotree.org.uk; 10.45 pm; closed Sat L; no smoking area.

Matsuri SW1   £ 52   ★
15 Bury St   7839 1101   2–3D
The *"authentic"* teppan-yaki makes a *"great show"* at this *"reliable"* St James's oriental (which also serves *"excellent sushi"*); the setting is a touch *"sterile"*, but regulars say *"you get used to it"*. / **Sample dishes:** *chicken yakitori; seafood teppan-yaki; toffee ice cream.* **Details:** www.matsuri-restaurant.com; 10.30 pm; closed Sun.

Mesclun N16   £ 28   𝔸★★
24 Stoke Newington Church St   7249 5029
"Wow!", *"a find"* – *"'food as good as many West End restaurants, but at a fraction of the cost"* (with *"attentive"* service too) is winning an ever-wider north London following for this *"friendly"* and *"understated"* Stoke Newington spot. / **Sample dishes:** *Gorgonzola polenta with roasted peppers; calves' liver & smoked bacon; raspberry crème brûlée.* **Details:** 11 pm; no Amex.

Mezzo W1   £ 45   ✗
100 Wardour St   7314 4000   2–2D
"Conran complacency shines through" at this *"noisy"* and *"cavernous"* Soho tourist-trap; *"surly"* service and *"slapdash"* cooking too often make it *"a waste of time and money"*. / **Sample dishes:** *trout pâté with beetroot jam; roast pork with armagnac prunes; passion fruit cheesecake.* **Value tip:** *set weekday L, Sun L & pre-th.£28(FP).* **Details:** www.conran.com; midnight, Thu-Sat 1 am (bar food until 3 am); closed Mon L, Tue L & Sat L.

Mildreds W1   £ 22   𝔸★
58 Greek St   7494 1634   3–2A
"The best veggie food in Soho" – and in *"big portions"* too – ensures disproportionate popularity for this *"tiny"* and *"cramped"* café. / **Sample dishes:** *spinach & goats cheese wontons; white bean burger with salsa & fries; treacle tart.* **Details:** 11 pm; closed Sun D; no credit cards; no smoking; no booking.

Mirabelle W1   £ 52   𝔸★
56 Curzon St   7499 4636   2–4B
"Thirties-style glamour", *"good-value"* Gallic cooking, an *"impressive"* wine list and *"slick service"* make a smooth cocktail – one that continues to win huge popularity for MPW's Mayfair classic. / **Sample dishes:** *warm salad of smoked eel & bacon; steak & kidney pudding with swede purée; peppered pineapple tarte Tatin.* **Details:** www.whitestarline.org.uk; 10.45 pm; no smoking area.

Mitsukoshi SW1   £ 53   ★
14-20 Lower Regent St   7930 0317   2–3D
The *"dated"* décor truly is *"dreadful"*, but the sushi counter offers *"beautiful food for introverts"* at this *"traditional"* West End Japanese; it also makes a serviceable venue for business. / **Sample dishes:** *octopus salad with lemon soy dressing; grilled beef teriyaki; fruit salad.* **Value tip:** *set weekday L £20(FP).* **Details:** 9.30 pm; closed Sun.

Mju SW1 £ 70

17 Sloane St 7235 4377 4–1D

*Is there enough money – even in Knightsbridge's glitter gulch – to sustain Tetsuya Wakuda's Franco-Japanese fusion newcomer?; we enjoyed our July '01 visit to this comfortable hotel dining room, and service charmed, but prices – even for the beautifully-arranged protein morsels – seemed unjustified. / **Sample dishes:** lobster mousse with wasabi jelly; rack of lamb with miso & water chestnuts; orange, honey & black pepper sorbet. **Value tip:** set weekday L £33(FP). **Details:** 10 pm; no smoking.*

Momo W1 £ 44 A

25 Heddon St 7434 4040 2–2C

*"Intriguing" and "exotic" (and "a bit cliquey") – Mourad Mazouz's "low-lit" and "romantic" Mayfair Moroccan still bewitches the faithful, even thought the grub is decidedly "average". / **Sample dishes:** cod carpaccio with alfalfa & caviar; seared tuna with chickpea polenta; quince & clementines with rose water. **Details:** 10.30 pm.*

Monkeys SW3 £ 62 A★

1 Cale St 7352 4711 4–2C

*"Great" staff help create a "wonderful" atmosphere at this "discreet" Chelsea fixture, where game is the speciality; for "an old-fashioned, delicious, traditional meal" – and with a serious wine list to match – it has few equals. / **Sample dishes:** lobster & leek terrine; roast partridge with traditional trimmings; sorbet. **Details:** 10 pm; closed Sat & Sun; no Amex.*

Monsieur Max TW12 £ 50 A★★

133 High St, Hampton Hill 8979 5546

*"Sublime" Gallic cooking (and "excellent" service too) have long succeeded in making Max Renzland's "classy" joint an improbable destination in suburban Hampton Hill; let's hope it's not too thrown by the summer '01 loss of chef Morgan Meunier. / **Sample dishes:** foie gras & duck terrine with Sauternes jelly; John Dory with champagne & sorrel risotto; liqorice meringue. **Details:** 9.30 pm; closed Mon, Sat L & Sun D.*

Moro EC1 £ 33 A★★

34-36 Exmouth Mkt 7833 8336 5–1A

*"Thrilling and imaginative" Southern Med/Moorish cooking, "friendly and helpful" service and a "buzzy" (if "crowded") ambience are propelling this unpretentious Clerkenwell four-year old to ever-greater prominence. / **Sample dishes:** Russian salad with smoked anchovies; lamb with roast beetroot & parsley sauce; chocolate & apricot tart. **Details:** 10.30 pm; closed Sat L & Sun.*

Mr Chow SW1 £ 48 A

151 Knightsbridge 7589 7347 4–1D

*Sceptics dismiss the cooking as "almost oriental" – and the whole experience as "ordinary in most ways" – but this Knightsbridge "living legend" is highly praised by many for its "first class, if pricey food", its "keen" (Italian) service and its "great" atmosphere. / **Sample dishes:** scallop, chicken & prawn stir-fry; lamb with pak choy; pear tart. **Details:** midnight.*

Mr Kong WC2 £ 20 ★

21 Lisle St 7437 7341 3–3A

*Some of the best dishes are "carefully hidden on the list of specials" at this "excellent and cheap" Chinatown "fixture"; it's a bit "shabby", and the "awful" basement is best avoided. / **Sample dishes:** stewed oysters with pork & mushrooms; sweet & sour pork; no puddings. **Details:** 2.45 am.*

Mr Wing SW5   **£ 40**   A★

242-244 Old Brompton Rd   7370 4450   4–2A
"Jungle-o-rama!" – *"dazzling tropical fish and plants"* set the scene
at this *"special"* Earl's Court basement; it's long been seen as
a great party or romantic venue, but *"don't let the greenery distract
you from the food"* – its current form puts it *"among the best
Chineses in town"*. / **Sample dishes:** *courgette tempura & prawn toast;
Sczechuan shredded chilli beef; toffee banana with sesame seeds.*
Details: *midnight.*

Nahm SW1   **£ 65**   ★

5 Halkin St   7333 1234   1–3A
*This Belgravia hotel dining room has been given an expensively
understated – or should that be 'underpowered'? – makeover,
and is now home to celebrated Aussie chef David Thompson;
his sock-it-to-'em Thai cooking impressed us on our July '01 visit,
but ill-conceived puds took the gloss off the meal which came at
a hefty price. / **Sample dishes:** crisp salted trout; monkfish 'jungle curry'
with deep-fried shallots; black sticky rice with cocnut cream. **Details:** 11 pm;
closed Sat L & Sun L.*

Nautilus NW6   **£ 22**   ★

27-29 Fortune Green Rd   7435 2532
"Ignore the '60s décor", and you can hope to find *"the best fish
and chips in north west London"* at this *"excellent"* West
Hampstead chippie. / **Sample dishes:** *prawn cocktail; deep-fried cod in
matzo meal with chips; lemon sorbet.* **Details:** *10 pm; closed Sun; no Amex;
no booking.*

Nobu W1   **£ 55**   A★★

Old Park Lane   7447 4747   2–4A
"Amazing" Japanese/South American cooking justifies the
"unbelievable expense" – and the *"pain of getting a booking"* – at
this *"very sexy"* Mayfair dining room; as a *"superb venue for
star-spotting"*, it has few equals. / **Sample dishes:** *'new-style' sashimi;
black cod with miso; chocolate Bento box.* **Details:** *10.15 pm, Fri & Sat
11 pm; closed Sat L & Sun L; no smoking area.*

Odette's NW1   **£ 39**   A★

130 Regent's Park Rd   7586 5486
*This *"gracious"* and *"romantic"* Primrose Hill fixture is best known
for its *"amazing"* (*"mirrors everywhere"*) décor; it offers more than
just looks, though – the *"traditional-with-a-twist"* cooking is *"very
well executed"*, the wine list is excellent, and service *"charms"*.
/ **Sample dishes:** sea scallop risotto; roast lamb with tempura courgettes;
chocolate mousse. **Value tip:** set weekday L £22(FP). **Details:** 11 pm; closed
Sat L & Sun.*

Odin's W1   **£ 40**   A★

27 Devonshire St   7935 7296   1–1A
"The sort of place my parents would love", this *"civilised"*
Marylebone veteran may be, but it's praised by young and old,
business-types and romantics alike for its *"very comfortable"*
ambience, its *"old-fashioned"* service and its *"high-standard"*
(if *"not innovative"*) Anglo/French cuisine. / **Sample dishes:** *smoked eel
mousse with horseradish; Cumberland sausages with mash & onion sauce;
date & ginger pudding.* **Details:** *www.langansrestaurants.co.uk; 11 pm; closed
Sat & Sun; no smoking area.*

1 Lombard Street EC3 £ 48

1 Lombard St 7929 6611 5–3C

It's "one for the expense account", but Herbert Berger's "efficient business venue", by Bank, is "a solid all-rounder" with "quality" modern French cooking, "slick" service and a "bustling" ("loud") setting. / **Sample dishes:** smoked haddock with quail's eggs & mustard sauce; veal with caramelised artichokes & truffles; liquorice crème brûlée with blackcurrant coulis. **Details:** www.1lombardstreet.com; 10 pm; closed Sat & Sun.

L'Oranger SW1 £ 55   A ★

5 St James's St 7839 3774 2–4D

A "first-rate all rounder", this "comfortable" St James's establishment offers an all-too-rare combination of "old-fashioned comfort", "excellent French cuisine" and "impeccable" service. / **Sample dishes:** salt cod & potato tartlet; roast pork with bacon & sage; hazelnut soufflé. **Details:** 11 pm; closed Sat L & Sun.

Orrery W1 £ 52   A ★

55 Marylebone High St 7616 8000 1–1A

"The only Conran worth bothering with"; this "quiet" dining room, overlooking a Marylebone churchyard, may be "expensive", but it's "worth it" for the "meticulously-presented" modern French cooking and its sometimes "fantastic" service. / **Sample dishes:** Bayonne ham with celeriac; seared tuna with coco beans; peach soufflé. **Details:** www.orrery.co.uk; 10.30 pm.

Oxo Tower SE1 £ 55   A ✕

Barge House St 7803 3888 5–3A

The view is "stunning", but it "can't compensate for the dreadful, highly-priced food" served on the eighth floor of this South Bank landmark; the cheaper brasserie is a marginally better bet than the restaurant. / **Sample dishes:** snails with mushrooms and smoked bacon; roast pheasant with caramelised endive; lemon parfait with rhubarb. **Details:** www.harveynichols.com; 11.15 pm.

Ozer W1 £ 35

4-5 Langham Pl 7323 0505 2–1C

This innovative Turkish yearling by Broadcasting House still wins praise for its "sexy décor" and its "excellent value" (particularly the set menus), but there's a feeling that the "food has declined since opening", and service likewise. / **Sample dishes:** parsley salad; lamb kofte; yoghurt with honey & nuts. **Value tip:** set £22(FP). **Details:** midnight; no jeans.

Il Pagliaccio SW6 £ 22   A

184 Wandsworth Bridge Rd 7371 5253 6–1B

It can be "bedlam" at this "crowded" Italian in deepest Fulham, but the locals applaud its "very friendly" service and its "cheap" pizza and other fare. / **Sample dishes:** mussels with beans; seafood pasta; tiramisu. **Details:** midnight; no Amex.

Le Palais du Jardin WC2 £ 39   A

136 Long Acre 7379 5353 3–3C

This vast and "buzzy" Covent Garden brasserie still makes a "reliable" central rendezvous, particularly "pre-theatre"; "consistently good fish" – notably the "amazing seafood platter" – is a highlight. / **Sample dishes:** smoked salmon with potato cake; fillet steak & roast tomatoes; Tia Maria crème brûlée. **Details:** 11.45 pm.

Parade W5   **£ 35**   A★

18-19 The Mall   8810 0202

For "excellent value in the suburbs", this large yearling in the "wastelands" of Ealing is hard to beat; like its Barnes sibling, Sonny's, it delivers a good all-round package, including "well-priced" food and a "pleasant", setting. / Sample dishes: chicken, black pudding & egg salad; skate with borlotti beans; baked egg custard tart.
Details: 11 pm; closed Sun D.

Pasha SW7   **£ 40**   A

1 Gloucester Rd   7589 7969   4–1B

"You feel like you're in Morocco" at this "very enticing", "low-lit" Kensington basement; it's quite "expensive for what it is", however, and both the "enjoyable" cooking and the service get a rather mixed press. / Sample dishes: mezze; chicken with preserved lemons; Turkish delight crème brûlée. **Details:** 11 pm; closed Sun L.

Pasha N1   **£ 27**   A★

301 Upper St   7226 1454

"Great food at easy prices" wins a big north London fan club for this "jolly" Islington Turk; at busy times, "they cram you in", though. / Sample dishes: courgette fritters; kleftiko; rosewater rice pudding. **Details:** 11.30 pm, Fri & Sat midnight; no Switch.

Passione W1   **£ 41**   A★★

10 Charlotte St   7636 2833   1–1C

Blossoming in its second year of operation, this agreeably "unpretentious" Fitzrovia spot offers "interesting" and "beautifully-cooked" Italian dishes, and "lovely" service. / Sample dishes: cuttlefish with preserved vegetables; mixed game ravioli with truffle sauce; limoncello ice cream. **Details:** www.passione.co.uk; 10.15 pm; closed Sat L & Sun.

Pâtisserie Valerie   **£ 20**   A

105 Marylebone High St, W1   7935 6240
44 Old Compton St, W1   7437 3466
8 Russell St, WC2   7240 0064
215 Brompton Rd, SW3   7823 9971

"What a great start to the day", say fans of the "piggy but delicious" treats on offer at this Gallic café chain; declining ratings, however, support those who say they're "not quite as good as they were a few years ago". / Sample dishes: quiche lorraine; smoked salmon & scrambled eggs; chocolate eclair.
Details: www.patisserie-valerie.co.uk; 7 pm-11 pm, Sun 6 pm (Soho 7 pm); no smoking area; no booking.

Paul WC2   **£ 9**   A★

29-30 Bedford St   7836 3304   3–3C

"A real boulangerie and pâtisserie"; this new Covent Garden outpost of a major Gallic chain serves "delicious cakes", "wonderful breads" and "good coffee" in a comfortable tearoom setting that puts most native offerings to shame. / Sample dishes: soup with sourdough bread; leek & lardon tartlet with salad; citron tart.
Details: 8.30 pm; no smoking.

Pétrus SW1   **£ 65**   ★★

33 St James's St   7930 4272   2–4C

The "delicate, subtle and pure flavours" of Marcus Wareing's modern French cooking – and a wine list living up to the place's name – are establishing this "comfortable" but "slightly clinical" St James's dining room as one of the most notable in town; some find service "oppressive". / Sample dishes: tuna carpaccio with coriander salad; pork belly with wild mushrooms; peach clafoutis.
Details: www.petrus-restaurant.com; 10.45 pm; closed Sat L & Sun; booking: max 6.

Phoenicia W8   **£ 36**

11-13 Abingdon Rd   7937 0120   4–1A

This "very friendly" Lebanese is a Kensington fixture, whose
"attentive" staff deliver food that's "unexceptional but good".
/ **Sample dishes:** stuffed vine leaves; spicy Lebanese sausage; pancakes
with ricotta & pistachios. **Details:** 11.45 pm; no smoking area.

Pied à Terre W1   **£ 72**   ★

34 Charlotte St   7636 1178   1–1C

Shane Osborn's "classical but imaginative" Gallic cooking and an
"excellent range of interesting wines" make this Fitzrovia fixture
one of London's foremost foodie temples; service can be "distant",
though, and the setting is "so-so". / **Sample dishes:** celeriac, chive &
salt cod soup; braised lamb with deep-fried tongue & olives; mandarin parfait
with lemon curd. **Value tip:** set weekday L £41(FP).
Details: www.pied.a.terre.co.uk; 10.45 pm; closed Sat L & Sun.

Pizza Metro SW11   **£ 29**   𝔸★★

64 Battersea Rise   7228 3812   6–2C

"It helps to be Italian when booking", as "it's very hard to get
a table" at this "cramped but fun" Battersea joint; it's known for
"the best pizza outside Napoli" (sold by the metre), but "incredible
antipasti and fish" are also served. / **Sample dishes:** antipasti; pizza
with salami & olives; tiramisu. **Details:** 11 pm; closed Mon, Tue-Fri D only,
Sat & Sun open L & D.

Pizzeria Castello SE1   **£ 20**   𝔸★

20 Walworth Rd   7703 2556

"The garlic hits you straight away", as you enter the Elephant
& Castle's leading contribution to the capital's gastronomy; hordes
of supporters from far and wide hail "the best pizza in town",
"cheerful" staff and the "urban buzz". / **Sample dishes:** prawns in
garlic; four cheese pizza; cheesecake. **Details:** www.pizzeria-castello.co.uk;
11 pm, Fri & Sat 11.30 pm; closed Sat L & Sun.

Poissonnerie de l'Avenue SW3   **£ 51**   ★

82 Sloane Ave   7589 2457   4–2C

"As good and pricey as ever", this Brompton Cross stalwart
continues to please its "older clientèle" with the "excellent seafood"
served in its cosy but "cramped" dining room. / **Sample
dishes:** lobster & salmon ravioli in cream sauce; seared tuna with salsa; lemon
tart. **Details:** 11.30 pm; closed Sun.

Popeseye   **£ 34**   ★★

108 Blythe Rd, W14   7610 4578
277 Upper Richmond Rd, SW15   8788 7733

"If you crave excellent steak, this is the place"; "top" meat and
a "fantastic list of keenly-priced old-world wines" makes for
a winning formula at this duo of "friendly" but basic bistros, in
Olympia and Putney. / **Sample dishes:** no starters; Aberdeen Angus steak
with chips & salad; farmhouse cheeses. **Details:** 10.30 pm; D only; closed
Sun; no credit cards.

La Porte des Indes W1   **£ 43**   𝔸★

32 Bryanston St   7224 0055   1–2A

Given the "out-of-this-world" décor of this lavish Indian, near
Marble Arch, it's no surprise that prices here can seem "inflated" –
the "exquisite" cooking, however, is at last living up to the setting.
/ **Sample dishes:** deep-fried prawns with coconut chutney; 'aphrodisiac' lamb
chops; ice cream & mango coulis. **Value tip:** set daily buffet £29(FP).
Details: www.la-porte-des-indes.com; midnight; closed Sat L.

La Poule au Pot SW1   £ 40   A★
231 Ebury St   7730 7763   4–2D
*"Still the best for romance" – this old Pimlico charmer is still
sweeping 'em off their feet with its candle-lit, "dingy-but-good"
farmhouse décor, its "hearty French grub" and its "authentic"
("nonchalant") service. / **Sample dishes:** pork & foie gras terrine; roast
lamb with green beans; chocolate mousse. **Value tip:** set weekday L £26(FP).
Details: 11.15 pm.*

Prism EC3   £ 50
147 Leadenhall St   7256 3888   5–2D
*It's "utterly suitable for business", but otherwise reports about
Harvey Nichols's City outpost – with its "nothing special" cooking,
and its rather "soulless" ex-banking hall setting – are getting more
and more ambivalent. / **Sample dishes:** mushroom consommé with oxtail
ravioili; roast cod with squid & mash; coffee & hazelnut parfait.
Details: www.harveynichols.com; 10 pm; closed Sat & Sun.*

The Providores W1   £ 42   ★
109 Marylebone High St   7935 6175   1–1A
*Peter Gordon, the original chef at the Sugar Club, launched his new
fusion café/restaurant in Marylebone as we were going to press;
our first-week impressions, formed on an August '01 visit to the
ground-floor Tapa Room, were of a welcoming establishment of
serious culinary endeavour – the plainly-decorated first-floor dining
room, however, is rather cramped. / **Sample dishes:** octopus with
deep-fried quail's egg & shallot laksa; venison with smoked paprika stew &
quince aoili; green tea pannacotta with lychee jelly.
Details: www.theprovidores.co.uk; 10.45 pm; no smoking in dining room.*

Quaglino's SW1   £ 44   ✗
16 Bury St   7930 6767   2–3D
*With its "overpriced but very standard grub", its "sloppy" service
and its "impersonal" atmosphere, this Conran brasserie in
St James's has now "gone totally downhill". / **Sample dishes:** foie gras
terrine with fig jam; roast guinea fowl with buttered spinach; pineapple with
ginger & basil. **Value tip:** set weekday L, Sun L & pre-th. £26(FP).
Details: www.conran.com; midnight, Fri & Sat 1 am.*

Ranoush W2   £ 20   ★★
43 Edgware Rd   7723 5929
*"The best kebabs in town" and "excellent juices" have long made
this "slice of Beirut" a popular central destination, particularly late
at night; go to the cash machine first, though – it's strictly readies
only. / **Sample dishes:** houmous & crudités; grilled meat skewers; baklava.
Details: www.maroush.com; 2.45 am; no credit cards.*

Rapscallion SW4   £ 32   A★
75 Venn St   7787 6555   6–2D
*This "bustling" joint by Clapham Picture House is "great for a quick
yet quality bite", but "the tables are very close together" and some
find the setting just "too loud". / **Sample dishes:** falafel with yoghurt
dressing; poached salmon with chilli noodles; chocolate brownie ice cream.
Details: 10.30 pm, Fri & Sat 11.30 pm.*

Rasa   £ 30   ★★
6 Dering St, W1   7629 1346
55 Stoke Newington Church St, N16   7249 0431
*"Everyone would be a veggie if all the food was this good" – the
"sublime" cooking served by this Keralan duo ensures that "they
are certainly not just for the sandals brigade"; service is very
"helpful" too. / **Sample dishes:** peppery lentil broth; mango & green
banana in spiced yoghurt; crisp apple cheesecake.
Details: www.rasarestaurants.com; 10.30 pm; N16 closed Mon L-Thu L –
W1 closed Sun; no smoking.*

Rasa Samudra W1 £ 39 ★★
5 Charlotte St 7637 0222 1–1C
"Try not to get stuck in one of the back rooms", if you visit this "weird sprawl" of a Fitzrovian; wherever you go, however, you should find some of "the best Indian vegetarian cooking in London", and "inventive Keralan fish dishes". / **Sample dishes:** *spicy seafood soup; crab with pickled vegetables; banana pancake.*
Details: *www.rasarestaurants.com; 10.30 pm; closed Sun L; no smoking area.*

The Real Greek N1 £ 38 ★
15 Hoxton Market 7739 8212 5–1D
"Fantastic Greek food with a twist" and a "brilliant wine list" have won a heady reputation for this "trendy" Hoxton two-year old; is it "going downhill", though? – the declining ratings support those who fear that it is. / **Sample dishes:** *pork, leek & prune terrine; pork stuffed with spiced peaches & feta; baklava with peaches & ouzo sorbet.*
Details: *www.therealgreek.co.uk; 10.30 pm; closed Sun; no Amex.*

Restaurant One-O-One SW1 £ 59 ★★
William St, 101 Knightsbridge 7290 7101 4–1D
Knightsbridge is an odd place to find a 'hidden gem', but the term fits this "spacious" hotel dining room; it doesn't attract a vast amount of feedback, but almost all reports confirm the "excellence" of the Gallic fish cooking, and praise the "outstanding" service. / **Sample dishes:** *salmon carpaccio; peppered fillet steak; strawberry cheesecake.* **Value tip:** *set weekday L £33(FP).* **Details:** *10.30 pm.*

Rhodes in the Square SW1 £ 54 ★
Dolphin Sq, Chichester St 7798 6767 1–4C
Some feel it "lacks finesse", but most applaud the high-quality cooking at this "grown up" Pimlico dining room; "generously spaced" tables and an out-of-the-way location (in a large apartment complex) make it a discreet venue for business. / **Sample dishes:** *scallops & prawns with fennel marmalade; pork with morels & sage cream; apple tart with blackberry ice cream.* **Value tip:** *set weekday L £35(FP).* **Details:** *10 pm; closed Mon, Sat L & Sun D.*

The Ritz W1 £ 78 🄰
150 Piccadilly 7493 8181 2–4C
The cooking is "overpriced" and "not especially memorable", but – for romantics – the "wonderful" décor of this "grand" and "beautiful" dining room "just about makes up" for it. / **Sample dishes:** *spiced potted lobster; monkfish with potato cakes & pancetta; prune & armagnac parfait.* **Details:** *www.theritzlondon.com; 11 pm; jacket & tie required.*

Riva SW13 £ 39 ★★
169 Church Rd 8748 0434 6–1A
"Knocks the River Café into a cocked hat"; Andreas Riva's "discreet" (but slightly "soulless") Barnes fixture still divides opinion, but the many vaunting its "amazingly creative and delicious" Italian cooking were much more to the fore this year. / **Sample dishes:** *San Daniele ham with apple & quince; veal & pork osso buco; pannacotta with nutmeg ice cream.* **Details:** *11 pm, Fri & Sat 11.30 pm; closed Sat L.*

The River Café W6 £ 56 ★
Thames Whf, Rainville Rd 7386 4200
"Buy a ticket to Tuscany instead", say critics – given the "stupid prices" at this famous Hammersmith Italian, it wouldn't cost much more; for many reporters, a visit here is still "worth it", but the ranks of those who think the place "overblown" and "disappointing" continue to swell. / **Sample dishes:** *asparagus risotto; crispy Bresse pigeon; chocolate nemesis.* **Details:** *9.30 pm; closed Sun D.*

Roussillon SW1 £ 43 ★★

16 St Barnabas St   7730 5550   4–2D

*"Brilliant", "nicely idiosyncratic" Gallic cooking is winning a growing following for this "understated" Pimlico establishment; as ever, there's a strange gulf between those who say there's "no ambience" and other who proclaim it "perfect". / **Sample dishes:** millefeuille of asparagus & morels; crunchy-skin sea bass with salsify in ham; blood orange tart.* **Value tip:** *set weekday L £28(FP).* **Details:** *www.roussillon.co.uk; 10.45 pm; closed Sat L & Sun; no smoking area.*

Royal China SW15 £ 27 ★★

3 Chelverton Rd   8788 0907   6–2B

*"For dim sum, it's as good as the one on Queensway" (now under separate ownership), say supporters of this "fantastic" Putney Chinese, where "the slightly faded glamour of the '70s nightclub décor just adds to the fun". / **Sample dishes:** pork & chive dumplings with turnip paste; prawns in steamed rice pasta with soy; green tea.* **Details:** *11 pm; only Amex; need 7+ to book, Sun L.*

Royal China £ 33 ★★

40 Baker St, W1   7487 4688
13 Queensway, W2   7221 2535
68 Queen's Grove, NW8   7586 4280
30 Westferry Circus, E14   7719 0888

*The food's "as near to real Chinese as you can get", and the dim sum are "the best in London", so it's no surprise that you often have to queue (especially on Sundays) for these "amusingly kitsch" orientals, done out "like '70s discos". / **Sample dishes:** deep-fried crispy oysters; pork chop with mandarin sauce; toffee banana.* **Details:** *10.45 pm, Fri & Sat 11.30 pm.*

Rules WC2 £ 48 Ⓐ

35 Maiden Ln   7836 5314   3–3D

*"Tradition at its best" – not least the menu of game, grills and solid puds – comes combined with "a surprising degree of modern flair" to make London's oldest restaurant (1798) too good to waste on out-of-towners; the recent ban on cigarette smoking, though, has some patrons up in arms. / **Sample dishes:** Stilton & celeriac soup; rabbit casserole with broad beans & mustard mash; champagne sabayon.* **Details:** *www.rules.co.uk; 11.30 pm; no smoking.*

Sakonis £ 16 ★★

129 Ealing Rd, HA0   8903 9601
180-186 Upper Tooting Rd, SW17   8772 4774

*"This is the real thing" – you won't find better value in the capital than these fabulous Indian veggie cafeterias; the Wembley original, in particular, gets "very busy", and a new branch has just opened in Tooting; no alcohol. / **Sample dishes:** vegetable samosas; biryani with poori & dahl; coconut shell kulfi.* **Details:** *www.sakonis.co.uk; 9.30 pm; SW17 closed Tue; no Amex; no smoking.*

Salloos SW1 £ 45 ★★

62-64 Kinnerton St   7235 4444   4–1D

*The décor is "rather dull" and prices are "high", but this Belgravia mews stalwart has long been a "consistent" performer, and many still reckon it serves "the best Indian/Pakistani food in the UK". / **Sample dishes:** mulligatawny soup; tandoori lamb with saffron rice; cardamom ice cream.* **Value tip:** *set weekday L £27(FP).* **Details:** *11.15 pm; closed Sun.*

Sarastro WC2   £ 30   𝔸 ✕

126 Drury Ln   7836 0101   1–2D

There's "plenty to criticise on the food front", but this "completely bizarre and kitsch" Theatreland Turk is well worth at least one visit for its "magical" and "OTT" décor (which comes complete with "romantic alcoves"). / **Sample dishes:** grilled sardines; kofte lamb meatballs with rice; cassata ice cream. **Value tip:** set brunch £17(FP). **Details:** www.sarastro-restaurant.com; 11.30 pm; no smoking area.

Sarkhel's SW18   £ 26   ★★

199 Replingham Rd   8870 1483   6–2B

Is this "the best Indian in London"?; Udit Sarkhel was formerly head chef at the Bombay Brasserie, and – thanks to his "wonderfully light and inventive cooking" – it's not a ridiculous claim to make for this "delightful" Southfields venture. / **Sample dishes:** deep-fried spiced paneer; Goan prawn masala; mango kulfi. **Details:** 10.30 pm, Fri & Sat 11 pm; closed Mon; no smoking area.

Savoy Grill WC2   £ 70

Strand   7420 2066   3–3D

It's no longer THE power lunching venue, but this gracious panelled dining room is still a "great business setting", sustained by staff who "anticipate and act on every whim"; the "so-so" traditional fare remains rather beside the point. / **Sample dishes:** seared tuna with coriander couscous; roast chicken with truffles & port sauce; apple & rhubarb crumble. **Value tip:** pre-th. £45(FP). **Details:** www.savoygroup.com; 11.15 pm; closed Sat L & Sun; jacket & tie required.

Seashell NW1   £ 23   ★

49 Lisson Grove   7224 9000

"Smashing" fish and chips (and "great mushy peas" too) maintain this "traditional" fixture's name as "the best chippy around"; "it's on the tourist trail, though", and it's looking pretty "tired". / **Sample dishes:** prawns in garlic; haddock & chips; treacle sponge pudding. **Details:** 10.30 pm; closed Sun; no smoking area; no booking.

Shanghai E8   £ 23   𝔸 ★

41 Kingsland High St   7254 2878

Make sure you sit in the front section (which was once an impressive pie 'n' eel shop) if you visit this "very good neighbourhood Chinese" in Dalston; "great buffet lunches" are a particular attraction. / **Sample dishes:** mussels in black bean sauce; sea bass with fried bean curd & peppers; toffee apple. **Details:** 11 pm; no Amex.

J Sheekey WC2   £ 42   𝔸 ★★

28-32 St Martin's Ct   7240 2565   3–3B

"The kingpin of fish cooking at the moment" – this chicly revitalised Theatreland seafood parlour has become "a real winner" since the Ivy/Caprice people began to work their magic; this year, for the first time, it joins its siblings in the 'Top 10' restaurants reporters talk about the most. / **Sample dishes:** seared tuna; Dover sole with asparagus; spotted dick. **Value tip:** set Sun L £25(FP). **Details:** midnight.

Shogun W1   £ 50   ★

Adam's Row   7493 1255   2–3A

"Excellent traditional cooking" (including "wonderful sushi") makes this "very expensive" Mayfair veteran one of the top Japaneses in town; some think its "dark" cellar setting has "great atmosphere", but it doesn't do it for everyone. / **Sample dishes:** seafood tempura; beef teriyaki; fruit & ice cream. **Details:** 11 pm; D only, closed Mon; no Switch.

Simpsons-in-the-Strand WC2   £ 49
100 Strand   7836 9112   3–3D
"Dated" standards – reminiscent of the "school canteen" – mean
you tend to find a rather "touristy" clientèle nowadays at what was
once the most famous of English restaurants; its "luxurious"
breakfasts, however, are commended. / **Sample dishes:** potted brown
shrimps & toast; pigeon with braised red cabbage; treacle sponge & custard.
Value tip: set weekday L £32(FP). **Details:** www.savoygroup.com; 11 pm, Sun
9 pm; closed Sat L; jacket required.

Smiths of Smithfield EC1   £ 48   A
67-77 Charterhouse St   7236 6666   5–1A
"An 'in' place that's almost passed the test of time"; this "trendy"
Manhattan-inspired complex, in an "interesting" building
overlooking Smithfield Market, successfully covers a variety of bases
– from bar snacks, via brunch in the brasserie (FP £32), to business
lunching in the rooftop restaurant (to which the price given relates).
/ **Sample dishes:** lobster omelette with star anise; roast Old Spot pork with
crackling & apple sauce; Sauternes custard with armagnac prunes. **Value
tip:** set weekday L £30(FP). **Details:** www.smithsofsmithfield.co.uk; 11 pm;
closed Sat L (café open all day).

Sonny's SW13   £ 38   A★
94 Church Rd   8748 0393   6–1A
"Excellent quality" cooking, "sensible" pricing, "thoughtful" service
and a "buzzy" atmosphere – this "well-loved local", now back on
form, is quite an asset in sleepy old Barnes. / **Sample dishes:** duck
liver parfait with sweet pickle; salmon with red lentils & samphire; apple &
sultana tart. **Details:** 11 pm; closed Sun D.

Le Soufflé W1   £ 66   ★
1 Hamilton Pl   7409 3131   2–4A
September '01 sees the departure of Peter Kromberg, who has
been chef at this soulless Mayfair dining room since 1975;
his successor must surely at some point be presented with the
revamp Mr K's cooking has so long deserved. / **Sample
dishes:** lobster & ginger tartlet; sea bass with caper & tomato jus; lemon tart
with lemon tea ice cream. **Value tip:** set weekday L £43(FP).
Details: www.interconti.com; 10.30 pm, Sat 11.15 pm; closed Mon, Sat L &
Sun D; no smoking area.

Souk WC2   £ 25   A
27 Litchfield St   7240 1796   3–3B
"Great little place, almost next to The Ivy", whose "fabulous", "fun"
atmosphere and affordable prices make it a good bet for romance,
and "excellent for parties"; the Moroccan grub is "decent enough".
/ **Sample dishes:** roast pepper & tpmato salad; Merguez sausages &
couscous; mint baklava. **Details:** 11.30 pm; no Amex.

Soulard N1   £ 28   A★
113 Mortimer Rd   7254 1314
"A hidden gem and a real bistro" – this "piece of France" in north
Islington charms with its "personal service", "excellent cuisine",
and "dim-lit romance". / **Sample dishes:** grilled goats cheese with honey;
smoed haddock with saffron sauce; crème brûlée. **Details:** 10 pm; D only,
closed Mon & Sun; no Amex.

Spoon + W1   £ 75   ✕
50 Berners St   7300 1444   2–1D
It may offer a "people-watching extravaganza", but the dining
room of Ian Schrager's north-of-Oxford-Street design-hotel is an
extremely "pretentious" place, with a "daft" menu and "crazy"
prices. / **Sample dishes:** iced tomato soup; steamed shrimp with green
mango & Thai dressing; meringue cake with summer berries. **Details:** 11 pm.

The Square W1 £ 71 ★

6-10 Bruton St   7495 7100   2–2C

With Philip Howard's "exquisite" modern French cooking, and a first-rate wine list, this "slick" Mayfair dining room is simply "the ultimate" for many reporters; it's "best on expenses", however, and "supercilious" service is a recurrent complaint. / **Sample dishes:** pea & ham soup with morels; sea bass with risotto; blood orange soufflé with chocolate ice cream. **Value tip:** set weekday L £43(FP). **Details:** 10.45 pm; closed Sat L & Sun L.

The Stepping Stone SW8 £ 35 A★★

123 Queenstown Rd   7622 0555   6–1C

The epitome of an "excellent local", this "stylish" but "relaxed" Battersea "all-rounder" is universally hailed for its "imaginative" and "careful" cooking, and its "attentive" service. / **Sample dishes:** smoked salmon & balsamic grapes; roast duck with chorizo & chickpeas; orange & bay leaf pannacotta. **Details:** 11 pm, Mon 10.30 pm; closed Sat L & Sun D; no Amex; no smoking area.

Sticky Fingers W8 £ 28

1a Phillimore Gdns   7938 5338   4–1A

"Stick to the burgers, as other options can disappoint", is one veteran's advice regarding this "nostalgia rock" Kensington diner (previously owned by Bill Wyman) – it has long been a popular destination for those with kids in tow. / **Sample dishes:** nachos with guacamole & salsa; bacon & cheeseburger with chips; ice cream. **Details:** 11.30 pm.

The Sugar Club W1 £ 47 ★★

21 Warwick St   7437 7776   2–2D

"Wonderful" Pacific Rim cooking, with "sumptuous" flavours, is making this "minimalist" – some say "stark" – Soho venture an ever-greater success. / **Sample dishes:** Indian prawn fishcakes with mango; venison with apple & pistachio pancakes; banoffi pie with galangal sorbet. **Details:** www.thesugarclub.co.uk; 11 pm; no smoking area.

Suntory SW1 £ 75

72 St James's St   7409 0201   2–4D

This tediously grand St James's veteran is "a favourite for visiting Japanese businessmen", and the cooking "maintains its high standards"; it's "hellishly expensive", though, and the level of service is surprisingly "poor". / **Sample dishes:** sea urchin on sushi rice; sea bass with foie gras & aubergine; summer fruits. **Value tip:** set weekday L £37(FP). **Details:** 10 pm; closed Sun L.

Sushi-Say NW2 £ 31 ★

33b Walm Ln   8459 7512

This "super, family-run Japanese" makes an excellent find in distant Willesden Green; the menu highlight is "top-class sushi", and service is "charming". / **Sample dishes:** clear soup with picked vegetables; salmon, tuna & eel sushi; ice cream. **Details:** 10.30 pm; closed Mon, Tue-Fri D only, Sat & Sun open L & D; no smoking area.

Sweetings EC4 £ 36 A★

39 Queen Victoria St   7248 3062   5–3B

For "great fish in a traditional setting", this "splendid" Victorian "relic" is "a perennial City favourite" (arrive at noon to be sure of a seat); the head chef became the new proprietor in July '01, so the policy of "excellence in simplicity" seems unlikely to change. / **Sample dishes:** crab cocktail; deep-fried halibut & chips; baked jam sponge. **Details:** L only, closed Sat & Sun; no credit cards; no booking.

Talad Thai SW15 £ 24 ★★

320 Upper Richmond Rd   8789 8084   6–2A

A "terrific" Putney canteen that's "hard to beat" – "if you don't mind queuing". / **Sample dishes:** spring rolls; chicken wrapped in pandan leaves; no puddings. **Details:** 10 pm; no credit cards; no smoking; no booking.

Tamarind W1 £ 44 A★★

20 Queen St   7629 3561   2–3B

"Chic and sophisticated" décor provides a backdrop for some "very refined" cooking at this Mayfair subcontinental, which is among the elite group "taking Indian cuisine to a new level". / **Sample dishes:** prawn & scallop tandoori with sour grapes; curried lamb shank with paratha bread; mango kulfi. **Value tip:** set weekday L & Sun L £27(FP). **Details:** 11.15 pm; closed Sat L.

Tas £ 20 A★

33 The Cut, SE1   7928 2111
72 Borough High St, SE1   7403 7200

This "tightly-packed" Turkish duo – by the Young Vic, and now near Borough Market – have now got the South Bank covered, and their "excellent-value mezze" make them ideal for "quick and cheerful" meals; despite a complete absence of PR ballyhoo, their top-value charms made them the second most-mentioned new restaurant in this years' survey. / **Sample dishes:** artichokes in garlic olive oil; lamb casserole; upside-down pudding. **Details:** 11.30 pm.

Tatsuso EC2 £ 68 ★★

32 Broadgate Circle   7638 5863   5–2D

"The prices kill your appetite", so "let your broker pay" at this City Japanese, which is the best in town; on the ground floor "awesomely fresh meat and fish" are grilled on the teppan-yaki, while the humbler basement serves "brilliant" sushi and other "exquisite" delicacies. / **Sample dishes:** seafood tempura; beef teriyaki; fruit salad with ice cream. **Details:** 9 pm; closed Sat & Sun.

Teca W1 £ 41 ★★

54 Brooks Mews   7495 4774   2–2B

"If Zafferano is booked, Teca is a good alternative" – "really top-notch" cooking and staff who "try hard" are elevating this Mayfair mews Italian (also part of A-Z Restaurants) to the first rank, even if the setting is "a bit on the bland side"; "there's a rare selection of fine Italian wines". / **Sample dishes:** foie gras terrine with cherry bread; bream with red pepper sauce & fried basil; tiramisu. **Details:** 10.30 pm; closed Sun.

The Tenth W8 £ 52 A★

Kensington High St   7361 1910   4–1A

A "well-kept secret"; this 10th-floor dining room not only has "fabulous views" (over Kensington Gardens) but also offers "beautifully presented" cooking and "very attentive" service. / **Sample dishes:** quail with black truffles; monkfish, tiger prawn & coconut broth with rice; chocolate pudding with Bailey's ice cream. **Value tip:** set weekday L £34(FP). **Details:** www.royalgardenhotel.co.uk; 11 pm; closed Sat L & Sun; no smoking area.

Thailand SE14 £ 28 ★★

15 Lewisham Way   8691 4040

"The best Thai outside Thailand" – well, almost – is found at this "small", "crowded" oriental, in a "less than pleasant" corner of Lewisham. / **Sample dishes:** tom yam soup with chicken; whole fish stuffed with Lao herbs; sticky rice & mango. **Value tip:** set weekday L £15(FP). **Details:** 11 pm; D only, closed Mon; no Amex; no smoking.

Titanic W1 £ 42 X

81 Brewer St   7437 1912   2–3D

Yes, it's "a disaster!"; with its "sub-standard comfort food", its "indifferent" service and "zero" atmosphere, MPW's subterranean brasserie, near Piccadilly Circus, strikes many reporters as little short of "shocking". / **Sample dishes:** wild mushrooms on toast; fish & chips with pea purée; Black Forest gâteau. **Details:** 11 pm; closed Mon & Sun.

Tootsies £ 25

35 James St, W1   7486 1611
177 New King's Rd, SW6   7736 4023
107 Old Brompton Rd, SW7   7581 8942
120 Holland Park Ave, W11   7229 8567
148 Chiswick High Rd, W4   8747 1869
198 Haverstock Hill, NW3   7431 3812
147 Church Rd, SW13   8748 3630
36-38 Abbeville Rd, SW4   8772 6646
"Kids love it", and there's *"something for everyone"* at this
café/diner chain, where *"consistently good"* burgers and *"very
good"* shakes are menu mainstays. / **Sample dishes:** *Thai chicken
cakes; beefburger with blue cheese sauce & chips; lemon meringue pie.*
Details: *11 pm-11.30 pm, Fri & Sat midnight; no smoking areas at SW13,
W11 & W4; booking at certain times only.*

Toto's SW1 £ 45   A★

Lennox Gardens Mews   7589 0075   4–2D
"Beautiful" and *"hidden away"*, this long-established Knightsbridge
Italian is one of the best all-rounders in town – *"great pasta"* is
the highlight of the *"consistent"* menu, service is *"patient and
attentive"*, and there's even a *"quiet terrace for a sunny day"*.
/ **Sample dishes:** *lamb carpaccio; monkfish with artichokes & pesto; mango
mousse.* **Details:** *11.30 pm.*

Les Trois Garçons E1 £ 42   A

1 Club Row   7613 1924
"The most amazing restaurant décor in London" – *"OTT"* and
"very cool", all at the same time – lends a *"marvellous
atmosphere"* to this converted East End boozer; the *"classic"*
French cooking is heftily priced, but surprisingly *"good"*. / **Sample
dishes:** *snails in garlic butter; steak with red wine jus and greens; French
cheese platter.* **Details:** *www.lestroisgarcons.com; 10 pm, Thu-Sat 10.30 pm;
closed Sat L & Sun.*

La Trompette W4 £ 39   A★★

5-7 Devonshire Rd   8747 1836
"More like Mayfair than Chiswick" – Nigel Platts-Martin (Chez
Bruce etc) has done it again with this stellar newcomer, on the
site of La Dordogne (RIP); *"sensational quality and value"* and
"first-class service" are among the qualities that make the whole
set-up seem very *"glamorous"*, especially *"for an out-of-town
place"*. / **Sample dishes:** *grilled sardine tart with gremolata; duck with foie
gras & madeira sauce; chocolate profiteroles.* **Details:** *11 pm; no smoking
area; booking: max 8.*

Troubadour SW5 £ 24   A★

265 Old Brompton Rd   7370 1434   4–3A
This *"snug"* and *"eccentric"* Earl's Court coffee shop is a south west
London rarity – a haunt for Bohemians and artistic types; you don't
have to look 'deep' if you stop off for breakfast, a coffee or
a snack... but it helps. / **Sample dishes:** *crab & melon salad; bangers &
mash; crème brûlée.* **Details:** *11 pm; no credit cards; no booking.*

Twentyfour EC2 £ 52   A

Old Broad St   7877 2424   5–2C
*"The City landscape makes a perfect backdrop to a business
meal"*, at this 24th-floor eyrie in the former NatWest Tower;
the food is *"not exceptional"*, but the *"bill matches the altitude"*.
/ **Sample dishes:** *seared scallops with pea sauce; tuna with aubergine
purée & spinach; chocolate fondant with capuccino ice cream.*
Details: *9.30 pm; closed Sat & Sun; no jeans.*

Ubon E14　　　　　　　　　　　**£ 55**　　　★
34 Westferry Circus　7719 7800
It utterly "lacks the glamour of Nobu", but this new, rather "corporate" East End cousin of the famed West Ender does at least bring some "dazzling" Japanese-inspired fare to Canary Wharf; it's easy to miss the "amazing" view, but it does offer some compensation for prices, which "make you cry". / **Sample dishes:** toro tartare with caviar; rock shrimp donburi (one-pot rice dish); fresh fruit Bento box. **Details:** 10.15 pm; closed Sat L & Sun; no smoking area.

Vama SW10　　　　　　　　　**£ 38**　　★★
438 King's Rd　7351 4118　4–3B
A "gourmet" Chelsea curry house, near World's End, whose "very fresh", "perfectly spiced" Indian cooking ranks it amongst "the best in town". / **Sample dishes:** tandoori prawns; chicken murgh tikka; kulfi. **Value tip:** set Sun L £25(FP). **Details:** www.vama.co.uk; 11 pm.

Viet-Anh NW1　　　　　　　　**£ 17**　　★★
41 Parkway　7284 4082
"Is this the best Vietnamese this side of Paris?" – "lovely" staff (who "take the trouble to explain things") add lustre to this small and "basic" Camden Town newcomer, whose cooking is "genuine" and "good value". / **Sample dishes:** spring rolls; spicy chicken broth with glass noodles; lychees. **Details:** 11 pm; no smoking area.

Vijay NW6　　　　　　　　　　**£ 18**　　★★
49 Willesden Ln　7328 1087
Who cares about the "awful" décor? – it's "worth the journey" to this "simply wonderful" West Hampstead spot for its "fresh" and "unusual" south Indian cooking, and its "friendly" service. / **Sample dishes:** king prawn tikka; chilli chicken; ice cream & mango. **Details:** 10.45 pm, Fri & Sat 11.45 pm; no smoking area.

Vong SW1　　　　　　　　　　**£ 54**　　　★
Wilton Pl　7235 1010　4–1D
"The plates are works of art", at this Belgravian outpost of the famous NYC Thai/French establishment, whose "elegant and delicious" cooking wins much applause; some find the food "over-slick and overpriced", however, and the atmosphere can seem "soulless". / **Sample dishes:** chilled tomato, cucumber & watermelon soup; steak with gingered mushrooms & soy caramel sauce; Valrhona chocolate cake. **Details:** www.jean-georges.com; 11.30 pm; no smoking area.

Vrisaki N22　　　　　　　　　**£ 26**　　　★
73 Myddleton Rd　8889 8760
"The biggest mezze ever" is the claim to fame of this big, "fun" Greek, which is "hard to find" in the backwaters of Bounds Green. / **Sample dishes:** smoked trout & pitta bread; moussaka; Greek yoghurt with honey. **Details:** midnight; closed Sun.

The Walmer Castle W11　　　**£ 26**　　Ⓐ★
58 Ledbury Rd　7229 4620
"Good and spicy Thai cooking" and a "great buzz" win ringing endorsements for this "charming room above a Notting HIll pub" – a fave rave for "trendy" twentysomethings. / **Sample dishes:** sweetcorn fritters; stir-fried prawns & vegetables; mango sorbet. **Details:** 10.30 pm; closed weekday L.

Wapping Food E1　　　　　　**£ 35**　　Ⓐ
Wapping Pumping Hs, Wapping Wall　7680 2080
Occupying an "outstanding space" – a converted East End machine hall, near the famous Prospect of Whitby – this "exciting" new venture offers a "good", if "rather limited", menu, accompanied by an impressive range of Antipodean wines. / **Sample dishes:** pork with Manchego cheese & sherry vinegar; fillet steak with leeks & pancetta; lavender pannacotta. **Details:** 10.30 pm; closed Sun D.

West Street Restaurant WC2　　　£ 42

13-15 West St　7010 8600　3–2B

It's only a few paces from the Ivy, so let's hope that this ambitious new bar/brasserie/restaurant (from the owners of Kensington Place, the Avenue et al) lives up to its aspirations when it opens in September '01 – if not, there will be unrivalled scope for odious comparisons! / **Details:** *midnight; closed Sun.*

Windows on the World W1　　　£ 72　　🄰 ✗

22 Park Ln　7208 4021　2–4A

"A breathtaking view is not enough" – this 24th-floor Mayfair eyrie has "massive" potential, but its current performance is "completely amateur in all respects". / **Sample dishes:** *chicken soup with curry glaze; roast lamb with coconut rice & citrus sauce; cherry clafoutis.* **Details:** *10.30 pm, Fri & Sat 11.30 pm; closed Sat L & Sun D; jacket & tie required at D; no smoking at breakfast.*

Windsor Castle W8　　　£ 27　　　　🄰

114 Campden Hill Rd　7243 9551

With its "brilliant garden", not to mention an ancient and atmospheric interior, this Kensington boozer is many a Londoner's idea of the "perfect" pub, and the "simple" cooking generally satisfies. / **Sample dishes:** *oysters; steak & ale pie; chocolate sponge pudding.* **Details:** *9.30 pm; no smoking area at L; no booking.*

The Wine Library EC3　　　£ 15　　　🄰

43 Trinity Sq　7481 0415　5–3D

"Not for food, but for wine"; "a good cheese and pâté selection" is on hand to help you sink your choice from the "massive" range of bottles (at merchant's price, plus £3.50 corkage) at these "intimate" and very atmospheric City cellars; you "need to book". / **Sample dishes:** *liver pâté & toast; quiche lorraine & salad; fresh fruit.* **Details:** *8 pm; L & early evening only, closed Sat & Sun.*

Yoshino W1　　　£ 33　　　★★

3 Piccadilly Pl　7287 6622　2–3D

"Just like Japan" – this "smart" little bar, hidden-away near Piccadilly Circus, is so "authentic" that it only relatively recently introduced a menu in English; it offers "the best sashimi in town", and is praised for its "outstanding value", particularly at lunch. / **Sample dishes:** *assorted sashimi; tempura prawns with chilli & wasabi salt dips; green tea ice cream.* **Value tip:** *set weekday L £19(FP).* **Details:** *9 pm; closed Sun; no smoking area.*

Yum Yum N16　　　£ 24　　　🄰 ★

30 Stoke Newington Church St　7254 6751

Some find the atmosphere a bit "noisy" and "impersonal", but this Stoke Newington favourite consistently delivers "well executed" Thai dishes and "friendly" service. / **Sample dishes:** *deep-fried seafood with plum sauce; spicy beef salad with Thai herbs; banana fritters.* **Value tip:** *set weekday L £14(FP).* **Details:** *www.yumyum.co.uk; 10.45 pm, Fri & Sat 11.15 pm.*

Zafferano SW1　　　£ 48　　　🄰 ★★

15 Lowndes St　7235 5800　4–1D

"Unchanged, despite the changes" – "Italian cooking at its classical best" matched by "cracking service" has survived the departure of Giorgio Locatelli from this wonderful Belgravian; it's still "too difficult to get into", and the seating is still rather "squashed". / **Sample dishes:** *saffon risotto; monkfish with walnuts & caper sauce; figs with mint sorbet.* **Details:** *11 pm.*

Zaika W8 £ 47

1 Kensington High St   7795 6533   4–1A

*It is a brave move for A-Z Restaurants to transfer this inspiring Indian – London's best – from its "sophisticated" Chelsea home to the cavernous Kensington site vacated by L'Anis (RIP); let's hope Vineet Bhatia's "superb and creative" cooking survives the transition. / **Sample dishes:** tamarind chicken with milk fritters; crab & spiced scallops with Indian risotto; deep-fried stuffed dates. **Value tip:** set weekday L £29(FP). **Details:** www.zaika-restaurant.co.uk; 10.45 pm; closed Sat L.*

Zaika Bazaar SW3 £ 27   ★★

2a Pond Pl   7584 6655   4–2C

*Zaika's pared-down new basement offshoot (on the site of the short-lived El Rincon, RIP) may not have huge charm, but the simple Indian menu is prepared to a standard that – on an early-days, July '01 visit – offered spectacular value, especially by Brompton Cross standards. / **Sample dishes:** tandoori broccoli & cauliflower; lamb with cinnamon & cloves; cardamom rice pudding. **Details:** 10.45 pm; closed Sat L & Sun.*

Ziani SW3 £ 35   𝔸★

45-47 Radnor Walk   7352 2698   4–3C

*"Great fun, if too crowded" – this small Chelsea backstreet Italian has long maintained a disproportionately large fan club, thanks to its "reliable" cooking and its "relaxed" approach. / **Sample dishes:** scallop & rocket salad; macaroni with wild boar sausage & aubergine; pannacotta. **Details:** 11.30 pm.*

LONDON
AREA OVERVIEWS
INDEXES
MAPS

CENTRAL

Soho, Covent Garden & Bloomsbury
(Parts of W1, all WC2 and WC1)

£70+	Savoy Grill	*British, Traditional*	-
£60+	Conrad Gallagher	*British, Modern*	𝔸★
	Lindsay House	*"*	𝔸
	Asia de Cuba	*East/West*	✗
£50+	Indigo	*British, Modern*	𝔸★
	The Criterion	*French*	𝔸
£40+	Bank	*British, Modern*	-
	The Ivy	*"*	𝔸★
	Mezzo	*"*	✗
	West Street Restaurant	*"*	-
	Rules	*British, Traditional*	𝔸
	Simpsons-in-the-Strand	*"*	-
	L'Escargot	*French*	𝔸★
	Incognico	*"*	★
	The Sugar Club	*East/West*	★★
	J Sheekey	*Fish & seafood*	𝔸★★
£35+	Aurora	*British, Modern*	𝔸★
	Le Palais du Jardin	*French*	𝔸
	Joe Allen	*American*	𝔸
£30+	Andrew Edmunds	*British, Modern*	𝔸★
	Sarastro	*International*	𝔸✗
	Balans	*"*	-
	Fung Shing	*Chinese*	★★
	Chiang Mai	*Thai*	★★
£25+	Souk	*North African*	𝔸
	Abeno	*Japanese*	★
£20+	Gordon's Wine Bar	*International*	𝔸
	Mildreds	*Vegetarian*	𝔸★
	Pâtisserie Valerie	*Sandwiches, cakes, etc*	𝔸
	Mr Kong	*Chinese*	★
£15+	Food for Thought	*Vegetarian*	★
£5+	Paul	*Sandwiches, cakes, etc*	𝔸★
	Bar Italia	*"*	𝔸

Mayfair & St James's
(Parts of W1 and SW1)

£80+	Connaught	*British, Traditional*	𝔸
	Le Gavroche	*French*	★★

	Gordon Ramsay (Claridges)	"	-
	Dorchester, Oriental	Chinese	★
£70+	The Square	French	★
	The Ritz	"	𝔸
	Windows on the World	"	𝔸✗
	Suntory	Japanese	-
£60+	Dorchester Grill	British, Traditional	𝔸
	Pétrus	French	★★
	Le Soufflé	"	★
£50+	Rhodes in the Square	British, Modern	★
	Greenhouse	"	-
	Mirabelle	French	𝔸★
	L'Oranger	"	𝔸★
	Nobu	East/West	𝔸★★
	Matsuri	Japanese	★
	Mitsukoshi	"	★
	Shogun	"	★
£40+	Le Caprice	British, Modern	𝔸★
	Quaglino's	"	✗
	Teca	Italian	★★
	Titanic	International	✗
	Momo	Moroccan	𝔸
	Hakkasan	Chinese	𝔸★
	Kai	"	𝔸★
	Tamarind	Indian	𝔸★★
£30+	Rasa	Indian	★★
	Yoshino	Japanese	★★
£25+	Hard Rock Café	Burgers, etc	𝔸

Fitzrovia & Marylebone (Part of W1)

£70+	Pied à Terre	French	★
	Spoon +	International	✗
£50+	Orrery	French	𝔸★
	Archipelago	East/West	𝔸★
	Defune	Japanese	★★
£40+	Odin's	British, Traditional	𝔸★
	Passione	Italian	𝔸★★
	The Providores	East/West	★
	La Porte des Indes	Indian	𝔸★
£35+	Back to Basics	Fish & seafood	★★
	Ozer	Turkish	-

	Rasa Samudra	*Indian*	★★
£30+	Café Bagatelle	*French*	𝔸
	Royal China	*Chinese*	★★
£25+	Giraffe	*British, Modern*	𝔸
	Fairuz	*Lebanese*	-
	Tootsies	*Burgers, etc*	-
£20+	Pâtisserie Valerie	*Sandwiches, cakes, etc*	𝔸

Belgravia, Victoria & Pimlico (SW1, except St James's)

£70+	Mju	*East/West*	-
£60+	Foliage	*French*	★
	Nahm	*Thai*	★
£50+	The Lanesborough	*British, Modern*	𝔸
	Goring Hotel	*British, Traditional*	𝔸
	Restaurant One-O-One	*French*	★★
	Vong	*East/West*	★
£40+	Roussillon	*French*	★★
	La Poule au Pot	*"*	𝔸★
	Zafferano	*Italian*	𝔸★★
	Toto's	*"*	𝔸★
	Ken Lo's Memories	*Chinese*	★★
	Mr Chow	*"*	𝔸
	The Cinnamon Club	*Indian*	𝔸★★
	Salloos	*"*	★★
	Mango Tree	*Thai*	-
£35+	Caraffini	*Italian*	𝔸★
	Il Convivio	*"*	𝔸★
£30+	Hunan	*Chinese*	★★
£25+	Blue Jade	*Thai*	𝔸★

WEST

Chelsea, South Kensington, Kensington, Earl's Court & Fulham (SW3, SW5, SW6, SW7, SW10 & W8)

£80+	Gordon Ramsay	*French*	𝔸★★
	Blakes Hotel	*International*	𝔸
£70+	Capital Hotel	*French*	★
£60+	Babylon	*British, Modern*	𝔸✗
	Monkeys	*French*	𝔸★
	Aubergine	*"*	★
	Bibendum	*"*	-
£50+	Clarke's	*British, Modern*	𝔸★★
	The Tenth	*"*	𝔸★
	Belvedere	*French*	𝔸
	Poissonnerie de l'Avenue	*Fish & seafood*	★
£40+	Launceston Place	*British, Modern*	𝔸★
	Bluebird	*"*	✗
	Chezmax	*French*	𝔸★★
	Pasha	*Moroccan*	𝔸
	Mr Wing	*Chinese*	𝔸★
	Bombay Brasserie	*Indian*	𝔸★
	Chutney Mary	*"*	★
	Zaika	*"*	-
	Blue Elephant	*Thai*	𝔸★
£35+	Admiral Codrington	*British, Modern*	-
	Lundum's	*Danish*	𝔸★
	Ziani	*Italian*	𝔸★
	Cambio de Tercio	*Spanish*	𝔸★
	Bibendum Oyster Bar	*Fish & seafood*	𝔸★★
	Phoenicia	*Lebanese*	-
	Vama	*Indian*	★★
£30+	De Cecco	*Italian*	𝔸★
	Elistano	*"*	𝔸★
	Balans	*International*	-
£25+	The Builder's Arms	*British, Modern*	𝔸★
	Lots Road	*"*	𝔸★
	Windsor Castle	*International*	𝔸
	Sticky Fingers	*Burgers, etc*	-
	Tootsies	*"*	-
	Basilico	*Pizza*	★★
	Zaika Bazaar	*Indian*	★★
£20+	Il Pagliaccio	*Italian*	𝔸

	Lomo	*Spanish*	𝔸
	Troubadour	*Sandwiches, cakes, etc*	𝔸 ★
	Pâtisserie Valerie	*"*	𝔸
£15+	Churchill Arms	*Thai*	𝔸 ★

Notting Hill, Holland Park, Bayswater, North Kensington & Maida Vale (W2, W9, W10, W11)

£40+	Julie's	*British, Modern*	𝔸
	Chez Moi	*French*	𝔸 ★
	Assaggi	*Italian*	𝔸 ★★
	Dakota	*American*	-
£35+	The Cow	*British, Modern*	𝔸 ★
£30+	The Ladbroke Arms	*British, Modern*	★
	Royal China	*Chinese*	★★
	Inaho	*Japanese*	★★
£25+	Tootsies	*Burgers, etc*	-
	Mandarin Kitchen	*Chinese*	★★
	The Walmer Castle	*Thai*	𝔸 ★
£20+	Ranoush	*Lebanese*	★★
£15+	Beirut Express	*Lebanese*	★★
£5+	Lisboa Patisserie	*Sandwiches, cakes, etc*	★★

Hammersmith, Shepherd's Bush Chiswick & Olympia (W4, W5, W6, W12, W14)

£50+	The River Café	*Italian*	★
£35+	Parade	*British, Modern*	𝔸 ★
	La Trompette	*French*	𝔸 ★★
	Chinon	*"*	★★
£30+	Popeseye	*Steaks & grills*	★★
	The Gate	*Vegetarian*	𝔸 ★★
£25+	The Anglesea Arms	*British, Modern*	★★
	The Havelock Tavern	*"*	★★
	Tootsies	*Burgers, etc*	-
	Esarn Kheaw	*Thai*	★★
£20+	Blah! Blah! Blah!	*Vegetarian*	★★

NORTH

Hampstead, West Hampstead, St John's Wood, Regent's Park, Kilburn & Camden Town (NW postcodes)

£40+	L'Aventure	*French*	𝔸★★
£35+	Odette's	*British, Modern*	𝔸★
	The Engineer	*"*	𝔸
£30+	The Gate	*Vegetarian*	𝔸★★
	Royal China	*Chinese*	★★
	Feng Shang	*"*	𝔸★
	Jin Kichi	*Japanese*	★★
	Sushi-Say	*"*	★
£25+	Giraffe	*British, Modern*	𝔸
	Tootsies	*Burgers, etc*	-
	Gung-Ho	*Chinese*	𝔸★
	Café Japan	*Japanese*	★★
£20+	Daphne	*Greek*	-
	Nautilus	*Fish & chips*	★
	Seashell	*"*	★
£15+	Geeta	*Indian*	★★
	Vijay	*"*	★★
	Sakonis	*"*	★★
	Viet-Anh	*Vietnamese*	★★

Islington, Highgate, Crouch End, Stoke Newington, Finsbury Park, Muswell Hill & Finchley (N postcodes)

£35+	Frederick's	*British, Modern*	𝔸★
	The Real Greek	*Greek*	★
£30+	The Duke of Cambridge	*British, Modern*	𝔸
	Chez Liline	*Fish & seafood*	★★
	Rasa	*Indian*	★★
£25+	Mesclun	*British, Modern*	𝔸★★
	Giraffe	*"*	𝔸
	Les Associés	*French*	𝔸★
	Soulard	*"*	𝔸★
	Vrisaki	*Greek*	★
	Pasha	*Turkish*	𝔸★
£20+	Iznik	*Turkish*	𝔸
	Yum Yum	*Thai*	𝔸★

SOUTH

South Bank
(SE1)

£50+	Oxo Tower	*British, Modern*	𝔸 ✗
£25+	Champor-Champor	*East/West*	𝔸 ★★
£20+	Pizzeria Castello	*Pizza*	𝔸 ★
	Tas	*Turkish*	𝔸 ★

Battersea, Clapham, Wandsworth, Barnes, Putney, Brixton & Lewisham
(All postcodes south of the river except SE1)

£50+	Monsieur Max	*French*	𝔸 ★★
£40+	Chez Bruce	*British, Modern*	𝔸 ★★
£35+	The Glasshouse	*British, Modern*	𝔸 ★★
	The Stepping Stone	"	𝔸 ★★
	Sonny's	"	𝔸 ★
	Riva	*Italian*	★★
	Enoteca Turi	"	𝔸 ★
£30+	Kennington Lane	*British, Modern*	𝔸 ★
	Rapscallion	"	𝔸 ★
	Cantinetta Venegazzú	*Italian*	𝔸 ★
	Popeseye	*Steaks & grills*	★★
	Bombay Bicycle Club	*Indian*	𝔸 ★
	Café Spice Namaste	"	𝔸 ★
£25+	Chez Lindsay	*French*	𝔸 ★
	Tootsies	*Burgers, etc*	-
	Pizza Metro	*Pizza*	𝔸 ★★
	Basilico	"	★★
	Royal China	*Chinese*	★★
	Sarkhel's	*Indian*	★★
	Thailand	*Thai*	★★
£20+	Arancia	*Italian*	-
	Talad Thai	*Thai*	★★
£15+	Gourmet Burger Kitchen	*Burgers, etc*	★
	Boiled Egg & Soldiers	*Sandwiches, cakes, etc*	-
	Kastoori	*Indian*	★★
	Sakonis	"	★★

EAST

Smithfield & Farringdon (EC1)

£40+	Club Gascon	*French*	𝔸★★
	Bleeding Heart	*"*	𝔸★
	Gaudi	*Spanish*	-
	Smiths of Smithfield	*Steaks & grills*	𝔸
£35+	Café du Marché	*French*	𝔸★
	Alba	*Italian*	★
£30+	Moro	*Moroccan*	𝔸★★
	Cicada	*Pan-Asian*	𝔸★
£20+	Fox & Anchor	*British, Traditional*	𝔸
	The Eagle	*Mediterranean*	𝔸★

The City & East End (All E and EC postcodes, except EC1)

£60+	Tatsuso	*Japanese*	★★
£50+	City Rhodes	*British, Modern*	★
	Prism	*"*	-
	Coq d'Argent	*French*	✕
	Twentyfour	*International*	𝔸
	Ubon	*East/West*	★
	City Miyama	*Japanese*	★★
£40+	The Don	*British, Modern*	𝔸★
	1 Lombard Street	*"*	-
	Les Trois Garçons	*French*	𝔸
£35+	Wapping Food	*International*	𝔸
	Sweetings	*Fish & seafood*	𝔸★
£30+	Il Bordello	*Italian*	𝔸★
	Royal China	*Chinese*	★★
	Café Spice Namaste	*Indian*	𝔸★
£20+	Faulkner's	*Fish & chips*	★★
	Shanghai	*Chinese*	𝔸★
	K10	*Japanese*	𝔸★★
£15+	The Wine Library	*British, Traditional*	𝔸
	Lahore Kebab House	*Indian*	★★
£1+	Brick Lane Beigel Bake	*Sandwiches, cakes, etc*	★★

BREAKFAST
(with opening times)

Central
Aurora *(8)*
Balans: *W1 (8)*
Bank *(7.30)*
Bar Italia *(7)*
Café Bagatelle *(10)*
The Cinnamon Club *(7.30 Mon-Fri)*
Connaught *(7.30)*
Dorchester Grill *(7, Sun 7.30)*
Food for Thought *(9.30)*
Giraffe: *all branches (8, Sat & Sun 9)*
Goring Hotel *(7)*
Indigo *(6.30)*
The Lanesborough *(7)*
Pâtisserie Valerie: *Old Compton St W1 (7.30, Sun 9); Marylebone High St W1 (8, Sun 9); WC2 (9.30, Sun 9)*
Paul *(7.30)*
The Providores *(8, Sat & Sun 10)*
Restaurant One-O-One *(7)*
The Ritz *(7)*
Simpsons-in-the-Strand *(7.30 Mon-Fri)*
Spoon + *(7)*
Windows on the World *(7)*

West
Balans: *SW3, SW5 (8)*
Basilico: *all branches (11)*
Beirut Express *(7.30)*
Blakes Hotel *(7.30)*
Capital Hotel *(7, Sun 7.30)*
Lisboa Patisserie *(7.45)*
Pâtisserie Valerie: *SW3 (7.30, Sun 8)*
Ranoush *(9)*
Tootsies: *SW6, SW7, W4 (10, Sat & Sun); W11 (8, Sat & Sun 9)*
Troubadour *(9)*

North
The Engineer *(9)*
Giraffe: *all branches (8, Sat & Sun 9)*
Iznik *(Sat & Sun only, 9)*
Tootsies: *NW3 (8, Sat & Sun 9)*

South
Basilico: *all branches (11)*
Boiled Egg *(9, Sun 10)*
Rapscallion *(10.30)*
Tootsies: *SW4 (10, Sat & Sun)*

East
Brick Lane Beigel Bake *(24 hrs)*
Coq d'Argent *(7.30 Mon-Fri)*
Fox & Anchor *(7)*
1 Lombard Street *(7.30)*
Smiths of Smithfield *(7, café)*
Wapping Food *(10)*

BRUNCH MENUS

Central
Aurora
Balans: *W1*
Bank
Le Caprice
Dorchester Grill
Giraffe: *all branches*
The Ivy
Joe Allen
The Lanesborough
Mirabelle
Momo
Pâtisserie Valerie: *both W1*
Restaurant One-O-One
The Sugar Club
Tootsies: *W1*
Vong
Windows on the World

West
Balans: *SW3, SW5*
Bluebird
Capital Hotel
The Cow
Dakota
Pâtisserie Valerie: *SW3*
Tootsies: *all west branches*

North
The Duke of Cambridge
The Engineer
Giraffe: *all branches*
Iznik
Tootsies: *NW3*

South
Boiled Egg
Kennington Lane
The Stepping Stone
Tootsies: *SW13*

East
Smiths of Smithfield

BUSINESS

Central
Bank
Le Caprice
Connaught
The Criterion
Dorchester Grill
Dorchester, Oriental
L'Escargot
Foliage
Le Gavroche
Goring Hotel
Greenhouse
Indigo
The Ivy
Ken Lo's Memories
The Lanesborough
Lindsay House

BYO
(Bring your own wine)

CHILDREN
**(h – high or special chairs
m – children's menu
p – children's portions
e – weekend entertainments
o – other facilities)**

Windows on the World (h)
Zafferano (hp)

West
Admiral Codrington (h)
The Anglesea Arms (hp)
Assaggi (p)
Aubergine (p)
Babylon (no children under 12)
Balans: SW3 (h); SW5 (hp)
Beirut Express (h)
Belvedere (h)
Bibendum (h)
Bibendum Oyster Bar (h)
Blakes Hotel (h)
Blue Elephant (he)
Bluebird (hmo)
Bombay Brasserie (h)
Chezmax (hp)
Chinon (p)
Chutney Mary (hm)
Dakota (hm)
Elistano (p)
The Gate: W6 (h)
The Havelock Tavern (hp)
Julie's (ho)
Lundum's (p)
Mandarin Kitchen (h)
Il Pagliaccio (h)
Parade (he)
Phoenicia (h)
Poissonnerie de l'Avenue (p)
Ranoush (m)
The River Café (hp)
Sticky Fingers (hme)
The Tenth (h)
Tootsies: all branches (hmo)
La Trompette (h)
Troubadour (h)
Vama (hp)
The Walmer Castle (h)

North
L'Aventure (h)
Daphne (p)
The Duke of Cambridge (hp)
The Engineer (hm)
Frederick's (hm)
The Gate: NW3 (hp)
Geeta (h)
Giraffe: all branches (h)
Mesclun (h)
Nautilus (h)
Royal China: NW8 (h)
Seashell (hm)
Soulard (p)
Tootsies: all branches (hmo)
Viet-Anh (m)
Vijay (h)
Yum Yum (h)

South
Boiled Egg (hme)
Café Spice Namaste: all branches (hp)
Cantinetta Venegazzú (hp)
Champor-Champor (hp)
Chez Bruce (h)
Chez Lindsay (h)
Enoteca Turi (hm)
The Glasshouse (h)
Gourmet Burger Kitchen (h)
Kastoori (h)
Pizza Metro (h)
Pizzeria Castello (h)
Rapscallion (p)
Riva (hm)
Royal China (h)
Sarkhel's (h)
Sonny's (h)
The Stepping Stone (hmo)
Tootsies: all branches (hmo)

East
Alba (hp)
Bleeding Heart (p)
Il Bordello (h)
Café Spice Namaste: all branches (hp)
Faulkner's (hm)
Gaudi (p)
Moro (hp)
Shanghai (hp)
Smiths of Smithfield (h)
Tatsuso (p)
Ubon (hp)
Wapping Food (h)

ENTERTAINMENT
(Check times before you go)

Central
Bank
(jazz, Sat)
Le Caprice
(pianist, nightly)
The Criterion
(magician, Wed-Sat)
Foliage
(jazz, Mon-Sat in bar)
Goring Hotel
(piano, nightly)
Hakkasan
(DJ, Fri & Sat)
Kai
(harpist, Thu & Sat nights)
The Lanesborough
(supper dances, Fri & Sat; jazz Sun brunch)
Mezzo
(music, nightly)
Momo
(live world music, Mon-Wed)
La Porte des Indes
(jazz, Sun brunch)
Quaglino's
(jazz, nightly in bar; pianist at L)
Restaurant One-O-One
(guitarist Fri & Sat)
The Ritz
(band, Fri & Sat pm (every night in Dec))
Sarastro
(opera, Mon & Sun)
Le Soufflé
(string trio, Sun L)

Souk
(belly dancer & DJ, Fri & Sat)
Titanic
(DJ, Thu-Sat)
Windows on the World
(dinner dance, Fri & Sat; jazz, Sun brunch)

West
Bombay Brasserie
(pianist & singer, nightly; jazz Sat & Sun L)
Chutney Mary
(jazz, Sun L)
Mr Wing
(jazz, Thu-Sat)
The Tenth
(jazz trio, Sat; dinner dance, once a month)
Vama
(jazz, Sun)

North
Les Associés
(accordion, 1st Fri of month)

South
Pizzeria Castello
(salsa, Mon pm)
Tas: *Borough High St SE1*
(guitarist, nightly); The Cut SE1
(music, nightly)

East
Café du Marché
(pianist & bass, nightly)
Coq d'Argent
(pianist Sat D: jazz Fri pm & Sun L)
1 Lombard Street
(jazz, Wed pm)

LATE
(open till midnight or later as shown; may be earlier Sunday)

Central
Asia de Cuba *(midnight, Sat 1 am)*
Balans: *W1 (5 am, Sun 1 am)*
Bar Italia *(4 am, Fri & Sat open 24 hours)*
Le Caprice
Hard Rock Café *(12.30 am, Fri & Sat 1 am)*
Incognico
The Ivy
Joe Allen *(12.45 am)*
The Lanesborough
Mezzo *(midnight, Thu-Sat 1 am (crustacea till 3 am))*
Mr Chow
Mr Kong *(2.45 am)*
Ozer
La Porte des Indes
Quaglino's *(midnight, Fri & Sat 1 am)*
J Sheekey
Tootsies: *all branches (Fri & Sat only)*

West
Balans: *W8 (1 am); SW3, SW5 (1 am)*
Beirut Express *(1.45 am)*
Blue Elephant
Bombay Brasserie

Mr Wing
Il Pagliaccio
Ranoush *(3 am)*
Tootsies: *all branches (Fri & Sat only)*

North
Pasha *(Fri & Sat only)*
Rasa: *N16 (Fri & Sat only)*
Tootsies: *all branches (Fri & Sat only)*
Vrisaki

South
Tootsies: *all branches (Fri & Sat only)*

East
Brick Lane Beigel Bake *(24 hours)*
Lahore Kebab House

NO-SMOKING AREAS
(* completely no smoking)

Central
Abeno
Archipelago
Café Bagatelle*
Chiang Mai
The Cinnamon Club
Connaught
Defune*
Foliage
Food for Thought*
Hakkasan
Hard Rock Café
Hunan
Joe Allen
Mildreds*
Mirabelle
Mju*
Nobu
Odin's
Paul*
Rasa: *all branches**
Rasa Samudra
Roussillon
Rules*
Sarastro
Le Soufflé
The Sugar Club
Vong
Yoshino

West
Chutney Mary
Phoenicia
The Tenth
La Trompette

North
Café Japan
The Duke of Cambridge*
Frederick's
Giraffe: *NW3**
Rasa: *all branches**
Seashell
Sushi-Say

Viet-Anh
Vijay

South
Gourmet Burger Kitchen*
Sarkhel's
The Stepping Stone
Talad Thai*
Thailand*

East
Brick Lane Beigel Bake*
Cicada
Faulkner's
K10*
Ubon

OUTSIDE TABLES
(* particularly recommended)

Central
Andrew Edmunds
Archipelago
Aurora*
Back to Basics
Balans: W1
Bar Italia
Caraffini
Il Convivio
Fairuz
Giraffe: W1
Gordon's Wine Bar*
Hard Rock Café
Hunan
Mildreds
Mirabelle*
Momo
L'Oranger
Orrery
Ozer
Le Palais du Jardin
Passione
Pâtisserie Valerie: WC2
La Poule au Pot*
The Ritz*
Spoon +*
Teca
Tootsies: all branches
Toto's*

West
Admiral Codrington*
The Anglesea Arms
Babylon*
Balans: SW3, SW5
Belvedere*
Bibendum Oyster Bar
Blakes Hotel*
Bombay Brasserie
The Builder's Arms
Cambio de Tercio
Chez Moi
Chinon
Dakota*
De Cecco*

Elistano
The Gate: W6*
The Havelock Tavern
Julie's
The Ladbroke Arms*
Lisboa Patisserie
Lundum's
Il Pagliaccio
Poissonnerie
  de l'Avenue
The River Café*
Tootsies: all branches
La Trompette
Troubadour
Vama
Windsor Castle*

North
Les Associés
L'Aventure*
Daphne*
The Duke of Cambridge
The Engineer*
Frederick's*
Odette's
Pasha
The Real Greek
Soulard
Tootsies: all branches
Viet-Anh

South
Arancia
Boiled Egg*
Café Spice Namaste: SW11
Cantinetta Venegazzú*
Enoteca Turi
Gourmet Burger Kitchen
Kastoori
Kennington Lane*
Oxo Tower*
Pizza Metro
Popeseye: SW15
Riva
Tootsies: all branches

East
Bleeding Heart*
Cicada
Coq d'Argent*
The Eagle
Fox & Anchor
Moro
Smiths of Smithfield*
Wapping Food

ROMANTIC

Central
Andrew Edmunds
Archipelago
Asia de Cuba
Aurora
Le Caprice
Connaught

Conrad Gallagher
Il Convivio
The Criterion
Dorchester Grill
L'Escargot
Le Gavroche
Greenhouse
Hakkasan
The Ivy
The Lanesborough
Lindsay House
Mirabelle
Momo
Nobu
Odin's
L'Oranger
Orrery
Le Palais du Jardin
Passione
La Porte des Indes
La Poule au Pot
Rhodes in the Sq
The Ritz
Roussillon
Salloos
Sarastro
J Sheekey
Shogun
Souk
Toto's
Vong
Windows on the World
Zafferano

West
Admiral Codrington
Assaggi
Aubergine
Babylon
Belvedere
Bibendum
Blakes Hotel
Blue Elephant
Bombay Brasserie
Cambio de Tercio
Chez Moi
Chezmax
Chinon
Clarke's
Dakota
Gordon Ramsay
Julie's
Launceston Place
Monkeys
Mr Wing
Pasha
The River Café
La Trompette
Zaika

North
L'Aventure
The Engineer
Frederick's
Mesclun

Odette's
The Real Greek
Soulard

South
Arancia
Champor-Champor
Chez Bruce
Enoteca Turi
The Glasshouse
Monsieur Max
Oxo Tower
Riva
Sonny's
The Stepping Stone

East
Bleeding Heart
Café du Marché
Club Gascon
Moro
Smiths of Smithfield
Les Trois Garçons

ROOMS WITH A VIEW

Central
Orrery
The Ritz
Windows on the World

West
Babylon
Belvedere
The Tenth

South
Oxo Tower

East
Coq d'Argent
Twentyfour
Ubon

MAP 1 – WEST END OVERVIEW

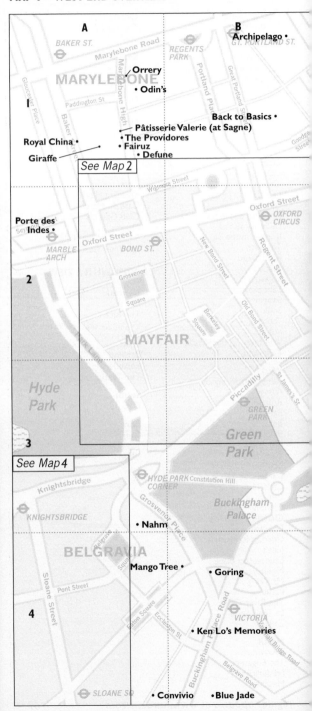

MAP 1 – WEST END OVERVIEW

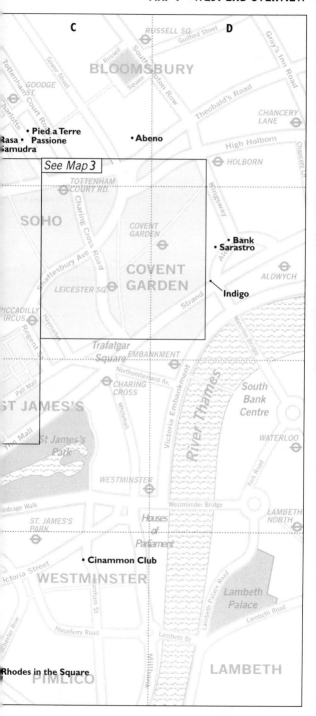

C
D

RUSSELL SQ.
Guilford Street

Gray's Inn Road

Russell
Square

BLOOMSBURY

Gower Street

Southampton Row

Tottenham Court Road

GOODGE
ST.

Theobald's Road

CHANCERY
LANE

Charlotte

• Pied a Terre
Rasa • Passione
Samudra

• Abeno

High Holborn

Chancery Ln.

HOLBORN

See Map 3

TOTTENHAM
COURT RD.

Kingsway

Charing Cross Road

SOHO

COVENT
GARDEN

COVENT
GARDEN

• Bank
• Sarastro

Shaftesbury Ave

ALDWYCH

LEICESTER SQ.

Indigo

PICCADILLY
CIRCUS

Strand

Regent St.

Haymarket

Trafalgar
Square

EMBANKMENT

Waterloo Bridge

Pall Mall

Northumberland Av.

ST JAMES'S

CHARING
CROSS

River Thames

South
Bank
Centre

The Mall

St James's
Park

Whitehall

Victoria Embankment

WATERLOO

York Road

Birdcage Walk

WESTMINSTER

ST. JAMES'S
PARK

Westminster Bridge

LAMBETH
NORTH

Houses
of
Parliament

Victoria Street

• Cinammon Club

WESTMINSTER

Marsham St.

Lambeth Palace Road

Lambeth
Palace

Lambeth Road

Chester Row

Horseferry Road

Lambeth Br.

Millbank

Rhodes in the Square

PIMLICO

LAMBETH

MAP 2 – MAYFAIR, ST JAMES'S & WEST SOHO

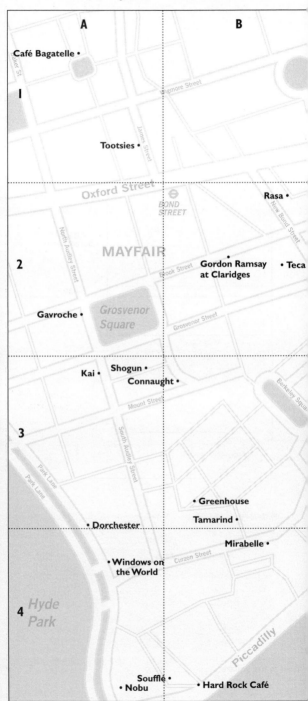

MAP 2 – MAYFAIR, ST JAMES'S & WEST SOHO

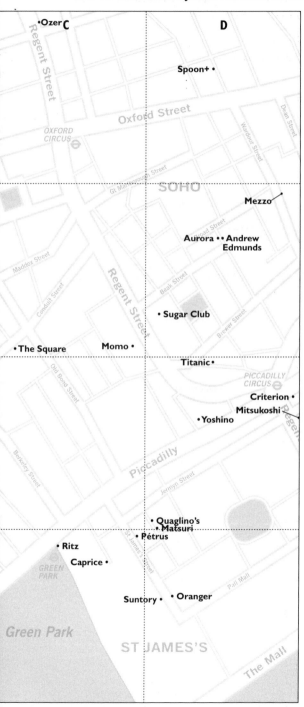

MAP 3 – EAST SOHO, CHINATOWN & COVENT GARDEN

MAP 3 – EAST SOHO, CHINATOWN & COVENT GARDEN

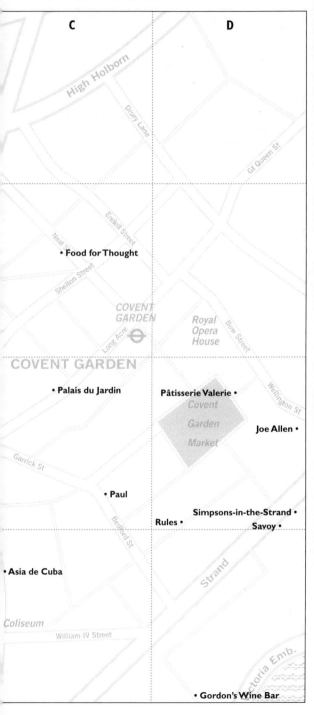

MAP 4 – KNIGHTSBRIDGE, CHELSEA & SOUTH KENSINGTON

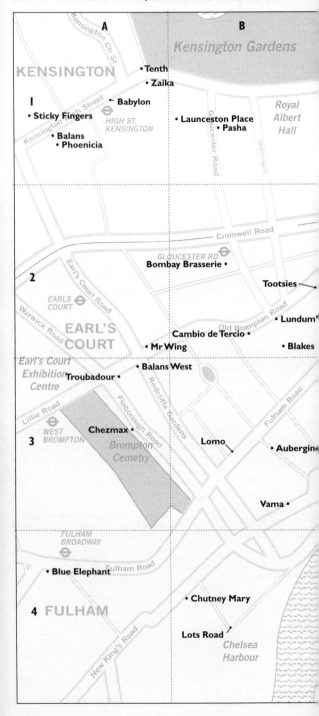

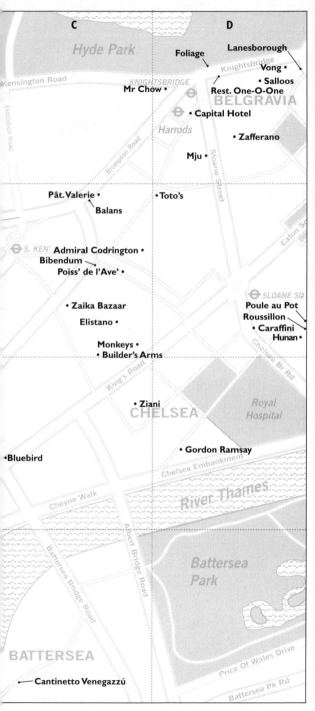

MAP 4 – KNIGHTSBRIDGE, CHELSEA & SOUTH KENSINGTON

Hyde Park

Foliage

Lanesborough

Knightsbridge

Vong •

• Salloos

KNIGHTSBRIDGE

Mr Chow •

Rest. One-O-One

Kensington Road

Exhibition Road

BELGRAVIA

• Capital Hotel

Harrods

Brompton Road

• Zafferano

Mju •

Sloane Street

Pât.Valerie •

•Toto's

Balans

Eaton Sq

⊖ *S. KEN'* Admiral Codrington •

Bibendum

Poiss' de l'Ave' •

⊖ *SLOANE SQ*

Poule au Pot

Roussillon

• Zaika Bazaar

• Caraffini

Elistano •

Hunan •

Chelsea Br Rd

Monkeys •

• Builder's Arms

King's Road

*Royal
Hospital*

• Ziani

CHELSEA

• Gordon Ramsay

Chelsea Embankment

•Bluebird

Cheyne Walk

River Thames

Albert Bridge Road

*Battersea
Park*

Battersea Bridge Road

BATTERSEA

Price Of Wales Drive

— Cantinetto Venegazzú

Battersea Pk Rd

MAP 5 – THE CITY

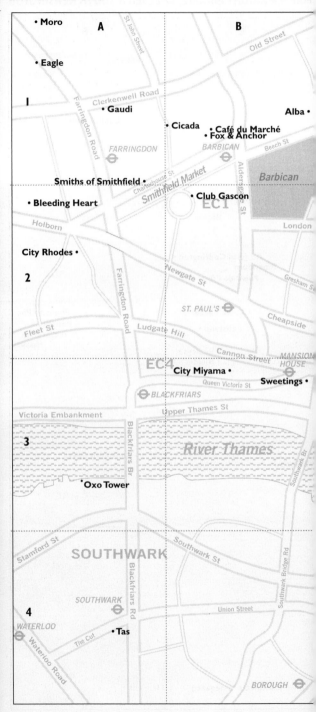

MAP 5 – THE CITY

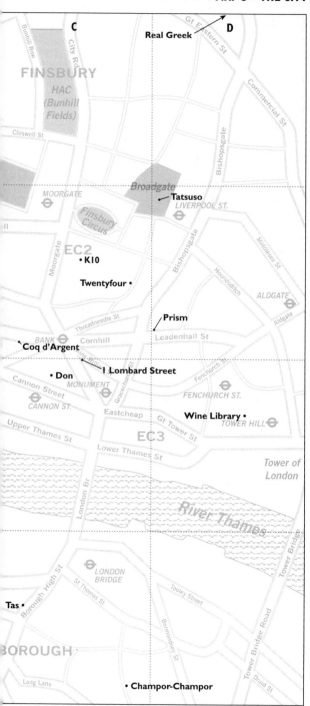

C **D**

Real Greek

Gt Eastern St

FINSBURY

Bunhill Row

City Rd

HAC
(Bunhill
Fields)

Chiswell St

Commercial St

Bishopsgate

MOORGATE

Broadgate

← **Tatsuso**

LIVERPOOL ST.

Finsbury
Circus

EC2

Moorgate

• **K10**

Twentyfour •

Bishopsgate

Houndsditch

Middlesex St

ALDGATE

Aldgate

Threadneedle St

→ **Prism**

BANK ⊖ Cornhill

Leadenhall St

• **Coq d'Argent**

← **1 Lombard Street**

• **Don**

MONUMENT

Gracechurch

Fenchurch

FENCHURCH ST.

Cannon Street

Wine Library •

CANNON ST.

Eastcheap

Gt Tower St

TOWER HILL ⊖

Upper Thames St

EC3

Lower Thames St

Tower of
London

River Thames

London Br

LONDON
BRIDGE

Tooley Street

Tower Bridge Road

Tower Bridge

Tas •

Borough High St

St Thomas St

Bermondsey St

Druid St

BOROUGH

Long Lane

• **Champor-Champor**

MAP 6 – SOUTH LONDON (& FULHAM)

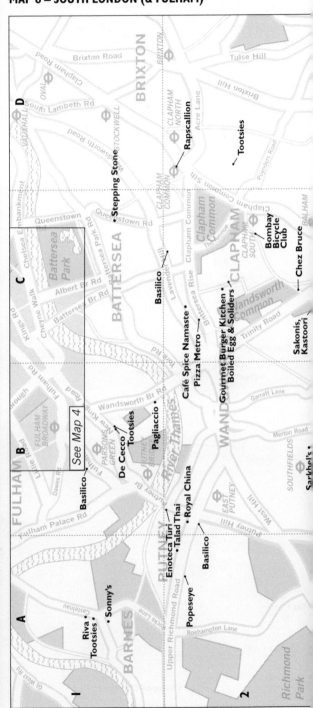

UK SURVEY RESULTS
& TOP SCORERS

PLACES PEOPLE TALK ABOUT

Restaurants outside London mentioned most frequently in the survey (last year's position shown in brackets):

1	Manoir aux Quat' Saisons (2)	*Great Milton, Oxon*
2	Yang Sing (1)	*Manchester*
3	Le Petit Blanc (3)	*Oxford*
4	Seafood Restaurant (9)	*Padstow, Cornwall*
5	Waterside Inn (8)	*Bray, Berks*
6	Terre à Terre (7)	*Brighton*
7	Le Petit Blanc (16)	*Birmingham*
8	Simply Heathcotes (11)	*Manchester*
9	The Angel (10)	*Hetton, N Yorks*
10	Walnut Tree (17)	*Llandewi Skirrid, Mon'shire*
11=	The Lime Tree (19)	*Manchester*
11=	Fat Duck (-)	*Bray*
11=	Sharrow Bay (-)	*Ullswater*
14	Chaing Mai (5)	*Oxford*
15	The Crown (18)	*Southwold, Suffolk*
16	Harts (-)	*Nottingham*
17	Merchant House (-)	*Ludlow*
18	Magpie (-)	*Whitby*
19	Browns (6)	*Oxford*
20=	Mumtaz Paan House (3)	*Bradford*
20=	Le Petit Blanc (-)	*Manchester*

TOP SCORERS

All restaurants whose food rating is ★★; plus restaurants whose price is £50+ with a food rating of ★:

£100+ Waterside Inn *(Bray)* ★
Le Manoir aux Quat' Saisons *(Great Milton)* ★

£80+ Altnaharrie Inn *(Ullapool)* ★★A
Gidleigh Park *(Chagford)* ★A
Patrick Guilbaud *(Dublin)* ★

£70+ Thorntons *(Dublin)* ★

£60+ Sharrow Bay *(Ullswater)* ★★A
Winteringham Fields *(Winteringham)* ★★A
Harry's Place *(Great Gonerby)* ★★
Airds Hotel *(Port Appin)* ★A
Gravetye Manor *(East Grinstead)* ★A
Turnberry Hotel *(Turnberry)* ★A

£55+ Michael's Nook *(Grasmere)* ★★
Charlton House *(Shepton Mallet)* ★A
Hambleton Hall *(Hambleton)* ★A
Lords of the Manor *(Upper Slaughter)* ★A

£50+ Chavignol at The Old Mill *(Shipston-on-Stour)* ★★
Northcote Manor *(Langho)* ★★
Old Chesil Rectory *(Winchester)* ★★
Shanks *(Bangor)* ★★
Amaryllis *(Glasgow)* ★A
Bodysgallen Hall *(Llandudno)* ★A
Clarence Hotel (Tea Rooms) *(Dublin)* ★A
Horn of Plenty *(Gulworthy)* ★A
Kinnaird House *(Dunkeld)* ★A
Pink Geranium *(Melbourn)* ★A
Read's *(Faversham)* ★A
Newbury Manor *(Newbury)* ★
Number One *(Edinburgh)* ★
Old Beams *(Waterhouses)* ★
One Paston Place *(Brighton)* ★
Pool Court at 42 *(Leeds)* ★

£45+ Bodidris Hall Hotel *(Llandegla)* ★★A
Fleur de Sel *(Storrington)* ★★A
Three Chimneys *(Dunvegan)* ★★A
La Potinière *(Gullane)* ★★
La Terrasse *(Sandgate)* ★★
The Mirabelle *(Eastbourne)* ★★

£40+ Brockencote Hall *(Chaddesley Corbett)* ★★A
Fairyhill *(Reynoldston)* ★★A
Gilpin Lodge *(Windermere)* ★★A
Monsieur Max *(Hampton Hill)* ★★A

TOP SCORERS

Morston Hall *(Morston)*		★★A
Plas Bodegroes *(Pwllheli)*		★★A
Summer Isles *(Achiltibuie)*		★★A
Wesley House *(Winchcombe)*		★★A
Yorke Arms *(Ramsgill-in-Nidderdale)*		★★A
Bosquet *(Kenilworth)*		★★
Croque en Bouche *(Malvern Wells)*		★★
Merchant House *(Ludlow)*		★★
Restaurant Martin Wishart *(Edinburgh)*		★★
Three Lions *(Stuckton)*		★★
Three Main Street *(Fishguard)*		★★
The Plumed Horse *(Castle Douglas)*		★★
£35+	Inn at Whitewell *(Clitheroe)*	★★A
	Three Choirs Vineyards *(Newent)*	★★A
	The Angel *(Hetton)*	★★
	Gamba *(Glasgow)*	★★
	Markwick's *(Bristol)*	★★
	Moody Goose *(Bath)*	★★
	Nutter's *(Cheesden)*	★★
	22 Mill Street *(Chagford)*	★★
£30+	Comme Ça *(Chichester)*	★★A
	Crannog *(Fort William)*	★★A
	White Hart *(Lydgate)*	★★A
	Crooked Billet *(Newton Longville)*	★★
	Gingerman *(Brighton)*	★★
	Melton's *(York)*	★★
	Rowan Tree *(Askrigg)*	★★
	Siam Thai *(Birmingham)*	★★
£20+	Chaing Mai *(Oxford)*	★★A
	Quince & Medlar *(Cockermouth)*	★★A
	Tomlins *(Penarth)*	★★A
	Café 21 *(Newcastle upon Tyne)*	★★
	Drum & Monkey *(Harrogate)*	★★
	Leela's *(Newcastle upon Tyne)*	★★
	Little Yang Sing *(Manchester)*	★★
	Mussel Inn *(Edinburgh)*	★★
	Magpie Café *(Whitby)*	★★
	Nantyffin Cider Mill *(Crickhowell)*	★★
	The Punch Bowl *(Crosthwaite)*	★★
	Wheeler's Oyster Bar *(Whitstable)*	★★
	Yang Sing *(Manchester)*	★★
£15+	Casa Mia Grande *(Leeds)*	★★A
	Gurkha Grill *(Manchester)*	★★
	Mumtaz Paan House *(Bradford)*	★★
	Rajput *(Harrogate)*	★★

UK DIRECTORY

Comments in "double quotation-marks" were made by reporters.

Foyer
Trinity Church £ 26 ★

82a Crown Street AB11 6ET (01224) 582277

Part of a laudible (getting people back into the) community and arts centre it may be, but it's the "excellent value" of the "well prepared and presented" fare (much of it veggie) at this café in Trinity Church that wins reporters' support. / **Sample dishes:** peppercorn & pork terrine with gooseberry chutney; baked sea bream with tabbouleh; lavender shortcake with raspberries. **Details:** 10 pm; closed Mon & Sun; no Amex; no smoking area; children: 14+ after 8 pm.

Royal Thai £ 28 ★

29 Crown Ter AB11 6HD (01224) 212922

"Wonderful food, shame about the décor" – the story's the same as ever at this popular oriental. / **Sample dishes:** mixed satay kebabs; Thai chicken green curry; fruit salad. **Details:** www.royal-thai.co.uk; off Crown St; 11 pm.

Sawadee £ 28

16-17 Bon Accord Cr AB11 6DE (01224) 582828

A "very pleasant" Thai restaurant, worth knowing about in this under-provided city. / **Sample dishes:** satay kebabs; lemongrass seafood; fresh mixed fruit salad. **Details:** 11 pm; closed Sun L; no smoking area.

Penhelig Arms £ 27 A★

LL35 0LT (01654) 767215

"On the seafront, overlooking the Dyfi estuary", this "friendly" inn with "lots of character" receives consistent praise for its traditional fare – "London-quality food offered at Welsh coastal prices". / **Sample dishes:** pan-fried squid with parsley & tomatoes; swordfish & salad; apricot frangipane tart. **Value tip:** set 2-crs L £9.95. **Details:** www.penheligarms.com; 9 pm; no Amex; no smoking in dining room. **Accommodation:** 14 rooms, from £70.

Walnut Tree £ 42 ★

Llandewi Skirrid NP7 8AW (01873) 852797

Franco Taruschio's 37-year stint at the stoves made this uncomfortably "tightly packed" and "tricky-to-get-to" inn the best-known place in Wales; perhaps inevitably since Stephen Terry took over in January 2001 – and put a more "nouvelle" spin on the "rustic Italian food with a Welsh twist" – the place hasn't provoked quite the passionate praise it once did; even some who say "the food has slipped", however, still say they had their best meal of the year here. / **Sample dishes:** crispy belly pork with lemon & caperberries; lamb with roast artichokes; pannacotta with raspberry jelly. **Details:** www.thewalnuttreeinn.com; 3m NE of Abergavenny on B4521; 10.30 pm; closed Mon & Sun D; no Amex.

Summer Isles £ 44 A★★

IV26 2YG (01854) 622282

It has a "stunning", remote seaside location – with wonderful views towards the Islands after which it is named – but this family-run hotel has also earned a big reputation on account of its "fantastic", "fresh" and original cooking. / **Sample dishes:** grilled mushrooms with Parmesan croutons; grilled turbot with capers & lime; lemon soufflé crepes. **Details:** 25m N of Ullapool on A835; 8 pm; no Amex; no smoking in dining room; booking essential; children: 6+. **Accommodation:** 13 rooms, from £98.

ALCISTON, EAST SUSSEX   3–4B

Rose Cottage Inn   **£ 25**   ★

BN26 6UW   (01323) 870377

"Honest" food – including "very good fish and game" – wins solid
support for this "cosy" 16th-century inn on the edge of the South
Downs. / **Sample dishes:** hot Sussex smokie; loin of pork; meringue with
summer berries. **Details:** off A27 nr Drusillas Park; 9 pm; closed Sun D;
no smoking; children: 6+. **Accommodation:** 1 room, at about £45.

ALDEBURGH, SUFFOLK   3–1D

Café 152   **£ 28**   ★

152 High St IP15 5AX   (01728) 454152

An "interesting" menu "that aims higher than you'd expect and
often hits the mark" helps make this "small, quaint and civilised"
bistro a uniformly popular recommendation; "local freshly-caught
fish" is a highlight. / **Sample dishes:** goat's cheese crostini with balsamic
onions; roast lamb with grilled polenta & Mediterranean vegetables; lemon &
lime posset with shortbread. **Details:** www.lawsons152.co.uk; 10 pm (9 pm in
winter); closed Tue; no Amex; no smoking area; children: before 8 pm only.

Lighthouse   **£ 26**   ★

77 High St IP15 5AU   (01728) 453377

"Fresh" fish and a "friendly", "laid-back" approach have combined
to make Peter and Sarah Hill's "pleasant" bistro a fashionable
destination (it's "worth booking") and it continues to be the most
popular place in town; it can get "too crowded", however, and there
were also one or two gripes this year of "declining standards".
/ **Sample dishes:** duck liver parfait with plum chutney; cod & spinach with
lemon oil; boozy banana pancakes. **Details:** on High St, by cinema; 10 pm;
open L&D all week; closed for 2 weeks in Jan & 1 week in Oct; no Amex;
no smoking area.

Regatta   **£ 26**   ★

171 High St IP15 5AN   (01728) 452011

It "never disappoints" say fans of this "reliable" establishment
whose "excellent fresh fish" is (as with everywhere in town) the
best bet; the atmosphere is "informal" and the place is "great for
kids". / **Sample dishes:** smoked prawns; duck with French beans; crème
brûlée. **Value tip:** set 2-crs pre-th £8. **Details:** 10 pm; no smoking area.

ALDFORD, CHESHIRE   5–3A

The Grosvenor Arms   **£ 27**   Ⓐ

Chester Rd CH3 6HJ   (01244) 620228

This "upmarket" pub/restaurant – near one of the gates to the
Duke of Westminster's estate – is a popular destination near
Chester, offering a "wide choice of interesting pub meals" in a
"characterful and relaxed" country setting. / **Sample dishes:** roasted
duck with red onion marmalade; spicy lamb kebabs with pitta bread & salad;
coffee & whisky cheesecake. **Details:** 6m S of Chester on B5130; 10 pm;
no smoking area; children: 14+ after 6 pm.

ALEXANDRIA, WEST DUNBARTONSHIRE   9–4B

Cameron House   **£ 61**

G83 8QZ   (01389) 755565

If you like "formal dining with a high level of silver service", the
grand Georgian Room at this "magnificently-located" hotel (on the
banks of Loch Lomond) may be for you; the place is undoubtedly
"old-fashioned", however, and there are those who find it "a bit
overrated". / **Sample dishes:** marinated seafood with lemongrass; veal in
butter bean stew with mustard jus; banana terrine with banana crisps.
Details: www.cameronhouse.co.uk; over Erskine Bridge to A82, follow signs to
Crianlarich; 9.45 pm; D only, closed Mon; jacket & tie required; no smoking;
children: 12+. **Accommodation:** 96 rooms, from £185.

Brig O'Doon House Hotel   £ 29   A★
Murdochs Ln KA7 4PQ   (01292) 442466
Burns's birthplace is a location worthy of poetry, and the cooking at the riverside hotel now housed there offers reliably "good value" ("despite the laminated menus"). / **Sample dishes:** haddock, bacon & potato soup; salmon with saffron & chive cream sauce; chocolate & orange sponge pudding. **Details:** www.costley-hotels.co.uk; 10 mins from Prestwick Airport, 45 mins from Glasgow Airport; 9 pm; no smoking in dining room. **Accommodation:** 5 rooms, from £100.

Franc's   £ 27
2 Goose Grn WA14 1DW   (0161) 941 3954
"Reminiscent of French holidays past", this "classic" bistro (which has a popular sibling in Chester) offers an "extensive menu" of "good-value" dishes. / **Sample dishes:** salmon dauphinoise; chicken in coconut & lime; chocolate praline tartlet. **Value tip:** set 3-crs pre-th £9.50. **Details:** www.francs-altrincham.com; 10.30 pm, Fri & Sat 11 pm; no smoking area.

French Restaurant   £ 31
25 The Downs WA14 2QD   (0161) 941 3355
A "dip in form" is apparent in reports on this "laid-back" suburban restaurant, which attracted too many gripes this year of "poor food, badly served". / **Sample dishes:** wild mushrooms in garlic; spicy penne with chicken; crème brûlée. **Value tip:** set 2-crs L £8.95. **Details:** 10 pm; closed Mon.

Jamfish   £ 31   ✗
28-32 Greenwood St WA14 1RZ   (0161) 928 6677
"Furnishings are so modern the place looks half-finished" at this trendy yearling, where there's a feeling that "it can't work out whether it's a restaurant or a late night bar" – this is reflected by food that "aims high, but delivers low". / **Sample dishes:** sticky beef; tuna & mango tian with ginger salsa; burnt Cambridge cream. **Value tip:** set 1-crs Sun L £7.95. **Details:** www.jamfish.co.uk; 10 pm; closed Mon.

Juniper   £ 52
21 The Downs WA14 2QD   (0161) 929 4008
The "original combinations" on the menu at this "unimposing" foodie destination regularly "push at the boundaries", and, sometimes "sublime" results made this the North West's most notable destination in the late-'90s; standards then fell, reflecting the fact (it now seems) that the restaurant was for sale; in 2001, however, chef Paul Kitching found the backing to buy the place, expand the kitchen and refurbish – there's every hope that this former star may now regain its brilliance. / **Sample dishes:** scallops with curried pea sauce; roast lamb with raisins & sweetbreads in espresso sauce; lemon tart with Florida fruit cocktail. **Value tip:** set 3-crs L £18. **Details:** 9.30 pm; closed Mon, Sat L & Sun; no smoking.

Amberley Castle   £ 48   A
BN18 9ND   (01798) 831992
"Eating in a castle is an experience never to be forgotten", and this "richly furnished" and "very romantic" venue is undoubtedly "a joy to behold"; it's a shame, then, that the cooking is perennially "variable", and that the service can be plain "surly". / **Sample dishes:** crab sausage with Jerusalem artichokes; rabbit with grain mustard mash; rhubarb & mango tart. **Value tip:** set 2-crs L £15. **Details:** www.amberleycastle.co.uk; N of Arundel on B2139; 9.30 pm; jacket & tie required; no smoking; booking: max 8; children: 12+. **Accommodation:** 19 rooms, from £145.

Drunken Duck   **£ 29**
Barngates LA22 0NG   (01539) 436347
*The beautiful Lakeland vistas are as impressive as ever, but satisfaction with this well-known pub/brewery/restaurant declined somewhat this year – the view that it offers "pub food at its very best" risks being drowned out by those saying it is becoming "overpriced" and "pretentious". / **Sample dishes:** chicken with sugar snap peas; quail stuffed with prune risotto; lemon torte with spiced oranges. **Details:** www.drunkenduckinn.co.uk; 3m from Ambleside, towards Hawkshead; 8.45 pm; no smoking. **Accommodation:** 11 rooms, from £100.*

The Glasshouse   **£ 26**   Ⓐ
Rydal Rd LA22 9AN   (01539) 432137
*Recently taken over by former manager Neil Farrell, there's no reason to expect any great change in the appeal of this notably "beautiful" ("pleasantly un-countryish" and "trendy") venue whose "stylishly presented" dishes have won the place a broad following. / **Sample dishes:** sun-dried tomato & aubergine fritters; coq au vin with buttered mash; blueberry cobbler. **Details:** www.theglasshouserestaurant.co.uk; behind Little Bridge House; 10 pm; no Amex; no smoking.*

Sheila's Cottage   **£ 30**   Ⓐ
The Slack   (01539) 433079
*Some note "variability of standards" at this "very attractive" Lake District spot – "a good coffee shop, which turns into a restaurant in the evening" – but its cooking, which includes "interesting local specialities" generally wins praise. / **Sample dishes:** apple & black pudding with mustard cream; smoked haddock with spinach & poached egg; bread & butter pudding. **Details:** www.amblesideonline.co.uk; 9 pm; no Amex.*

Zeffirelli's   **£ 22**
Compston Rd LA22 9DN   (01539) 433845
*"Café, restaurant and cinema, and even excellent vegetarian fare…" – this unusual complex is "much more than just the pizza house" it might at first appear, and its "good wholesome food is ideal after a day's walking". / **Sample dishes:** polenta with tapenade; cannelloni with roasted peppers; rich chocolate torte. **Details:** www.zeffirellis.co.uk; 9.45 pm; D only; no Amex; no smoking.*

Famous Fish   **£ 30**
11 Market Sq HP7 ODF   (01494) 728665
*The setting may be "loud", "crowded" and "basic", but thanks to the "creative" cooking of its South African owners, "you need to book ahead" for this "very popular" fish restaurant. / **Sample dishes:** lobster bisque; seafood kebabs; crème brûlée. **Details:** in Old Amersham (1m from Amersham); 10 pm; closed Sun; no smoking; booking essential.*

Gilbey's   **£ 30**
1 Market Sq HP7 0DF   (01494) 727242
*"Excellent wine at shop prices", "friendly" service and cooking that – if no great shakes – is "always consistent" provide compensation for the "somewhat overcrowded" conditions at this brasserie, "opposite the old clock tower", which maintains a strong local fan club. / **Sample dishes:** pork & prune roulade; grilled sea bass; raspberry & lime cheesecake. **Value tip:** set 2-crs Sun L £10.50. **Details:** www.gilbeygroup.co.uk; in Old Amersham (1m from Amersham); 9.45 pm.*

Kings Arms   £ 29
30 High St HP7 0DJ   (01494) 726333
"Ancient beamed pub" on the main drag that's *"popular in a
gastro-desert"*; the atmosphere is *"stilted"*, though, and the food
"can disappoint". / **Sample dishes:** salmon & trout with strawberry
vinaigrette; monkfish with Chinese spices & black linguini; pear belle-Hélène.
Details: www.kingsarmsamersham.co.uk; in Old Amersham (1m from
Amersham); 9.30 pm; closed Mon & Sun D.

Santhi   £ 24   𝔸
16 Hill Ave HP6 5BW   (01494) 432621
"A good-standard curry for out-of-town" is to be had at this
"unusual", glitzily-decorated Indian, near the terminus of the
Metropolitan line. / **Sample dishes:** prawn purée & poppadoms;
hot, sweet & sour chicken curry; chocolate mousse.
Details: www.santhirestaurant.co.uk; take A40 to A413 towards Amersham;
10.45 pm; no smoking area.

ANSTRUTHER, FIFE   9–4D

Cellar   £ 40   𝔸★
24 East Grn KY10 3AA   (01333) 310378
"What dining out should be", Peter and Susan Jukes's
"comfortable" restaurant – in the cellar of a 17th-century stone
house, behind the Scottish Fisheries museum – offers *"beautiful
fresh fish"* and *"excellent local beef"*, twinned with *"friendly"* but
"professional" service. / **Sample dishes:** asparagus & leek soup; roast
pesto-crusted cod; hazelnut praline parfait. **Details:** in the harbour area;
9.30 pm; closed Mon L & Tue L (& Sun in winter); no smoking area;
children: 8+.

APPLECROSS, HIGHLAND   9–2B

Applecross Inn   £ 29   ★
Shore St IV54 8LR   (01520) 744262
"Seafood fresh from the boat outside" and *"exceptional views"*
reward those who make the pilgrimage to this rural inn, *"remotely
situated in beautiful country"*; it's *"a cosy place"*, too, *"especially
off-season"*. / **Sample dishes:** local oysters; hand-dived king scallops with
bacon; raspberry crannachan. **Details:** off A896, S of Shieldaig; 9 pm;
no Amex; no smoking. **Accommodation:** 7 rooms, from £50.

APPLETHWAITE, CUMBRIA   7–3C

Underscar Manor   £ 49   𝔸★
CA12 4PH   (01768) 775000
"Formal" but *"friendly"*, and benefiting from a *"wonderful"* location
on a hillside – the dining room of this small country house hotel
offers *"high-class"* cooking which is unanimously praised by
reporters. / **Sample dishes:** calves liver with soft onions; roast duck &
Chinese pancakes with pak choy; crème fraîche mousse with brandy-soaked
strawberries. **Details:** on A66, 17m W of M6, J40; 8.30 pm; jacket required;
no smoking; children: 12+. **Accommodation:** 11 rooms, from £170, incl D.

ARDEN, ARGYLL & BUTE   9–4B

Duck Bay Hotel & Marina   £ 33
Duck Bay G83 8QZ   (01389) 751234
"Good views inside and out", and *"excellent service"* helps
make this lochside hotel restaurant a unanimous *"thumbs-up"*
recommendation. / **Sample dishes:** kromesky (deep-fried meat parcels);
roast lamb; mocha chocolate mousse. **Value tip:** set 2-crs L £9.95.
Details: www.duckbay.co.uk; 10 pm. **Accommodation:** 18 rooms, from £79.

Ascot Oriental   £ 31   𝐴

London Rd   SL5 0PU   (01344) 621877

"A great stop near Ascot"; this smart Chinese benefits from excellent service and is complimented on its solid cooking and "relaxing" atmosphere. / **Sample dishes:** tempura prawns; seared tuna with Asian greens; coconut & mango tart. **Details:** in Windsor Great Park; 10.30 pm.

The Thatched Tavern   £ 35

Cheapside Rd   SL5 7QG   (01344) 620874

It's rather "squashed" in this part-thatched 17th-century building; local fans "love" it on account of its reliable, no-nonsense "French/English cuisine" at prices that are modest for the area, but even so there are some who find it a mite "overpriced" for what it is. / **Sample dishes:** chicken liver & pistachio pâté; roast lamb with rosemary & thyme jus; lemon & ginger crunch. **Details:** 2m from Ascot, signed to Cheapside Village; 10 pm.

The Crab & Lobster   £ 28

Dishforth Rd   YO7 3QL   (01845) 577286

It's difficult to know which has contributed more to the huge success of this "eccentric" thatched inn, its "brilliant seafood dishes" or its amazing, "dark-grotto-of-ephemera" interior; it would score top marks, but at the time of writing it was up for sale so a rating seems inappropriate. / **Sample dishes:** Irish oysters on ice; crab-crusted salmon with saffron mash; chocolate torte. **Value tip:** set 2-crs L £10. **Details:** www.craband lobster.co.uk; at junction of Asenby Rd & Topcliffe Rd; 9.30 pm; no smoking in dining room. **Accommodation:** 12 rooms, from £100.

Holne Chase Hotel   £ 46   𝐴

TQ13 7NS   (01364) 631471

"A really wonderful setting" – a converted hunting lodge in extensive grounds just outside the Dartmoor National Park – helps make this country house hotel a "great" destination; it generated limited feedback, mostly to the effect that the "superb" cooking matches the impressive surroundings. / **Sample dishes:** oak-smoked duck & hazelnut salad; roast herbed lamb with Madeira sauce; strawberry & custard fool. **Details:** www.holne-chase.co.uk; 2nd Ashburton turnoff onto A38 coming from Plymouth; 8.45 pm; no Amex; children: 12+ at D. **Accommodation:** 17 rooms, from £130.

The King's Arms   £ 26   𝐴

Market Pl   DL8 3HQ   (01969) 650817

It will always be most famous for its screen role – as 'The Drovers' in 'All Creatures Great & Small' – but it's also worth visiting this cosy inn for its "above-average pub food". / **Sample dishes:** spicy salmon fishcakes; chicken & cheese wrapped in smoked bacon; sticky toffee pudding. **Details:** 9 pm; no Amex; no smoking.

Rowan Tree   £ 31   ★★

Market Pl   DL8 3HT   (01969) 650536

It's so "tiny" that it's something of "a secret", but for "a relaxing gourmet experience" Mr and Mrs Wylie's 22-seater "never disappoints", thanks to its absolutely "exquisite" cooking. / **Sample dishes:** Asian crab cakes with Thai dip; roast lamb with lentil cassoulet; passion fruit & apricot roulade. **Details:** 4m from Aysgarth falls; 8.30 pm; closed Mon, Tue–Sat D only, closed Sun D; no credit cards; no smoking until coffee; children: 7+.

Pecks   £ 37   ★
Newcastle Rd CW12 4SB   (01260) 275161
"A set menu at a set time, but what a meal" – the "marvellous"
results at this unusual, quite upmarket BYO set-up are unanimously
approved; lunch is a recent innovation. / **Sample dishes:** chicken
consommé with black beans; roast lamb with rosemary & redcurrant sauce;
rum & raisin cheesecake. **Details:** www.pecksrest.co.uk; off A34; 8 pm (one
sitting only); closed Mon & Sun; no smoking until coffee; booking essential.

Hartwell House   £ 59
Oxford Rd HP17 8NL   (01296) 747444
This "lovely" part-Jacobean country house set in parkland is
undoubtedly a "magnificent hotel"; there is a strong sentiment,
though, that the "ambience of the dining room doesn't match up
to the rest of the establishment", not helped by "appallingly stiff"
service and "mediocre" cooking. / **Sample dishes:** Atlantic fish soup with
aniseed; roast duck with braised red cabbage; plum parfait & tuile biscuits.
Value tip: set 2-crs L £22. **Details:** www.hartwell-house.com; 2m W of
Aylesbury on A418; 9.45 pm; no Amex; jacket & tie required; no smoking in
dining room; children: 8+. **Accommodation:** 46 rooms, from £225.

Babington House   £ 36
BA11 3RW   (01373) 812266
Soho comes to Somerset at this country outpost of a trendy London
club – a "very relaxed", five-year-old venture in a listed Georgian
house that also opens to non-members who are staying in the
hotel; the food tends to the "average", but "attentive" service
contributes to a favourable overall impression. / **Sample
dishes:** crab & avocado salad with dill bread; confit duck with balsamic honey
glaze; trio of herb sorbets. **Details:** www.babingtonhouse.co.uk; 11 pm; open
to residents & members only for L&D all week; booking essential.
Accommodation: 28 rooms, from £210.

Aitch's Wine Bar   £ 32   ★
4 Buxton Rd DE45 1DA   (01629) 813895
There's "always an interesting, International menu" at this "vibrant"
wine bar, and the "excellent value for money" attracts a clientèle
that's quite "cosmopolitan" by local standards. / **Sample dishes:** spicy
Thai fishcakes with salad; crispy duck with stir-fried vegetables; champagne
cheesecake with cassis ice cream. **Value tip:** set 2-crs L £7.95.
Details: www.aitchswinebar.co.uk; 10 pm; closed Sun; no Amex.

Renaissance   £ 29   𝔸★
Bath St DE45 1BX   (01629) 812687
"A refreshing change from the usual Bakewell tourist traps",
Monsieur Piedaniel's "comfortable" and "cottagey" establishment
is resoundingly praised for its "sheer culinary brilliance" and its
"wonderfully friendly service". / **Sample dishes:** trout terrine with lobster;
potato & cheese gnocchi with tomato coulis; ginger mousse with orange sauce.
Details: 9.30 pm; closed Mon & Sun D; no Amex; no smoking.

BALLATER, ABERDEEN

9–3C

Green Inn £ 42 ★

9 Victoria Rd AB35 5QQ (01339) 755701

"Outstanding use of Scottish ingredients" (with "a focus on fish") ensures that a visit to Jeffrey and Carol Purves's "friendly" dining room is always a "memorable" experience; they've been in business since 1990, but supporters insist that the place "gets better every year"; (note – though the building was once a temperance hotel, you can BYO!) / **Sample dishes:** smoked haddock cheesecake; venison & beef with mushroom ragout; lemon gratin with basil ice cream. **Details:** www.green-inn.com; in centre of village, on the green; 9.30 pm; D only; no smoking at D. **Accommodation:** 3 rooms, from £119, incl D.

BANBURY, OXFORDSHIRE

2–1D

Thai Orchid £ 29

56 Northbar St OX16 0TL (01295) 270833

With its "pretty" setting ("plants, pools, goldfish"), this popular oriental is especially "good for large groups"; some question the authenticity of the cooking, but even critics say it's of a "good" quality. / **Sample dishes:** chicken satay; Thai green curry; Thai custard. **Details:** next to St Marys church; 10.30 pm; closed Fri L & Sat L; no smoking area.

BANGOR, COUNTY DOWN

10–1D

Shanks £ 50 ★★

150 Crawfordsburn Rd BT19 1GB (028) 9185 3313

The setting is rather odd – the Conran-designed dining room of a golf club outside Belfast – but Robin Millar's "exciting" modern cooking and "fabulous" presentation make this stylish rural restaurant Northern Ireland's top culinary destination. / **Sample dishes:** foie gras ravioli in chicken broth; duck with spiced Mediterranean vegetables; fig puff with lavender ice cream. **Value tip:** set 2-crs L £15.95. **Details:** A2 to Bangor, follow signs for The Blackwood; 10 pm; closed Mon, Sat L & Sun.

BANGOR, GWYNEDD

4–1C

The Fat Cat Café Bar £ 21

161 High St LL57 1NU (01248) 370445

In an "area largely free of decent restaurants", this "busy café bar" (the first in a northerly mini-chain) is worth knowing about for its "usually good" food. / **Sample dishes:** chicken quesadillas; tuna with stir-fried vegetables in oyster sauce; Caribbean banana charlotte. **Details:** nr Cathedral; 10 pm; no smoking area; no booking, Fri & Sat; children: not permitted.

BARTON UPON HUMBER, NORTH LINCOLNSHIRE

6–2A

Rafters £ 25 ★

24 High St DN18 5PD (01652) 660669

The décor may be "rather frugal", but the food at this "unpretentious" market town restaurant is "well cooked and presented". / **Sample dishes:** antipasto & avocado salad; curried pork with dried fruits; chocolate Scotch pancakes. **Value tip:** set 3-crs L £8.95. **Details:** www.rafters.co.uk; 0.5m S of Humber Bridge off A15; 10 pm; closed Mon & Sun D; smoking in bar only.

BASINGSTOKE, HAMPSHIRE

2–3D

Hees Chinese £ 29

23 Westminster Hs RG21 7LS (01256) 464410

For "good, basic Chinese" this long established local destination is worth knowing about, in a very thin area. / **Sample dishes:** satay chicken; king prawns in black bean sauce; toffee bananas. **Details:** next to library; 10.30 pm; closed Sun L; children: 6+.

Fischers at Baslow Hall   £ 48   A ★
Calver Rd DE45 IRR   (01246) 583259
*"Simply terrific" cooking and a "beautiful situation" make this
Edwardian Gothic country house hotel a very popular "special
occasion" destination; there remain one or two reporters for whom
it hits the wrong note, but feedback is generally characterised by its
consistently upbeat tone. / **Sample dishes:** red snapper with spring salad;
roast Dutch rabbit with mash; selection of mini desserts. **Details:** on A623
Stockport Rd, 0.5m past village church; 9.30 pm; closed Sun D; jacket required
at D; no smoking in dining room; children: 12+ after 7 pm.
Accommodation: 11 rooms, from £150.*

BATH, BATH & NE SOMERSET   2–2B

Bath has a huge number of restaurants, probably more per
head than any other city in the UK. Given the exterior beauty
of the city, however, it's surprising that only one restaurant
(the venerable *Hole in the Wall*) achieves an atmosphere of
particular charm. (Unless you would be satisfied by afternoon
tea or a light lunch, in which case the Pump Rooms, not listed
below and adjacent to the Baths themselves, are worth
queueing for – or book on 01225 444477.)

The local scene has been much impoverished by the surprise
closure of Lettonie, which was one of England's best
restaurants. The baton now passes to the excellent *Moody
Goose*, with only the *Olive Tree* (and perhaps *Martin Blunos
at Fitzroy's*) seriously in contention.

Browns   £ 28   X
Old Police Station, Orange Grove BA1 1LP   (01225) 461199
*"Bland, bland, bland" – even by the dirgeful standards of this Six
Continents-owned chain, this potentially atmospheric branch raises
mediocrity to a new level with its "uninspired" and "predictable"
food, its "disinterested" and "indifferent" service and a setting that
"no longer has the charm it had of old". / **Sample dishes:** buffalo
mozzarella & plum tomatoes; steak, mushroom & Guinness pie; sticky toffee
pudding. **Details:** www.browns-restaurants.com; nr Pulteney Bridge; 11.30 pm;
no smoking area; no booking.*

Demuth's   £ 29   ★
2 North Parade Passage BA1 1NX   (01225) 446059
*"Well-crafted vegetarian food in bright surroundings" has long
made this a very popular destination, and fans say it's still
"evolving and improving"; "uneven" or "aloof" service coloured a
number of reports this year, however, and contributed to a decline
in overall satisfaction. / **Sample dishes:** chermoula kebabs; southern
Indian thali; poached peaches with redcurrants. **Details:** www.demuths.co.uk;
off Abbey Green; 10 pm; no smoking; booking: max 4, Fri & Sat; children: 6+
after 7 pm.*

The Eastern Eye   £ 24
8a Quiet St BA1 2JS   (01225) 422323
*With its "opulent" setting in a large Georgian building (with
some "sensational ceiling décor"), this central Indian offers
"a good variety of dishes at good-value prices, well served".
/ **Sample dishes:** mixed tandoori kebabs; lamb korma; kulfi.
Details: www.easterneye.co.uk; off Milsom St; 11 pm; no smoking area.*

Firehouse Rotisserie £ 35

2 John St BA1 2JL (01225) 482070

"California-style cooking" – "proper pizzas" a speciality – has
made this "bistro-type" central spot "very popular"; there is a
growing sense in some quarters, though, that the place is "overhyped" and "overpriced". / **Sample dishes:** brie & grape quesadilla;
Pacific crab & smoked salmon cakes; chocolate pecan pie.
Details: www.firehouserotisserie.co.uk; 11 pm; closed Sun.

Fishworks £ 42

6 Green St BA1 2JY (01225) 448707

This recently refitted restaurant "above, and run by, a super fish
shop" has made quite a "local reputation"; there is a widespread
feeling, though, even amongst some fans, that it is now "a bit
overpriced" and that "the food is not as good as it was" – perhaps
it's the distractions of opening offshoots in Bristol and Christchurch,
and preparing for a TV series (plus, of course, the inevitable
cookbook). / **Sample dishes:** crab salad with tarragon mayonnaise; cod with
mash & parsley sauce; Sicilian lemon tart. **Details:** www.fishworks.co.uk;
10 pm; closed Mon & Sun; no smoking.

Hole in the Wall £ 33 Ⓐ

16 George St BA1 2EN (01225) 425242

This "revived former favourite" occupies a "cosy" basement dining
room which is one of the UK's most venerable restaurant sites, and
is quite "lively" in its latest incarnation; some feel the place "trades
on its high profile", but the "homely" cooking for the most part
wins the thumbs-up. / **Sample dishes:** warm scallop & bacon salad;
guinea fowl with beetroot & garlic sauce; caramelised pears with coffee ice
cream. **Value tip:** 2-crs set L £8.50. **Details:** 10 pm; closed Sun; no smoking
area.

Mai Thai £ 24

6 Pierrepont St BA1 1LB (01225) 445557

Cooking with "varied" and "delicate" flavours makes this
"authentic" (and rather "noisy") Thai restaurant a popular local
recommendation. / **Sample dishes:** chicken satay; Thai green chicken
curry; banana fritters with ice cream. **Details:** 10.30 pm, Fri & Sat 10.45 pm;
children: 9+.

Martin Blunos at Fitzroy's
Duke's Hotel £ 34

Great Pulteney St BA2 4DN (01225) 463512

With the recent unexpected closure of Lettonie, those who wish to
sample the cooking of Bath's leading chef will now only have the
option of this 'diffusion' outlet, which comes complete with walled
garden, in the centre of the town; it opened too late for our survey
– let's hope its food does justice to the Blunos name. / **Sample
dishes:** scallops & fennel in butter sauce; lamb with haricots & onion compote;
bread & butter pudding with apricots. **Value tip:** set 2-crs L £12.95.
Details: www.dukesbath.co.uk; 10 pm. **Accommodation:** 18 rooms,
from £145.

Moody Goose £ 39 ★★

74 Kingsmead Sq BA1 2AB (01225) 466688

"I never knew provincial restaurants could be this good!" – "there's
nothing to divert attention from the food" in what some find a
slightly "claustrophobic" basement, but fortunately Stephen Shore's
"inventive" approach achieves "terrific" results, and the service is
of a "very good standard" too. / **Sample dishes:** crab, squid & red
mullet pie; beef with watercress purée, bacon & lentils; lemon tart with basil
sorbet. **Value tip:** set 2-crs L & pre-th £12. **Details:** www.moody-goose.com;
9.30 pm; closed Sun; no smoking in dining room.

Olive Tree
Queensberry Hotel   £ 41   ★
Russel St BA1 2QF   (01225) 447928
*"Always good and sometimes exciting", say fans of the "light",
"well-presented" Mediterranean cooking at this well-known hotel
basement, who would "go back every week" if they could; a "lack
of atmosphere" is a persistent gripe, however, and a few found the
place "not quite as good as hoped".* **Sample dishes:** grilled red
mullet & roast aubergine; braised pork with morels & savoy cabbage; roast
peach tart. **Value tip:** set 3-crs L £15.50. **Details:** www.batholivetree.com;
10 pm; closed Sun L; no Amex; no smoking. **Accommodation:** 29 rooms,
from £135.

Rajpoot   £ 21
4 Argyle St BA2 2BA   (01225) 466833
*"The front of the restaurant gives no hint as to what is below
decks" at this "busy" basement curry house whose vaulted interior
delivers "a fascinating architectural experience" for some reporters;
others think the décor is "tacky", though, and the cooking can be
"variable".* / **Sample dishes:** chicken tikka; hot chicken curry; mango kulfi.
Value tip: set 3-crs L £6.95. **Details:** www.rajpoot.com; 11 pm, Fri & Sat
11.30 pm.

Richmond Arms   £ 24   ★
7 Richmond Pl BA1 5PZ   (01225) 316725
*The dining space in this "cramped" Lansdown pub may be
"modest", but the "experimental" and "creative" ("Aussie/Asian")
cooking ensures "incredible popularity" – "weekend booking" is
advised.* / **Sample dishes:** Thai fishcakes; kangaroo with sweet chilli
mayonnaise; blueberry iced terrine. **Details:** 1m from centre; 8.30 pm, Fri &
Sat 9 pm; closed Mon & Sun D; children: 14+.

Sukhothai   £ 24
90a Walcot St BA1 5BG   (01225) 462463
*"Consistent", "varied", "tasty" Thai cooking wins a dedicated
following for this "great little restaurant", and it's a "fun" place too.*
/ **Sample dishes:** Thai soup; green chicken Thai curry; banana fritters.
Details: 10.30 pm; closed Sun L; no smoking area; children: 7+ at D.

Tilley's Bistro   £ 26
3 North Parade Pas BA1 1NX   (01225) 484200
*"The pavement level's better than the basement" at David and
Dawn Mott's small, central bistro, "tucked away near Sally Lunn's";
devoted fans applaud the "interesting" menu, made up of tapas-
style dishes and puddings, but sceptics find the food
"disappointing".* / **Sample dishes:** French onion soup; pork with Roquefort;
lemon posset trifle. **Details:** www.tilleysbistro.co.uk; 11 pm; closed Sun;
no Amex; no smoking area.

Woods   £ 31
9-13 Alfred St BA1 2QX   (01225) 314812
*It doesn't aim to set the world alight, but the "traditional" Gallic
cooking is "usually reliable" at this "congenial" Bath brasserie of
long standing; the best value comes from its "bargain offers".*
/ **Sample dishes:** duck & chicken terrine with kumquats; sea bass with
chilli & lime dressing; chocolate torte. **Details:** 10 pm; closed Sun D; no Amex.

BAWTRY, SOUTH YORKSHIRE   5–2D
China Rose   £ 30
16 South Parade DN10 6JH   (01302) 710461
*Even fans admit it isn't a place that would suit everyone – "its size
and openness might put you off" – but this "busy" Chinese attracts
widespread support for its "attentive" service and dependable
cooking from an "extensive" menu.* / **Sample dishes:** mussels in black
bean sauce; Szechuan chicken; Korean apples. **Details:** 10.30 pm; D only;
no smoking in dining room.

Leigh House £ 29
53 Wycombe End HP9 1LX (01494) 676348
A "good, reliable local Chinese that's somewhat smarter than the norm". / **Sample dishes:** sesame prawn toast; spicy lemon prawns with rice; toffee apples. **Details:** 10 pm; no smoking area.

BEAUMARIS, ISLE OF ANGLESEY 4–1C

Ye Olde Bull's Head £ 42 ★
Castle St LL58 8AP (01248) 810329
"Consistently high standards" are maintained at this historic coaching inn; in addition to the restaurant "up the creaky old stairs", a "good-value" brasserie was added a couple of years ago, and the same "attention to detail" is evident throughout. / **Sample dishes:** quail confit with red plum compote; monkfish brochette with wild rice risotto; crème brûlée & raspberries. **Details:** www.bullsheadinn.co.uk; 9.30 pm; closed Sun; no smoking; children: 7+. **Accommodation:** 15 rooms, from £85.

BEDFORD, BEDFORDSHIRE 3–1A

St Helena's £ 42 𝔸★
MK42 9XP (01234) 344848
This unusually "good all-rounder" occupies an old house in a small village just outside the town itself; the "Mediterranean" cuisine, the "excellent" service and the "peaceful" location all attract little but praise, but there is the odd complaint of "inflated" prices. / **Sample dishes:** scallop, mushroom & quail's egg salad; crispy duck with blueberry & peppercorn sauce; three-fruit crème brûlées. **Details:** 9 pm; closed Mon, Sat L & Sun; jacket & tie required; no smoking; children: 12+.

BEETHAM, CUMBRIA 7–4D

The Wheatsheaf £ 29
LA7 7AL (01539) 562123
This must be a holding entry for this "pretty" and popular (but "pricey") pub – it moved into new ownership just as this year's survey was getting under way, and we look forward to reporting on the new regime next year. / **Sample dishes:** steamed mussels; lamb chop with garlic & thyme mash; cappuccino & pistachio iced parfait. **Details:** 5m N of A6, J35; 9 pm; no Amex; no smoking. **Accommodation:** 4 rooms, from £60.

BELFAST, COUNTY ANTRIM 10–1D

Though Belfast's dining scene is hardly huge, it includes a number of quality restaurants of note, all in a style which might be described as 'modern British' (Aldens, Nick's Warehouse) or trendier (Cayenne). For the very best food, the trip to Bangor's Shanks is likely to be justified.

Aldens £ 31 ★
229 Upper Newtownards Rd BT4 3JF (028) 9065 0079
Its location (a former supermarket) is hardly propitious, but most hail the "creative" menu and the "top-class" results at this "excellent" modern venture. / **Sample dishes:** smoked salmon frittata; crumbed chicken with baby leeks & goat's cheese; rhubarb granita with apple brandy. **Details:** 2m from Stormont Buildings; 10 pm, Fri & Sat 11 pm; closed Sat L & Sun; no smoking area.

Cayenne £ 31 ★

7 Lesley Hs, Shaftesbury Sq BT27 7DB (028) 9033 1532

For some it's "just like any trendy London 'fusion' eatery", but most reporters say TV chef Paul Rankin's "revamped Roscoff" (as the place was formerly called) is beginning to get into a more satisfactory stride, offering an "imaginative" menu and generally "high" standards; "very closely-packed tables" and a "high noise level", however, can still take the edge off the experience. / Sample dishes: salt & chilli squid; chicken with avocado & black bean salsa; dark chocolate brownie. Details: nr Botanic Railway Station; 11.15 pm; closed Sat L & Sun; no smoking area.

Deanes £ 33

34-40 Howard St BT1 6PE (028) 9056 0000

For fans, this big and bustling central brasserie (with a quieter fine dining restaurant above, formula price £48) is "still the best" in town, thanks to its "excellent and well-presented" cooking; performance has been inconsistent of late, though, and one reporter notes "a 50/50 chance of having something wonderful or something deeply uninspiring". / Sample dishes: goat's cheese with salami & asparagus; ground beef with onion mash & spiced ketchup; steamed pineapple pudding. Details: www.deanesbelfast.com; nr Grand Opera House; 11 pm; closed Sun; no smoking area.

Imperial City £ 24

96 Botanic Ave (028) 9080 8833

This "quality" Chinese destination has something of a reputation for its "good-value" fare, with seafood a speciality. / Sample dishes: chilli squid; chicken in black bean sauce; vanilla ice cream. Details: 11 pm.

Nick's Warehouse £ 33 ★

35 Hill St BT1 2LB (028) 9043 9690

This ever-popular, modern wine bar-cum-restaurant is most mentioned by reporters for its "terrific" lunches ("though it can be excellent in the evening too, if it's not too busy"); the menu is "interesting" at any time, and there's a "good wine list", but some find the service "sloppy". / Sample dishes: Caesar salad with marinated duck; lamb chops with caramelised onion mash; crème brûlée. Details: www.nickswarehouse.co.uk; behind St Anne's Cathedral; 10 pm; closed Mon D, Sat L & Sun; children: before 9 pm only.

Shu £ 32

253 Lisburn Rd BT9 7EN (028) 9038 1655

One or two say its "pretentious", but for most reporters this "beautiful" year-old "Japanese/Western" restaurant makes a "very chic" destination, with interesting "fusion" cooking. / Sample dishes: artichoke & new potato salad; roast hake with noodle cakes, pak choy & salsa; coconut rice spring rolls with ginger. Details: www.shu-restaurant.com; by Windsor Park; 10 pm; closed Sun; children: 12+.

BERKSWELL, WARWICKSHIRE 5–4C

Bear Inn £ 22

Spencer Ln CV7 7BB (01676) 533202

A "traditional" pub, with low ceilings and log fires whose "wide choice of freshly cooked dishes" is uniformly praised. / Sample dishes: fishcakes; minted lamb with lime sauce; caramel tart. Details: off A45 through Meriden; 10 pm; no smoking area; no booking; children: 14+ in bar.

BEVERLEY, EAST RIDING OF YORKSHIRE 6–1A

Wednesdays £ 29

8 Wednesday Mkt HU17 0DG (01482) 869727

This "homely" and "cheerful" spot remained a popular local destination amongst reporters this year, notwithstanding the odd 'off' report. / Sample dishes: celeriac remoulade with prosciutto; Indonesian spiced chicken; vanilla cream tart with rhubarb. Value tip: set 2-crs L £10. Details: nr Beverley Minster; 9.30 pm; closed Sun.

BIGBURY, DEVON 1–4D

Oyster Shack £ 24 𝔸

Millburn Orchard Farm, Stakes Hills TQ7 4BE
(01548) 810876

"The oysters may no longer be from their own beds, but they are beautiful nonetheless", says one fan of this "very friendly" small seafood restaurant, whose seaside location offers "paradisical views over Burgh Island and the coast". / **Sample dishes:** grilled oysters with cream; smoked fish medley with salad; raspberry pavlova. **Details:** L only in summer (closed Tue & Wed, but open Sat D in winter); no Amex; no smoking; booking essential; children: no children at D.

BIRCHOVER, DERBYSHIRE 5–3C

Druid Inn £ 24 ★

Main St DE4 2BL (01629) 650302

"The huge blackboard offers varieties to appeal to most tastes", and "big platefuls" come "well cooked" at this "delightful" creeper-clad pub. / **Sample dishes:** garlic mushrooms in cream; Olde English beef with dumplings; Dime bar crunch pie. **Details:** www.birchovervillage.co.uk; NE of Ashbourne off B5056; 9 pm; no smoking area; children: 10+.

BIRKENHEAD, MERSEYSIDE 5–2A

Capitol £ 23 ★

24 Argyle St CH41 6AE (0151) 647 9212

"Very good food" is the lynchpin of the continuing success of this popular Chinese, of over three decades' standing. / **Sample dishes:** crispy Peking duck; lamb with spring onions; pineapple fritters. **Details:** www.capitol-restaurant.co.uk; 2m from Liverpool city centre; 11 pm; no smoking area.

BIRMINGHAM, WEST MIDLANDS 5–4C

There's so much happening in Birmingham, that it's very tempting to assume that much of it must be good. In fact, much of the middle-market 'excitement' is the result of the vacuum which existed until a couple of years ago being filled by an influx of large 'factory-restaurants' – a style which, in London at least, is fast approaching its sell-by date. In this category, Brum has recently seen the arrival of branches of *Bank*, *fish!* and *Le Petit Blanc* – none of which has found unqualified acclaim among reporters. This city has also recently seen the opening (too late for reporters to comment) of an *Hotel du Vin et Bistro* – part of a group whose aims are worthy, but whose realisation is rather variable.

It's perhaps significant that the most successful of the new Brindleyplace restaurants, so far as reporters are concerned, is *Thai Edge* – this may be a large and ambitious place, but it's backed by a local entrepreneur. Otherwise, Brum's best restaurants remain the few they always were – *San Carlo*, the Italian which is still the city-centre's most notable non-ethnic, and quite a range of Indians and balti houses. As a handy central lunch destination, the *Café Ikon* stands out.

Adils £ 14 ★

148-150 Stoney Ln B12 8AJ (0121) 449 0335

"Don't just judge a restaurant by its décor!"; this is "one of the original Brum curry houses", and though it's "cheap", it has a "happy atmosphere" and "there's no better place for this type of meal". / **Sample dishes:** chicken tikka; prawn rogan josh; rosmalai (Indian rice pudding). **Details:** www.adilbalti.co.uk; 3m from city centre on A41; 12.30 am; no smoking area.

Bank   **£ 28**

4 Brindleyplace B1 2JB   (0121) 633 4466

After a shaky start a year ago, this city-centre mega-brasserie is winning rather more plaudits nowadays as "a successful transfer from London"; as with the original in the capital, however, opinions are mixed, and those praising its "delicious" cooking and its "large and trendy" style vie with those decrying "sterile food and sterile surroundings". / **Sample dishes:** *salt cod fritters; chicken on polenta with sweet & sour onions; Valrhona chocolate cake.* **Value tip:** *set 3-crs meal £12.50.* **Details:** *www.bankrestaurants.com; 2 mins from ICC; 11 pm, Fri & Sat 11.30 pm; closed Sun D; no smoking area.*

Café Ikon   **£ 21**   ★

Ikon Gallery B1 2HS   (0121) 248 3226

A "stylish setting" — "as you might hope for in a modern art gallery" — not to mention "smashing" tapas and "paella to kill for" have helped make this "small, but very pleasant" tapas bar "the best snack lunch venue in town". / **Sample dishes:** *Spanish omelette; mixed seafood paella; ice cream.* **Details:** *10.30 pm; closed Mon & Sun D; no Amex; no smoking area; children: before 9 pm only.*

California Pizza Factory   **£ 22**

42 High St B17 9NE   (0121) 428 2636

"Yummy" pizza makes this family-friendly Harborne hang-out a useful destination. / **Sample dishes:** *Greek salad; spinach florentine pizza; spiced apple cake.* **Details:** *nr Botanical Gardens; 10.45 pm; no Amex; no smoking area.*

Chez Jules   **£ 22**

5a Ethel St, off New St B2 4BG   (0121) 633 4664

A reputation for "down-to-earth" prices and "simple, freshly cooked food" ensures quite a following for this "useful" Gallic canteen, just off New Street, although, some had "expected a bit more pizzazz". / **Sample dishes:** *chicken liver & mushroom pâté; pork in honey & grain mustard sauce; crème brûlée.* **Details:** *11 pm; closed Sun; no smoking area.*

Chung Ying Garden   **£ 30**

17 Thorp St B5 4AT   (0121) 666 6622

"Popular with the local Chinese community" — this huge, recently-revamped Chinatown emporium (and its older sibling at 16-18 Wrottesly Street, tel 0121 622 5669) serves a humungous menu "promptly, but unsmilingly"; "delicious dim sum" receives a particular thumbs-up, but the overall verdict is of cooking that is reliable, but nothing more. / **Sample dishes:** *crispy chicken wings; fried lamb in hot & spicy sauce; ice cream.* **Details:** *www.chungying.co.uk; 11.30 pm.*

52 Degrees North   **£ 32**

Arcadian Centre, Hurst St B5 4TD   (0121) 622 5250

This "cool" and "stylish" venue, opposite the Hippodrome is "one of the best modern restaurants in Birmingham" (not, in itself, a great achievement), and the bar is a popular destination in its own right; even fans admit the place is rather "expensive" for what it is. / **Sample dishes:** *black pudding & pancetta salad; lamb with cardamom sauce & basil mash; raspberry crème brûlée.*
Details: *www.fiftytwodegreesnorth.co.uk; 2 am; D only; children: not permitted.*

fish! £ 34

The Mailbox, 156-158 Wharfside St B1 1RQ
(020) 7234 3333

"A good location by the canal" is the only undisputed strength of this new branch of an expanding national chain, which comes over as *"a basic place with mild pretensions to trendiness"*; some think it succeeds in its aim of *"good-quality fish, simply cooked"*, but *"poorly trained"* staff and *"London prices"* limit enthusiasm; (a Solihull branch recently opened in the Touchwood Centre, same tel).
/ *Sample dishes:* smoked haddock with Welsh rarebit; steamed swordfish with red wine gravy; summer pudding. **Value tip:** set 2-crs pre-th £9.95 (Mon-Fri).
Details: www.fishdiner.co.uk; 10.30 pm; no smoking area.

Giovanni's £ 29

27 Poplar Rd B14 7AA (0121) 443 2391

"Great food if you go for the fish and specials" is claimed by supporters of this *"eccentric"* Italian establishment of long standing, near Highbury Park. / *Sample dishes:* spinach & ricotta cannelloni; red snapper with vegetables; tiramisu. **Details:** 10.30 pm; closed Mon, Sat L & Sun.

Henry's Cantonese £ 27 ★

27 St Paul's Sq B3 1RB (0121) 200 1136

"Simple", *"small"* Cantonese, in the city-centre, praised by a small but ardent fan club for its *"good food at a good price"* and *"family atmosphere"*. / *Sample dishes:* sesame prawn toast; Dover sole with ginger & spring onions; ice cream. **Details:** www.henrysrestaurant.co.uk; 11 pm.

Hotel du Vin et Bistro £ 38

Church St B3 2NR (0121) 236 0559

The newest branch of this popular chain of boutique hotels opened in a former Victorian eye hospital in mid-2001 – too late for any survey commentary; given the group's general standards elsewhere, it should certainly be a very useful addition to the local scene.
/ *Sample dishes:* beef carpaccio with rocket & Parmesan; stuffed pigs trotter with black pudding & mushrooms; chocolate tart with espresso ice cream.
Details: www.hotelduvin.com; 10 pm. **Accommodation:** 66 rooms, from £110.

Imran's £ 10 ★

264-266 Ladypool Rd B12 8JU (0121) 449 6440

"If you can stand the bright lights, the food is fantastic", say fans of this simple Sparkbrook balti house. / *Sample dishes:* chicken pakora; prawn biryani; kulfi. **Details:** www.imrans.co.uk; midnight; no smoking area.

Jonathans £ 41 ✗

16-24 Wolverhampton Rd B68 OLH (0121) 429 3757

Fans say that this locally eminent Victorian-style dining room is *"currently going through a good phase"*; given the ferocity of the negative reports – relating to *"poor"* cooking, *"disgraceful"* service, and *"ridiculous"* prices – one has to wonder what the bad times must be like! / *Sample dishes:* 'Market day' broth; wild berry chicken; bread & butter pudding. **Details:** www.jonathans.co.uk; on junction with Hagley Road; 10 pm; closed Sat L & Sun D; no jeans or trainers; no smoking area. **Accommodation:** 48 rooms, from £98.

Jyoti £ 15 ★

569-571 Stratford Rd B11 4LS (0121) 766 7199

"Incredibly tasty and cheap vegetarian food" keeps reporters coming back to this BYO Sparkhill Gujerati, even if *"it could do with a visit from the decorators"*. / *Sample dishes:* samosas; aubergine masala; mango kulfi. **Details:** 8.30 pm; closed Mon, Tue L & Wed L; no Amex; no smoking.

Kababish £ 20 ★

29 Woodbridge Rd B13 8EH (0121) 449 5556

"Consistently good" cooking (including the *"best naan bread ever"*) helps this *"friendly local balti house"* stand out, even amongst all the Moseley competition. / **Sample dishes:** tandoori fish; chicken masala & coriander naan; pistachio kulfi. **Details:** 11.15 pm; D only, closed Sun.

Maharaja £ 24 ★

23 Hurst St B5 4SA (0121) 622 2641

This long-established city-centre Indian still pleases with its *"good-quality ingredients"* and its *"fresh and subtle"* spicing; *"lovely"* service helps one overlook the rather dated surroundings. / **Sample dishes:** onion bhaji; spiced chicken in yoghurt; kulfi. **Details:** nr Hippodrome; 11 pm; closed Sun.

Malt Shovel £ 16

1 Newton Rd B43 6HN (0121) 357 1148

"Always full and buzzing" – this *"country pub/restaurant"* on the city's northern outskirts wins praise for its *"super"* atmosphere, and *"consistent"* nosh. / **Sample dishes:** roast pork & traditional trimmings; ice cream selection. **Details:** 8.45 pm, Fri & Sat 9.15 pm.

Le Petit Blanc £ 34

9 Brindleyplace B1 2HS (0121) 633 7333

Raymond Blanc's large and *"stylish"* canalside Gallic brasserie attracts much commentary, and most reports are of results somewhere between *"worthwhile"* and *"top-class"*; some find the place *"low on ambience"*, though, and too many reports of *"average"* cooking rob it of an unequivocal endorsement. / **Sample dishes:** tomato risotto; sea bream with artichoke, squid & sun-dried tomato; tarte Tatin. **Value tip:** set 2-crs L & pre-th £12.50. **Details:** www.petitblanc.com; 11.30 pm; no smoking area.

Rajdoot £ 22 A★

12-22 Albert St B4 7UD (0121) 643 8749

The cooking *"never disappoints"* and the setting is *"comfortable, welcoming, calm and friendly"* at this comparatively *"classy"* city-centre Indian. / **Sample dishes:** fish tikka; chicken tikka masala; kulfi. **Details:** www.rajdoot.co.uk; 11.15 pm; closed Sat L & Sun L.

Royal Naim £ 14 ★

417-419 Stratford Rd B11 4JZ (0121) 766 7849

"The food is much better than average" at this BYO Sparkhill spot, praised by its small fan club for the *"sensational value"* it offers. / **Sample dishes:** mixed kebabs; chicken balti; pistachio kulfi. **Details:** 2 mins from city centre on A34; midnight.

San Carlo £ 34 A★

4 Temple St B2 5BN (0121) 633 0251

Still the most consistently successful restaurant in Brum, this *"buzzing"*, *"very posh"* (going on glitzy) city-centre spot is a *"genuine"* Italian, much praised for its *"wonderful"* food – including *"great, fresh pasta"* – and for its *"friendly"* service. / **Sample dishes:** barbecue spare ribs; veal in wine, mushroom & cream sauce; coffee bean ice cream. **Details:** behind Cathedral; 10.45 pm; children: 5+.

Shimla Pinks £ 28

214 Broad St B15 1AY (0121) 633 0366

It remains the most talked-about restaurant in town, but (in line with the financial difficulties of the national chain that it spawned) this *"noisy"* and *"showy"* city-centre subcontinental is *"slipping"* – the *"aromatic"* cooking seems increasingly *"overpriced"* and *"designer-clad"* staff can be *"arrogant"*. / **Sample dishes:** pink salmon in spicy sauce; tandoori chicken & rice; mango dessert. **Details:** www.shimlapinks.bite2enjoy.com; nr Symphony Hall; 11 pm; closed Sat L & Sun L.

Siam Thai £ 32 ★★

7a High St B14 7BB (0121) 444 0906

"Opening times are irregular", and *"you may have to book well in advance"* (that goes for some of the dishes, too), but the *"freshness of the ingredients"* and the *"care in their preparation"* makes this *"authentic"* and very personal Thai restaurant well worth planning ahead for. / **Sample dishes:** Thai chicken satay; king prawn green curry; Thai custard. **Details:** www.siamrestaurant.co.uk; 10.30 pm; D only, closed Mon & Sun; no Amex; booking essential.

Thai Edge £ 28 𝔸 ★

Brindleyplace B1 2HS (0121) 643 3993

This *"smart"* new canalside Thai has quickly established itself as a *"fantastic"* hit, thanks to its *"very good"* food at *"reasonable prices"*, and its *"beautiful setting and décor"*. / **Sample dishes:** prawn satay; green chicken curry; coconut jelly. **Details:** 11 pm, Fri & Sat 11.30 pm.

BISHOPS TACHBROOK, WARWICKSHIRE 5–4C

Mallory Court £ 59

Harbury Ln CV33 9QB (01926) 330214

For *"formal"* dining, this *"very professional"* and *"civilised"* country house hotel – with its *"lovely location in beautiful grounds"* – receives many good recommendations even from those who find the décor a bit *"heavy and old fashioned"*, and the food *"comforting rather than exciting"*. / **Sample dishes:** scallops in pancetta with vegetable nage; beef with foie gras & truffles in Madeira sauce; lemongrass brûlée with mango sorbet. **Value tip:** set 2-crs L £19. **Details:** www.mallory.co.uk; 2m S of Leamington Spa, off B4087; 10 pm, Sat 10.30 pm; no smoking in dining room; children: 9+. **Accommodation:** 18 rooms, from £185.

BISPHAM GREEN, LANCASHIRE 5–1A

Eagle & Child £ 25

Maltkiln Ln L40 3SG (01257) 462297

A *"proper"* country pub, serving *"proper"* food, say fans of this *"relaxed"* establishment; note that the *"local"* dishes are *"ideal for carnivores"*, but veggie reporters can emerge feeling very poorly treated indeed. / **Sample dishes:** deep-fried goat's cheese; toasted chicken & red pepper panini; sticky toffee pudding. **Details:** M6, J27; 8.15 pm; no Amex; no smoking area.

BLACKPOOL, LANCASHIRE 5–1A

September Brasserie £ 31 ★

15-17 Queen St FY1 1PU (01253) 623282

A *"delightful"* restaurant in this kiss-me-quick town *"may sound like a contradiction"* but all reports continue to agree that there's *"good and interesting cooking"* (*"and wine too"*) to be had at this *"small and cosy"* first-floor fixture (located *"above a hairdressers"*). / **Sample dishes:** hot chicken liver pâté; duck cassoulet; white chocolate bavarois. **Details:** just past North Pier, opp Cenotaph; 10 pm; closed Mon & Sun.

BLAIRGOWRIE, PERTH & KINROSS 9–3C

Kinloch House £ 41 ★

PH10 6SG (01250) 884237

"Although it's a country house hotel, they seem to entertain many locals" at this *"delightful"* (and rather formal) establishment – presumably it's because they know that the *"excellent Scottish fayre"* is well worth seeking out. / **Sample dishes:** Highland salmon marinated in whisky; Angus beef with foie gras & savoy cabbage; chocolate truffle cake with mint cream. **Details:** www.kinlochhouse.com; 9.15 pm; jacket & tie required at D; no smoking; children: 12+ at D. **Accommodation:** 20 rooms, from £155.

The White Horse Hotel   £ 35   ★
4 High St NR25 7AL   (01263) 740574
"They try hard" at this 17th-century inn, which fans say is a *"gem"*
in the marshlands on account of the *"ambitious"* pub grub on offer
at *"moderate prices"* in its conservatory restaurant. / **Sample
dishes:** *crab & radishes with Thai mayonnaise; roast lamb with aubergine
purée; raspberry tart.* **Details:** *9 pm; D only, closed Mon & Sun; children: 6+.*
Accommodation: *10 rooms, from £60.*

Church House Inn   £ 23
Church St SK10 5PY   (01625) 574014
This *"traditional"* pub is an *"excellent, warm and friendly local, with
food to match"*. / **Sample dishes:** *garlic mushrooms; steak diane with Dijon
mustard sauce; hot almond tart.* **Details:** *close to Strickley Hall Hotel;
9.30 pm; no Amex; no smoking area; no booking in main bar.*
Accommodation: *5 rooms, from £45.*

Devonshire Arms   £ 62   ✗
Grassington Rd BD23 6AJ   (01756) 710441
It's hard not to conclude that this imposing coaching inn *"trades
on its links with the Duchess of Devonshire"* – though culinary
standards have improved fractionally from their previously dire
levels, there are still too many who experience *"mediocre"* cooking
and *"unbelievably incompetent"* service. / **Sample dishes:** *goat's
cheese with red onion marmalade; pan-roasted beef with red wine gravy; iced
white chocolate nougatine.* **Value tip:** *set 3-crs Sun L £19.50.* **Details:** *on
A59, 5m NE of Skipton; 10 pm; D only, except Sun open L & D; no smoking.*
Accommodation: *41 rooms, from £165.*

Strawberry Duck   £ 19   Ⓐ
Overshores Rd, Turton BL7 0LU   (01204) 852013
"Lovely old pub" on the Pennines fringe, where new owners seem
to be maintaining a *"good"* standard of cooking; *"if it's busy there
can be a long wait"*, though. / **Sample dishes:** *black pudding tower;
ostrich with chilli, tomatoes & cream; syrup sponge & custard.* **Details:** *100
yds from Entwistle railway station; 9.30 pm, Sat 10 pm; no Amex.*
Accommodation: *4 rooms, from £45.*

Spice Box   £ 28   Ⓐ★
152 High St LS23 6BW   (01937) 842558
"Fish of the highest quality" is the highlight among the *"innovative"*
and *"fairly priced"* selection which has created a very strong
following for this *"small and cosy, brasserie-style restaurant"*;
success has recently brought expansion, in the form of a new
branch at 24 King's Rd, Harrogate (tel 01423 568600). / **Sample
dishes:** *fishcakes with Thai sauce; duck with bacon & thyme potatoes;
chocolate truffle.* **Details:** *www.spiceboxrestaurant.co.uk; 2 E of A1, on A659;
9.30 pm; closed Mon L & Sun; no smoking.*

Eastwell Manor   £ 39
Eastwell Pk TN25 4HR   (01233) 213000
"Well-presented food, elegantly served in an historic atmosphere"
was more consistently praised this year at this impressive-looking
country house hotel; there were still some, though, who found the
cooking a *"disappointment"*. / **Sample dishes:** *cured salmon with orange
butter sauce; roast lamb with pearl barley risotto; apricot savarin with vanilla
cream.* **Value tip:** *set 2-crs L £10.* **Details:** *www.eastwellmanor.co.uk; 3m N
of Ashford on A251; 10 pm; closed Sun D; no jeans; no smoking in dining room.*
Accommodation: *62 rooms, from £190.*

Bistro on the Beach   £ 25   Ⓐ
Solent Promenade BH6 4BE   (01202) 431473
*The name says it all about this "caff by day, bistro by night" (it is
indeed "right on the beach"), which offers "good-value set menus".*
/ **Sample dishes:** *smoked salmon & prawn terrine; braised lamb with mint
mash; bread & butter pudding.* **Details:** *9.30 pm; D only, closed Sun-Tue;
no smoking.*

Chez Fred   £ 15
10 Seamoor Rd BH4 9AN   (01202) 761023
*It's "nothing fancy" but this "first-class chippy" is well worth
knowing about; it's "where the stars eat" when they're in town,
apparently.* / **Sample dishes:** *no starters; cod & chips with mushy peas;
treacle sponge & custard.* **Details:** *www.chezfred.co.uk; 1m W of town centre;
9.45 pm; closed Sun L; no Amex; no smoking; no booking.*

Clarks   £ 39   ★
350-352 Charminster Rd BH8 9RX   (01202) 240310
*It was only established in 1999, but "word has spread" about Gary
and Lucinda Clark's small establishment on the town's outskirts,
whose "delicious" cooking fans vaunt as "the best within 25 miles".*
/ **Sample dishes:** *asparagus & truffle tart; roast lamb & sweetbreads with
summer vegetables; banana pannacotta with walnut praline.* **Details:** *off
Cooperdean roundabout; 10 pm; closed Mon, Tue L, Sat L & Sun; no smoking
before 10 pm; children: 10+.*

Ocean Palace   £ 26   ★
8 Priory Rd BH2 5DG   (01202) 559127
*"Bournemouth's best Chinese" has quite a following, and its
"incredible selection of fish and vegetarian dishes" attracts
particular praise; "there's a good atmosphere" too, "especially
in the conservatory".* / **Sample dishes:** *deep-fried chicken in chilli sauce;
crispy aromatic duck with pancakes; banana fritters.*
Details: *www.oceanpalace.co.uk; 11 pm.*

Miller Howe   £ 53   Ⓐ
Rayrigg Rd LA23 1EY   (01539) 442536
*"Come back Tovey!"; though some reporters say that the food
at this country house hotel known for its lakeland views is "still
wonderful under the new regime", more strident are the complaints
of those who – citing "dreadful" cooking or "oppressive" service –
say the place is "living on its reputation".* / **Sample dishes:** *roast
asparagus spears; roast maize-fed chicken; sticky toffee pudding & toffee
sauce.* **Value tip:** *set 3-crs L £17.50.* **Details:** *www.millerhowe.com; on A592
between Windermere & Bowness; 8 pm; open L&D all week; closed for 2
weeks in Jan; no smoking in dining room; children: 8+.* **Accommodation:** *12
rooms, from £140, incl D.*

Porthole   £ 40   A★

3 Ash St LA23 3EB   (01539) 442793

*The odd misgiving was expressed this year, but most reporters still praise Gianni & Judy Berton's "Cumbrian institution" – currently celebrating its thirtieth anniversary – for the "long-standing excellence" of its cooking and for the "lovely" surroundings of its 17th-century town-centre setting; there's also a good terrace for the summer. / **Sample dishes:** antipasto; veal with mushrooms; sticky toffee pudding. **Details:** www.porthole.fsworld.co.uk; near Old England Hotel; 10.30 pm; closed Tue & Sat L.*

BRADFORD ON AVON, WILTSHIRE   2–2B

Thai Barn   £ 23   ★

24 Bridge St BA15 1BY   (01225) 866443

*"Great food" and "friendly service" win consistent support for this "completely unexpected" oriental, in a converted 18th-century barn; there's "good provision for non-meat-eaters" too. / **Sample dishes:** 'Thai Barn' platter; roast duck in 'Thai Barn' sauce; ginger ice cream. **Details:** opp Bridge St car park; 11 pm; closed Mon & Tue L; no Amex; no smoking area.*

BRADFORD, WEST YORKSHIRE   5–1C

Aagrah   £ 23   ★

483 Bradford Rd LS28 8ED   (01274) 668818

*"Good consistent food, with distinctive individual flavours" is praised here, as at other branches of this excellent chain of Yorkshire Indians, and it's "always very busy". / **Sample dishes:** paneer tikka; lamb chops with korma sauce; mango kulfi. **Details:** www.aagrah.com; on A647, 3m from city centre; 11.30 pm, Fri & Sat midnight; D only; no smoking area.*

Akbars Balti   £ 18   A★

1276 Leeds Rd BD3 3LF   (01274) 773311

*"Great big 'family' naans" help set the convivial tone at this "buzzing", "exceptionally good" and "very popular" Thornbury Indian – "in the land of curry houses, this one stands out". / **Sample dishes:** fish pakoras; chicken balti & rice; kulfi. **Details:** www.akbars.co.uk; midnight; D only; no credit cards; no smoking area.*

Clarks   £ 28

46-50 Highgate BD9 4BE   (01274) 499890

*As "a rare non-Asian eatery in Bradford", this "busy bistro" is "amazingly popular", thanks to its "eclectic" menu and its "sensibly priced" wine; critics, though, discern a tendency to "over-elaboration". / **Sample dishes:** warm salad of calves liver; garlic king prawns with braised chicory; treacle tart. **Value tip:** set 2-crs L £7.95. **Details:** www.clarksrestaurant.co.uk; 5 mins from city centre on A650 to Shipley; 10 pm; closed Sat L & Sun L; no smoking area.*

Karachi   £ 9   ★

15-17 Neal St BD5 0BX   (01274) 732015

*"It hasn't changed in 25 years", but fans say the "authentic", "dirt-cheap" cooking at this "grotty" curry house in central Bradford remains extremely "consistent". / **Sample dishes:** samosas; chicken curry; gulab jaman (Indian sweets). **Details:** nr ice skating rink off Little Horton Lane; 1 am, Fri & Sat 2 am; no credit cards.*

Kashmir   £ 11   ★

27 Morley St BD7 1AG   (01274) 726513

*Bradford's oldest curry house remains a well-liked, "authentic" destination – "you eat with your hands" and "surroundings are basic", but "who cares, it's such good value for money". / **Sample dishes:** mushroom bhaji; chicken Kashmiri; rasmalai (cream cheese dessert). **Details:** nr Alhambra Theatre; 3 am; no Amex; no smoking area.*

Mumtaz Paan House £ 15 ★★

Great Horton Rd BD7 3HS (01274) 571861

*"Without doubt, the best Asian cuisine I have ever experienced" –
for almost all reporters, a visit to this phenomenally popular
Kashmiri (which is one of the UK's top subcontinentals) is "an
experience to be relished", and one that a total absence of alcohol
does remarkably little to dim.* / **Sample dishes:** *spiced chicken &
sweetcorn in pastry; spiced cod with pomegranate; mango ice cream.*
Details: *www.mumtaz.co.uk; nr Alhambra Theatre & Photographic Museum;
1 am; no smoking area.*

Nawaab £ 22 ★

32 Manor Rw BD1 4QE (01274) 720371

*"Currytastic!" – "an excellent menu-choice" and "better décor than
the Mumtaz" (plus, perhaps, the fact that "they serve alcohol")
leads some reporters to nominate this "pleasant", well-known city-
centre Indian as their top choice in town.* / **Sample dishes:** *paneer
tikka; potato & aubergine balti; kulfi.* **Details:** *www.nawaab.com; 11 pm;
no smoking area.*

BRANCASTER, NORFOLK 6–3B

White Horse £ 29

Main Rd PE31 8BY (01485) 210262

*"Spectacular views overlooking the Norfolk Coastal Path" and
"surprisingly good" food can make for a memorable visit at this
"very popular" pub-plus-conservatory-restaurant.* / **Sample
dishes:** *spiced chicken terrine with salsa; sea bass with Puy lentils & deep-fried
leeks; strawberry shortbread.* **Details:** *www.whitehorsebrancaster.co.uk; on
A149; 8.45 pm.* **Accommodation:** *8 rooms, from £60.*

BRANSCOMBE, DEVON 2–4A

Masons Arms £ 26 Ⓐ

Main St EX12 3DJ (01297) 680300

*A "welcoming" pub that's "full of character" and with "a terrific
selection of real ale"; once again, reporters judge its varied grub
as "OK".* / **Sample dishes:** *steamed scallops; crispy roast duckling; sherry
trifle.* **Details:** *www.masonsarms.co.uk; 8.45 pm; D only; no smoking.*
Accommodation: *27 rooms, from £44.*

BRAY, WINDSOR & MAIDENHEAD 3–3A

The Fat Duck £ 76

High St SL6 2AQ (01628) 580333

*Genius or egotist? – views on Heston Blumenthal's "extraordinary"
cooking admit of no Third Way; fans (a bare majority) vaunt the
"breathtaking" results from his "daring", even "outrageous" menus,
but doubters deride "pretentious combinations", "off-hand" service,
a "cold and unwelcoming" atmosphere and "silly" prices; (a new
brasserie sibling is planned as we go to press).* / **Sample dishes:** *foie
gras with smoked eel & jasmine; lamb with garlic & coffee dentelle; smoked
bacon ice-cream.* **Value tip:** *set 3-crs L £25.75.* **Details:** *2m from M4 J8 or
J9; 9.30 pm, Sat 10 pm; closed Mon & Sun D; closed 2 weeks at New Year;
no smoking area.*

Fish £ 44 ★

Old Mill Ln SL6 2BG (01628) 781111

*Some say the service is iffy and think the atmosphere a
"downside", but all-in-all this converted pub (which does "good
real ale", despite its gentrification) "maintains a high standard" –
especially when it comes to its "wide range of fish dishes" – and
the place is "modestly priced (at least by local standards)".*
/ **Sample dishes:** *oysters; char-grilled tuna with black olive mash; chocolate
truffle cake.* **Details:** *www.fishatbray.co.uk; 9.15 pm; closed Sun D; no smoking
area; children: 12+ at D.*

Waterside Inn   **£100**   ★

Ferry Rd SL6 2AT   (01628) 620691

"Impeccable" cuisine, "cosseting" service (considerably improved
since last year) and a "beautiful", "restful" riverside setting help
make Michel Roux's long-established Thames Valley fixture "just
the most perfect eating experience" in many people's books;
"you pay heavily", however, and if there's a failing, it's an
atmosphere some find rather "snooty" or "corporate".
/ **Sample dishes:** pappardelle with quail & watercress; sweetbreads & veal
ravioli with fondant potatoes; raspberry soufflé. **Value tip:** set 3-crs L £33.50
(Sun L £49). **Details:** www.waterside-inn.co.uk; off A308 between Windsor &
Maidenhead; 10 pm; closed Mon & Tue (open Tue D Jun-Aug); children: 12+.
Accommodation: 9 rooms, from £150.

BREARTON, NORTH YORKSHIRE   8–4B

The Malt Shovel   **£ 20**   Ⓐ★

HG3 3BX   (01423) 862929

"No pretensions – just what pub grub should be"; "consistently
tasty" food, "well-kept real ale" and a "nice" environment makes
this one-time barn a top local recommendation. / **Sample
dishes:** mussels; game pie; treacle tart. **Details:** off A61, 6m N of Harrogate;
9 pm; closed Mon & Sun D; no credit cards; no booking.

BRIDPORT, DORSET   2–4B

Riverside   **£ 34**

West Bay DT6 4EZ   (01308) 422011

"The freshest fish, imaginatively presented" has made this
"unpretentious" café a popular fixture for over thirty years now;
even some fans feel it's "a bit too crowded and 'in' these days",
though, adding to a sense that it is becoming "pricey" and "smug".
/ **Sample dishes:** mussels with shallots; skate wing with brown
butter & capers; knickerbocker glory. **Value tip:** set 2-crs L £12.50.
Details: www.riverside-restaurant.co.uk; in centre of West Bay; 9 pm; closed
Mon & Sun D; no Amex; smoking discouraged.

BRIGHTON, EAST SUSSEX   3–4B

From first impressions, it's easy enough to dismiss Brighton
(& Hove) as a place full of restaurants none of which is any
good. Fortunately that's too simplistic, and the city in fact
offers enough choice of quality restaurants to satisfy the
repeat visitor.

At the top end, One Paston Place stands unchallenged, but
those looking to spend rather less should consider particularly
Gingerman, and also Strand or Whytes. Vegetarians are
especially well catered for, with Terre à Terre a leading name
nationally and the most notable of a string of good places. For
quintessential seaside seafood, the Regency is hard to beat.

Those looking for the more obvious ethnic cuisines will
find an unusually wide choice of relatively inexpensive
establishments of good quality. There are also some famous
tourist traps, which are best avoided.

Al Duomo   **£ 20**

7 Pavilion Building BN1 1EE   (01273) 326741

"A long-established landmark", this "cramped" and "lively" Italian
near the Royal Pavilion continues to pack 'em in; pizza from the
wood-burning oven is a speciality. / **Sample dishes:** calamari; fusilli
with tomatoes & anchovies; tiramisu. **Value tip:** set 3-crs meal £8.95.
Details: www.alduomo.co.uk; near the pier; 11 pm.

Ashoka   £ 22   ★
95-97 Church Rd BN3 2BA (01273) 736463
"Good-quality" cooking, "brisk" service and a "pleasant"
atmosphere win continuing support for this "reliable" Indian, near
*Hove Town Hall. / **Sample dishes:** lamb kebab; chicken bhuna; kulfi.*
***Details:** 11.45 pm; no smoking area.*

Aumthong Thai   £ 24   ★
60 Western Rd BN3 1JD (01273) 773922
A popular Thai restaurant in Hove, where there's "little to fault in
*food or service". / **Sample dishes:** spicy prawn cakes; Thai green chicken*
*curry; Thai coconut flan. **Value tip:** set 4-crs D £20.*
***Details:** www.aumthong.com; 10.30 pm; closed Mon.*

Basketmakers Arms   £ 15
12 Gloucester Rd BN1 4AD (01273) 689006
"Cheap and plentiful" pub food – "great burgers" especially – not
to mention "superb beer" win consistently warm reviews for this
*boozer near the railway station. / **Sample dishes:** tomato & Mozzarella*
*salad; sirloin steak & chips; chocolate tart. **Details:** 8.30 pm; closed Sat D &*
Sun D; no booking; children: before 8 pm only.

Black Chapati   £ 30
12 Circus Pde, New England Rd BN1 4GW (01273) 699011
"Maverick, seriously non-conformist cooking that plunders Asia
and beyond" has made quite a name for this "sterile-looking"
and "grottily-located" backstreet venture; the results strike some
as "careless", though, and the "volatile" service veers from
*"interesting" to plain "abusive". / **Sample dishes:** hot & sour soup with*
sea bass; braised pork with caramelised garlic & pak choy; Turkish coffee
*ice-cream. **Details:** 1m from seafront; 10 pm; D only, closed Mon & Sun;*
smoking discouraged; booking: max 8.

Bombay Aloo   £ 13   ★
39 Ship St BN1 1AB (01273) 771089
The "exceptionally cheap", "eat-as-much-as-you-like" buffet formula
seems like "astonishing value" to most reporters on this popular
Indian vegetarian; "the upstairs room has rather more ambience
*than downstairs". / **Sample dishes:** onion bhaji; mixed vegetable curry with*
*garlic naan; Indian rice pudding. **Details:** near the Lanes; 11 pm; no Amex;*
no smoking area; need 6+ to book; children: under 6s eat free.

Browns   £ 28   ✗
314 Duke St BN1 1AH (01273) 323501
"Each year it seems to disappoint more" – what was an "old
favourite" (and the original) branch of this well-known brasserie
chain exhibits the same "disappointing" standards as elsewhere;
even those who say it's "still a friendly meeting house" say the
"food leaves a lot to be desired", and service can be "very poor".
*/ **Sample dishes:** smoked salmon with soda bread; chicken & leek pie; sticky*
*toffee pudding. **Details:** www.browns-restaurants.com; 11.30 pm; no smoking*
area.

Chilka House   £ 23
69 St James St BN2 1PJ (01273) 677085
With its "very wide menu of Indian food" and a "Goan slant" to
many dishes, this basic subcontinental delivers "delicious" results
according to its fans; one or two reporters didn't fare so well this
*year, however. / **Sample dishes:** king prawn pakora; duck vindaloo; fresh*
*mango. **Details:** 10 pm; D only.*

China Garden £ 27

88-90 Preston St BN1 2HG (01273) 325124

This "large", "café-style" Chinese, on the corner of Preston Park, is still Brighton's best-known oriental, but even some supporters acknowledge that the food "is slipping with increased popularity"; "great dim sum" are much approved nonetheless. / **Sample dishes:** aromatic duck pancakes; sizzling Cantonese steak; toffee apples. **Details:** on seafront nr Grand Hotel & Metropole Hotel; 11 pm.

Donatello £ 22

1-3 Brighton Pl BN1 1HJ (01273) 775477

This "staple" Italian in the Lanes remains "really busy" and fans like its "great buzz" and rapid turnarounds; the cooking is "hit-and-miss", however, and to critics its "extremely impersonal" service smacks of a "cattle market" approach. / **Sample dishes:** garlic & parsley mushrooms; rigatoni with four cheeses; tiramisu. **Details:** www.donatello.co.uk; 11.30 pm; no smoking area.

English's £ 38 ✗

29-31 East St BN1 1HL (01273) 327980

"Unchanged" and ever-"crowded", this venerable Lanes institution is one of the oldest restaurants in the UK; many think it "a lovely old fashioned place", and some traditionalists also laud its "fantastic fresh seafood", but – as ever – there are far too many complaints of "dull" cooking , of "rushed" service, and that it's "very expensive". / **Sample dishes:** crab & apple terrine with crispy whitebait; monkfish goujons with vodka & strawberries; deep-fried pineapple with butterscotch sauce. **Value tip:** set 2-crs pre-th £7.95 (not Sun). **Details:** www.englishs.co.uk; 10 pm.

Food for Friends £ 16

17-18 Prince Albert St BN1 1HF (01273) 202310

"Be prepared to queue" for this "very popular" vegetarian haunt near the Town Hall, whose fans hail the "wonderful and extensive" menu; there's a minority that just "hates the place", though, finding it "pretentious" and "over-rated", and with "unbelievably bad service". / **Sample dishes:** Jerusalem artichoke soup; Senegalese groundnut stew; banana trifle. **Details:** www.foodforfriends.com; 10 pm; no Amex; no smoking area.

La Fourchette £ 30

101 Western Rd BN3 36H (01273) 722556

This "idiosyncratic", modern French restaurant produces some "well-prepared", quite "imaginative" food; service can be "surly", though, and the "small" premises are "noisy" and "tight on space". / **Sample dishes:** quail ravioli; roast veal; citron tart. **Details:** 10.30 pm; closed Mon L & Sun.

Gars £ 24

19 Prince Albert St BN1 1HF (01273) 321321

"The set menus represent excellent value for money" at this busy Chinese, near the seafront. / **Sample dishes:** mushroom satay; Szechuan chicken; banana fritters. **Details:** beside the Lanes; 11 pm; children: 7+ after 7 pm.

The George £ 20

5 Trafalgar St BN1 4EQ (01273) 681055

"Good veggie pub grub" ensures huge popularity for this "big and friendly" boozer near Brighton station, perhaps explaining why service can be "painfully slow". / **Sample dishes:** nachos with cheese; smoked Applewood rarebit; tarte Tatin. **Details:** near the railway station; 9.30 pm, Fri-Sun 8 pm; no booking, Fri-Sun.

Gingerman £ 33 ★★
21a Norfolk Square BN1 2PD   (01273) 326688
"The location takes some finding", but it's worth seeking out this *"small"*, *"quality"* establishment, on the Brighton/Hove border; staff make you feel *"wanted"*, and ex-Paston Place chef Ben McKellar produces some *"totally superb"*, *"imaginative"* cooking at a *"good-value"* prices. / **Sample dishes:** gnocchi with watercress, broad beans & Parmesan; veal with dried ham & olive oil mash; caramelised pineapple tart. **Details:** off Norfolk Square; 10 pm; closed Mon & Sun.

The Grand £ 49 Ⓐ
97-99 Kings Rd BN1 2FW   (01273) 224300
It's no great surprise that lunch or dinner at this huge, five star seaside landmark can be *"a let-down"*, but it's *"a lovely place for afternoon tea"*. / **Sample dishes:** prawns in garlic & coriander butter; duck with oriental noodles; raspberry crème brûlée.
Details: www.grandbrighton.co.uk; 10 pm; jacket & tie required at weekends & tea dances; no smoking before 9 pm. **Accommodation:** 200 rooms, from £220.

Havana £ 42 ✕
32 Duke St BN1 1AG   (01273) 773388
Even some advocates acknowledge that this *"stylish"* Lanes spot offers a *"variable experience"*, and there are one too many detractors who say they *"try a bit too hard to make it trendy"*, complaining of *"pretentious"* cooking and *"arrogant"* staff. / **Sample dishes:** haddock & poached egg tartlet; roasted & poached venison; Baileys parfait with biscuits. **Details:** 10.15 pm, Fri & Sat 10.45 pm; no trainers; children: 6+ after 7 pm.

Kambi £ 18
107 Western Rd BN1 2AA   (01273) 327934
An *"excellent range of Middle Eastern fare"* makes this *"friendly"* spot, near Hove seafront, a popular destination; *"BYO is a bonus in keeping down the bill"*. / **Sample dishes:** mezze; chicken marinated in lemon & garlic; honey halva. **Details:** 11.30 pm.

One Paston Place £ 53 ★
1 Paston Pl BN2 1HA   (01273) 606933
"Still Brighton's No 1", this *"elegant"* Kempstown townhouse is run by *"perfectionists"*, and its Gallic cooking is still rated by many as *"the finest on the South Coast"*; some, however, complain that it all comes at *"London prices"*, and the *"quiet"* ambience strikes some as a mite *"boring"*. / **Sample dishes:** stuffed quail with morel bouillon; grilled brill & smoked haddock with fennel sauce; chocolate desserts. **Value tip:** set 2-crs L £16.50. **Details:** between the pier & marina; 9.45 pm; closed Mon & Sun; children: 2+.

Regency £ 17 ★
131 Kings Rd BN1 2HH   (01273) 325014
"Much loved" by trippers of all ages for its *"unpretentious"* approach, this *"very pleasant upmarket chippy"* offers *"very good"*, if *"basic"*, fish dishes and *"friendly"* service. / **Sample dishes:** oysters; dressed crab salad; peach melba. **Details:** opp West Pier; 11 pm; no smoking area. **Accommodation:** 25 rooms, from £50.

Saucy £ 30
8a Church Rd BN3 2FL   (01273) 324080
It's *"very Brighton"* (well Hove, actually), and this *"adventurous"* restaurant is applauded by fans for its *"funky"* and *"chilled"* setting and its *"original twist"* on British cooking; it takes flak from sceptics, though, for food that's *"lacking"* and *"a need to build atmosphere"*. / **Sample dishes:** 'Saucy' fishcakes; liver & bacon; crêpes Suzette. **Value tip:** set 2-crs L & pre-th £10.
Details: www.saucyrestaurant.com; 10.30 pm; no Amex; booking: max 6, Fri & Sat.

Strand £ 26 ★

6 Little East St BN1 1HT (01273) 747096

"Great staff" help create a *"chilled"* atmosphere at this trendy spot, near the Royal Pavilion, where *"creative"*, *"global"* cuisine – *"with the emphasis on vegetarian and fish dishes"* – is realised to a *"solid"* standard. / **Sample dishes:** Thai fishcakes; duck with sweet potato mash; toffee apples & custard. **Details:** 10 pm, Fri & Sat 10.30 pm; closed Mon L.

Terre à Terre £ 29 ★

71 East St BN1 1NQ (01273) 729051

Long in contention as the UK's top veggie – this *"exciting"* and *"lively"* Lanes institution owes its phenomenal popularity to its *"inspiring"*, *"robust"* but *"unstodgy"* cooking; *"despite its reputation"*, though, *"some meals are not exceptional"*, and there is some feeling that the place is *"not as good as it used to be"*. / **Sample dishes:** smoked soba salad; goat's cheese ballotine; pineapple parfait. **Details:** 10.30 pm; closed Mon L; no smoking area.

Trogs £ 33

124 Kings Rd BN1 2FA (01273) 204655

There's something of a *"home-from-home"* atmosphere at this *"friendly"* basement bar/restaurant; reactions to the veggie/vegan fare remain mixed however – to some its *"imaginative"*, to others *"disappointing"*. / **Sample dishes:** Thai coconut, chilli & lime patties; steamed wild mushroom pudding; passion fruit brûlée. **Details:** opp West Pier, by Metropole Hotel; 9.30 pm; no smoking.

Tsing Tao £ 26 ★

33 Preston St BN1 2HP (01273) 202708

This well-established oriental, near the West Pier, is known for being *"where the Chinese eat"* locally; *"cheerful"* staff offer an *"extensive"* menu, and the place numbers *"the best dim sum"* and a *"good veggie selection"* among its attractions. / **Sample dishes:** mixed hors d'oeuvres; crispy duck with pancakes; lychees. **Details:** on seafront nr West Pier; 11 pm.

Whytes £ 34 ★

33 Western St BN1 2PG (01273) 776618

"Fresh" and *"original"* cooking is twinned with *"enthusiastic"* service to make this *"intimate"* dining room on the Brighton/Hove border one of the best in town; advice on the wine front is *"brilliant"* too. / **Sample dishes:** citrus-cured gravadlax; duck with blackberries & truffle jus; chocolate fondant with cherry & basil sorbet. **Details:** www.whytesrestaurant.com; 9.30 pm; D only, closed Mon & Sun.

BRIMFIELD, SHROPSHIRE 5–4A

The Roebuck Inn £ 32 ★

SY8 4NE (01584) 711230

"Everything is freshly prepared" at this *"tiny old pub"*, where the *"consistently good value"* of the cooking and the *"smiling"* service make it a unanimously popular recommendation. / **Sample dishes:** Dartmouth crab gateaux; brill with sea asparagus & hollandaise; brioche bread & butter pudding. **Details:** www.roebuckinn.demon.co.uk; 9.30 pm; no Amex; no smoking. **Accommodation:** 3 rooms, from £60.

The Three Crowns £ 25 ★

The Street SN15 5AF (01666) 510366

"Terrific" pub fare from an "extensive", largely traditional menu (enlivened by a few "adventurous" choices such as crocodile) makes this "utterly dependable" boozer off the M4 extremely popular – there is no booking for its attractive dining conservatory, and many reports note the difficulty of getting a table.
/ **Sample dishes:** no starters; roast crocodile with rice; flambéed bananas.
Details: www.threecrowns.co.uk; on village green; 9.30 pm; no smoking area; no booking.

BRISTOL, CITY OF BRISTOL 2–2B

With *Markwick's* as cheerleader, Bristol has a number of establishments of some note. It is, for example, lucky to boast what is almost certainly the best of the country's four *Hotels du Vin et Bistro*, as well as *Glasnost*, another very satisfactory all-rounder.

Many of the best-known restaurants boast settings which are strikingly designed and potentially atmospheric. Unfortunately – to an extent which is currently unique among provincial English cities – many seem to be able and willing to exploit these advantages to offer an overall quality of experience that reporters judge unacceptably poor.

Anthem £ 26 🅰

27-29 St Michaels Hl BS2 8DZ (0117) 929 2834

"Unusual, quirky, enjoyable" – this sweet little place, in a 17th century building near the city centre, has a "relaxed" atmosphere and offers an "interesting" fusion menu that's a bit "different".
/ **Sample dishes:** smoked duck with gin & orange dressing; lamb in pastry with mint & pea mash; chocolate truffle terrine. **Details:** 10.30 pm; D only, closed Mon & Sun; no Amex.

Belgo £ 27 ✗

The Old Granary, Queen Charlotte St BS1 4SB
(0117) 905 8000

"Formulaic" and "overpriced" outpost of the Belgian mussels and beer emporium chain, with notably "lazy" service; partially redeeming features include being "good with children", and the fixed-price lunch menu. / **Sample dishes:** lobster soup; moules marinière & chips; Belgian waffles. **Value tip:** set 1-crs L £5 (incl beer).
Details: www.belgo-restaurants.com; 11 pm.

Bell's Diner £ 32 🅰

1 York Rd BS6 5QB (0117) 924 0357

Fans "never tire of the atmosphere" at this "cosy" old "stand-by in the backstreets of Montpelier", with its "cheerful and helpful" service; the number vaunting its cooking as "top class", however, has declined on yesteryear, and though some still say the food is "consistently delicious", others feel it "tries too hard" and doesn't quite deliver. / **Sample dishes:** grilled Cornish squid; roast turbot with herb salad; peach melba soufflé. **Details:** by Acton St, off A38; 10 pm; closed Mon L, Sat L & Sun D; no smoking.

Boston Tea Party £ 16 A★

75 Park St BS1 5PF (0117) 929 8601

"A lovely terraced garden with heaters" is the highlight at this extremely popular café, which serves "an excellent range" of "big sandwiches, soups and cakes", together with "great coffee" and "real tea (with leaves!)". / **Sample dishes:** carrot & coriander soup; Spanish chicken; rum & raisin cheesecake.
Details: www.thebostonteaparty.co.uk; 10 pm, Sun 7 pm; closed Mon D; no smoking.

Browns £ 28

38 Queens Rd BS8 1RE (0117) 930 4777

With its "buzzy", "slightly studenty" atmosphere, this prominently-located outpost of Six Continents' brasserie chain is "convenient" and can be "fun for a casual eat"; as at other branches, however, the overwhelming impression is a too often of an overly "commercial" venue where "overpriced, badly cooked, formulaic food" is served by "disinterested" and "surly" staff. / **Sample dishes:** duck liver parfait; swordfish with pesto salsa; chocolate mousse cake.
Details: www.browns-restaurants.com; 11.30 pm; no smoking area.

Brunel Raj £ 21

Waterloo St BS8 4BT (0117) 973 2641

A "good, cosy Indian restaurant in the heart of Clifton village", whose "varied menu" of "freshly cooked" dishes attracts a number of approving local mentions. / **Sample dishes:** fish tikka; Brunel Raj king prawns; Indian ice cream. **Details:** 11 pm.

Budokan £ 16

31 Colston St BS1 5AH (0117) 914 1488

This "pan-Asian fuelling station" (which now has a sibling in Clifton Down, tel 0117 949 3030) became a big local hit when it opened a few years ago and some still find it a "reliable and stylish" destination; it's getting "lazy" though, with complaints of "small" portions, "dodgy" service and "high" prices. / **Sample dishes:** Thai fishcakes; Thai green curry; no puddings. **Details:** www.budokan.co.uk; 11 pm; closed Sun; no Amex; no smoking; need 10+ to book.

Byzantium £ 39 A

2 Portwall Ln BS1 6NB (0117) 922 1883

With its "Moroccan-casbah, theatrically-styled" décor this trendy joint is "a beautiful venue", built to a standard seldom seen outside London; the cooking perennially "doesn't live up to expectations", however, and is "poor value". / **Sample dishes:** crab, chilli & coriander tart; smoked roast lamb with Swiss chard gratin; chocolate & Grand Marnier mousse. **Details:** www.byzantium-restaurant.co.uk; nr Temple Meads, opp St Mary's Redcliffe church; 11 pm; D only, closed Sun (open for L in Dec); no smoking area.

Glasnost £ 26 A★

1 William St BS3 4TU (0117) 972 0938

"What a wonderful experience – especially the kangaroo"; "an interesting and varied" menu is a key feature at this "lively" and "good value" backstreet favourite, where "they care about the food" and service has "a keen eye for detail". / **Sample dishes:** mushrooms stuffed with Stilton; pork in Parma ham with peach compote; chocolate & praline soufflé. **Details:** 10 pm; D only, closed Mon & Sun; no Amex.

The Glass Boat £ 34 **X**
Welsh Back BS1 4SB (0117) 929 0704
*It may have "lovely views" from its "great location in the city-centre
docks", but this moored restaurant continues to be "totally over-
rated and a let-down in all respects" – "I've eaten there ten times
and always been disappointed!"* / **Sample dishes:** *goat's cheese with
radish & chive salad; roast duck & duck spring roll with warm mango;
Szechuan peppered crème brûlée.* **Value tip:** *set 2-crs L £14.50.*
Details: *www.glassboat.co.uk; below Bristol Bridge, 10 mins from Temple
Meads; 9.30 pm; closed Sat L & Sun; no smoking area.*

Harveys £ 60
12 Denmark St BS1 5DQ (0117) 927 5034
*"Its reputation as a first-class restaurant" is justified, say devotees
of the "rich" cooking (and impressive wine list) at these long-
established dining rooms, in quirkily decorated cellars under the
wine museum of the famous sherry-shippers; many continue to
complain of its "complacent" standards, however – let's hope that
the recent take-over by caterers Searcy's will pep things up (though
the London precedents are not encouraging).* / **Sample dishes:** *warm
tomato tart with crab salad; roast monkfish with broad beans; pistachio soufflé
with apricot sorbet.* **Value tip:** *set 2-crs L £16.50.*
Details: *www.j-harvey.co.uk; 9.30 pm; no smoking at D.*

Hope & Anchor £ 20 Ⓐ
38 Jacobs Wells Rd BS8 1DR (0117) 929 2987
*An "excellent garden" helps keep this "atmospheric" and "friendly"
pub "extremely busy"; the "simple", "hearty" fare has perhaps
"slipped" somewhat of late, but still comes in "generous portions"
and at "reasonable prices".* / **Sample dishes:** *crayfish tail & anchovy
salad; lamb & rosemary pie; sticky toffee pudding & custard.* **Details:** *10 pm;
no credit cards; no booking; children: 14+ in bar.*

Hotel du Vin et Bistro £ 37 Ⓐ★
The Sugar Hs, Narrow Lewins Mead BS1 2NU
(0117) 925 5577
*With its "amazing transformation of an old sugar warehouse",
this "lovely", "very buzzy" two-year old is – in all-round terms –
arguably "Bristol's best" (showing "none of the tiredness of the
Winchester branch"); the "capable" staff really "know their
onions", the "gutsy" French "country cooking" is dependably
realised, and (as you might hope) there's an "excellent wine list".*
/ **Sample dishes:** *seared scallops with crispy pancetta; roast salmon with
creamed cabbage; chocolate St Emilion with mixed berries.* **Value tip:** *set 2-crs
L £15.* **Details:** *www.hotelduvin.com; 9.45 pm; booking: max 10.*
Accommodation: *40 rooms, from £109.*

Hullaballoos £ 24
85 Park St BS1 5PJ (0117) 907 7540
*"The BYO policy is the chief asset" that makes this chain restaurant
"attractive for cheaper dining"; otherwise, it's a "noisy" place, with
a "slightly uninspiring" menu and "service which can be very slow".*
/ **Sample dishes:** *deep-fried cucumber with blueberry confit; salmon in saffron
butter with prawn linguini; lemon tart with citrus sauce.*
Details: *www.hullaballoos.co.uk; nr University buildings; 10.30 pm; closed
Sun D; no smoking area.*

Johns £ 25
27 Midland Rd BS2 0JT (0117) 955 0333
*"Newly enlarged", John Wright's slightly quirky, long-established
venture still serves "decent" Thai dishes, as well as traditional
British puds & "legendary" Sunday roasts.* / **Sample dishes:** *crispy
duck salad; northern chicken curry; chocolate pecan pie.* **Details:** *10 pm;
closed Mon, Tue–Sat D only, Sun open L & D; no Amex; no smoking.*

Markwick's £ 39 ★★
43 Corn St BS1 1HT (0117) 926 2658

Stephen Markwick's "formidable", "classic" French cooking "goes from strength to strength", and – with its "excellent" wine list – this Merchant Quarter fixture is arguably "under-rated" for one of the West Country's leading gastronomic lights; some find the "comfortable" setting "slightly stuffy", though, and a touch "claustrophobic" – there's only so much you can do with a converted bank vault. / **Sample dishes:** Cornish crab tart; beef with foie gras & Madeira sauce; passion fruit meringue tart. **Details:** 10 pm; closed Mon, Sat L & Sun.

Melbournes £ 27
74 Park St BS1 5JX (0117) 922 6996

Aided by its BYO policy, this somewhat dated central bistro enjoys a local reputation as a "good-value", "relaxed" stand-by. / **Sample dishes:** melon, pear & walnut salad; pork with mushroom stroganoff sauce; banoffi ice cream. **Details:** nr University; 10.30 pm; D only, closed Sun.

Mud Dock £ 27 A
40 The Grove BS1 4RB (0117) 934 9734

With its odd location ("above a bike shop"), there are "excellent views" to be had from this "relaxing" riverside café; food and service are "variable, but generally OK". / **Sample dishes:** tagliatelle with rocket & ricotta; tuna steak with roasted vegetables; banoffi pie. **Details:** www.mud-dock.com; close to the Industrial Museum & Arnolfini Gallery; 10 pm; closed Mon D; no smoking area; no booking.

Over The Moon £ 27
117 St George's Rd BS1 5UW (0117) 927 2653

Although "good-value" menus have made quite a name for these "unpretentious" and "welcoming" modern bistros (a second branch is at 76 Victoria Street, tel 0117 922 6688), there is a feeling that standards "are not what they were". / **Sample dishes:** spinach & mushroom filo parcel; pan-fried duck with roasted vegetables; cherry & almond tart. **Details:** nr Cathedral; 10.30 pm; D only, closed Sun; no Amex.

Primrose Café £ 27 A
1 Boyces Ave BS8 4AA (0117) 946 6577

"Clean, bright and buzzy" café whose "innovative" fish dishes (as well as good sandwiches and cakes) continue to make it a "special" place for some locals. / **Sample dishes:** pumpkin tortellini & sage butter sauce; char-grilled sea bass with salsa verde; treacle pudding & liquorice ice cream. **Details:** close to suspension bridge; 9.30 pm; closed Mon D & Sun D; no Amex; no smoking area; no booking at L.

Quartier Vert £ 36
85 Whiteladies Rd BS8 2NT (0117) 973 4482

A couple of years after the name change, this Clifton fixture ("Rocinantes as was") is putting in a good-in-parts performance; fans hail its "super" wine, "good tapas" in the bar and "delicious, organic, Mediterranean-ish" cooking in the restaurant, but others continue to think it all "very expensive". / **Sample dishes:** spinach soup with Parmesan croutons; veal with risotto Milanese & broad beans; orange crème caramel. **Value tip:** set 2-crs L £12.95. **Details:** www.quartiervert.co.uk; 10.30 pm.

Rajdoot £ 25
83 Park St BS1 5PJ (0117) 926 8033

The atmosphere is a touch "subdued", but "discreet" service, dependable cooking and décor that's smarter-than-average for a curry house help make this long-established Indian a useful central option. / **Sample dishes:** chicken shashlik; lamb tikka masala; kulfi. **Details:** www.rajdoot.co.uk; nr University; 11.30 pm; closed Sun L.

Rajpoot £ 32 ★

52 Upper Belgrave Rd BS8 2XP (0117) 973 3515

*With its "high-class Raj atmosphere" this eminent subcontinental is "far from being your usual curry house" – "the only drawback is the cost". / **Sample dishes:** calamari; chicken tikka masala; kulfi.* **Details:** *11 pm; closed Sun; no smoking.*

Red Snapper £ 32 ★

1 Chandos Rd BS6 6PG (0117) 973 7999

*"It's rare to find fish this good", says one of the many supporters of this "excellent 'local' restaurant", whose Clifton premises have recently been enlarged. / **Sample dishes:** leek, wild garlic & potato soup; hake with mash, capers & fennel; mango & muscat crème brûlée. **Value tip:** set 2-crs L £10.50.* **Details:** *on M32, follow signs to BRI Hospital then Redland; 10 pm; closed Mon L & Sun D.*

riverstation £ 31 ✕

The Grove BS1 4RB (0117) 914 4434

*A "wonderful setting in a prime position" makes this strikingly-designed, "light" and "airy" riverside landmark the most talked-about restaurant in town; even some supporters say it can be "unpredictable", though too many say "don't believe the hype" about this "noisy", "unfriendly" and "overpriced" establishment. / **Sample dishes:** sautéed morels & asparagus; sea trout with summer vegetables & aioli; gooseberry & elderflower fool. **Value tip:** set 2-crs L £11.50.* **Details:** *10.30 pm, Fri & Sat 11 pm; closed Sat L; no Amex; no smoking area; no booking in deli bar.*

Severnshed £ 29

The Grove, Harbourside BS1 4RB (0117) 925 1212

*A "beautiful riverside setting" and a striking building have helped make a big name for this "too trendy" venture, with its North African and Middle Eastern cooking; at the time of our survey it moved into new ownership, so perhaps its food and service will become rather less "hit and miss". / **Sample dishes:** seafood filo parcels; butternut squash stuffed with goats cheese; chocolate St Emilion.* **Details:** *www.severnshed.co.uk; 10.30 pm; closed Sun D; no smoking.*

Teohs £ 15 ★

26-34 Lower Ashley Rd BS2 9NP (0117) 907 1191

*"Pack 'em in, serve it well, make it good value" – a "basic and quick" package of "pan-Asian street food", that's "so cheap" served in a "cheerful", no-nonsense canteen setting is proving a winning formula for this "expanding chain of neighbourhood eateries" (which – as well as the original listed – now has a branch at the Old Tobacco Factory, Bedminster, tel 0117 902 1122). / **Sample dishes:** fishcakes & noodles with spicy sauce; crispy duck pancakes; ice cream.* **Details:** *100 yds from M32, J3; 10.30 pm; closed Mon; no smoking.*

Thai Classic £ 28

87 Whiteladies Rd BS8 2NT (0117) 973 8930

*A Clifton fixture, whose "very competent" Thai and Malaysian dishes continue to win it consistent support. / **Sample dishes:** mixed Thai starters; stir-fried seafood with noodles; mango & sticky rice.* **Details:** *11.30 pm; no smoking area.*

Tico Tico £ 31

24 Alma Vale Rd BS8 2HY (0117) 923 8700

*"Known for its unusual combinations", this "small" and "intimate" Clifton restaurant serves "good-quality" food from a "regularly changing" menu; the occasional "let-down" is not unheard of, however. / **Sample dishes:** pumpkin & fennel risotto; sea bass with Thai spices; cherry & chocolate mousse cake.* **Details:** *10 pm; closed Mon D & Sun; no Amex.*

The Goose £ 37

OX49 5LG (01491) 612304

It may have received "rave reviews" – in other publications – but this "foodie pub", run by the Prince of Wales's former chef, gets a 'thumbs-down' from too many reporters, who criticise a "cold" place that's "very expensive" for what it is, and whose food is "not all it's cracked up to be". / **Sample dishes:** gratin of scallops florentine; venison with creamed leeks & shallots; chocolate mousse. **Value tip:** set 3-crs L £10. **Details:** www.thegoose.freeserve.co.uk; M40, J6 nr Watlington; 9 pm; closed Mon & Sun D; no Amex; no smoking.

Druidstone Hotel £ 27 𝔸

Druid Haven SA62 3NE (01437) 781221

This "family-run" clifftop hotel has an ardent fan club, who praise its "wonderful fresh food served simply", its "warm" service and its "lovely" atmosphere; it doesn't please everyone, though, and newcomers can find the style a bit "cliquey and hippy". / **Sample dishes:** terrine de campagne; brill with spring onions, artichokes & vermouth; lemon & passion fruit cheesecake. **Details:** www.druidstone.co.uk; from B4341 at Broad Haven turn right, then left after 1.5m; 9.30 pm; D only, except Sun when L only; no smoking in dining room. **Accommodation:** 9 rooms, from £33.50.

Drewe Arms £ 37 ★

EX14 3NF (01404) 841267

There is a "fine" array of "fantastic" fish served at this "cosy", "picture postcard" pub in a pretty thatched village; "it gets very booked up". / **Sample dishes:** mixed seafood selection; grilled turbot with hollandaise; bread pudding with whisky butter sauce. **Details:** 5m from M5, J28, on A373 to Honiton; 9.30 pm; closed Sun D; no Amex; no smoking.

Lygon Arms £ 61 𝔸

High St WR12 7DU (01386) 852255

The Savoy Group's Elizabethan outpost in the Cotswolds offers "grand" cuisine in a "beautiful" and "elaborate" setting; the cooking is "pricey" for what it is, though, and some find the whole "fussy" approach ultimately rather "disappointing". / **Sample dishes:** leek & mushroom lasagne with truffle oil; sea bass with creamed leeks & chorizo; plum crumble soufflé with liquorice ice-cream. **Details:** www.savoygroup.com; just off A44; 9.15 pm, Fri & Sat 10 pm; no smoking; children: 8+. **Accommodation:** 70 rooms, from £180.

Buckland Manor £ 61

WR12 7LY (01386) 852626

Some say it's "an all-round fantastic experience" to visit this "elegant" and "luxurious" 13th-century Cotswold manor house hotel; for others, though, visits can be spoilt by "over-wrought and unimaginative" cooking and "overbearing" service. / **Sample dishes:** roast scallops with endive salad; maize-fed chicken with pasta & asparagus; blueberry soufflé with lavender ice cream. **Value tip:** set 3-crs Sun L £24.50. **Details:** www.bucklandmanor.com; 2m SW of Broadway on B4632; 9 pm; jacket & tie required at D; no smoking in dining room; children: 12+. **Accommodation:** 13 rooms, from £210.

Lamb at Buckland   £ 33
Lamb Ln SN7 8QN   (01367) 870484
*"Consistently good standards" – including of the "tasty, fresh food
in huge portions" – make this "pricey" gastropub a consistently
popular destination. / **Sample dishes:** lemon sole with chive & butter
sauce; pan-fried skate wing; peach & almond flan. **Details:** on A420 between
Uxford & Swindon; 9 pm; no smoking. **Accommodation:** 4 rooms,
from £42.50.*

The Lamb   £ 35   Ⓐ
Sheep St OX18 4LR   (01993) 823155
*Primarily, it's the "classy, yet relaxed" ambience (complete with
"cosy fires in inglenooks"), which makes this "fabulous", ancient
Cotswold tavern an extremely popular destination, where "superior
pub grub" is "reliable". / **Sample dishes:** halibut, gravadlax & crab tian
with shrimp mousse; rib-eye steak with lyonnaise potatoes; pear tarte Tatin.
Details: 9 pm; D only, except Sun open L & D; no Amex; no smoking.
Accommodation: 15 rooms, from £105.*

David Woolley's   £ 34   ★
78 Main St LS29 7BT   (01943) 864602
*Dinner chez Woolley is "like having dinner at a friend's house", and the
"consistently good modern British cooking" is complemented by
service which is "humorous" and "attentive". / **Sample dishes:** salmon
platter; blackened duck with orange & honey; brown bread parfait with
butterscotch sauce. **Details:** www.davidwoolleysrestaurant.co.uk; 10 pm; closed
Sun; no Amex; no smoking area.*

Fishes   £ 31
Market Pl PE31 8HE (01328) 738588
*This long-established spot – with quite a name for "fresh fish,
simply prepared" – was taken over by Caroline and Matthew
Owsley-Brown in September '01, and the premises are to be
refurbished in early-2002; Mr Brown's experience working for
Rick Stein should stand him in good stead, but a rating is
inappropriate in the circumstances. / **Sample dishes:** potted brown
shrimps; monkfish with fennel & cream sauce; strawberry mousse.
Value tip: set 3-crs L £12.95. **Details:** 9 pm, Sat 9.30 pm; closed Mon &
Sun L; no smoking; children: 5+ after 8.30 pm.*

Hoste Arms   £ 31
The Green PE31 8HD (01328) 738777
*This "charming hostelry" has long been a well-known destination,
often praised for its "first-class food" (with "local fish" a speciality),
its "excellent beer" and its "imaginative wine list"; on the downside,
it can seem "too popular" for its own good, and rather "London-
pricey" – given the origin of many of the customers, this is perhaps
not very surprising. / **Sample dishes:** salmon & chilli fishcakes; sea bass
with wilted spinach; sabayon of glazed fruits. **Details:** www.hostearms.co.uk;
6m W of Wells-next-the-Sea; 9 pm; no Amex; no smoking area.
Accommodation: 28 rooms, from £64.*

BURNSALL, NORTH YORKSHIRE 8–4B

Red Lion £ 31 Ⓐ
BD23 6BU (01756) 720204
With its "picture postcard" Dales riverside setting, it's no surprise
that this "traditional" (but "idiosyncratic") old inn is "an enduring
favourite"; most reporters say the superior pub fare is "good" too,
"both in the bar and the restaurant". / *Sample dishes:* duck liver
parfait with brioche; pot-roasted pork & shallots with apple sauce; chocolate &
hazelnut parfait. **Details:** www.redlion.co.uk; off A59; 9.30 pm; D only, except
Sun open L & D; no smoking. **Accommodation:** 13 rooms, from £100.

BURPHAM, WEST SUSSEX 3–4A

George & Dragon £ 38 ★
BN18 9RR (01903) 883131
"Lovely countryside nearby" is just one of the attractions of this
traditional inn on the South Downs; the "great food" – served "in
both the comfortable bar and in the more formal restaurant" –
received much improved reports this year. / *Sample
dishes:* langoustine & sea scallop tortellini; roast rib of Scottish beef; chocolate
mousse with basil sorbet. **Details:** 3m from Arundel station, off A27; 9.30 pm;
D only, except Sun when L only; smoking discouraged; children: 8+.

BURY ST EDMUNDS, SUFFOLK 3–1C

Maison Bleue £ 31 ★
30-31 Churchgate St IP33 1RG (01284) 760623
This "very friendly French fish restaurant" – an offshoot of
The Great House at Lavenham – receives only positive reports,
and the set lunch, in particular, is thought "good value". / *Sample
dishes:* langoustines; grilled Dover sole; crème brûlée with Pernod. **Value
tip:** set 2-crs L £9.95. **Details:** www.maisonbleue.co.uk; 9.30 pm; closed
Mon & Sun; no smoking.

BUSHEY, HERTFORDSHIRE 3–2A

St James £ 39
30 High St WD2 3DN (020) 8950 2480
It may be "a beacon in a culinary desert", and a "friendly" one too,
but the compliments attracted by this "modern" establishment in
the 'burbs tend to have a hint of qualification about them, in
particular regarding its "unadventurous" cooking and slight "lack
of atmosphere". / *Sample dishes:* warm satay salad; chicken fricassée
with roasted vegetables; Toblerone cheesecake. **Details:** opp St James Church;
9.45 pm; closed Sun; no smoking area.

CADNAM, HAMPSHIRE 2–3C

White Hart £ 28 ★
Old Romsey Rd SO40 2NP (023) 8081 2277
There's "fine" food to be had at this New Forest pub, though some
do find the ambience "very cramped and smoky". / *Sample
dishes:* dressed crab with Mediterranean sauce; guinea fowl stuffed with
couscous; crêpes Suzette. **Details:** signposted off M27, J1; 9.30 pm; no Amex;
no smoking area.

CALVER, DERBYSHIRE 5–2C

Chequers £ 22 Ⓐ
Froggatt Edge, Hope Valley S32 3ZJ (01433) 630231
In "a beautiful part of the Peak District", this "good dining pub"
boasts a "nice garden" and offers a "wide-ranging" menu of "high
quality food". / *Sample dishes:* spicy tomato soup; pan-fried mullet; sticky
toffee pudding. **Details:** on road between Sheffield & Bakewell; 9 pm;
no Amex; no smoking area. **Accommodation:** 5 rooms, from £72.

Perhaps Cambridge's restaurants exist to contribute to Oxonians' (usually) unwarranted sense of superiority? The diligent reader will see that the Fenland university town's restaurants together muster a measly two stars – one apiece for a noodle-bar (*Dojo*) and a budget boozer (*Wrestlers Pub*) – and not a single commendation for atmosphere. *Midsummer House* is the closest the city comes to a flagship destination, but many find it just too expensive for what it is.

Browns   £ 28
23 Trumpington St CB2 1QA   (01223) 461655
"It used to be an old favourite, but now the food seems very average and the place drab" is sadly typical of reports on this branch – and indeed most others – of this English brasserie chain (now owned by Six Continents); a "buzzy" ambience lingers, not helped by the "conveyor-belt" attitude of the "lethargic" staff. / **Sample dishes:** *Caesar salad; steak, mushroom & Guinness pie; hot fudge brownie.* **Details:** www.browns-restaurants.com; opp Fitzwilliam Museum; 11.30 pm; no smoking area.

Curry Queen   £ 19
106 Mill Rd CB1 2BD   (01223) 351027
"Typical Indian fare, but done well" makes this "predictable, but ultra-reliable" curry house something of a classic varsity fixture. / **Sample dishes:** *onion bhaji; chicken tikka masala; kulfi.* **Details:** midnight; no Switch.

Dojo   £ 13   ★
1-2 Millers Yd, Mill Ln CB2 1RQ   (01223) 363471
A "central", "friendly" and "very popular" noodle joint, where the food is "not bad, quick and cheap". / **Sample dishes:** *tempura prawns with teriyaki sauce; prawn dumplings with pad Thai; no puddings.* **Details:** www.dojonoodlebar.co.uk; off Clanlington St; 10.45 pm; no Amex; no smoking; no booking.

Loch Fyne Oyster Bar   £ 28
37 Trumpington St CB2 1QY   (01223) 362433
For some, "good fresh fish" and "friendly service" make this offshoot of the famous Scottish seafood parlours "the best bet" in this under-served town; even supporters note that "portions are quite small", though, and there are too many who just find disappointment across the board. / **Sample dishes:** *queen scallops; lobster platter; ice cream.* **Details:** www.loch-fyne.com; opp Fitzwilliam Museum; 10 pm; no smoking in dining room.

Maharaja   £ 16
9-13 Castle St CB3 0AH   (01223) 358399
It may be "pretty standard", but this is amongst "the best of the mediocre bunch of Cambridge curry houses". / **Sample dishes:** *chicken & lamb tikka; chicken jalfrezi; banana fritters.* **Details:** midnight.

Michels Brasserie   £ 32
21-24 Northampton St CB3 0AD   (01223) 353110
That this uninspired (but "friendly") spot, at the back of John's, is "one of the best restaurants in Cambridge" speaks volumes about culinary standards in the Fens; for those not looking for too much in the way of excitement, it's undoubtedly a useful destination. / **Sample dishes:** *charcuterie with rustic pickles; fish kebabs with samphire; chocolate bread & butter pudding.* **Value tip:** set 3-crs L £8.95. **Details:** close to A1303; 10 pm; no smoking area.

Midsummer House £ 54

Midsummer Common CB4 1HA (01223) 369299

"A gorgeous location" is the undisputed highlight at this *"pretty
Victorian villa on the banks of the Cam, and overlooking the
common"*; many reporters also vaunt the *"interesting"* cooking,
but even fans acknowledge that the place is *"expensive"* and
there's a vocal minority who think it thoroughly *"over-rated"*.
/ **Sample dishes:** snails with bacon, celery & frog's legs; braised pig's head
with spices & parsley potatoes; passion fruit soufflé with orange sorbet. **Value
tip:** set 2-crs L £15. **Details:** facing University Boathouse; 9.45 pm; closed
Mon & Sun; no jeans; no smoking.

Peking Restaurant £ 33

21 Burleigh St CB1 1DG (01223) 354755

"Often described as the best Chinese restaurant in Cambridge",
this establishment near the Grafton Centre is certainly *"the most
expensive"*, but not all reporters are convinced that the premium
is justified. / **Sample dishes:** deep-fried squid in chilli; Szechuan chicken;
toffee bananas. **Details:** nr Grafton Centre; 10.30 pm; no credit cards;
no smoking area.

Sala Thong £ 21

35 Newnham Rd CB3 9EY (01223) 323178

It may be rather *"cramped"*, but this *"unpretentious"* and
"straightforward" Thai is praised for its *"good"* and *"plentiful"* fare
and its *"friendly"* service. / **Sample dishes:** prawn satay; Thai green
chicken curry; ice cream with mango sauce. **Value tip:** set 2-crs pre-th £7.50.
Details: nr mill pond; 9.45 pm; closed Mon; no Amex; no smoking.

22 Chesterton Road £ 35

22 Chesterton Rd CB4 3AX (01223) 351880

The *"small"*, *"cramped"* dining room of this Edwardian house has
a somewhat *"sedate"* atmosphere enlivened by *"charming service"*;
some say the *"short but regularly-changing"* modern British menu
is *"lovely"*, but the consensus is that it's a mite *"over-rated"*.
/ **Sample dishes:** fish kebabs with hollandaise sauce; roast lamb with mint &
parsley jus; prune tart with praline ice-cream.
Details: www.restaurant22.co.uk; 9.45 pm; D only, closed Mon & Sun;
no smoking at D; children: 12+.

Venue £ 33

66 Regent St CB2 1DP (01223) 367333

"After a promising start", *"standards have slipped rather"* at this
"stark", *"contemporary"* restaurant, which some feel is already
"a bit '90s", with food that *"tries to be clever but fails"*; jazz piano
music (after 10pm) offers some consolation. / **Sample dishes:** Thai
style mussels; butternut squash gnocchi; dark chocolate truffle cake.
Details: www.venuerestaurant.com; 11 pm; D only; no Amex; no smoking
area.

Wrestlers Pub £ 18 ★

337 Newmarket Rd CB5 8JE (01223) 566553

There are *"no frills"* at this *"noisy"* boozer, but its *"authentic"* Thai
dishes are consistently praised. / **Sample dishes:** prawn crackers; chicken
fried rice; hot bananas & pineapple. **Details:** www.wrestlers.co.uk; 9 pm;
closed Sun (for food); no Amex.

CAMPSEA ASHE, SUFFOLK 3–1D

Old Rectory £ 28 🄰★

IP13 0PU (01728) 746524

Lots of *"olde worlde"* charm is not the only attraction of this small
Georgian rectory, next to the church – the *"delicious"* cooking from
patron Stewart Bassett's no-choice menu offers *"outstanding value"*
too. / **Sample dishes:** sea bass with spinach mousse; grilled duck with sharp
plum sauce; fruit roulade. **Details:** 8.45 pm; D only, closed Sun; no smoking.
Accommodation: 8 rooms, from £60.

Augustines £ 31 ★

1-2 Longport CT1 IPE (01227) 453063

"Very good French food at very reasonable prices" is winning quite a following for Tom and Robert Grimer's small Gallic establishment, where most reports speak of a "delightful" overall experience. / **Sample dishes:** Singapore chicken laksa soup; Aberdeen Angus beef with roasted shallots; passion fruit tart with coconut ice cream. **Value tip:** set 3-crs L £9.95. **Details:** nr the Cathedral; 9.30 pm; closed Mon & Sun D; no smoking; booking: max 7; children: no babies.

Cafe des Amis £ 25 Ⓐ

95 St Dunstan's St CT2 8AA (01227) 464390

"Cramped but worth it", this "busy, rather noisy and fun" diner is a double rarity – "an above-average Mexican" and a good choice in this under-provided city. / **Sample dishes:** pan-fried king prawns with garlic; crispy duck burger & mash; pineapple tarte Tatin. **Details:** by Westgate Towers; 10 pm; no smoking area; booking: max 6, Fri & Sat.

Bryn Tyrch £ 23 ★

LL24 0EL (01690) 720223

With its "cosy sofas" and "open fires", this "small inn within the Snowdonia National Park" is "the place to go after a day's walking", and its supporters say it offers "excellent" vegetarian food. / **Sample dishes:** smoked duck with orange & apricot chutney; Greek feta & spinach pie; bread & butter pudding. **Details:** on A5; 9 pm; no smoking area. **Accommodation:** 15 rooms, from £19.50.

The Welsh capital remains very under-served culinarily speaking. Its star-performer – Le Gallois in Canton – has rightly emerged as the city's leading light, but in another town it might seem a good middle-ranker.

Nowhere has emerged to be the destination demanded by the regeneration of the Bay. Tides is one of the most-mentioned places, but attracts almost as many brickbats as it does bouquets. The establishment which gathers most all-round support from reporters is a year-old re-creation of a rural Japanese tavern, Izakaya.

Armless Dragon £ 27

97 Wyeverne Rd CF2 4BG (029) 2038 2357

It's "not quite as good as under the previous regime", but most say it's still "a pleasure to find" this long-established backstreet bistro – "an oasis of civilised eating in the gastronomic desert that is Cardiff". / **Sample dishes:** liver parfait with date chutney; roast chicken with leeks & truffle oil; crème brûlée. **Value tip:** set 3-crs L £10. **Details:** off Salsbury Road; 9.30 pm, Sat 10.30 pm; closed Mon & Sun; no Amex; no smoking in dining room.

La Brasserie £ 30 Ⓐ

60 St Mary St CF10 1FE (029) 2037 2164

"Steak and fish, and good atmosphere" accurately summarises the key attractions of Benigno Martinez's enormous, rambling city-centre institution, where you choose from the cold cabinets what is to be cooked and how. / **Sample dishes:** frogs legs with garlic mayonnaise; beef sirloin & chips; apple tart. **Value tip:** set 2-crs L £5.95. **Details:** www.le-monde.co.uk/brasserie.html; nr Marriott Hotel; midnight; closed Sun; no booking.

Le Cassoulet £ 39

5 Romilly Cr CF11 9NP (029) 2022 1905

"A bit of Toulouse in Cardiff", say long-term fans of this quite "smart", "very traditional" Gallic fixture in a converted Canton shop, who praise its "patient and friendly" service and "excellent" fare; there continue to be one or two doubters, though, who say the grub is "only OK". / **Sample dishes:** watercress soup with goat's cheese ravioli; beef with red wine & pink peppercorn sauce; spice bread soufflé. **Value tip:** set 3-crs L £13.50. **Details:** 10 mins W of city centre; 10 pm; closed Mon & Sun.

Le Gallois £ 33 ★

6-10 Romilly Cr CF11 9NR (029) 2034 1264

"Easily Cardiff's best" – Graham and Ann Jones's "interesting mix of French and Welsh cuisine" has propelled this "bright, smart and lively" establishment, "on the outskirts of the city-centre", to deserved local stardom; success has its perils, though, and some question whether they are starting to "rely on their fashionable reputation". / **Sample dishes:** crab, brown shrimp & pea risotto; pot-roasted pork with bacon & truffle mash; pear tarte Tatin. **Value tip:** set 2-crs L £10.95. **Details:** www.legallois.co.uk; 1.5m W of Cardiff Castle; 10.30 pm; closed Mon & Sun.

The Greenhouse Café £ 23 ★

38 Woodville Rd CF24 4EB (029) 2023 5731

"A little-known gem" – this veggie/seafood café near the University may be "tiny", but its "limited" menu crams in "so much flair and novelty" as to make it some reporters' top tip in town. / **Sample dishes:** mackerel with lime pesto; marinated tofu with honey; banoffi pie. **Details:** nr Cardiff University; 10.30 pm; closed Mon; no Amex; no smoking in dining room.

Happy Gathering £ 23

233 Cowbridge Road East CF11 9AL (029) 2039 7531

"When it gets busy it can be a bit noisy", but most agree that this is a "fun venue" for "traditional" Chinese food. / **Sample dishes:** chicken satay & crispy seaweed; steamed duck in orange sauce; crispy toffee banana. **Details:** nr the Castle; 10.45 pm.

Izakaya £ 26 Ⓐ★

Mermaid Quay CF10 5BW (029) 2049 2939

Cardiff Bay might not seem the most natural habitat for a re-creation of a rural Japanese tavern, but this year-old venture of a Welshman and his Japanese wife is a "welcoming" place which offers "great food, and great fun" at communal tables. / **Sample dishes:** sashimi; pan-fried tuna with shiitake mushrooms; green tea ice cream. **Details:** www.izakaya-japanese-tavern.com; 10.30 pm; no smoking area; children: children: 10+.

King Balti £ 19

131 Albany Rd CF24 3NS (029) 2048 2890

Though some "mention it for the food and nothing else" – others are more enthusiastic about the somewhat eccentric, American-style approach of this pan-Asian diner. / **Sample dishes:** spiced potatoes; chicken tikka masala; Indian ice cream. **Details:** off Newport Road; 11.45 pm; D only; no smoking area.

Le Monde £ 30

62 St Mary St CF10 1FE (029) 2038 7376

'Upstairs at La Brasserie' – as the place might equally well be called – is the poshest section of the city-centre's huge Hispanic dining complex; it's a "pleasant" and "friendly" venue, with a similar you-pick-it-they-grill-it formula. / **Sample dishes:** marinated seafood salad; venison with port wine sauce; Welsh cheeses. **Details:** www.le-monde.co.uk; midnight; closed Sun; no jeans; no booking.

Noble House £ 23

9-11 St Davids Hs, Wood St CF1 4ER (029) 2038 8430

*"Highly commended", say fans (particularly locals) of this "good"
and "friendly" Chinese.* / **Sample dishes:** *beef & chicken satay; crispy
duck with fried rice; lemon sorbet.* **Details:** *next to Millennium stadium;
11 pm.*

Tides

St David's Hotel & Spa £ 43 ✗

Havannah St CF10 5SD (029) 2031 3018

*There are those who say this swanky new hotel ("with great views
of the harbour") is "a credit to Rocco Forte"; overall, however, the
many complaints of "dull hotel cooking" in the awkwardly-located
dining room are more evocative of the good-old-bad-old Trust
House days.* / **Sample dishes:** *goat's cheese soufflé; sea bass with fennel &
new potatoes; whisky parfait & cherry compote.* **Details:** *www.rfhotels.com; in
Cardiff Bay; 10.30 pm; no jeans or trainers; no smoking.*
Accommodation: *132 rooms, from £170.*

Woods Brasserie £ 37

Pilotage Building, Stuart St CF10 5BW (029) 2049 2400

*"A good effort at metropolitan dining" – this Cardiff Bay spot is one
of the few hereabouts to offer "modern"-style cooking in "relaxed",
"buzzy" surroundings; that said, some find the fare "formulaic" and
service "variable".* / **Sample dishes:** *leek & Gruyère tart; aubergine
parmigiana with pesto; treacle tart & custard.* **Details:** *in the Inner Harbour;
10 pm; closed Mon & Sun D.*

CARTERWAY HEADS, NORTHUMBERLAND 8–3B

Manor House £ 25 ★

DH8 9LX (01207) 255268

*Thin reports this year on this old, "well situated" pub/restaurant;
such as they are continue to praise its "imaginative and well cooked
food".* / **Sample dishes:** *spicy mushrooms with rosemary & tomato; veal with
blood orange & whisky sauce; ginger cake.* **Details:** *A68 just past turn-off for
Shotley Bridge; 9.30 pm; no smoking area; children: 9+ at D.*
Accommodation: *4 rooms, from £55.*

CARTMEL FELL, CUMBRIA 7–4D

Masons Arms £ 26 Ⓐ ★

Strawberry Bank LA11 6NW (01539) 568486

*There's "an extraordinary range of good beers, and food too" at
this "fantastic" microbrewery/pub, which offers some great views
too; "the only problem is getting in".* / **Sample dishes:** *pile of ribs;
chicken & mushroom pie; butterscotch crumble.*
Details: *www.masonsarms.uk.com; W from Bowland Bridge, off A5074;
8.45 pm; need 12+ to book.* **Accommodation:** *6 rooms, from £30.*

CASTLE DOUGLAS, DUMFRIES & GALLOWAY 7–2B

The Plumed Horse £ 42 ★★

Crossmicheal DG7 3AU (01556) 670333

*"Outstanding international cuisine, with a local flavour" has
attracted the attention of the men from the French tyre company
to this smart village restaurant; it's also been lavishly praised by
reporters, but some fear that the arrogance that sometimes goes
with a Michelin accolade is already setting in.* / **Sample dishes:** *foie
gras with sultana & Madeira brioche; salmon with langoustine tortellini; banana
brûlée with butterscotch sauce.* **Value tip:** *set 3-crs L £14.95.*
Details: *www.plumed-horse.co.uk; 9 pm; closed Mon, Sat L & Sun D;
no Amex; no smoking.*

Castle Inn £ 21 ★

Castle St S33 8WG (01433) 620578

A "traditional-style" pub/hotel in the heart of the Peak District, where "interesting" cooking (always including at least one "good veggie choice") contributes to general satisfaction. / **Sample dishes:** field mushrooms with garlic toast; butterfly chicken with tomato risotto; toffee bread & butter pudding. **Details:** www.peakland.com/thecastle; 10 pm; no smoking area; no booking. **Accommodation:** 12 rooms, from £50.

Creel Inn £ 25 A★

AB39 2UL (01569) 750254

"Honest food using local seafood and veg" makes this romantically located, clifftop-village inn a favourite local destination. / **Sample dishes:** garlic crab claws; pot-roasted wild venison; sticky apple & carrot pudding. **Details:** 4m S of Stonehaven on A92; 9.30 pm; closed Tue; no Amex; no smoking. **Accommodation:** 2 rooms, from £50.

Caunton Beck £ 27

Main St NG23 6AB (01636) 636793

"Consistently good", "brasserie-type" food (from breakfast to dinner), served in a "good pub ambience", makes this "relaxed" rural offshoot of Lincoln's Wig & Mitre unanimously popular, especially as a "sunny day" recommendation. / **Sample dishes:** mushroom risotto with Parmesan crisps; roast guinea fowl; banana curd parfait. **Value tip:** set 2-crs L £9. **Details:** 6m NW of Newark past British Sugar factory on A616; 10 pm; no smoking.

Brockencote Hall £ 41 A★★

DY10 4PY (01562) 777876

"The closest to a meal in a French château you'll find in England" – the dining room of this "excellent", country house hotel (in an impressive converted Victorian mansion) is "known as the best for miles around", and rightly so on the basis of the uniformly positive commentary inspired by its "modern cuisine with a Gallic flavour". / **Sample dishes:** poached mackerel with basil mousse; braised lamb shank; apple & almond cream tart. **Value tip:** set 3-crs L £15. **Details:** www.brockencotehall.com; on A448, just outside village; 9.30 pm; closed Sat L; no smoking. **Accommodation:** 17 rooms, from £135.

Gidleigh Park £ 80 A★

TQ13 8HH (01647) 432367

The Gallic cooking at Kay and Paul Henderson's mega-pricey ,"very relaxed", country house hotel – built in the '30s on the fringe of Dartmoor – is "stunningly good" and, like the rest of the operation, receives a hymn of praise for its "amazing attention to detail"; "there are beautiful grounds for that post-prandial stroll". / **Sample dishes:** salmon & red mullet terrine with aubergine caviar; roast pigeon with potato galette & Madeira sauce; hot apple tart. **Value tip:** set 2-crs L £25. **Details:** www.gidleigh.com; from village, right at Lloyds TSB, take right fork to end of lane; 9 pm; no Amex; no smoking; children: 7+ at D. **Accommodation:** 15 rooms, from £385 incl D.

22 Mill Street   £ 36   ★★

22 Mill St TQ13 8AW   (01647) 432244

"Well worth the journey"; chef Duncan Walker offers *"a menu just like Gidleigh Park's"* (where he used to work) for roughly half the price at this *"small"* establishment, also praised for its *"brilliant attitude to customers"*. / **Sample dishes:** tuna with anchovy & quail's egg salad; roast squab pigeon with puréed peas; chocolate & raspberry tart. **Value tip:** set 3-crs L £19.50. **Details:** 9 pm; closed Mon L, Tue L, Sat D & Sun; no Amex; no smoking area; children: 14+. **Accommodation:** 2 rooms, from £45.

CHAPELTOWN, SOUTH YORKSHIRE   5–2C

Greenhead House   £ 42   A★

84 Burncross Rd S35 1SF   (0114) 246 9004

"Simple but imaginative" cooking, *"friendly and efficient"* service and a *"wonderful ambience"* – commentary on Neil and Anne Allen's seventeenth-century house is as uniformly complimentary as ever. / **Sample dishes:** moules marinière; roast chicken with chanterelle mushrooms; raspberry meringues. **Details:** 1m from M1, J35; 9 pm; closed Mon, Tue, Wed L, Sat L & Sun; no smoking in dining room; children: 5+.

CHEADLE, STAFFORDSHIRE   5–3B

Thornbury Hall Rasoi   £ 23   A★

Lockwood Rd ST10 2DH   (01538) 750831

A *"converted manor house in a rural location"* provides a *"great"*, almost colonial setting for Mr & Mrs Siddique's excellent one-off Indian, whose *"superb"* Pakistani cooking wins consistent approval. / **Sample dishes:** vegetable samosas; bitter chicken with onions & ginger; pecan honey ice cream. **Details:** nr Alton Towers; 10.30 pm; no Amex; no smoking area.

CHEESDEN, LANCASHIRE   5–1B

Nutter's   £ 38   ★★

Edenfield Rd OL12 7TY   (01706) 650167

For once, a TV chef's establishment which *"lives up to the hype"*; Andrew Nutter's cooking is *"brilliant"* and *"well presented"*, and his *"old-style"*, family-run venture in a rural converted pub has a truly *"friendly"* feel; reporters' top tip? – *"you must try the tour of the cheeseboard"*. / **Sample dishes:** salmon with mesclun salad; monkfish with mango & coriander noodles; peanut butter cheesecake. **Details:** between Edenfield & Nordon on A680; 9.30 pm; closed Tue; no smoking.

CHELMSFORD, ESSEX   3–2C

Siam Cottage   £ 29

44 Moulsham St CM2 0HY   (01245) 352245

"Pity about the décor and ambience" (and the tables which are *"too close"*), but *"varied"* and *"beautifully presented"* Thai dishes make this a popular local oriental. / **Sample dishes:** mixed starters; green chicken curry; Siam Cottage ice cream. **Details:** www.siamcottage.com; 10.30 pm; closed Sun L; no Amex.

CHELTENHAM, GLOUCESTERSHIRE   2–1C

Champignon Sauvage   £ 48   ★

24-26 Suffolk Rd GL50 2AQ   (01242) 573449

An *"abrupt"* manner (especially on the 'phone), *"over-fussiness"* (of food and service) and *"zero atmosphere"* are the sort of drawbacks which can disenchant visitors to David and Helen Everitt Mathias's small restaurant; it's such a shame, as many reporters heartily endorse the *"innovative"* cooking, the *"meticulous attention to detail"* and the *"interesting, good-value wine list"*. / **Sample dishes:** eel tortellini with watercress cream; red mullet; lemon mousse with milk sorbet. **Value tip:** set 2-crs L £16.50. **Details:** on A40 to Oxford, nr Boys' College; 9.15 pm; closed Mon, Thu & Sun; no smoking before 10.30 pm.

Daffodil £ 33 ⒜

18-20 Suffolk Parade GL50 2AE   (01242) 700055

All agree that this former Art Deco cinema has been "beautifully restored" and provides a "terrific setting", but "there's too much emphasis on the look of the place" – the food is often "mediocre", and service can be "appalling". / *Sample dishes:* salmon ravioli with mussels; Dorchester lamb; strawberry gateau. *Details:* just off Suffolk Square; 10.30 pm; closed Sun; no smoking.

Mayflower £ 26

32-34 Clarence St GL50 3NX   (01242) 522426

An "interesting" menu of "tasty" dishes (including an "excellent range of vegetarian options") makes Mr and Mrs Kong's long-established Chinese restaurant a popular recommendation. / *Sample dishes:* garlic & chilli frog's legs; roast duck with beansprouts; toffee bananas. *Details:* 10 pm; closed Sun L.

Le Petit Blanc £ 30 ✕

Promenade GL50 1NN   (01242) 266800

Monsieur Blanc knows how to run a good restaurant (see Great Milton), so it's a mystery why he is content with the too-often "truly awful" standards of his spin-off brand; as with the Oxford Petit Blanc, fans think this "noisy" and "overcrowded" town-centre brasserie is "cool", but it inspires numerous complaints of "unfriendly" staff and "mediocre" cooking. / *Sample dishes:* polenta gnocchi with tomato coulis; navarin of lamb with seasonal vegetables; pistachio soufflé. *Value tip:* set 2-crs L & pre-th £12.50. *Details:* www.petit-blanc.co.uk; 10.30 pm; no smoking in dining room.

Ruby £ 29

52 Suffolk Rd GL50 2AQ   (01242) 250909

Most praise the "delicious" and "well-priced" cooking at this "good all-round" Chinese, particularly the "cheap early-evening menus" (not served at weekends). / *Sample dishes:* crispy aromatic duck; stir-fried monkfish in wine sauce; toffee bananas. *Details:* nr Cheltenham Boys College; 11.30 pm; no smoking area.

Storyteller £ 28 ⒜★

11 North Pl GL50 4DW   (01242) 250343

"Interesting" dishes – including "an excellent range from North and South America" – contribute to the "good all-round experience" of a visit to this slightly theme-y joint, just off the high street; (they have a wine room in which you can browse for your choice, and also regular tastings). / *Sample dishes:* Mauritian beef skewers; tower of lamb with new potatoes; chocolate mud pie. *Value tip:* set 3-crs L £9.95. *Details:* www.storyteller.co.uk; 10 pm.

CHESTER, CHESHIRE 5–2A

Albion Inn £ 16

Park St CH1 1RN   (01244) 340345

"One of a dying breed" – "pre-war" décor and "heaped plates" of "home-cooked pub grub" (it's a "chip-free zone") is an old-fashioned formula that generally finds favour at this "individualistic" boozer, tucked away near the Newgate. / *Sample dishes:* no starters; steak & kidney pie; bread & butter pudding. *Details:* between Eastgate clock & the river; 8 pm; no credit cards; need 6+ to book; children: discouraged.

Arkle
Chester Grosvenor Hotel   £ 60
Eastgate CH1 1LT (01244) 324024
*By the relaxed standards of the North West, the "formality" of
the dining room at this five-star city-centre hotel (owned by the
Duke of Westminster) is something of "a different world"; for
many reporters that's a plus, but the minority who say it's "stuffy",
"outdated" and "seriously overpriced" is much too vocal to ignore.*
/ **Sample dishes:** quail & foie gras terrine; lamb cutlets with sweet pepper
gnocchi; chocolate truffle & passion fruit. **Details:** www.chestergrosvenor.co.uk;
by the Eastgate Clock; 9.30 pm; closed Mon & Sun D; jacket & tie required;
no smoking. **Accommodation:** 85 rooms, from £195.

Blue Bell   £ 32   A
Northgate St CH1 2HQ (01244) 317758
*A "lovely" atmosphere, "charming" service and "very nice" food
make this "olde worlde" pub (est 1494) near the Northgate a
"consistently good" option for a meal in the city centre.* / **Sample
dishes:** smoked salmon gnocchi; roast lamb shank; raspberry cheesecake.
Value tip: set 3-crs L £10. **Details:** www.blue-bell-restaurant.co.uk; 9.45 pm;
no Amex; no smoking.

The Fat Cat Café Bar   £ 24   A
85 Watergate St CH1 2LF (01244) 316100
*A "varied" and "reasonably priced" menu makes it worth knowing
about this "cosy" but "loud" outpost of a northerly mini-chain.*
/ **Sample dishes:** Mexican nachos; Fat Cat burger with French fries;
Devonshire flan with custard. **Details:** 10 pm; no smoking area at L; children:
not permitted.

Francs   £ 22   A
14 Cuppin St CH1 2BN (01244) 317952
*"Chester needs more good restaurants", like this "pleasant" and
"reasonably priced" bistro, which has become something of a local
"classic", thanks to its "you-could-be-in-France seasonal menus"
and its "Gallic staff who sometimes even smile".* / **Sample dishes:** red
salad; salmon with spring vegetables; summer fruits in bourbon.
Details: www.francs.co.uk; 11 pm; no smoking.

CHICHESTER, WEST SUSSEX   3–4A

Comme Ça   £ 33   A★★
67 Broyle Rd BO19 4BD (01243) 788724
*"A big welcome" is assured at Jane and Michel Navet's "very
attractive", rustically-converted spot (with a "pretty courtyard"),
where "totally French" staff dish up some "exceptionally tasty"
and "superbly-presented" Gallic cooking.* / **Sample dishes:** asparagus
with hollandaise sauce; Scottish cured salmon; summer pudding.
Details: www.commeca.co.uk; 0.5m N of city centre; 10.30 pm; closed Mon &
Sun D; no smoking area.

CHILGROVE, WEST SUSSEX   3–4A

White Horse   £ 36   ★
High St PO18 9HX (01243) 535219
*A several-hundred-bin wine list is the acknowledged "marvel" of this
"beautifully-located" South Downs pub, where "delicious fresh fish"
is the highlight amongst the "wonderful bar snacks".* / **Sample
dishes:** goats cheese & leek filo parcels; lamb & spinach with Madeira sauce;
warm chocolate gâteaux. **Details:** 8m NW of Chichester on B2141; 9.30 pm;
closed Mon & Sun D; no smoking.

---

regular updates at www.hardens.com

Sir Charles Napier £ 36 Ⓐ

Spriggs Alley OX9 4BX (01494) 483011

With its "glorious Chilterns setting", this "small restaurant/pub in the middle of nowhere" is best known as "a great escape from London", and its "junk shop" décor helps make it a "quirky" destination; its many fans say that it "never disappoints" with its "seriously delicious" cuisine, but – as ever – there's a group of refusniks who find the whole place "overpriced" and "rather smug". / **Sample dishes:** *pumpkin soup with chestnuts; rabbit with ricotta & spinach; date cake with toffee sauce.* **Details:** *M40, J6 into Chinnor, turn right at roundabout; 10 pm; closed Mon & Sun D; no smoking area; children: 6+ at D.*

Eight Bells £ 28

Church St GL55 6JG (01386) 840371

"A lovely location and great place to eat outside on a sunny day" – this classic, "olde worlde" stone pub in the Cotswolds offers "consistent", "good-value" cooking. / **Sample dishes:** *twice-baked cheese soufflé; braised lamb with julienne vegetables; dark chocolate cheesecake.* **Details:** *www.eightbellsinn.co.uk; 10m S of Stratford-upon-Avon; 9 pm, Fri & Sat 9.30 pm; no Amex; no smoking area.* **Accommodation:** *6 rooms, from £70.*

Chav Brasserie £ 32

7 Horsefair OX7 5AL (01608) 645968

These tiny tea-room premises have adopted a simpler brasserie style (now that the Maguires have moved Marchus Ashenford and their main operation Chavignol to nearby Shipston-on-Stour); feedback on the new formula is sparse, but even a reporter who says the "new team has less experience than the old" reports "a couple of good meals". / **Sample dishes:** *scallop & salmon sushi with tempura cauliflower; roast lamb with tomato & basil couscous; peach tart with liquorice ice cream.* **Details:** *www.chavignol.co.uk; 10 pm; closed Mon L & Sun; no Amex; no smoking.*

Quails £ 34

1 Bagshot Rd GU24 8BP (01276) 858491

"Long-established" in a neo-Georgian building in the town-centre, this "small" and "rather formal" establishment offers dishes that almost all reporters agree are "really well produced", if from a somewhat "limited" menu. / **Sample dishes:** *bruschetta with tomato & goat's cheese; glazed wood pigeon with honey-roasted vegetables; raspberry brûlée.* **Value tip:** *set 2-crs L £11.95.* **Details:** *2m SE of M3, J3; 9.30 pm; closed Mon, Sat L & Sun.*

Splinters £ 42 ★

12 Church St BH23 1BW (01202) 483454

"Careful" is a word which crops up in reports on both the "very good" cooking and the service at this attractively-located spot, near the Priory; if there is a criticism, it is that results are a touch predictable. / **Sample dishes:** *crab & mango with coriander dressing; sea bass ravioli with spring onion salsa; iced nougatine parfait.* **Details:** *on cobbled street near the priory; 10.30 pm; closed Mon & Sun; no smoking.*

CIRENCESTER, GLOUCESTERSHIRE 2–2C

Tatyan's £ 23

27 Castle St GL7 1QD (01285) 653529

*"Not your average provincial Chinese" – it's "quite a stylish place",
and its menu is hailed for its "wide range" and "good value".
/ **Sample dishes:** Szechuan chicken; sizzling prawns with ginger; banana
fritters. **Details:** www.tatyans.com; nr junction of A417 & A345; 10.30 pm;
closed Sun.*

CLACHAN, ARGYLL & BUTE 9–3B

Loch Fyne Oyster Bar £ 25 ★

PA26 8BL (01499) 600236

*"Excellently cooked and simple seafood, just as it ought to be" and
a "stunning location" on the Loch have won fame for this "most
unpretentious" spot of long-standing, and it "can be hard to get a
table"; (it's actually under semi-separate ownership from the
national chain that it inspired). / **Sample dishes:** smoked haddock
chowder; king scallops; ice cream. **Details:** www.loch-fyne.com; 10m E of
Inveraray on A83; 8.30 pm; open L&D all week (Nov-Mar D only); no smoking
area.*

CLANFIELD, OXFORDSHIRE 2–2C

Plough £ 32 Ⓐ

Bourton Rd OX18 2RB (01367) 810222

*"Log fires in winter" set the tone at this Elizabethan manor house
on the edge of the Cotswolds, where "unintrusive" but "efficient"
service contributed to a very high overall level of satisfaction for the
few who reported on it. / **Sample dishes:** salmon fishcakes; roast duck
with berry compote; almond ice-cream. **Details:** 9 pm; no smoking; children:
12+ at D. **Accommodation:** 13 rooms, from £95.*

CLAVERING, ESSEX 3–2B

The Cricketers £ 33

Wicken Rd CB11 4QT (01799) 550442

*Is this "a good pub, run professionally" or a "mediocre
establishment, which trades on the fact that it's run by the mum
and dad of the Naked Chef"? – both schools of thought are well
represented, though the more positive view just prevails. / **Sample
dishes:** squid with crispy onions & bacon; pork meatballs & fusilli; chocolate
cheesecake. **Details:** www.thecricketers.co.uk; on B1038 between Newport &
Buntingford; 10 pm; closed Sun D; smoking in bar only. **Accommodation:** 8
rooms, from £90.*

CLAYGATE, SURREY 3–3A

Le Petit Pierrot £ 35 ★

4 The Parade KT10 0NU (01372) 465105

*"Still as good as ever", this "little bistro-style restaurant" is a
"personal" establishment (run by Annie and Jean Pierre Brichot),
and its "provincial French cuisine" is of "a consistently good level".
/ **Sample dishes:** grilled asparagus & smoked chicken salad; pan-fried calves
liver with raspberries; crispy waffles with lemon cream. **Value tip:** set 2-crs L
£12.25. **Details:** nr station; 9.30 pm; closed Sat L & Sun; children: 8+.*

CLECKHEATON, WEST YORKSHIRE 5–1C

Aakash £ 26

Providence Pl, Bradford Rd BD19 3PN (01274) 870011

*The former congregational chapel is now a temple to curry, having
been converted into what claims to be the largest Indian restaurant
in the world (with nearly 900 seats); its opening, in summer '01,
was too late for it to figure in the survey. / **Sample dishes:** chicken
soup with cloves & saffron; lamb kebabs marinated in yoghurt; paneer
dumplings with pistachio. **Details:** www.aakashrestaurant.com; A638 towards
Dewsbury from M62, J26; 11 pm; D only; no smoking area.*

CLENT, WORCESTERSHIRE   5–4B

The Fountain Inn   £ 27   ★

Adams HI DY9 9PU   (01562) 883286

*"Country pub with oak beams and open fires" – this "quiet" place, attracts consistent reports for its "very good" cooking. / **Sample dishes:** deep-fried goat's cheese with raspberry coulis; chicken Wellington; summer fruit cheesecake. **Details:** 2m from Hagley by Clent Hills; 9.30 pm; no Amex; no smoking area.*

CLEOBURY MORTIMER, SHROPSHIRE   5–4B

Spice Empire   £ 19   ★

17 High St DY14 8DG   (01299) 270419

*"A delightful find" – "you get a surprisingly good curry in this tiny Shropshire town", at this innovative Indian. / **Sample dishes:** chicken kebabs; chilli beef; banana fritters. **Details:** 11 pm; closed Mon & Sun L.*

CLEVEDON, NORTH SOMERSET   2–2A

Junior Poon   £ 28   ★

16 Hill Rd BS21 7NZ   (01275) 341900

*"Superior Chinese food" and "impeccable" service combine to make this "reliable but fairly pricey" pier-side spot a consistently popular local destination. / **Sample dishes:** crispy lamb in spiced garlic sauce; sweet & sour pork in batter; lychee fritters. **Details:** nr Clevedon Pier; 10 pm; D only, closed Sun; no jeans or trainers.*

CLIMPING, WEST SUSSEX   3–4A

Bailiffscourt Hotel   £ 53   𝔸

BN17 5RW   (01903) 723511

*This "beautifully-converted" 'ancient' manor house – in fact, a '30s creation from old materials – has an "intimate" banqueting hall with an "extremely romantic" atmosphere; staff are "relaxed but very efficient", too, so it's all the more unfortunate that the food can be quite a let-down. / **Sample dishes:** seared tuna with wasabi; clams, mussels & scallops in aniseed broth; tarte Tatin.*
***Details:** www.hshotels.co.uk; 9.45 pm; no smoking; children: 7+.*
***Accommodation:** 31 rooms, from £150.*

CLIPSHAM, RUTLAND   6–4A

Olive Branch   £ 28   𝔸 ★

Main St LE15 7SH   (01780) 410355

*"A fine example of a gastropub", this "comfortable" and "refined" – but "lively" – yearling has achieved instant and wide-ranging popularity on account of its "interesting, but ungimmicky" cooking, backed up by a "good choice of wine". / **Sample dishes:** prawn & avocado cocktail; roast brill with chive mash; cappuccino mousse with Amaretto biscuits. **Details:** 2m from A1; 9.30 pm; closed Sun D; no Amex; no smoking area.*

CLITHEROE, LANCASHIRE   5–1B

Inn at Whitewell   £ 37   𝔸 ★ ★

Forest of Bowland BD7 3AT   (01200) 448222

*"An excellent retreat in the Forest of Bowland", this "wonderful", "traditional" country pub pretty much has it all – a "beautiful" location, "attentive and friendly" service, a "charming" atmosphere, and "delicious cooking with a distinct regional bias"; if you plan to stay, book well ahead. / **Sample dishes:** goat's cheese cannelloni with rocket; roast lamb with grilled black pudding; passion fruit cake.*
***Details:** 9.30 pm; D only (bar meals only at L). **Accommodation:** 17 rooms, from £80.*

Clytha Arms £ 30 ★
NP7 9BW (01873) 840206
Some find a contrast between "the warm cottage/pub style" and the "serious" cooking at Andrew Canning's "pleasant" spot, "in the heart of rural South Wales", but all pronounce the "wide-ranging" menu realised to very good effect. / Sample dishes: melon & avocado salad; roast hake with herb salsa; Sauternes cream with spiced prunes. Value tip: set 2-crs meal £12.95. Details: on Old Abergavenny Road; 9.30 pm; closed Mon D & Sun D; no smoking. Accommodation: 4 rooms, from £60.

La Capanna £ 39
48 High St KT11 3EF (01932) 862121
Service can be "friendly" – but also very "arrogant" – at this long-established Italian, where commentary on all aspects of what some still find a "cheerful" and "attractive" destination becomes ever more mixed. / Sample dishes: fresh crab salad; veal & scallops with mushroom sauce; profiteroles. Details: 10.45 pm; closed Sat L.

Cricketers £ 36
Downside Common Rd KT11 3NX (01932) 862105
With its "lovely setting on the green", this village boozer offers "good-value, restaurant-style pub food". / Sample dishes: smoked haddock & salmon with poached egg; roast lamb with garlic & rosemary; fresh cheesecake. Details: 2m from Cobham High St; 9.30 pm; closed Mon & Sun D.

Quince & Medlar £ 28 Ⓐ★★
13 Castlegate CA13 9EU (01900) 823579
"Interesting and imaginative" vegetarian cooking wins enthusiastic praise for the "informal" panelled dining room of Colin and Louise Le Voi's Georgian house. / Sample dishes: spinach, olive & Brie tartlet; curried vegetable coulibiac; lemon cheesecake. Details: next to Cockermouth Castle; 9.30 pm; D only, closed Mon & Sun; no Amex; no smoking; children: 5+.

Baumann's Brasserie £ 35
4-6 Stoneham St CO6 1TT (01376) 561453
Fans of this "surprisingly sophisticated" spot note that the owner was a past associate of the late and great Peter Langan – and say "it shows"; especially given the "lovely linen and art", however, the atmosphere can seem strangely lacklustre, and the realisation of the rather "pretentious" menu is no better than "average plus". / Sample dishes: prawn & leek filo parcels; Dover sole with new potatoes; dark chocolate truffle cake. Value tip: set 3-crs L £12.50. Details: opposite the clock tower; 9.30 pm; closed Mon & Tue; no smoking area.

Lemon Tree £ 22 Ⓐ★
48 St Johns St CO2 7AD (01206) 767337
"Roman walls add to the ambience" of this "busy" town-centre restaurant, praised for its quality, moderately-priced modern cooking and its "unobtrusive staff who know their stuff". / Sample dishes: goats cheese & red pepper tart; sea bass with basil butter & samphire; baked cheesecake with black cherries. Details: www.the-lemon-tree.com; 10 pm; closed Sun; no smoking; children: 5+.

Lucknam Park £ 64 Ⓐ

SN14 8AZ (01225) 742777

A "lovely" Georgian hotel and stud farm in "a parkland setting", where many report that a meal in the "beautiful" dining room – with its "courteous, but unobtrusive" service – is "a really high-quality dining experience"; its middle-of-the-road ratings, however, continue to suggest it's rather pricey even so. / **Sample dishes:** crab tortellini with marinated cucumber; sea bass with roasted vegetables; millefeuille of lime & rhubarb. **Details:** www.lucknampark.co.uk; 6m NE of Bath; 9.30 pm; D only, except Sun open L & D; jacket & tie required; no smoking; children: 12+ at D. **Accommodation:** 41 rooms, from £190.

Martins Arms Inn £ 40 Ⓐ

School Ln NG12 3FD (01949) 81361

A "lovely unspoilt old country pub"; it's well-known locally for its "inventive" cooking, but even supporters can find it "rather expensive". / **Sample dishes:** warm salad of squid & chorizo; halibut with chicory, orange & rosemary sauce; trio of lemon desserts. **Details:** 2 miles off A46; 9.30 pm; closed Sun D; no Amex; children: 14+.

The Withies Inn £ 36 Ⓐ

Withies Ln GU3 1JA (01483) 421158

This "old beamed pub" is "full of character", and some laud its cooking for its "excellent variety" and its "very good value"; it is "rather variable", though. / **Sample dishes:** asparagus with hollandaise butter; roast suckling pig with apple sauce; treacle tart & custard. **Details:** off A3 near Guildford, signposted on B3000; 10 pm; closed Sun D; booking essential.

Trengilly Wartha Inn £ 34

Nancenoy TR11 5RP (01326) 340332

It's "difficult to find" this "out-of-the-way" pub and restaurant, but most reporters reckon its worth it particularly for its "interesting bar food", "superb cellar" and "friendly, family orientated" approach; as ever, though, positive reports are mixed with the occasional 'off' experience. / **Sample dishes:** scallop ravioli; flamiche with herb salad; chocolate delice. **Details:** www.trengilly.co.uk; 1m outside village; 9.30 pm; D only. **Accommodation:** 8 rooms, from £72.

Bel & The Dragon £ 34 Ⓐ

High St SL6 9SQ (01628) 521263

There's a "great atmosphere" at this popular, "gothicky" 15th-century inn (which owes much of its ambience to a refit in recent times); it serves "well-prepared" food from an "imaginative" and "varied" menu that's "really too ambitious to be called pub grub". / **Sample dishes:** goat's cheese & spinach strudel; roast lamb with herb mash & raspberry jus; banoffi cheesecake.
Details: www.belandthedragon.co.uk; opp Stanley Spencer Gallery; 9.45 pm; no smoking area.

CORBRIDGE, NORTHUMBERLAND

The Valley £ 24
Old Station Hs NE45 5AY (01434) 633434
"This ain't no ordinary curry, pet"; for the full experience, this "fun" Indian is best enjoyed as part of a 'Package to India', from Newcastle, whereby you have a drink and order on a special train and your dinner awaits your arrival; it's "better for groups".
/ **Sample dishes:** green peppers stuffed with spicy prawns; Mediterranean lamb with green peppers & coriander; pineapple paradise.
Details: www.northeastonline.co.uk/valley; at Corbridge railway station; 10.30 pm; D only, closed Sun; no smoking area.

CORSCOMBE, DORSET

Fox Inn £ 33 𝔸★
DT2 0NS (01935) 891330
"Hospitable" and "delightfully-situated" village boozer; its motto is 'no chips or microwaves', and its "generous portions" of "good home cooking" win unanimous approval. / **Sample dishes:** roast aubergines with tomato & Mozzarella; Barbary duck with soy & honey sauce; lemon crème brûlée. **Details:** www.fox-inn.co.uk; 5 mins off A37; 9 pm, Fri & Sat 9.30 pm; no smoking area. **Accommodation:** 3 rooms, from £65.

CORSE LAWN, GLOUCESTERSHIRE

Corse Lawn Hotel £ 39 ★
GL19 4LZ (01452) 780771
"Reliable", "professional", "charming" – the same concepts keep cropping up in reviews of the Hine family's country house hotel (occupying a very picturesque Queen Anne building), not least as regards its "well-prepared", quite "rich" cuisine. / **Sample dishes:** wild mushroom pancake; pan-fried guinea fowl with split peas; poached fruits with vanilla cream. **Details:** www.corselawnhousehotel.co.uk; 5m SW of Tewkesbury on B4211; 9.30 pm; no smoking; children: 6+ at D.
Accommodation: 19 rooms, from £125.

COVENTRY, WEST MIDLANDS

Thai Dusit £ 25
39 London Rd CV1 2JP (024) 7622 7788
An "excellent host and staff" are the star features at this "very friendly" Thai restaurant – it attracts a good range of favourable commentary, even if its food does tend to "standard". / **Sample dishes:** chicken satay; green Thai curry & jasmine rice; mango & ice cream. **Details:** 11 pm; closed Sun L; no Amex.

COWBRIDGE, VALE OF GLAMORGAN

Farthings £ 26
54 High St CF71 7AH (01446) 772990
An "excellent range" of "both light and heavy dishes" makes Natalie & Nick Dobson's two-year-old brasserie a very "popular" destination; "fantastic desserts" are a highlight. / **Sample dishes:** crab & avocado tartlets; halibut with char-grilled asparagus; hazelnut & raspberry meringue. **Details:** 10 pm; closed Mon D & Sun D; no Amex; no smoking area.

COWLING, WEST YORKSHIRE

Harlequin £ 29
139 Keighley Rd BD22 0AH (01535) 633277
A wine bar and "informal" restaurant that makes an "always-reliable" destination, thanks to its "individual" cuisine and its overall "good value". / **Sample dishes:** scallop & smoked bacon tart; roast duckling with apple & plum purée; nougatine parfait with macaroons. **Value tip:** set 3-crs Sun L £12.50. **Details:** on A6068 towards Colne; 9.30 pm; closed Mon & Tue; no smoking; children: 7+ at D.

COXWOLD, NORTH YORKSHIRE 8–4C
Fauconberg Arms £ 27
YO61 4AD (01347) 868214

This may be "just a village pub", but it's an "atmospheric" place, beautifully situated in the Hambleton Hills; new management aim to take it upmarket a bit (hence the lack of rating) – let's hope they don't wreck the "tasty, home-made food" reporters said was "definitely worth seeking out". / *Sample dishes:* quail, black pudding & apple salad; steak & ale pie with buttercrust pastry; meringue with raspberries & peaches. *Details:* 9.30 pm; restaurant open only Wed D-Sat D & Sun L, pub open L&D all week; no Amex; no smoking. *Accommodation:* 4 rooms, from £60.

CRANBORNE, DORSET 2–4C
La Fosse £ 29
The Square BH21 5PR (01725) 517604

"Always enjoyable, always busy", this simple family-run restaurant-with-rooms receives nothing but praise, especially for its "unhurried and friendly" service and "great-value lunches". / *Sample dishes:* lobster thermidor; roast deer & vegetables with redcurrants; tropical fruit parfait. *Value tip:* set 3-crs L £8.95. *Details:* www.la-fosse.com; 10 pm; closed Mon, Sat L & Sun D; no smoking. *Accommodation:* 3 rooms, from £65.

CRASTER, NORTHUMBERLAND 8–1B
Jolly Fisherman £ 12
NE66 3TR (01665) 576461

"Good crab soup" and "salmon sandwiches" are the sort of dishes which complement the "wonderful views of the sea" at this popular inn. / *Sample dishes:* crab soup; smoked salmon sandwiches; blackcurrant crumble with custard. *Details:* nr Dunstanburgh Castle; 8 pm; no credit cards; no smoking area.

CREIGAU, CARDIFF 2–2A
Caesars Arms £ 28
Cardiff Rd CF15 9NN (029) 2089 0486

Choosing from the "glass counter display of fish, meat and shellfish" is the "simple but effective" formula which makes this "rurally-located" brasserie-cum-pub ("from the same stable as Cardiff's Le Monde") a "pleasant" destination; "good Spanish and New World wines" too. / *Sample dishes:* smoked salmon with eggs & capers; honey-roasted duckling; raspberry pavlova. *Details:* beyond Creigau, past golf club; 10.30 pm; closed Sun D.

CRICKHOWELL, POWYS 2–1A
The Bear £ 32 ★
High St NP8 1BW (01873) 810408

"It's worth a long drive out of your way", say most reporters, for the "traditional Welsh/English" cooking, "old-fashioned" service and "comfortable", "cosy" atmosphere of this well-known coaching inn (and it's a "nice place to stay" too); the occasional misfire, however, is not unknown. / *Sample dishes:* seared king scallops with noodles; swordfish with wild rice; summer fruit pudding. *Details:* NW of Abergavenny on A40; 9.30 pm; D only, except Sun when L only; no smoking in bar; children: 7+. *Accommodation:* 34 rooms, from £68.

Nantyffin Cider Mill £ 26 ★★
Brecon Rd NP8 1SG (01873) 810775

"What a surprise that such a touristy-looking place can have such good cooking"; the "serious" cuisine at this "unusual" mill-conversion is "well above the standard you'd expect at these prices" and includes "a wide mix of the modern and the traditional". / *Sample dishes:* Loch Fyne langoustines with herb butter; gingered red mullet with pak choy; Drambuie pannacotta with figs. *Details:* www.cidermill.co.uk; on A40 between Brecon & Crickhowell; 9.30 pm; closed Mon; no smoking area.

The Punch Bowl   **£ 26**   ★★
LA8 8HR   (01539) 568237
"The value-for-money factor is very high" at Steven and Marjorie
Doherty's "charming" gastropub, "beautifully located" in the Lakes;
portions are "generous" from the "extensive" and "imaginative"
menu, and the "superb" results "more than compensate for the
slight starkness of the décor". / **Sample dishes:** pasta in spicy tomato
sauce; grilled aubergine with polenta; chocolate nemesis.
Details: www.punchbowl.fsnet.co.uk; off A5074 towards Bowness, turn right
after Lyth Hotel; 9 pm; closed Mon & Sun D; no Amex; no smoking.
Accommodation: 3 rooms, from £55 (£97.50 incl D).

Ockenden Manor   **£ 43**
Ockenden Ln RH17 5LD   (01444) 416111
Especially if you don't like the "silver covers and salvers" style, you
may find dining at this Elizabethan manor house "pompous and
pretentious"; it's set in "fine gardens" and "with beautiful views of
the South Downs", though, and the majority of reporters think the
cooking is "good and fresh". / **Sample dishes:** truffle risotto; grilled beef
with mustard sauce; warm apple fritters. **Value tip:** set 2-crs L £12.95.
Details: www.hshotels.co.uk; 9.30 pm; no smoking. **Accommodation:** 22
rooms, from £132.

Bear & Ragged Staff   **£ 28**
Appleton Rd OX2 9QH   (01865) 862329
"A cut above the standard village pub restaurant", this beamed
14th century inn just outside Oxford is a "nice", "cosy" place, with
quite an "imaginative" menu. / **Sample dishes:** creamed oyster
mushrooms; crepes with garlic & basil-roasted vegetables; sticky toffee &
banana pudding. **Details:** 9.30 pm; no smoking area.

Ostlers Close   **£ 41**
25 Bonnygate KY15 4BU   (01334) 655574
This small, family-run restaurant of two decades' standing remains
a consistently popular destination; its enthusiastic fan club say it
offers "the best French food north of London" and its dishes are
certainly "well cooked and nicely presented". / **Sample dishes:** seared
scallops with salt cod brandade; duck with Puy lentils & plum sauce; lemon tart
with tangerine sorbet. **Details:** www.ostlersclose.co.uk; 9.30 pm; closed Mon,
Tue L, Wed L, Thu L & Sun; no smoking; children: 6+.

The Peat Inn   **£ 42**   🅰
KY15 5LH   (01334) 840206
"Top-quality ingredients cooked with flair, and served with dignity"
have made the Wilsons' famous converted coaching inn "an
institution"; as ever, however, the general level of satisfaction is
undercut by the odd reports of "disappointing" experiences.
/ **Sample dishes:** roast scallops with leeks & smoked bacon;
roe deer fillet with cocoa bean purée; trio of caramel desserts.
Details: www.thepeatinn.co.uk; at junction of B940 & B941, SW of
St Andrews; 9.30 pm; closed Mon & Sun; no smoking.
Accommodation: 8 rooms, from £145.

Cott Inn   £ 27
TQ9 6HE   (01803) 863777
This "lovely olde worlde pub" has "deteriorated since being taken over by a chain" – too many reporters now speaking of "mediocre" cooking, and of service which is "slow" and "familiar". / **Sample dishes:** venison & game pâté; turkey à la king; treacle tart. **Details:** www.oldenglish.co.uk; up hill from Cider Press Centre; 9.30 pm; no smoking. **Accommodation:** 6 rooms, from £70.

Carved Angel   £ 51
2 South Embankment TQ6 9BH   (01803) 832465
Opinions divide on this sparsely furnished harbourside fixture (now with the same owners as Tavistock's Horn of Plenty); critics still say "it's not what it was under Joyce Molyneux", finding the new approach "pretentious" and "nouvelle-y", while advocates insist that "the new style is an improvement" and hail "beautiful" cooking ("especially fish", and most particularly the "great value lunch"). / **Sample dishes:** Dartmouth crab with smoked pepper relish; lamb with root vegetable strudel & cherry jus; rhubarb soufflé. **Details:** www.thecarvedangel.com; opp passenger ferry pontoon; 9.30 pm; closed Mon L & Sun D; no smoking; children: 10+ at D.

Carved Angel Café   £ 33   𝔸★
7 Foss St TQ6 9DW   (01803) 834842
"It's gone from strength to strength and is better value than its parent" is the general verdict on this new "café offshoot" of the famous restaurant (a street or so away), which wins praise for its "nice bistro atmosphere", "friendly staff" and "tasty and good value" food, from a "blackboard" menu; they've gone on to open offshoots in Exeter (Cathedral Green, tel 01392 210303) and Taunton (2 St James St, tel 01823 352033). / **Sample dishes:** grilled goats cheese with red onion confit; sea bass with spring onion mash & herb cream; chocolate & peanut brownie. **Details:** www.thecarvedangel.com; 11 pm; closed Mon D-Wed D & Sun; no smoking; no booking at L.

Fawsley Hall   £ 50   𝔸
NN11 3BA   (01327) 892000
"Experiences have varied" somewhat at this recently renovated Tudor hall, which all agree offers a "beautiful" setting and a "marvellous" ambience – it's often thought to be "quite good", but can be "bland". / **Sample dishes:** foie gras assiette; roast duck with caramelised turnips; miniature chocolate desserts. **Value tip:** set 2-crs L £15. **Details:** www.fawsleyhall.com; on A361 between Daventry & Banbury; 9.30 pm; no smoking in dining room. **Accommodation:** 30 rooms, from £179.

Le Talbooth   £ 46   𝔸
Gun Hill CO7 6HP   (01206) 323150
Deep in Constable Country, the Milsom family's well-known, long-established hotel benefits from a "beautiful" riverside location; it's a little bit "staid" for current tastes, though, and the old criticism that it serves "mediocre food at inflated prices" was more in evidence again this year. / **Sample dishes:** langoustines; guinea fowl stuffed with crab mousse; hot chocolate & orange fondant. **Value tip:** set 2-crs L £17.50. **Details:** www.talbooth.com; 5m N of Colchester on A12, take B1029; 9.30 pm. **Accommodation:** 10 rooms, from £155.

DENSHAW, GREATER MANCHESTER
Rams Head Inn   £ 27   A★   5–2B

OL3 5UN   (01457) 874802

It may be "bleakly situated" in the Pennines, but "friendly" service, "open fires" and a "well-stocked bar" help make this "pub-turned-restaurant" a welcoming sort of place, and its cooking is "imaginative" too. / **Sample dishes:** smoked salmon & asparagus salad; pan-fried venison with black cherry & orange sauce; chocolate & Bailey's cheesecake. **Details:** 2m from M63, J22 towards Oldham; 10 pm; closed Mon L; no Amex; no smoking area.

DERBY, DERBYSHIRE   5–3C
Darleys on the River   £ 37

Darley Abbey Mill   DE22 1DZ   (01332) 364987

This "nicely located" riverside mill-conversion is praised by many for its "very good meals in a thin area"; even some advocates think it "expensive", though, and perhaps a tad "complacent". / **Sample dishes:** duck & foie gras ballottine; poussin with new potatoes & grain mustard; toffee apple crumble. **Value tip:** set 2-crs L £13.50. **Details:** www.darleys.com; 2m N of city centre by River Derwent; 10 pm; closed Sun D; no smoking.

DEWSBURY, WEST YORKSHIRE   5–1C
West Riding Refreshment Rooms   £ 11

Railway Station, Wellington Rd   WFB 1HF   (01924) 459193

"Fantastic for a pub, particularly for vegetarians", say fans this well-reputed converted railway station; it does have its critics, though, who "would turn it back into a waiting room". / **Sample dishes:** vegetable soup & roll; beef in beer with parsnip mash; steamed sponge & custard. **Details:** www.yorkshire-ale.org.uk/west-riding; in old waiting room of railway station; 9 pm; L only, except Tue & Wed, when L&D; no credit cards; no smoking area.

DINTON, BUCKINGHAMSHIRE   2–3C
La Chouette   £ 45   ★

Westlington Grn   HP17 8UW   (01296) 747422

An "entertaining and unconventional Belgian host" sets the tone at this swell village restaurant, whose attractions include some good "Belgian-style food" – including "a variety of fish dishes" – and some "fine beers". / **Sample dishes:** salmon & strawberries; duck in elderflower sauce; chocolate soufflé. **Value tip:** set 3-crs L £11. **Details:** on A418 between Aylesbury & Thame; 9 pm; closed Sat L & Sun; no Amex.

DODDISCOMBSLEIGH, DEVON   1–3D
Nobody Inn   £ 24   A★

EX6 7PS   (01647) 252394

"A sensational selection of West Country cheeses", a "superb" wine list (over 1000 bins), an "amazing" array of single malts, "fabulous" hospitality ... – this "idyllic" 15th-century pub "out in the wilds" is "very memorable" and it's perhaps no great surprise that at times it can "suffer somewhat from its popularity". / **Sample dishes:** guinea fowl terrine with apple & tomato chutney; pheasant in rich red wine sauce; spotted dick & custard. **Details:** www.thenobodyinn.com; off A38 at Haldon Hill (signed Dunchidrock); 9 pm; closed Mon & Sun; no smoking area; children: 14+. **Accommodation:** 7 rooms, from £55.

DOGMERSFIELD, HAMPSHIRE   3–3A
Queen's Head   £ 24   ★

Pilcot Ln   RG27 8SY   (01252) 613531

"A good selection of first-rate food" at "reasonable prices" wins popularity for this "upmarket" pub. / **Sample dishes:** avocado & prawn salad; lamb chops with mint & cranberry gravy; treacle sponge & custard. **Details:** off A287 between Farnham & Odiham; 9 pm; closed Mon.

Lord Newborough £ 26 ★

Conway Rd LL32 8JX (01492) 660549

*"A rural ex-pub, with a high reputation", where "superb lamb dishes" are a highlight of a menu which makes much use of "local produce", and there's a "short but good wine list"; "insist on a table in the front bar". / **Sample dishes:** bacon & cheese salad; pan-fried chicken with leek & mushroom sauce; summer pudding. **Details:** 9 pm; closed Mon & Sun D; no smoking area.*

Partners £ 42

2-4 West St RH4 1BL (01306) 882826

*Though "excellent food, beautifully presented" is heartily praised by fans of this "quiet", "dark" and "intimate" establishment (in a beamed medieval building in the town centre), there remain doubters who opine that "it costs more than places of similar quality in the capital". / **Sample dishes:** whole quail; calves liver & black pudding with mash; apple & calvados brioche.* **Details:** www.scoot.co.uk/partners; 10 pm; closed Mon, Sat L & Sun; no smoking area.

Country Friends £ 40 ★

SY5 7JD (01743) 718707

*This mock-Tudor manor house, not far from Shrewsbury, may not be anything special to look at, but its "cosy" and "unpretentious" charms win it unanimous support – "superb and original vegetable dishes" and "exquisite desserts" come in for particular praise. / **Sample dishes:** twice-baked red pepper & pesto soufflé; venison with sloe gin sauce; queen of puddings. **Details:** 5m S of Shrewsbury on A49; 9 pm; closed Mon, Tue & Sun; no Amex; no smoking. **Accommodation:** 1 room, at about £130.*

DUBLIN, COUNTY DUBLIN, *ROI*

Though clearly not geographically within the ambit of a guide called UK Restaurants, we have included the Irish capital as it receives so many visitors from the UK, and is much reported on.

Dublin has emerged strongly as a restaurant centre over recent years, and for a city of its size offers an excellent selection. In keeping, however, with a history which (except in the last decade) involved more emigration than immigration, its strengh lies in European restaurants, and it boasts relatively few ethnic options of any note.

The classically-influenced *Patrick Guilbaud* remains the city's pre-eminent gastronomic venue (and scored one of the highest food ratings in the survey across the whole of the British Isles). With the closure of the long-established Ballsbridge landmark, Le Coq Hardi, there are now only two other establishments with ambitions to haute cuisine: *Peacock Alley* and *Thorntons*. Judged by the survey, neither is capable of unqualified recommendation.

For notable but more informal eating, there are a number of good choices. The *Mermaid Café*, the *Clarence Hotel Tea Rooms* and *Jacob's Ladder* all in differing ways answer to this description.

Reporters' favourites still tend to be places where the ambience outshines the cooking. Perhaps sadly, *Roly's Bistro* increasingly finds itself in this category. With its wonderful setting, *La Stampa* remains reporters' top tip for a celebratory evening.

Temple Bar is the best known touristy area, and – like London's Covent Garden – you will often eat better and more cheaply elsewhere.

Bang Café   IR £ 39
11 Merrion Row D2   (01) 676 0898
"Newly-opened and original, for Dublin" – this "contemporary"-looking, three-floor outfit generally gets the thumbs-up for its "well-cooked and presented" modern cooking and "friendly" service.
/ **Sample dishes:** *lobster, chorizo & baby corn salad; seared tuna with lentil salsa & spring leaves ; plum & lavender tarte Tatin.*
Details: *www.cafebang.com; 10.30 pm, Thu-Sat 11 pm; closed Sun; no Switch.*

Café Mao   IR £ 25   ★
2-3 Chatham Rw D2   (01) 670 4899
"Good fun and good food" is a combination that continues to win praise for this "consistent" venture – a "modern café/bar" off Grafton Street whose "wide selection of tasty pan-Asian dishes" draws a "cosmopolitan" younger crowd. / **Sample dishes:** *chilli squid; lemongrass & chilli tiger prawns; passion fruit syllabub.*
Details: *www.cafemao.com; just off Grafton St & St Stephen's Green; 11.30 pm; no Amex or Switch; no booking; children: 6+ after 7 pm.*

Clarence Hotel (Tea Rooms)   IR £ 51   𝔸★
6-8 Wellington Quay D2   (01) 670 7766
"Classy, relaxed, confident and modern" – the stylish dining hall at this hippest of hotels (owned by U2) is widely praised as a "memorable all round experience" that's "pricey but of a good standard"; (a small, but persistent minority are left cold, though, citing "unexceptional" food and a slightly "dead" ambience).
/ **Sample dishes:** *deep-fried potato & bacon cakes; Angus beef with wild mushrooms & mash; clementine & lemon trifle.* **Value tip:** *set 3-crs L £15.*
Details: *www.theclarence.ie; opp New Millennium Bridge; 10.45 pm; closed Sat L; no Switch; no smoking area.* **Accommodation:** *50 rooms, from £185.*

Cooke's Café   IR £ 43
12 South William Street D2   (01) 679 0536
Johnny Cooke's simple Mediterranean café has something of a reputation as a fashionable 'in'-crowd haunt; the uninitiated may be "disappointed", however (especially given the prices), and even some who praise the "great, light cuisine" find the setting "a bit boring". / **Sample dishes:** *warm goat's cheese salad; sea trout with Mediterranean vegetables; chocolate pecan tart.*
Details: *www.cookescafe.com; 11 pm; closed Mon & Sun; no Switch; no smoking area.*

L'Ecrivain   IR £ 51
109 Lower Baggot St D2   (01) 661 1919
The limited feedback we received was unanimously favourable this year, regarding Derry & Sally Anne Clarke's well-established fixture, praised all-round for its "enjoyable" modern Irish cooking and "superb" service. / **Sample dishes:** *baked rock oysters with cabbage & bacon; seared blue fin tuna; summer berry truffle cake.* **Value tip:** *set 3-crs L £20.* **Details:** *www.lecrivain.com; opp Bank of Ireland; 10.30 pm; closed Sat L & Sun; no Switch; no smoking area; booking essential.*

Eden   IR £ 39

Meeting House Sq   D2   (01) 670 5372

"Well-taught and knowledgeable staff" add to the enjoyment of
eating at this groovily-decorated café/restaurant, by Temple Bar's
Olympia Theatre; it serves *"straightforward"*, *"modern"* cuisine
at *"reasonable prices"*. / **Sample dishes:** smoked eel salad; organic
pork & apricot stew; crème brûlée. **Details:** nr Olympia Theatre; 10.30 pm;
no Switch; no smoking area.

Elephant & Castle   IR £ 34   A

18 Temple Bar   D2   (01) 679 1956

"Now an institution in Dublin" – this *"simple American-style
eatery"* (a characterful diner in Temple Bar) serves *"tasty food
for hungry young people"*, and makes a *"fantastic brunch venue"*
in particular. / **Sample dishes:** chicken wings; beefburger with cheese &
chips; carrot cake. **Details:** 11.30 pm; no Switch; no smoking area;
no booking.

Jacob's Ladder   IR £ 39   ★

4-5 Nassau St   D2   (01) 670 3865

"Something of a find" is the tenor of most feedback on this
'serious' establishment, overlooking the grounds of Trinity College,
which is praised for its *"excellent food"*; one or two found *"it didn't
live up to its promise"*, however. / **Sample dishes:** roast quail with
quail's eggs & celeriac cream; roast pigeon with lentils; rum & raisin brûlée.
Details: www.jacobsladder.ie; beside Trinity College; 10 pm; closed Mon &
Sun; no Switch; no smoking area.

King Sitric   IR £ 49

East Pier   (01) 832 5235

Overlooking a pretty fishing harbour (at the end of the DART),
this long-established seafood fixture is known for its *"good fish"*
and *"wonderful wine"*; even some fans say it's *"expensive"* for
what it is, though. / **Sample dishes:** Rossmore oysters; black sole meunière;
passion fruit delight. **Value tip:** set 3-crs L £18.50. **Details:** www.kingsitric.ie;
10.30 pm; closed Sat L & Sun; no Switch; no smoking area.
Accommodation: 8 rooms, from £90.

Mermaid Café   IR £ 40   ★

69-70 Dame Street   D2   (01) 670 8236

Even those complaining *"it wasn't as fantastic as I'd been led to
believe"* thought the food *"good"* at this simple-looking café, on the
fringe of Temple Bar; fans, meanwhile, are ecstatic in their praise of
the place's *"relaxed and informal"* ambience, its *"interesting wine"*
and its *"outstanding, sophisticated cooking that belies the décor's
rustic style"*. / **Sample dishes:** rabbit fillet with chickpea tajine; osso bucco
with Jerusalem artichokes & juniper; rum & raisin bread & butter pudding.
Details: www.mermaid.ie; nr Olympia Theatre; 11 pm, Sun 9 pm; no Amex or
Switch; no smoking area.

101 Talbot Street   IR £ 29   ★

100-102 Talbot St   D1   (01) 874 5011

"Simple cuisine with an interesting twist" makes it well worth
knowing about this *"relaxed"* Middle-Eastern-influenced café, just
off O'Connell Street. / **Sample dishes:** goat's cheese crostini with
aubergine pesto; duck with port & juniper sauce; white chocolate & Bailey's
cheesecake. **Details:** nr Abbey Theatre; 10.45 pm; D only, closed Sun & Mon;
no Switch; no smoking area.

Patrick Guilbaud
Merrion Hotel   IR £ 87   ★

21 Upper Merrion St D2   (01) 676 4192

"On a par with London's first rank, and hard to fault" – this spacious chamber is "the best in Ireland" in the estimation of many, offering "superb" classically-rooted cooking and a voluminous wine list; it's "an arm and a leg" job, naturally, and if there is a gripe, it's that "the atmosphere doesn't match up to that in the rest of the hotel". / **Sample dishes:** carpaccio style pig's trotter; squab pigeon with savoy cabbage; crème brûlée. **Value tip:** set 2-crs L £22 (not in Dec). **Details:** 10.15 pm; closed Mon & Sun; no Switch; no smoking area.

Peacock Alley   IR £ 86

Fitzwilliam Hotel, 119 St Stephen's Grn D2   (01) 677 0708

"Excellent, expensive… expensive, but excellent" – even fans focus on the prices at this esteemed establishment, which has put in a mixed performance while chef/patron Conrad Gallagher has been establishing his new London venture; let's hope that the late summer '01 arrival of well-reputed chef David Cavalier will steady the kitchen's output. / **Sample dishes:** sea scallops; pan-fried sole with black butter; lemon tart with raspberry coulis. **Value tip:** set 3-crs L £24. **Details:** www.restaurantpeacockalley.com; 10.30 pm; no Switch; no smoking area; children: 12+.

Roly's Bistro   IR £ 39   Ⓐ

7 Ballsbridge Ter D4   (01) 668 2611

"There's the feeling of a really good night out" at this "convivial", "buzzing" Ballsbridge brasserie, which is a perennially "trendy" favourite; it's known as a "quality" place that's "fairly" priced, but there were a number of reporters this year who said "it's poor, given how good it used to be". / **Sample dishes:** spiced crab with angel hair pasta; Dublin Bay prawns with tarragon rice; Jaffa Cake torte. **Value tip:** set 2-crs pre-th £12.95. **Details:** nr American Embassy; 9.45 pm; no Switch; no smoking area.

La Stampa   IR £ 49   Ⓐ

35 Dawson St D2   (01) 677 8611

"An outstanding evening out"; the décor is "stunning" and the atmosphere "unbelievable" at this memorable venue – a converted ballroom "reminiscent of a grand, Belle Epoque brasserie"; the cooking is rather "bland", though. / **Sample dishes:** pan-fried foie gras brioche; roast fillet of beef; chocolate fondant. **Details:** www.lastampa.ie; off St Stephen's Green; midnight, Sat 12.30 am; D only; no Switch; no smoking area.

Thorntons   IR £ 72   ★

1 Portobello Rd D8   (01) 454 9067

An off-the-beaten-track location (in a townhouse next to a canal south of the city centre) perhaps explains the slender feedback on this much-fêted foodie destination; such comment as we have is a trifle mixed, but enthusiastic praise is tempered only by quite muted criticisms. / **Sample dishes:** sautéed foie gras & scallops; roast suckling pig; apple tarte Tatin with butterscotch ice cream. **Details:** 2m S of city centre; 10.30 pm; D only, except Fri when L&D; closed Mon & Sun; no Switch; no smoking area; children: 3+.

Wagamama   IR £ 22

South King St D2   (01) 478 2152

"Fast, frantic atmosphere, but flavoursome and filling food" remains the verdict on this "fun", no-booking oriental refectory – a branch of the well-known 'ramen' noodles chain. / **Sample dishes:** grilled vegetable dumplings; chilli beef & ramen noodles in spicy soup; no puddings. **Details:** www.wagamama.com; opp Gaiety Theatre; 11 pm; no Switch; no smoking; no booking.

Bucks Head £ 31 A ★

77-79 Main St BT33 0LU (028) 43751868

An "excellent village inn", which offers a "varied" menu and "very good" service, in a "relaxed" and "charming" conservatory setting. / **Sample dishes:** Dundrum bay oysters; seafood crepes with herb oil; pannacotta with espresso-soaked prunes. **Value tip:** set 3-crs Sun L £14.50. **Details:** 3m N of Newcastle; 9 pm; no smoking area.

Kinnaird House £ 50 A ★

Kinnaird Estate PH8 0LB (01796) 482440

"Immaculately-trained staff" and "superb" cooking contribute to the great sense of well-being which envelops visitors to this "splendid country house hotel" – "one of the best in Scotland", it occupies a large estate "within easy reach of Edinburgh". / **Sample dishes:** squab pigeon salad; pan-fried John Dory with peas & fèves; hot pear soufflé. **Details:** www.kinnairdestate.com; 8m NW of Dunfield, off A9 onto B898; 9.30 pm; jacket & tie required; no smoking; children: 12+. **Accommodation:** 9 rooms, from £365.

Three Chimneys £ 48 A ★★

Colbost IV55 8ZT (01470) 511258

"Well worth the seven hour drive", this "perfect romantic location" – a converted crofter's cottage – is an "excellent" place, where Shirley and Eddie Spear's menu "makes fantastic use of local ingredients"; fish and seafood are, of course, the speciality. / **Sample dishes:** twice-baked crab soufflé; venison with potato cakes; hot marmalade pudding. **Value tip:** set 2-crs L £12.95. **Details:** www.threechimneys.co.uk; 5m from Dunvegan Castle on B884 to Glendale; 9.30 pm; closed Sun L; no smoking. **Accommodation:** 6 rooms, from £160.

The Ship £ 26

St James St IP17 3DT (01728) 648219

"Their fish and chips are out of this world" – and "the veggie choice is good" too – at this "pleasant" pub in a seaside village; on a sunny day in the garden, "a carnival atmosphere prevails". / **Sample dishes:** Stilton & walnut pâté; sole with potatoes & vegetables; profiteroles. **Details:** 7m S of Southwold, follow signs from A12; 9.30 pm; no Amex; no smoking; no booking at L. **Accommodation:** 4 rooms, from £55.

Bistro 21 £ 33 A ★

Aykley Heads Hs DH1 5TS (0191) 384 4354

This "cramped, but popular bistro" – an offshoot of Newcastle's Café 21 – provides "a haven in the culinary desert"; the cooking is quite "plain", but "never disappoints", while service is "attentive and pleasant". / **Sample dishes:** Cheddar & spinach soufflé; sautéed chicken with wild mushrooms; warm chocolate mousse. **Value tip:** set 2-crs L £12. **Details:** nr Durham Trinity School; 10.30 pm; closed Sun; no smoking.

Shaheens Indian Bistro £ 20 ★

The Old Post Office, 48 North Bailey DH1 3ET (0191) 386 0960

"Great" curries and staff who are "always very friendly" makes this popular Indian a useful option in this under-served city. / **Sample dishes:** garlic mushrooms; chicken rogan josh; banana split. **Details:** 11 pm; D only, closed Mon; no Amex or Switch; no smoking area.

Jolly Sportsman £ 30
BN7 3BA (01273) 890400
*The décor may be "a little Spartan", but there's "usually a jolly atmosphere" at this "off-the-beaten-track" pub/restaurant, whose "fresh", "modern" cooking generally wins the thumbs-up. / **Sample dishes:** tiger prawn, saffron & chive risotto; roast guinea fowl with spinach & almonds; sticky toffee pudding. **Value tip:** set 2-crs L £10. **Details:** NW of Lewes; 9 pm, Fri & Sat 10 pm; closed Mon & Sun D; no Amex; no smoking.*

Gravetye Manor £ 60 🅰★
Vowels Ln RH19 4LJ (01342) 810567
*This "memorable" family-run Elizabethan country house hotel – with its famously "beautiful" garden – certainly has the potential to offer the "perfect rural eating experience"; the standard of the cooking – not the key attraction in recent times – is currently on an up. / **Sample dishes:** pavé of foie gras; roast John Dory; pannetone with poached peaches. **Value tip:** set 2-crs L £23.
Details: www.gravetyemanor.co.uk; 2m outside Turner's Hill; 9.30 pm; no Amex; jacket & tie required; no smoking; children: babies and children 7+ welcome. **Accommodation:** 18 rooms, from £190.*

Drovers Inn £ 30
5 Bridge St EH40 3AG (01620) 860298
*Thin feedback this year on the upstairs restaurant at this coaching inn off the A1; such as there is praises "great pub food in the Scottish country tradition". / **Sample dishes:** griddled black pudding & bacon in pepper sauce; rabbit with caramelised carrots & shallots; meringue with red berry sauce. **Details:** by A1; 9.30 pm; no smoking area.*

Blue Lion £ 32 🅰★
DL8 4SN (01969) 624273
*"Hard to find, but worth the effort", this "very attractive" coaching inn has a huge fan club on account of its "peerless" combination of a "stunning" Dales location, "splendid" beer and "very good" food. / **Sample dishes:** mussels in white wine & garlic; sautéed beef with red wine & mushroom sauce; pineapple tarte Tatin with liquorice ice cream. **Details:** between Masham & Leyburn on A6108; 9.30 pm; no Amex. **Accommodation:** 12 rooms, from £69.*

The Mirabelle
The Grand Hotel £ 45 ★★
King Edwards Pde BN21 4EQ (01323) 412345
*"Surprisingly good"; the pukka dining room at this huge five-star hotel is that all too rare beast – a "confident", "truly grand", "fine dining" experience, and one to which "old-fashioned" and "attentive" service makes no small contribution. / **Sample dishes:** salmon terrine with sweet pepper coulis; pork with Cumberland stuffing & Bramley apple sauce; warm toffee & date pudding.
Details: www.grandeastbourne.co.uk; 10 pm; closed Mon & Sun; jacket & tie required at D; no smoking; children: 14+. **Accommodation:** 152 rooms, from £159.*

Haxted Mill £ 42

Haxted Rd TN8 6PU (01732) 862914

"Very good summer lunches by the mill pond" are just one feature of this former mill, picturesquely located in the Eden Valley, the quality of whose English cooking is regulars claim "a closely maintained local secret". / **Sample dishes:** spinach & watercress salad with Roquefort; Dover sole with lobster & prawn sauce; tarte Tatin of figs & honey. **Details:** www.haxtedmill.co.uk; between Edenbridge & Lingfield; 9 pm; closed Mon & Sun D (& Sat L in winter); no Amex; no smoking.

EDINBURGH, CITY OF EDINBURGH 9–4C

A few years ago, describing Edinburgh was easy – it had quite a lot of solid, slightly uninspiring, 'traditional' restaurants, but not much else. If you wanted trendy, you went to the *Atrium* (whose rarity value arguably won it a lot more attention than it deserved), and for a foodie treat you sought out the café behind *Valvona & Crolla*.

The traditional establishments are still going strong, and some of them are really quite good – *Café St-Honoré*, *Dubh Prais*, *Jacksons*, *Martins* and (in expense account territory) *Number One*. For an experience (if not necessarily a culinary one), the *Witchery by the Castle* has long been of note.

Recent years, however, have seen the establishment of *Restaurant Martin Wishart* – the modern culinary champion the city used so signally to lack, and, in the summer of 2001, *Rogue*. If press accounts are correct, this latter is a fusion of fashionable form and substance so successful that it would be notable even in the English capital. At a less heady level, places making waves include *Apartment* and *The Marque*.

As with other cities, fame does not necessarily equate to quality. With its views of the castle, *The Tower* attracts more commentary than any other establishment in the city – rather a lot of it saying that it should be better.

Leith's waterfront offers a concentration of good, mid-priced all-rounders rare in the UK, including *Fisher's Bistro*, *Shore* and *Skippers* and, a short walk away, the charming *Vintners Rooms*.

Vegetarians (*Bann UK*, *Black Bo's*) and curry-fans (*Kalpna*, *Khushi's*) are also well catered for.

Ann Purna £ 18

44-45 St Patrick's Sq EH8 9ET (0131) 662 1807

"Near the more-fêted Kalpna" – but not completely eclipsed by it – this "exceptionally friendly", if rather basic Gujerati vegetarian café is recommended for its "good" and "cheap" cuisine. / **Sample dishes:** mixed vegetable pakoras; okra masala; gulab jaman (Indian sweets). **Value tip:** set 3-crs L £5.95. **Details:** 10.30 pm; closed Sat L & Sun L; no Amex or Switch; no smoking; children: 10+.

Apartment £ 25 🄰★

7-13 Barclay Pl EH10 4HN (0131) 228 6456

With its "fast, funky and fun" environment and "affordable modern cuisine", this "youthful" and "innovative" yearling seems to have hit a more consistent stride, and continues to draw a strong following to its less-than-obvious location, in the far reaches of the Old Town. / **Sample dishes:** wild mushrooms with aubergine & sweet potato; peppered rib-eye steak & fries; profiteroles with Cointreau sauce. **Details:** between Tollcross & Bruntsfield; 11 pm; D only Mon-Fri, L only Sat & Sun; no Amex; no smoking area.

The Atrium   **£ 40**

10 Cambridge St EH1 2ED   (0131) 228 8882

Last year's better performance was, it seems, a blip at this well-known trendy venue; some still proclaim the place, particularly the ambience, as "totally wonderful", but all the old complaints – an "unappealing" menu, "off-hand" service and "poor" value – are once again very much in evidence. / **Sample dishes:** *scallops & crabs with glazed artichokes; roast pigeon with wilted spinach; warm autumn berries.* **Value tip:** *set 2-crs L £14.* **Details:** *by the Usher Hall; 10 pm; closed Sat L & Sun.*

Bann UK   **£ 30**   A★

5 Hunter Sq EH1 1QW   (0131) 226 1112

"Simple" and "well-cooked" fare served by "well-trained" staff in a "trendy", "modern" setting again proves a winning formula for this "smart veggie, just off the Royal Mile". / **Sample dishes:** *aubergine cannelloni; bangers & mash; coconut & lime brûlée.*
Details: *www.scoot.co.uk/bann1/; 11 pm; no smoking area.*

Black Bo's   **£ 29**   ★

57-61 Blackfriar's St EH1 1NB   (0131) 557 6136

"Imaginative veggie food in funky surroundings" is the proposition at this "rough and ready, but intimate" and "welcoming" bar/restaurant, near the Royal Mile. / **Sample dishes:** *sun-dried tomato & smoked tofu roulade; aubergine & leeks with Parmesan crust; almond tart.* **Details:** *www.blackbos.com; 10.30 pm; D only, except Fri & Sat open L & D; no Amex.*

blue bar café   **£ 30**

10 Cambridge St EH1 2ED   (0131) 221 1222

Although the food "can be very good" and "imaginative", the Atrium's less ambitious bar/café sibling suffers from an "echoey and unpleasantly noisy" setting and very indifferent service; fans don't mind, as the place remains "very trendy", but others find it "pretentious" and feel "you don't get value for money". / **Sample dishes:** *char-grilled tuna niçoise; sea bream with tomato & courgette galette; apple tart with calvados parfait.* **Value tip:** *set 2-crs L £9.* **Details:** *by the Usher Hall; 10.45 pm; closed Sun; no smoking area; children: before 8 pm only.*

Le Café St-Honoré   **£ 37**   A★

34 NW Thistle Street Ln EH2 1EA   (0131) 226 2211

"On a good day, you could be at a Parisian bistro", at this "charming" and "efficient" spot, hidden away in the New Town; the "good, traditional" French fare "never disappoints" its loyal clientèle, but the place does get "very busy" and can be "noisy". / **Sample dishes:** *duck with poached figs & orange mash; sea bass with chilli boxty bread; tarte Tatin.* **Value tip:** *set 2-crs pre-th £13.50.* **Details:** *between George St and Queen St; 10.15 pm; closed Sat L & Sun; no smoking area.*

La Cuisine d'Odile   **£ 15**   ★

13 Randolph Cr EH3 7TT   (0131) 225 5685

A "great" lunch (some say it's "the best value in town") is to be had at this basement café (with garden), which – as you might hope for part of the Insitut Français – offers "a real taste of France"; you can BYO at modest cost. / **Sample dishes:** *sardine & lemon pâté; duck & pigeon casserole with mushroom sauce; citrus, coconut & kiwi tart.* **Value tip:** *set 2-crs L £6.65.* **Details:** *between Dean Bridge & Charlotte Square; L only; closed Mon & Sun; no credit cards.*

Daniel's   **£ 25**

88 Commercial St EH6 6LX   (0131) 553 5933

Fans praise the "good", robust Alsatian dishes and "well-priced wine list" at this "noisy" and "brightly lit" Leith café, near the waterfront; as, ever, though, feedback is too variable to win it an unreserved recommendation. / **Sample dishes:** *tarte flambé; duck confit with spring greens; spicy ice cream terrine.*
Details: *www.edinburghrestaurants.co.uk/daniels.html; 10 pm; no smoking area.*

The Dial £ 23 ★

44 George IV Bridge EH1 1EJ (0131) 225 7179

*"High-quality", "modern Scottish" cuisine has earned a good name for this "post-modern" Old Town basement; its offbeat décor can seem a mite "sterile" nowadays, however, perhaps explaining why feedback is limited. / **Sample dishes:** trout & parsley fishcakes; Scottish salmon with citrus butter; white chocolate cheesecake. **Value tip:** set 3-crs L £8.95. **Details:** on George IV Bridge off the Royal Mile; 11 pm.*

Dubh Prais £ 34 ★

123b High St EH1 1SG (0131) 557 5732

*"Fabulous" Scottish cooking (making much use of local ingredients) and "great" service make it well worth seeking out this cramped, hidden-away basement, just off the Royal Mile; "a change of décor", though, might do the place no harm. / **Sample dishes:** kedgeree; lamb cutlets with tomato & rosemary sauce; lemon shortcake. **Value tip:** set 2-crs L £10. **Details:** www.bencraighouse.co.uk; 10.30 pm; closed Mon, Sat L & Sun.*

Fisher's Bistro £ 32 Ⓐ★

1 The Shore EH6 6QW (0131) 554 5666

*"Wonderful (if you have the foresight to book)" – "excellent seafood, varying daily" and a "fantastic" atmosphere draw a huge following to this "friendly", "lively" bistro, "trendily-located" on the Leith waterfront; it now has a larger offshoot in New Town, at 58 Thistle St (tel 0131 225 5109). / **Sample dishes:** seafood soup; Dover sole in garlic butter; Turkish delight in brandy snaps. **Details:** on Leith shorefront; 10.30 pm.*

(Fitz) Henry £ 35

19 Shore Pl EH6 6SW (0131) 555 6625

*Unsurprisingly, the year which saw a change of ownership saw unsettled feedback on this well-known, rather baroque warehouse-conversion, a short step from Leith's waterfront; the "imaginative" chef Hubert Lamort served under the previous regime, however, so let's hope the place will re-establish itself as a "consistently good" all-rounder. / **Sample dishes:** pan-fried ox tongue & asparagus salad; braised lamb with polenta & Parmesan mash; pine kernel tart with honey ice cream. **Value tip:** set 3-crs L £16.50. **Details:** www.fitzhenrys.com; 10 pm, Fri & Sat 10.30 pm; closed Sun.*

Henderson's £ 19

94 Hanover St EH2 1DR (0131) 225 2131

*Its dated formula doesn't please everyone, but this self-service "vegetarian extravaganza" – in business since 1965 – still wins more bouquets than brickbats for its "reliable" standards and "cheap" prices; its basement premises, near Princes Street, are enlivened by live music nightly. / **Sample dishes:** vegetable soup; baked aubergine & tomato topped with Mozzarella; banoffi pie. **Details:** www.hendersonsofedinburgh.co.uk; 10 pm; closed Sun; no smoking area.*

Indian Cavalry Club £ 25

3 Atholl Pl EH3 8HP (0131) 228 3282

*"Delicately flavoured dishes" still win support for this smart, colonial-style subcontinental; sometimes "shambolic" service, however, contributes to an impression that it's "not as consistent as it was". / **Sample dishes:** mixed kebabs; lamb passanda; Indian ice cream. **Details:** between Caledonian Hotel & Haymarket Station; 11.30 pm; no smoking area.*

Indigo (yard)　　　　　　　　£ 26

7 Charlotte Ln EH2 4QZ　(0131) 220 5603
"Forget the food" – it's the "bustling, young and lively" atmosphere
which makes this distinctively designed, all-day West End spot a
notably "hip" destination. / **Sample dishes:** moules marinière; seafood
tagliatelle with tomato & herbs; banoffi cheesecake.
Details: www.indigoyardedinburgh.co.uk; just off Queensferry St; 10 pm;
no smoking area; children: 12+.

Jacksons　　　　　　　　£ 36　　　★

209 High St EH1 1PZ　(0131) 225 1793
Tucked away in a "great" Royal Mile location – this long-established
basement spot may be "quite expensive", but it provides
"attentive" service and some "excellent" Scottish dishes. / **Sample
dishes:** warm salad of roast monkfish in prosciutto; saddle of lamb with garlic
pearls; crème brûlée with cinnamon shortbread. **Value tip:** set 3-crs L £9.
Details: www.jacksons-restaurant.com; 10.30 pm, Fri & Sat 11 pm.

Kalpna　　　　　　　　£ 18　　　★

2-3 St Patrick Sq EH8 9EZ　(0131) 667 9890
"Reputedly the best Indian in town" – though it's not much to look
at, and there is the odd let-down, most reporters heap praise on
the "fantastic" Gujerati vegetarian fare served at this "perennial
favourite", a hugely popular destination, near the University.
/ **Sample dishes:** paneer tikka; mushroom & spinach masala; mango kulfi.
Details: 10.30 pm; closed Sun L; no Amex or Switch; no smoking.

Khushi's　　　　　　　　£ 14　　　★

16 Drummond St EH8 9TX　(0131) 556 8996
"Everything is cooked from scratch" at this "cheap and cheerful",
family-run canteen near the University, which has been in business
for over half a century; "good meatballs", "excellent vegetable
dishes" and "the best chapatis" are typical of its simple Indian
scoff. / **Sample dishes:** vegetable pakoras; chicken curry; kulfi.
Details: next to New Festival Theatre; 9 pm; closed Sun; no credit cards.

Loon Fung　　　　　　　　£ 25

2 Warriston Pl EH3 5LE　(0131) 556 1781
*The interior of this Canonmills restaurant may be in "traditional"
style* – "British Chinese", that is – but its reliable cooking makes the
place "a firm favourite with the locals". / **Sample dishes:** chicken &
sweetcorn soup; beef in black bean sauce; ice cream. **Details:** nr Botanical
Gardens; 11.30 pm, Fri & Sat 12.30 am; closed Sat L & Sun L.

Maison Bleue　　　　　　　　£ 24

36-38 Victoria St EH1 2GW　(0131) 226 1900
*The "French but eclectic" cooking at this "slightly Spartan" little
chain* has quite a number of advocates, but others feel the food is
"not as good as you know it could be"; the other branches are at
8 Union St and 8 Gloucester St. / **Sample dishes:** calamari; seared tuna
with shrimps; banana cheesecake. **Value tip:** set 3-crs L £5.90 (£6.90 on
Sun). **Details:** 11 pm; no smoking area.

Malmaison　　　　　　　　£ 32　　　✗

1 Tower Place EH6 7DB　(0131) 468 5000
This Leith design-hotel has a "good sea-view", and offers a useful
combination of "restaurant, bar, wine bar and café"; like the rest of
this initially-promising chain, however, standards far too often just
"don't come up to scratch". / **Sample dishes:** prawn & avocado
tempura; chicken in bang-bang sauce; crème brûlée. **Value tip:** set 3-crs L
£11.95. **Details:** www.malmaison.com; 11 pm. **Accommodation:** 60 rooms,
from £110.

The Marque £ 35 ★

19-21 Causewayside EH9 1QF (0131) 466 6660

"Interesting" cooking (if from a fairly "limited" menu) is making a good name for this Southside three-year-old – indeed, it's been so successful that it has spawned an offshoot by the Royal Lyceum Theatre (tel 0131 229 9859); "very good-value" set lunches and pre-theatre dinners feature at both outlets. / Sample dishes: wild mushroom soup; pan-fried pigeon with lentils; iced peach parfait. Value tip: set 2-crs L & pre-th £12.50. Details: S of Meadows; 10 pm, Fri & Sat 11 pm; closed Mon; no smoking in dining room.

Martins £ 41 ★

70 Rose St, North Ln EH2 3DX (0131) 225 3106

"Everything a trendy place is not" – this "hard to find" New Town stalwart may "lack atmosphere", but it receives nothing but praise for its "outstanding" modern Scottish cooking and for its "amiable" (if somewhat "eccentric" and "occasionally OTT") service; "the cheese explanation is almost as good as the cheese". / Sample dishes: twice-baked goat's cheese soufflé; poached John Dory with rosti potatoes; pear & honey ice cream. Value tip: set 2-crs L £12.50. Details: between Frederick St & Castle St; 10 pm; closed Mon, Sat L & Sun; no smoking; children: 7+.

Mussel Inn £ 25 ★★

61-65 Rose St EH2 2HN (0131) 225 5979

"Mussels to sell your mother for (and scallops that are even better)" are amongst the "freshest" of seafood that make this unpretentious bistro an "exciting" destination. / Sample dishes: warm salmon Caesar salad; Moroccan mussels; banoffi pie. Details: 10 pm.

Number One
Balmoral Hotel £ 51 ★

1 Princes St EH2 2EQ (0131) 557 6727

Even those who say this grand hotel dining room is "still Edinburgh's premier restaurant" admit that its "businesslike" basement setting "can lack atmosphere"; it retains "high standards" though, and makes a particularly good-value lunch destination. / Sample dishes: crab & avocado salad with caviar; Dover sole roulade with langoustines; rice pudding with basil sorbet. Value tip: set 3-crs L £15.50. Details: www.thebalmoralhotel.com; above Waverley Station; 10 pm, Fri & Sat 10.30 pm; closed Sat L & Sun L; no smoking area. Accommodation: 189 rooms, from £215.

Le Petit Paris £ 27 Ⓐ

38-40 Grassmarket EH1 2JU (0131) 226 2442

With its "very French" feel, this "bijou bistro" near the Castle lives up to its name for most reporters; the menu is "limited", but generally offers "good value". / Sample dishes: goat's cheese & walnut salad; chicken in red wine sauce with baby onions; crème caramel. Details: www.petitparis-restaurant.co.uk; near the Castle; 11 pm; no Amex.

Point Hotel £ 20 Ⓐ

34 Bread St EH3 9AF (0131) 221 5555

An "arty", "modern" hotel dining room, which – with its "very reasonably priced", "straightforward" cooking and "very attentive" staff – "offers something for everyone". / Sample dishes: smoked chicken salad with pineapple salsa; frittata of courgette & broccoli; champagne sorbet with raspberries. Details: www.point-hotel.co.uk; 10 pm; closed Sun. Accommodation: 140 rooms, from £95.

Restaurant Martin Wishart £ 43 ★★
54 The Shore EH6 6RA (0131) 553 3557
Martin Wishart is "one of the UK's celebrity-chefs-to-be", and the "exquisite" and "exceptionally creative" cooking on display at his Leith waterfront establishment is "unlike anything else you can find in Edinburgh or Glasgow"; service is "friendly" and "efficient" too. / **Sample dishes:** guinea fowl with leek cream & veal sweetbreads; daube of beef with root vegetables; raspberry & almond tart. **Value tip:** set 3-crs L £15.50. **Details:** www.martin-wishart.co.uk; nr Royal Yacht Britannia; 10 pm; closed Mon, Sat L & Sun; no Amex; no smoking before 10 pm.

Rhodes & Co £ 31 ✗
3-15 Rose St EH2 2YU (0131) 220 9190
"Overpriced, mediocre, and unimaginative" – reporters are forthright in their denunciation of the "really poor" food too often served up at this "overstretched" operation in Jenners department store; "Gary, pay a visit!". / **Sample dishes:** smoked haddock tart; roast beef & Yorkshire pudding; pear parfait. **Details:** 10.30 pm; closed Sun.

Rogue £ 32
67 Morrison St EH3 8BU (0131) 228 2700
A summer opening precluded our reporters commenting on David Ramsden's (ex- (Fitz)Henry's) trendy new bar/restaurant in the Scottish Widows building, but it would be fair to say that – judging from the deluge of positive newspaper reviews – it's pretty darn cutting edge for Auld Reekie. / **Sample dishes:** ox tongue with Arran mustard sauce; guinea fowl with lemon & parsley couscous; summer fruits in jelly. **Details:** www.rogues-uk.com; 11 pm; closed Sun D.

Sept £ 30
7 Old Fishmarket Close EH1 1RW (0131) 225 5428
A "good location" – "down a cobbled lane" – adds lustre to this "small" and "cosy" bistro whose menu features an extensive selection of crêpes; fans say its "good-value prices" make it well suited "for a casual meal", but there are those very "disappointed" by its rather dated standards. / **Sample dishes:** grilled goat's cheese; rack of lamb with roast vegetables; banana & chocolate crepe. **Value tip:** set 3-crs L £7.50. **Details:** 10.30 pm, Fri 11.30 pm; no smoking area.

The Shore £ 28 🄰★
3-4 The Shore EH6 6QW (0131) 553 5080
With its "great" atmosphere, this "very crowded" bar/restaurant on the Leith waterfront also wins strong praise from fans who laud its "superb, simply cooked fresh seafood"; one or two "expected more" of the cooking, however, and the "welcoming" service can be "slow". / **Sample dishes:** carrot & tomato soup; lemon sole with parsley butter; mango & ginger cheesecake. **Value tip:** set 2-crs L £13. **Details:** www.edinburghrestaurants.co.uk/shore.html; 10 pm; no smoking in dining room.

Siam Erawan £ 27
48 Howe St EH3 6TH (0131) 226 3675
It attracts only a modest level of commentary, but this long-established New Town basement can deliver some "fresh" and "flavourful" Thai cooking. / **Sample dishes:** sweet marinated pork skewers; sea bass steamed with lime & lemongrass; banana waffle & ice cream. **Details:** 10.45 pm; no Amex.

Skippers £ 31 🄰★
1a Dock Pl EH6 6UY (0131) 554 1018
The setting may be "pokey", "oddly decorated" and rather "crowded", but this "intimate" and "relaxed" Leith bistro is "always friendly and welcoming", and serves "good quality, no-nonsense fish". / **Sample dishes:** grilled sardines with Parmesan toast; sautéed scallops with smoked haddock risotto; cheese & biscuits. **Value tip:** set 3-crs L £13.50. **Details:** www.skippers.co.uk; 10 pm.

Stac Polly £ 37

29-33 Dublin St EH3 6NL (0131) 556 2231

A loyal fan club says there's an "enjoyable atmosphere" and some "gorgeous" modern Scottish cooking to be had at this New Town stalwart; its ambience can seem rather "stark", though, and its also "not-terribly-fancy" West End basement sibling (8-10 Grindlay St, tel 0131 229 5405) is preferred by some. / Sample dishes: pork belly & streaky bacon terrine; swordfish with peppered asparagus; coconut sponge with lime syrup. Details: www.stacpolly.co.uk; 10.30 pm; closed Sun L; no smoking area.

Sukhothai £ 25 ★

23 Brougham Pl EH3 9JU (0131) 229 1531

"Great food at great prices" makes this Tollcross Thai a consistently popular destination. / Sample dishes: spring rolls; Thai green curry with aubergine; banana fritters. Details: nr Kings Theatre; 10.30 pm; closed Tue L.

Suruchi £ 25

14a Nicolson St EH8 9DH (0131) 556 6583

It's not just the "unusual menu in Scots dialect" which makes it worth knowing about this Indian opposite the Festival Theatre – the dishes offer some "interesting variations" on the recipes we all know and love, and are "impressively presented". / Sample dishes: pakoras; chicken tikka; kulfi. Details: opp Edinburgh Festival Theatre; 11.30 pm; closed Sun L; no Amex.

Susies £ 15 ★

51-53 West Nicolson St EH8 9DB (0131) 667 8729

"Solid veggie cooking" which "never lets you down" makes this rustic-looking, cafeteria-style spot a popular destination near the University; the place is licensed, but you can BYO. / Sample dishes: falafel with houmous; chilli bean enchiladas; pear frangipane flan. Details: opp Pear Tree pub; 9 pm; closed Sun (except Festival time); no credit cards; no smoking area; no booking.

Thai Orchid £ 28 ★

44 Grindlay St EH3 9AP (0131) 228 4438

"Spicy" but "well balanced" Thai cooking makes this small oriental off Lothian Road a handy local destination. / Sample dishes: mixed Thai starters; Thai green prawn curry; sticky rice & mango. Details: 10.45 pm; closed Sat L & Sun L.

Tinelli's £ 26

139 Easter Rd EH7 5QA (0131) 652 1932

It you're looking for a "basic" and "old-fashioned" neighbourhood Italian experience, Giancarlo Tinelli's fixture, near Leith Links, can produce some "delicious" results. / Sample dishes: pasta with spinach; sirloin steak with Parma ham; cassata. Details: 11 pm; closed Mon & Sun; no Switch.

The Tower
Museum of Scotland £ 40

Chambers St EH1 1JF (0131) 225 3003

"A great view of the Castle" certainly helps make this top-floor museum restaurant an "impressive" venue (and one that's particularly "romantic" at night); many find its approach distinctly "pretentious", though, and "snotty" service contributes to an overall assessment that it "does not live up to expectations". / Sample dishes: prawn cocktail; cured salmon with avocado salad; chocolate truffle torte. Value tip: set 2-crs pre-th £12. Details: www.tower-restaurant.com; at top of Museum of Scotland; 11 pm; no smoking.

Valvona & Crolla £ 34 ★
19 Elm Row EH7 4AA (0131) 556 6066
"Simple ingredients are served without fuss" at the "down-to-earth"
café adjoining this famous Italian deli and wine merchants of over
half a century's standing, and "excellent shop wines with
reasonable corkage" make it an œnophile's delight; it's "a mite
pricey", though, and the odd Sassenach heretic insists that "in
London, it would be thought ordinary". / Sample dishes: marinated
olives; Scottish beef salad; chocolate torte. Details: www.valvonacrolla.co.uk;
at top of Leith Walk, nr Playhouse Theatre; 5 pm; closed Sun; no smoking.

Vintners Rooms £ 40 𝔸★
87 Giles St EH6 6BZ (0131) 554 6767
"Very classy all round" – these "relaxed" and "atmospheric" 16th-
century Leith premises (with arguably "the most romantic dining
room in the UK") are "ideal for a special occasion"; most reporters
find the cooking "interesting" and "beautifully presented", too, but
'off' nights are not unknown. / Sample dishes: West coast oysters;
guinea fowl with spiced Puy lentils; summer pudding. Value tip: set 3-crs L
£15. Details: www.thevintnersrooms.demon.co.uk; 9.30 pm; closed Sun;
no smoking in dining room.

The Waterfront £ 29 𝔸
1c Dock Pl EH6 6LU (0131) 554 7427
"It's worth the wait for a table in the (non-smoking) conservatory"
at this popular fixture on the Leith waterfront; some are distinctly
unimpressed by the cooking, but others think it "surprisingly good
for a pub with a nice atmosphere and a view". / Sample
dishes: grilled sardines with feta & chickpeas; swordfish with hot & sour sauce;
white chocolate & Bailey's cheesecake. Details: nr Royal Yacht Britannia;
9.30 pm, Fri & Sat 10 pm; no smoking area; children: 5+ at D.

The Witchery by the Castle £ 45 𝔸
352 Castlehill, The Royal Mile EH1 2NF (0131) 225 5613
There's a "fantastically bewitching" atmosphere at this "magical"
and "opulent" hide-away, near the castle, both in the charming
'Secret Garden' and "dark and buzzy" Witchery proper; however
food that's "very average apart from the price" and "poor" service
makes a visit here "very disappointing" for quite a lot of reporters.
/ Sample dishes: Fife crab salad; lobster with herb butter & chips; rum baba.
Value tip: set 2-crs L & pre/post-th £9.95. Details: www.thewitchery.com;
11.30 pm. Accommodation: 2 rooms, from £195.

EGLINGHAM, NORTHUMBERLAND 8–1B

Tankerville Arms £ 25
15 The Village NE66 2TX (01665) 578444
You're "lucky to get a table on a Saturday evening" at this "friendly"
country coaching inn set in "lovely countryside", whose tasty nosh is
acclaimed by most (if not quite all) reporters. / Sample dishes: roast
sea bream salad; venison with oyster mushrooms; lemon & lime cheesecake.
Details: 9 pm; no smoking in dining room.

ELSTEAD, SURREY 3–3A

Woolpack £ 25
The Green GU8 6HD (01252) 703106
Is this "Surrey's best dining pub"? – many laud the "enormous
portions of delicious grub" and "consistent all-round performance"
here, though some fear "it's in danger of becoming too popular".
/ Sample dishes: deep-fried calamari; beef, ale & horseradish casserole; fruit
pavlova. Details: 7m SW of Guildford, on village green; 9.45 pm; no Amex;
no booking.

Old Fire Engine House £ 33

25 St Mary's St CB7 4ER (01353) 662582

This "friendly" and "homely" fixture of over 30 year's standing certainly still has many advocates who say it "brings traditional English cooking to life"; complaints remain, however, regarding the "unchanging menu", and sceptics say it's become a "flair-free" establishment, like "an expensive tea shop". / **Sample dishes:** smoked eel; roast lamb with mint & lemon stuffing; coffee meringue cake. **Details:** 9 pm; closed Sun D; no Amex; no smoking area.

36 on the Quay £ 49 ★

47 South St PO10 7EG (01243) 375592

"Exceptionally fine food" ("with high prices to match") makes this "charming harbour site" well worth seeking out; it's best to go in a relaxed frame of mind, though, as service can be "very slow". / **Sample dishes:** pan-fried mullet with pesto; scallops with chicken & goose liver sausage; quartet of lemon desserts. **Value tip:** set 3-crs L £20.95. **Details:** www.36onthequay.co.uk; off A27 between Portsmouth & Chichester; 10 pm; closed Mon L, Sat L & Sun; no smoking in dining room.

Epworth Tap £ 32

DN9 1EU (01427) 873333

This well-known rustic bistro became "something of an institution" under its former owners; under the new regime, many say that the "food is still of a good standard", but some say that the notable wine list is "not quite what it was". / **Sample dishes:** grilled goat's cheese with Waldorf salad; rack of lamb with roasted vegetable broth; steamed syrup pudding. **Details:** 3m from M180, J2; 9.30 pm; closed Mon, Tue, Thu L, Fri L, Sat L & Sun; no Amex; no smoking.

Good Earth £ 33

14-18 High St KT10 9RT (01372) 462489

"Good, if a little pricey" – the verdict on this "reliable" and "comfortable", if slightly "sterile", Chinese restaurant of long standing remains very much the same as it ever was. / **Sample dishes:** spicy spare ribs; Mongolian lamb; toffee apples & ice cream. **Details:** www.goodearthgroup.co.uk; 11 pm.

Gilbey's £ 30

82-83 High St SL4 6AF (01753) 855182

With "a large conservatory at the rear", the premises still known to some as the Eton Wine Bar (still under the same ownership) are much bigger than they at first appear; even some fans admit that the "workmanlike" cooking is "nothing special", but the emphasis on "good, fairly priced wine" remains, as does the "pleasant" and "relaxed" atmosphere. / **Sample dishes:** caramelised red onion & walnut salad; confit duck leg; deep-fried banana. **Details:** www.gilbeygroup.co.uk; 5 mins walk from Windsor Castle; 10.30 pm, Fri & Sat 11 pm.

EVERSHOT, DORSET

2–4B

Summer Lodge £ 50

Summer Lodge DT2 0JR (01935) 83424

Reports were a touch more mixed this year on the "formal" dining room of this rural country house hotel; to fans it remains an utter "treat of a place" on account of its "slick" and inventive food and its "lovely" setting (including a beautiful walled garden) – to critics it seems "not overly imaginative" and "a bit starchy". / Sample dishes: seared scallops with cauliflower fritters; venison with root vegetable purée; trio of chocolate desserts. Value tip: set 2-crs L £12.50. Details: www.summerlodgehotel.com; 12m NW of Dorchester on A37; 9.30 pm; jacket required; no smoking in dining room; children: 7+. Accommodation: 17 rooms, from £135.

EVESHAM, WORCESTERSHIRE

2–1C

Evesham Hotel £ 32 ★

Coopers Ln WR11 6DA (01386) 765566

"Family-run" and "friendly" – this "eccentric" hotel is "not part of a chain, and it shows", not least in the "quality and individuality" of its cooking, and the "incredible" wine list. / Sample dishes: Roquefort mousse with shortbread biscuits; monkfish with butter noodles; white chocolate cheesecake. Details: www.eveshamhotel.com; 9.30 pm; no smoking. Accommodation: 40 rooms, from £103.

EWEN, GLOUCESTERSHIRE

2–2C

Wild Duck £ 30 🅰

Drakes Island GL7 6BY (01285) 770310

It's the "great" atmosphere which is the special attraction of this bustling old inn – "the food is not especially exciting, but reasonably well done". / Sample dishes: crispy duck salad; swordfish with coriander couscous; roast figs with gingerbread biscuits. Details: www.thewildduckinn.co.uk; 10 pm. Accommodation: 11 rooms, from £80.

EXETER, DEVON

1–3D

Brazz £ 28 🅰

10-12 Palace Gate EX1 1JU (01392) 252525

"Vastly superior to the sister restaurant in Taunton" – this "stylish" new brasserie is highly praised as a "buzzing", "cool and trendy place in the heart of the town"; that said, though portions are "generous", both food and service can be "variable". / Sample dishes: mushroom brioche; chicken with lemon leeks & wild mushroom sauce; chocolate brownie with white chocolate sauce. Details: 10.30 pm, Fri & Sat 11 pm.

Double Locks £ 23 🅰

Canal Banks, Alphington EX2 6LT (01392) 256947

"What a setting!" – though that's not the only reason people praise this "highly entertaining" canalside pub near the centre of town, and its "extensive" menu is "very reasonably priced". / Sample dishes: mushrooms & blue cheese on toast; spinach pie; sticky toffee pudding. Details: through Marsh Barton industrial estate, follow dead-end track over bridges to end of towpath; 10.30 pm; no Amex.

Michael Caines
Royal Clarence Hotel £ 41 ★

Cathedral Yd EX1 1HD (01392) 310031

Consultant chef Michael Caines made his name at the most famous of West Country hotels (where he still works) – his "Gidleigh Park food at affordable prices" has made this "elegant" new restaurant "a very welcome addition to Exeter"; there were a few "disappointments", though, with "iffy" service the most common specific complaint. / Sample dishes: oyster & squid salad; roast brill with red wine sauce; chocolate & coffee tart. Value tip: set 2-crs L £15. Details: www.michaelcaines.com; 10 pm; no smoking. Accommodation: 56 rooms, from £110.

Thai Orchid   **£ 27**

5 Cathedral Yd EX1 1HJ   (01392) 214215

"Lovely set banquets" are particularly praised at this "authentic" oriental, which benefits from an "intimate" ambience and a "fantastic location right by the Cathedral".
/ **Sample dishes:** hot & sour mushroom soup; stir-fried pork & peppers; fresh pineapple. **Value tip:** 20% discount on all meals 6.30 pm-8.30 pm. **Details:** www.thaiorchid.co.uk; next to Exeter Cathedral; 10.30 pm; closed Sun; no Amex.

FARNHAM, SURREY   3–3A

Vienna   **£ 39**   ★

112 West St GU9 7HH   (01252) 722978

"Consistent" results from a "complex" menu – with an "exceptional fish" a highlight – make this "small town restaurant" quite a "crowd-puller"; some find the place a touch "stuffy", but the more general view is that it's "warm" and "cosy". / **Sample dishes:** crab cannelloni; chicken stuffed with salmon; cappuccino brûlée. **Details:** 10.30 pm; closed Sun; no Amex or Switch; no smoking area; children: 5+.

FAVERSHAM, KENT   3–3C

The Dove   **£ 32**   ★

Plum Pudding Ln ME13 9HB   (01227) 751360

This may look like a "simple village pub with a small stripped-pine dining room", but the "unusual", "varied" menu is "of restaurant quality", and it's "nicely presented" too. / **Sample dishes:** spring onion & crab risotto; duck with lentils & foie gras; baked chocolate pudding. **Details:** 9 pm; closed Mon, Tue D & Sun D; no Amex; booking essential.

Read's   **£ 51**   🅐★

MacNade Manor, Canterbury Rd ME13 8XE   (01795) 535344

Even in its old premises (a "hideous" converted supermarket) fans of this long-established, "family-run" fixture proclaimed a "very civilised" experience with "consistently good" cooking and "gracious" service; its new (since mid-2001) quarters – an eighteenth century Georgian manor house in four acres of garden – could hardly be in starker contrast, and this could now become quite a destination. / **Sample dishes:** smoked haddock platter; roast lamb with provençal vegetables; rice pudding crème brûlée. **Details:** www.reads.com; 9.30 pm; closed Mon & Sun. **Accommodation:** 6 rooms, from £125.

FERRENSBY, NORTH YORKSHIRE   8–4B

General Tarleton   **£ 35**

Boroughbridge Rd HG5 0QB   (01423) 340284

This "upmarket and unpubby" roadside bar/restaurant generated mixed feedback this year; many did still praise the "good food" and "excellent" wines you'd expect from an offshoot of the famous Angel at Hetton, but others declare it "not in same league", decrying "mediocre" cooking, "slow" service and a "poor" ambience. / **Sample dishes:** Pacific-style squid; char-grilled venison with fruit sauce; lemon tart & raspberry coulis. **Details:** www.generaltarleton.co.uk; 2m from A1, J48 towards Knaresborough; 9.30 pm; D only, except Sun when L only; no jeans; no smoking. **Accommodation:** 14 rooms, from £84.90.

FISHGUARD, PEMBROKESHIRE   4–4B

Three Main Street   **£ 40**   ★★

3 Main St SA65 9HG   (01348) 874275

Inez Ford & Marian Evans's small and "friendly" restaurant with rooms overlooking the harbour is an extremely "solid performer"; it offers "expertly cooked", "interesting, but unfussy" cooking, and at modest prices too. / **Sample dishes:** twice-baked crab soufflé; fillet of beef with mushrooms; orange & Grand Marnier jelly. **Details:** off town square on Newport to Cardigan road; 9 pm; closed Mon & Sun; no credit cards; no smoking in dining room. **Accommodation:** 3 rooms, from £65.

Moonfleet Manor   £ 35   ★

DT3 4ED   (01305) 786948

"Good modern cooking in an eccentric, child-friendly hotel" – one reporter neatly summarises all the key points of this Georgian manor house (with major extensions); fine views of Lyme Bay are a further attraction. / **Sample dishes:** duck liver & foie gras parfait; confit duck with olive mash & cherry sauce; caramelised rice pudding.
Details: www.moonfleetmanor.com; from Weymouth, B3157 then follow signs; 9.30 pm; no smoking; children: no children after 7.30 pm.
Accommodation: 39 rooms, from £95.

The Griffin Inn   £ 33

TN22 3SS   (01825) 722890

"A charming little traditional pub, with a more serious restaurant attached"; its "good fresh fish and the imaginative, changing menu" command widespread support, but the "occasional big disappointment" gives some cause to wonder if it's "trading on its reputation". / **Sample dishes:** pan-fried scallops with lemongrass lentils; monkfish tails with cumin, fennel & saffron sauce; pear turnover.
Details: www.thegriffininn.co.uk; off A272; 9.30 pm; closed Sun D in winter; no smoking area. **Accommodation:** 8 rooms, from £65.

White Hart Inn   £ 33

SN14 8RP   (01249) 782213

"Tucked away by a stream" – and handy for visitors to Castle Combe – this fine, "beautifully located" old inn strikes quite a number of reporters as "a real gem"; some regulars, though, note that it has "definitely suffered" since being taken into chain ownership (Eldridge Pope) a couple of years ago. / **Sample dishes:** chilli beef carpaccio with oriental pickles; roast duck & chicory in pearl barley broth; chocolate & raspberry tart. **Value tip:** set 2-crs L £10.95.
Details: on A420 between Chippenham & Bristol; 9.30 pm; no smoking area.
Accommodation: 11 rooms, from £84.

Crannog   £ 32   A★★

Town Pier PH33 7NG   (01397) 705589

"Marvellous", "fresh" seafood, "attentive" service and a "first-class" location (overlooking Loch Linnhe) make this former smokehouse a unanimously popular destination – "it can get crowded, though, and suffer accordingly". / **Sample dishes:** smoked salmon selection; fisherman's feast with dauphinoise potatoes; heather cream cheesecake. **Details:** www.crannog.net; 10 pm (9 pm Dec-Mar); no Amex; no smoking area.

Inverlochy Castle   £ 60   A

Torlundy PH33 6SN   (01397) 702177

"It surpassed all the recommendations!" – "very personal" service contributes to the overall expressions of contentment in the (relatively few) reports on this scenically-located baronial pile. / **Sample dishes:** roast duck confit & braised lentils; seared salmon with asparagus; chocolate & orange sponge. **Details:** www.inverlochy.co.uk; off A82; 9.15 pm; jacket & tie required; no smoking; children: 12+.
Accommodation: 17 rooms, from £255.

Chequers £ 26 ★
SG8 7SR (01763) 208369
This "cosy pub, steeped in history" has long had a reputation for its "outstanding" food – "well-presented game, fish and steak" and "superb puddings". / Sample dishes: Shetland mussels; grilled Dover sole; date sponge with toffee sauce. Details: on B1368 between Royston & Cambridge; 10 pm; no smoking area.

The Fox & Goose £ 32
IP21 5PB (01379) 586247
There were mixed reports this year on this well-known, "out-of-the-way" country inn; for some, it "never fails to come up trumps", while for others, its "hearty, old-school fare lacks refinement". / Sample dishes: grilled halloumi with pitta bread; roast cod with garlic mash; sticky toffee pudding. Details: off A140; 9 pm; no Amex; no smoking.

Alford Arms £ 29
HP1 3DD (01442) 864480
"Above-average" cooking and a "good welcome" help make this "upmarket pub/restaurant" a "busy" (and sometimes "noisy") destination. / Sample dishes: warm crispy duck & sesame salad; calves liver with beetroot mash; pannacotta with winter fruits. Details: nr Ashridge College, by vineyard; 10 pm; booking: max 12.

Netherton Hall £ 26 ★
Chester Rd WA6 6UL (01928) 732342
It's quite "expensive", but support remains solid for this "popular pub/restaurant" with its "interesting" range of dishes, "well-kept real ales" and "good wines by the glass". / Sample dishes: pork & duck terrine; chicken stuffed with Brie & Parma ham; Cointreau & chocolate mousse. Details: 4m from Stanlow service station; 9 pm; no smoking area.

Elephant Royale £ 31
579 Cranbrook Rd IG2 6JZ (020) 8551 7015
"Lovely flavours", "friendly service" and "live music" are among the contributors to the "great experience" reported by local supporters of this grimly-located suburban Thai (which has a new branch at the tip of the Isle of Dogs, tel 020 7987 7999). / Sample dishes: chicken satay; sweet & sour king prawns; steamed banana with coconut cream. Details: 11.30 pm.

Queen's Head £ 28
Llandudno Junction LL31 NJP (01492) 546570
A "good choice" of "consistent" cooking, "using local produce", makes this converted wheelwright's cottage worth seeking out in a thin area. / Sample dishes: asparagus & mushroom risotto; char-grilled chicken with chilli glaze; fruit pavlova. Details: 9 pm; no Amex; no smoking area; no booking, Sat D; children: 7+.

It's appropriate that Glasgow was the birthplace of Gordon Ramsay – the UK's leading chef of the moment – as the city boasts a long-established restaurant culture in a way foreign to English cities outside London. The 'big news' of the past year has been Mr Ramsay taking over at One Devonshire Gardens the restaurant now renamed *Amaryllis*, which looks set to retain its place as the city's finest.

That said, Glasgow is not currently in a 'Golden Age', and its recent superiority to Edinburgh as a restaurant destination is looking under threat. Its 'biggest' names, historically speaking – *Rogano* and the *Ubiquitous Chip* – have shone dimly in recent years. *Gamba*, however, is establishing itself as a notable destination for fish-lovers and *Stravaigin* continues to be a quirky, well-liked favourite.

On the ethnic front, the city has a lot to offer. It boasts the finest range of Indian restaurants outside London, including *Ashoka*, *Mother India*, *Mr Singh's India* and *Shish Mahal*. There are also good oriental options – *Amber Regent*, *Fusion*, *Ichiban* and *Thai Fountain* – and some good Italians, with the irrepressible *Sarti's* being a leading local institution.

Air Organic £ 26 ★
36 Kelvingrove G3 7SA (0141) 564 5200
The "rather futuristic" setting can seem "cold" nowadays, but the "fresh" and "tasty", "Pacific Rim-y" cuisine of this "trendy" Kelvingrove spot still wins almost universal acclaim. / **Sample dishes:** roast tomato & Mozzarella crostini; beef fillet bento box; white chocolate & lemon cheesecake. **Details:** nr Kelvingrove art galleries; 11 pm; no smoking area; booking: max 10 at weekends.

Amaryllis
One Devonshire Gardens £ 53 𝔸 ★
1 Devonshire Gardens G12 0UX (0141) 337 3434
Star London chef Gordon Ramsay has recently taken charge of the restaurant at this impressive townhouse hotel – already the city's top "posh" place; he's certainly raised its media profile, and an early report of the new regime suggests that chef-on-the-ground David Dempsey is maintaining the (already very high) standards set by the old one. / **Sample dishes:** lobster & langoustine ravioli in lobster bisque; venison with red cabbage & bitter chocolate sauce; chocolate fondant tart. **Details:** 1.5m from M8, J17; 11 pm; closed Sat L; no smoking; children: 12+. **Accommodation:** 35 rooms, from £145.

Amber Regent £ 35 ★
50 West Regent St G2 2RE (0141) 331 1655
An "extensive menu" and "top-class presentation" help make this city-centre spot the town's top Chinese – not, it has to be said, a contest in which there are many serious competitors. / **Sample dishes:** spring rolls; duck with garlic & plum sauce; toffee apples. **Details:** 500m from Central Station; 10.45 pm; closed Sun.

Arthouse £ 33
129 Bath St G2 2SY (0141) 221 6789
A year or so after opening, it's sad to record that this trendy hotel dining room, which started off so well, now strikes too many reporters as "so laid back it's not stylish – just lazy and pretentious". / **Sample dishes:** moules marinière; tuna with rosemary roasted sweet potatoes; berry & almond shortcake. **Value tip:** set 3-crs L £11.50. **Details:** www.arthousehotel.com; 11 pm; no smoking. **Accommodation:** 65 rooms, from £90.

Ashoka £ 26 ★

19 Ashton Ln G12 8SJ (0800) 454817

*Take note, this is not THE Ashoka – that is to say the original,
and possibly best, of Glasgow Indians of that name (which is at
108 Elderslie St, tel 0141 221 1761) – but rather the leading
member of the "excellent group of curry houses all over Glasgow"
which confusingly bears the same name (but is under different
ownership); it's a "firm family favourite" that's "highly reliable in
every sense" – fortunately, they all are!* / **Sample dishes:** vegetable &
fish pakoras; chicken in coconut & chilli sauce; 'death by chocolate' cake. **Value
tip:** set 3-crs L £5.95. **Details:** www.harlequin-leisure.co.uk; behind Hillhead
station; midnight; closed Sun L.

Babbity Bowster £ 29 Ⓐ

16-18 Blackfriar's St G1 1PE (0141) 552 5055

*"Traditional Scottish cooking (haggis, stovies, clootie dumpling
etc…)" is the culinary highlight at this "friendly" Merchant City
pub, which occupies a building designed by James Adam;
(upstairs, there's a "small, candle-lit and intimate" dining room
called Schottische, which serves some more ambitious grub along
similar lines).* / **Sample dishes:** poached Scottish oysters; beef with port &
foie gras sauce; chocolate terrine with Glayva. **Details:** 11 pm; closed Sat L &
Sun. **Accommodation:** 6 rooms, from £50.

Buttery £ 43

652 Argyle St G3 8UF (0141) 221 8188

*Though it has a pretty odd location (cut off from the city-centre
by the M8), this "formal" panelled restaurant, with its handiness
for the SECC, is still something of a natural business lunching
venue; service can be "fussy", however, and there continue to be
complaints of "food that doesn't taste as good as it looks".* / **Sample
dishes:** game terrine with pear & walnuts; salmon & smoked haddock with
chive sour cream; Scotch whisky tart with cinnamon custard. **Details:** under
Kingston Bridge; 10.30 pm; closed Sat L & Sun; no smoking area.

Café Gandolfi £ 26 Ⓐ★

64 Albion St G1 1NY (0141) 552 6813

*"You can eat a light or substantial meal" from a flexible modern
British menu at this cosy and "very enjoyable" Merchant City
favourite; "the new Buchanan Gallery branch in Habitat is also
good" (tel 0141 331 1254).* / **Sample dishes:** Piedmontese peppers
with sun-blush tomatoes; chicken fajitas with coriander salsa; lemon &
poppyseed cake. **Details:** nr Tron Theatre; 11.30 pm; no smoking area.

Café India £ 37

171 North St G3 7DA (0141) 248 4075

*This cavernous city-centre institution is one of the more "consistent"
performers in town – it serves a "brilliant selection" of "tasty"
dishes in quite a "stylish" setting.* / **Sample dishes:** pakoras; spiced lamb
with tomatoes; kulfi. **Value tip:** set 3-crs L £8.95.
Details: www.cafeindia-glasgow.com; next to Mitchell Library; midnight;
no smoking area.

Café Mao £ 25

84 Brunswick St G1 1ZZ (0141) 564 5161

*"Modern Euro-Asian food" that's mostly "fresh and interesting
(but occasionally disappoints)" has made this "trendy" spot "quite
a hit with Glasgow's jeunesse dôrée".* / **Sample dishes:** fried fishcakes;
lemongrass & chilli tiger prawns; frozen yoghurt. **Details:** www.cafemao.com;
11 pm; no smoking area.

City Merchant £ 33

97-99 Candleriggs G1 1NP (0141) 553 1577

In the heart of the Merchant City, this unpretentious spot has long been a popular destination, with quite a name for its simple seafood and game menu; this year, however, it only attracted a thin volume of reports, which spoke of "bland" food and "poorly trained" staff. / **Sample dishes:** silver anchovies; roast duck; bitter chocolate torte. **Value tip:** set 2-crs L & pre-th £12.75.
Details: www.citymerchant.co.uk; nr George Square; 11 pm; closed Sun L; no smoking area.

Crème de la Crème £ 26

1071 Argyle St G3 8LZ (0141) 221 3222

A converted cinema in a less-than-lovely area south of the West End provides the setting for one of the larger Indians in Scotland's curry capital (now under the same ownership as Café India); reporters generally approve the grub, most of which is served buffet-style. / **Sample dishes:** chicken with tomato & coriander sauce; Indian garlic chilli chicken; gulab jaman. **Details:** nr Scottish Exhibition Centre; 11 pm; closed Sun L; no smoking area.

Eurasia £ 49

150 St Vincent St G2 5NE (0141) 204 1150

Ferrier Richardson's "skilfully-prepared" and "creative" combinations can make for "an evening to remember" at his ambitious yearling in the financial district; there are those who find it "a let-down, after all the hype", however, who complain of a "colourless" ambience and "too many tastes" vying for attention. / **Sample dishes:** Thai beef broth with lime; char-grilled salmon teriyaki; banana soufflé with caramel sauce. **Value tip:** set 2-crs L £14.95.
Details: 2 mins from George Square; 11 pm; closed Sat L & Sun.

Fusion £ 19 ★

41 Byres Rd G11 5RG (0141) 339 3666

"Top sushi" and "great noodle dishes" are among the Japanese-inspired culinary attractions of this small West End oriental. / **Sample dishes:** seafood tempura; chicken yakitori; banana katsu.
Details: at very end of Byres Rd, at Dunbarton Road intersection; 10 pm, Fri & Sat 11 pm; closed Sun L; no smoking.

Gamba £ 39 ★★

225a West George St G2 2ND (0141) 572 0899

The "best and freshest seafood this side of Scotch Corner" from an "imaginative menu that works" and eminently "competent" service is a formula which "never fails to impress" almost all reporters on this "businesslike" two-year-old. / **Sample dishes:** smoked haddock & mussel tart; seared turbot with pesto mash; cinnamon sponge with sesame seed ice cream. **Value tip:** set 2-crs pre-th £10.95 (L £12.95).
Details: www.gamba.co.uk; 10.30 pm; closed Sun; children: 14+.

Gingerhill £ 28

1 Hillhead St G62 8AF (0141) 956 6515

"First-class fish" ("plus one excellent meat option") is already beginning to make something of a name for this "somewhat cramped" Milngavie spot (which, by day, is a café); chef Alan Burns formerly cooked at Paul Heathcote's establishment at Longridge. / **Sample dishes:** smoked duck with avocado & grapefruit; roasted cod & scallops with saffron leeks; Cabernet chocolate truffle with strawberries.
Details: 9.30 pm; closed Mon, Tue, Wed D & Sun D; no Amex; no smoking at D.

Gordon Yuill & Company £ 28

257 West Campbell St G2 4SQ   (0141) 572 4052

Backed by the former maître d' of Rogano's, this "bright" new brasserie is voted "best newcomer" by some reporters; doubters, however, find the food "lacking flair" and – rather ironically – suggest "more staff training" is needed; a West End sibling has opened (two are planned) at 2 Byres Rd, tel 0141 337 1145. / Sample dishes: crispy duck & watercress salad; sea bass with braised fennel; triple chocolate marquise. Details: www.gordonyuillandcompany.co.uk; 10.30 pm; closed Sun; children: 14+.

Grassroots Café £ 21

97 St Georges Rd G3 6JA   (0141) 333 0534

An "excellent" choice of "good", "fresh" dishes is winning a growing following for this veggie café, near St George's Cross – a spin-off from a nearby healthfood shop and deli. / Sample dishes: Greek dips & olives; Thai green curry; vegan chocolate cake. Details: 10 pm; mainly nonsmoking.

Groucho St Judes £ 36　Ⓐ

190 Bath St G2 4HG   (0141) 352 8800

The fusion cooking "seems to have gone off the boil", but this "relaxed" and "hip" relation of the famous London media club (here, they let in non-member riff-raff) still impresses many with its "understated elegance" and its "sophisticated" atmosphere. / Sample dishes: Gorgonzola pannacotta with figs; tiger prawn risotto; dark chocolate & cherry fudge cake. Value tip: set 2-crs L £9.50. Details: www.grouchosaintjudes.com; 10.30 pm; closed Sun L. Accommodation: 6 rooms, from £95.

Ichiban £ 14　Ⓐ★

50 Queen St G1 3DS   (0141) 204 4200

It's "not the place for a relaxed meal", but this "cheap and cheerful" noodle café is a "funky" spot, serving a wide and "interesting" range of oriental fare. / Sample dishes: assorted sushi; pork chop curry & rice; green tea. Details: www.ichiban.co.uk; 9.45 pm, Thu-Sat 10.45 pm; no smoking; no booking at weekends.

Insomnia £ 15

38-42 Woodlands Rd G3 6UR   (0141) 564 1530

"Londoners take note", says a (London-based) fan of this groovy café, near Kelvingrove Park – "an example of what 24hr dining should be". / Sample dishes: quesadillas; chicken & spinach lasagne; hot chocolate fudge cake. Details: open 24 hrs; no smoking area; no booking.

Kama Sutra £ 25　Ⓐ

331 Sauchiehall St G2 3HW   (0141) 332 0055

"A regular that doesn't let you down" – despite its OTT, camp décor, this Indian opposite the Centre for Contemporary Art wins praise for its "real style" and for cooking that's "well presented and prepared". / Sample dishes: chicken pakora; pan-fried machi fish & creamed spinach curry; ice cream. Details: www.kama-sutra-restaurant.com; midnight; closed Sun L.

Killermont Polo Club £ 23　Ⓐ

2022 Maryhill Rd G20 0AB   (0141) 946 5412

"Amazing", "beautiful" décor has helped turn this Maryhill Indian into a "very popular" destination; the "unusual" cooking is still generally praised, but incidents of "terrible", "forgetful" service contributed to a slide in ratings this year. / Sample dishes: prawn tikka; chicken stuffed with cheese & pomegranate; fruit pavlova. Details: www.killermont-polo-club.co.uk; nr Maryhill Station; 10.30 pm; closed Sun L; no smoking area.

Mitchell's   **£ 34**

157 North St G3 7DA   (0141) 204 4312

"Best when Angus Boyd is in the kitchen", this "bistro-type
restaurant" pleases some with its "unpretentious" dishes with
"a Scottish slant"; there is also a West End offshoot at 35 Ashton
Lane (tel 0141 339 2220). / *Sample dishes:* grilled squid with chorizo;
Scottish beef with crispy potatoes & mustard lentils; coconut tart with orange
sorbet. *Details:* 10.30 pm; closed Sat L & Sun; smoking discouraged; children:
12+.

Mother India   **£ 26**   ★

28 Westminster Ter G3 7RU   (0141) 221 1663

"Excellent and different" Indian cooking has made a very big name
for this "busy" (and "noisy") institution, and almost all reporters say
it "still offers the freshest, spiciest curries"; this year, however, there
were some who felt it "didn't live (fully) up to its reputation".
/ *Sample dishes:* aubergine fritters; chicken tikka passanda; gulab jaman.
Value tip: set 3-crs L £8.50. *Details:* beside Kelvingrove Hotel; 10.30 pm,
Fri & Sat 11 pm; closed Mon L, Sat L & Sun L; no Amex.

Mr Singh's India   **£ 22**   ★

149 Elderslie St G3 7JR   (0141) 204 0186

"Superb" presentation is one of the strengths of this somewhat
"unusual" Kelvingrove Park Indian, whose "very good regional
dishes" are consistently praised. / *Sample dishes:* pan-fried prawns with
lime; south Indian garlic spiced chicken; toffee pudding. *Details:* on Charing
Cross corner, nr art galleries; 11.30 pm.

Nairns   **£ 42**   ✗

13 Woodside Cr G3 7UL   (0141) 353 0707

Fans of TV-chef Nick Nairn's "designer" establishment in a
townhouse south of Kelvingrove Park hail its "imaginative" cooking
and "relaxed but stylish" atmosphere; there are still too many
critics, however, who – citing "pricey" food that's "not as good as
it looks in his books" and "grumpy" staff who "love themselves" –
write the whole performance off as "self-important tosh". / *Sample
dishes:* seafood & asparagus tartlet; potato & Brie samosa with tomato vierge;
chocolate fondant with white chocolate Mascarpone. *Value tip:* set 3-crs L
£12. *Details:* www.nairns.com; 9 pm; closed Mon & Sun; no smoking; children:
10+ at D.

Number 16   **£ 29**   ★

16 Byres Rd G11 5JY   (0141) 339 2544

It's "far too small" and "cramped", but you get "simple, first class"
food at "brilliant" prices at this "friendly" Scottish/French bistro,
near the Dumbarton Road. / *Sample dishes:* scallops & bacon with
avocado salsa; lamb with caper cream & rosemary jus; sticky toffee pudding.
Details: close to Dumbarton Rd; 10 pm; closed Sun; no Amex; no smoking
until coffee.

Parmigiana   **£ 28**

447 Great Western Rd G12 8HH   (0141) 334 0686

With its "slightly formal and old-fashioned" air, this "smart" and
"authentic" Italian of long standing marches happily on; some,
though, do rate the "decently priced" pre-theatre menu in
preference to the "expensive" à la carte. / *Sample dishes:* lobster
ravioli; fish & shellfish soup with bruschetta; lemon tart with cherries. *Value
tip:* set 3-crs pre-th £11.50. *Details:* www.laparmigiana.co.uk; at Kelvinbridge
underground station; 11 pm; closed Sun.

Puppet Theatre £ 40   A

11 Ruthven Ln G12 9BG (0141) 339 8444

"Delightful use of décor to create an intimate night-time setting" has given this interesting, rambling West End venue a name as *"a wonderful place for special occasions"*; even some fans say it's *"a bit pricey"*, but the food is usually *"reasonable"* and can be *"excellent"*. / *Sample dishes: fricassée of scallops & courgettes; lamb with fennel & potato purée; orange flower & cardamom tart.* **Details:** *nr Ashton Lane; 10.30 pm; closed Mon & Sat L; no smoking area; children: 12+.*

Rogano £ 45   A

11 Exchange Pl G1 3AN (0141) 248 4055

"Gorgeous Art Deco décor" helps make a visit to this famous establishment (modelled on the Queen Mary's staterooms) *"an incredible all-round dining experience"* for some reporters; the cooking is no better than *"reasonable"* however (especially as it's *"very expensive"*), and service can be *"slow"*.
/ *Sample dishes: tuna & salmon sushi; seared trout & noodles with Thai curry sauce; pear & peach tarte Tatin.* **Value tip:** *set 2-crs pre-th £10.95.*
Details: *www.rogano.co.uk; 10.30 pm; no smoking before 10 pm.*

Sarti's £ 26   A★

121 Bath St G2 2SZ (0141) 204 0440

"No trip to Glasgow is complete without a visit to Sarti's", declare fans of this *"cheap"*, *"friendly"* and *"wonderfully atmospheric"* institution – a *"deli-turned-restaurant"*, run by the same family for 50 years, serving *"terrific"* antipasti and pasta and *"the best pizza this side of Rome"*; it's licensed, but for modest corkage you can BYO. / *Sample dishes: minestrone soup; four cheese pizza; tiramisu.*
Details: *11 pm; no smoking area; no booking at L.*

78 St Vincent £ 38

78 St Vincent's St G2 5UB (0141) 248 7878

With its spacious surroundings, this elegant former banking hall in the city-centre can make an *"impressive"* venue; even some who say the cooking's excellent, think it's *"a touch overpriced"*, though, and others say it's *"very ordinary"* and that service is lacklustre.
/ *Sample dishes: rainbow trout with sweet pepper butter; halibut with braised fennel & rocket; white chocolate praline tart.* **Details:** *www.78stvincent.com; 2 mins from George St; 10 pm, Fri & Sat 10.30 pm; no smoking area.*

Shish Mahal £ 24   ★

66-68 Park Rd G4 (0141) 339 8256

"Still a gem after over 30 years" – *"a wide range of old favourites in hearty portions"* is served at this *"hardy perennial"* of a curry house, recently renovated in a *"modern"* style. /
Sample dishes: chicken & cashew nut curry; chicken tikka masala; gulab jaman (Indian sweets). **Details:** *www.shishmahal.co.uk; 11.30 pm; closed Sun L; no smoking area.*

Stravaigin £ 36   ★

28 Gibson St G12 8NX (0141) 334 2665

"Modern, casual and imaginative" – Colin Clydesdale's *"unpretentious but adventurous"* fixture near the University continues to be one of the favourite choices in town on account of his *"genuinely exciting"*, *"global eclectic menu with a Scottish flavour"* and the place's *"trendy"* atmosphere; there's a cheaper bar above the basement restaurant, and also a new branch nearby (Stravaigin 2, 8 Ruthven Ln, tel 0141 334 7165).
/ *Sample dishes: rabbit with sage gnocchi & tomato essence; spiced pear, pimento & walnut tortilla; chocolate & vanilla bread & butter pudding.*
Details: *www.stravaigin.com; 1 am; closed Mon, Tue L, Wed L & Thu L; no smoking before 10 pm.*

Thai Fountain £ 32 ★

2 Woodside Cr G3 7UL (0141) 332 1599

With its "impeccable" service and "exquisite, delicately-flavoured" food, Glasgow's original Thai restaurant is still a "classy" joint, and, in spite of being rather pricey, remains the most popular oriental in town. / **Sample dishes:** *spring rolls; Thai green curry; sticky rice.* **Details:** *www.thai-fountain.com; 11 pm, Fri & Sat midnight; closed Sun; children: 7+.*

Thirteenth Note £ 19

50-60 Kings St G1 5QT (0141) 553 1638

A "studenty" bar/venue where most reporters applaud "cheap" vegan food served in "ample" portions. / **Sample dishes:** *aubergine dip & pitta bread; veggie burger & salad; fruit crumble.* **Details:** *www.13thnote.com; 10 pm; no Amex; children: 18+ after 6.30 pm.*

Two Fat Ladies £ 37 ★

88 Dumbarton Rd G11 6NX (0141) 339 1944

"Really interesting" and "varied" food – "superb" fish is the speciality – and "charming" service have made quite a big name for this "tiny" and quirky fixture; fans say it's a "cosy" place, but others feel it "lacks atmosphere". / **Sample dishes:** *pan-fried herring salad; halibut with saffron & peppercorn sauce; flambéed banana & tequila pavlova.* **Details:** *10 pm; closed Mon, Tue L-Thu L & Sun L.*

Ubiquitous Chip £ 42 ✗

12 Ashton Ln G12 8SJ (0141) 334 5007

With its "fairytale" courtyard setting, Ronnie Clydesdale's famous West End institution (est 1971) is still thought a "stylish" haunt by diehard fans; truth to tell, though, it's "trading on its reputation", and much criticised by reporters for its "predictable", "overpriced" and over-rich Scottish cooking, and its "inept" service. / **Sample dishes:** *venison haggis 'n' neeps; shellfish custard with scallops & prawns; crannachan.* **Details:** *www.ubiquitouschip.co.uk; directly behind Hillhead underground; 11 pm.*

Yes! £ 44

22 West Nile St G1 2PW (0141) 221 8044

"Bright, crisp and formal", this well-known city-centre basement seems to be re-establishing itself after the ownership upheavals of the last couple of years – both the "beautifully-presented" modern cooking and "efficient", "individual" service were much more consistently praised this year. / **Sample dishes:** *haggis, neeps & tattie gateaux; Perthshire lamb with rosemary jus; brioche & gingerbread pudding.* **Details:** *10.30 pm; closed Mon, Tue & Sun; children: 10+.*

GODALMING, SURREY 3–3A

Bel & The Dragon £ 40 Ⓐ

Bridge St GU7 3DU (01483) 527333

This "brilliant conversion of a redundant church" is certainly "distinctive", and fans say it offers "a sumptuous setting for a meal"; cooking comes in "large portions", but some do find that "results fall short of expectations raised by the menu". / **Sample dishes:** *deep-fried Thai spring rolls; Madras chicken with yoghurt & mint; apricot & honeycomb cheesecake.* **Details:** *www.belandthedragon.co.uk; 10 pm.*

GOLCAR, WEST YORKSHIRE   5–1C

The Weavers Shed   £ 36   A ★

Knowl Rd HD7 4AN   (01484) 654284
*In an "excellent setting in old weaving shed", Steven Jackson's
"friendly" and "efficient" staff serve "tasty, locally-grown food"
that's "consistently well cooked" and "beautifully presented".
/ **Sample dishes:** warm smoked haddock mousseline; stuffed butternut
squash with winter greens; warm Eccles cake. **Value tip:** set 2-crs L £9.95.
Details: 10 pm; closed Mon, Sat L & Sun. **Accommodation:** 5 rooms,
from £55.*

GORING, BERKSHIRE   2–2D

Leatherne Bottel   £ 38   A

Bridleway RG8 OHS   (01491) 872667
*"Perfect for a summer evening", when it's a "fantastic" experience
to sit on the terrace of this comfortable Thames-side establishment
which boasts a "beautiful", tranquil setting; most reporters also
praise the "lovely", "innovative" cooking, though – as ever – there
are some who feel that the food is "not what it should be, given its
reputation and price". / **Sample dishes:** steamed shellfish with red curry;
char-grilled swordfish in Cajun spices; sticky toffee pudding.
Details: www.leathernebottel.co.uk; 0.5m outside Goring on B4009; 9 pm;
closed Sun D; children: 8+.*

GRAMPOUND, CORNWALL   1–4B

Eastern Promise   £ 27   ★

1 Moor View TR2 4RT   (01726) 883033
*A "long-established Chinese restaurant in a small Cornish village" –
and one which serves "very good food" – is quite a rarity, and if
you want a table at this "popular" establishment, you "always need
to book". / **Sample dishes:** crispy won-tons; chicken with cashew nuts;
banana fritters. **Details:** between Truro & St Austell on A390; 10 pm; closed
Mon L, Tue L, Wed, Thu L, Fri L, Sat L & Sun L; no smoking area.*

GRANGE MOOR, WEST YORKSHIRE   5–1C

Kaye Arms   £ 28   ★

29 Wakefield Rd WF4 4BG   (01924) 848385
*A "lovely pub turned restaurant" that's "hard to find, but worth it",
thanks to its "imaginative" cooking and "warm" welcome. / **Sample
dishes:** smoked duck with sweetcorn & walnuts; wild boar & Black Sheep ale
sausages; trio of desserts. **Details:** 7m W of Wakefield on A642; 9.30 pm;
no Amex; no smoking area; no booking, Sat; children: no children at D.*

GRASMERE, CUMBRIA   7–3D

Lancrigg Country House Hotel   £ 34   ★

Easedale Rd LA22 9QN   (01539) 435317
*"Vegetarian food worth coming down from the fells for" is served
at this small hotel with a charming location in the Easedale Valley.
/ **Sample dishes:** Parmesan & pine kernel soufflé; chestnut, wild mushroom &
cranberry tart; orange, sultana & pecan pudding. **Details:** www.lancrigg.co.uk;
8 pm; D only (bar meals only at L); no smoking in dining room.
Accommodation: 12 rooms, from £100, incl D.*

Michael's Nook   £ 59   ★★

LA22 9RQ   (01539) 435496
*It's "a relaxing and wonderful experience" to visit the Giffords'
long-established country house hotel, where the menus are
"exceptionally well prepared and presented" (and there's a "very
extensive wine list"); if there is a reservation, it's that the style is a
bit too "fancy" for some tastes. / **Sample dishes:** ragout of rabbit with
stuffed cabbage; roast quail with quail boudin; Bramley apple mousse.
Details: 9 pm; jacket & tie required; no smoking; children: 7+.
Accommodation: 14 rooms, from £135, incl D.*

GREAT AYTON, MIDDLESBOROUGH 8–3C

Dudley Arms £ 27

Ingleby Greenhow TS9 6LL (01642) 722526

"A country restaurant and bistro inside a popular pub"; the odd misfire is not unknown, but in general it's a "friendly" place offering "varied" and "reasonably priced" fare. / **Sample dishes:** home-cured gravadlax with dill mayonnaise; steak with salad & chips; raspberry crème brûlée. **Details:** 9.30 pm.

GREAT DUNMOW, ESSEX 3–2C

Starr £ 32 ★

Market Pl CM6 1AX (01371) 874321

"Knowledgeable" and "friendly" service helps set the right tone at this "very nice", "upmarket" pub "in the centre of the village", whose "good menu" is "always produced to a high standard". / **Sample dishes:** lobster, mango & baby spinach salad; baked halibut with parsley crust; steamed syrup pudding. **Details:** 8m E of M11, J8 on A120; 9.30 pm; closed Sun D; no jeans; no smoking. **Accommodation:** 8 rooms, from £100.

GREAT GONERBY, LINCOLNSHIRE 5–3D

Harry's Place £ 60 ★★

17 High St NG31 8JS (01476) 561780

Harry Hallam's "eccentric but amazing" dishes are "carefully prepared" using "top-quality ingredients", and served in an extraordinarily "intimate" (10-seater) setting – the dining room of the family's cottage; "if I was only allowed one meal out a year, this is where I'd go". / **Sample dishes:** mushroom soup with truffle oil; Lincolnshire woodcock with bacon & sage; chocolate mousse. **Details:** on B1174 1m N of Grantham; 9.30 pm; closed Mon & Sun; no Amex; no smoking; booking essential; children: 5+.

GREAT MILTON, OXFORDSHIRE 2–2D

Le Manoir aux Quat' Saisons £106 ★

Church Rd OX44 7PD (01844) 278881

It is "an artistic as well as a gastronomic experience" to eat at this "truly remarkable" manor house near Oxford, whose "exquisite" modern French cuisine is as much a flagship for cooking in England as it is for Raymond Blanc personally; it's "a pity about the prices", of course, and a few complain of an atmosphere verging on "Disneyesque". / **Sample dishes:** pigeon & veal kromesky with foie gras; spit-roast suckling pig with marjoram jus; strawberry jelly with rhubarb soup. **Value tip:** set 3-crs L £45. **Details:** from M40, J7 take A329; 9.30 pm; no smoking. **Accommodation:** 32 rooms, from £245.

GREAT YELDHAM, ESSEX 3–2C

White Hart £ 31 Ⓐ★

Poole St CO9 4HJ (01787) 237250

Reporters "wish there were more" like this "real gem" of a pub – a half-timbered fifteenth-century building, with "great" food, and a "fantastic" wine list; it "can get very busy". / **Sample dishes:** Galia melon & Parma ham salad; seared tuna with courgette & aubergine ragoût; baked apricot & almond tart. **Details:** between Haverhill & Halstead on A1017; 9.30 pm; no smoking.

GUERNSEY, CHANNEL ISLANDS

Christie's £ 28 Ⓐ

The Pollet GY1 W1Q (01481) 726624

This "big modern eatery" boasts a "bustling" atmosphere and "great views over the castle"; it offers a "vast" menu, realised to a "reliable" standard. / **Sample dishes:** poached egg, asparagus & salmon salad; swordfish with Mediterranean vegetables; spiced mango & coconut ice cream. **Details:** 10.30 pm.

Café de Paris   £ 30
35 Castle St GU1 3UQ (01483) 534896
*Opinions continue to differ on this "very, very French"
establishment – for fans, it offers an "it-could-be-Paris" experience,
but others find it "overpriced" for what it is , and recommend the
bistro as "better value than the restaurant". / **Sample dishes:** potato
rosti & smoked salmon; veal in butter & herbs; cheese platter.
Details: 10.30 pm; closed Sun.*

Cambio   £ 40
10 Chapel St GU1 3UH (01483) 577702
*For local reporters this "lovely" spot, in an ancient house near the
castle, is a "classic and true" Italian restaurant, serving "completely
fresh" cuisine; an 'off' experience of one non-local reporter,
however, sounds a warning note. / **Sample dishes:** Parma ham with
melon; deep-fried calamari with vegetable fritters; Amaretto mousse. **Value
tip:** set 2-crs L £10.50. **Details:** www.cambiorestaurant.co.uk; by Guildford
Castle; 10.30 pm, Fri & Sat 11 pm; closed Mon L, Sat L & Sun; no smoking in
dining room.*

fish!   £ 34
Rooftop, Sydenham Rd Car Pk GU1 3RT   (020) 7234 3333
*The location – on top of a car park – may offer a "great view", but
"disappointing service" (sometimes "rushed", sometimes "incredibly
slow") and a "soulless, noisy canteen feel" have won a poor
reception for this new branch of the "trendy" London-based fish
chain. / **Sample dishes:** devilled whitebait; grilled monkfish with olive oil
dressing; bread & butter pudding. **Value tip:** set 2-crs pre-th £9.95 (Mon-Fri).
Details: www.fishdiner.co.uk; 10.30 pm; closed Sun D; no smoking area.*

Rum Wong   £ 27   ★
16-18 London Rd GU1 2AF   (01483) 536092
*"Superb Thai food" is served "with a smile" at this "always
reliable" oriental; "it's a big place", though, and some find the
atmosphere "crowded and manic". / **Sample dishes:** chicken satay;
roast duck fried with cashew nuts; Thai custard. **Details:** www.rumwong.co.uk;
10.45 pm; closed Mon; no Amex or Switch; no smoking area.*

Harry Ramsden's   £ 21
White Cross LS20 8LZ   (01943) 874641
*Some still say you get "excellent traditional fish and chips in
1930's splendour" at this, the world's largest chippy (where nearly
1,000,000 customers a year pass through its doors); reporters are
largely left nonplussed, however – "what do people see in it?", "it's
like a giant service station". / **Sample dishes:** moules marinière; plaice &
chips; caramel apple granny. **Details:** www.harryramsdens.co.uk; off A65;
10 pm; no smoking; need 6+ to book.*

La Potinière   £ 46   ★★
Main St EH31 2AA   (01620) 843214
*Hilary and David Brown's small establishment may be improbably
located in "a chintzily converted garage", but the quality of its
French cuisine makes it "the most wonderful restaurant in
Scotland" for many reporters, and it has "an extraordinary wine
list"; NB – it was closed 'for a sabbatical' at press time, but it is
hoped to re-open in 2002. / **Sample dishes:** crispy salmon with vierge
sauce; honey-roast venison; lemon tart. **Details:** 17m E of Edinburgh, off
A198; 8 pm; open only Thu L, Fri D, Sat D & Sun L; no credit cards;
no smoking.*

Horn of Plenty   £ 51   A★

PL19 8JD   (01822) 832528

"Peter Gorton is famous, and with every justification", says one of the many fans of his "delectable" cooking at this "superb" restaurant with rooms, overlooking the Tamar valley; although this year's ratings were just a shade less lofty than last, the general view is that the place remains "marvellous" all round. / **Sample dishes:** millefeuille of smoked salmon & crab; roast lamb with mint & pesto tagliatelle; cappuccino parfait & coffee meringue. **Details:** www.thehornofplenty.co.uk; 3m W of Tavistock on A390; 9 pm; closed Mon L; no smoking; children: 13+. **Accommodation:** 10 rooms, from £115.

Design House   £ 29   ★

Dean Clough   HX3 5AX   (01422) 383242

"Good food in an unusual location" is the common theme of reports on this "stylish" spot, in a minimalistically-converted mill. / **Sample dishes:** courgette & aubergine tempura; tagliatelle carbonara; zabaglione parfait. **Value tip:** set 2-crs L £11.95. **Details:** from Halifax follow signs to Dean Clough Mills; 10 pm; closed Sat L & Sun; no smoking.

Hambleton Hall   £ 57   A★

LE15 8TH   (01572) 756991

Tim Hart's "lush country house hotel", has a wonderful location with "superb views over Rutland Water" – and most reporters find it "marvellous in every respect", not least the "imaginative and subtle" cooking; even some fans find it "expensive", however, and criticisms include food that is "too rich" and an ambience that can seem a mite "stilted". / **Sample dishes:** crab, avocado & green bean salad; braised turbot with leeks & herb risotto; pavé of white & dark chocolate. **Value tip:** set 2-crs L £16.50. **Details:** www.hambletonhall.com; 3m E of Oakham; 9.30 pm; no smoking. **Accommodation:** 17 rooms, from £195.

Monsieur Max   £ 43   A★★

133 High St   TW12 1NJ   (020) 8979 5546

"Sublime" Gallic cooking (and "excellent" service too) have long succeeded in making Max Renzland's "classy" joint an improbable destination in suburban Hampton Hill; let's hope it's not too thrown by the summer '01 loss of chef Morgan Meunier. / **Sample dishes:** Irish oysters with lemon shallot vinegar; ballottine of pigeon; orange & lemon tart with pineapple sorbet. **Details:** nr Teddington; 10.30 pm; closed Mon, Sat L & Sun D; children: 8+.

Star Inn   £ 33   A★

YO62 5JE   (01439) 770397

"The atmosphere is brilliant" at Andrew & Jacquie Pern's "very friendly", "olde worlde" thatched inn, where the "fabulous" cooking is "far above normal pub standards" and service is "charming and energetic"; its popularity is such that it "soon gets overcrowded". / **Sample dishes:** warm salad of black pudding & foie gras; wild turbot & green mustard fritter; Pimm's jelly with spearmint sorbet. **Details:** 3m SE of Helmsley off A170; 9.30 pm; closed Mon & Sun D; no Amex; no smoking. **Accommodation:** 3 rooms, from £90.

Chef Peking £ 26
5-6 Church Grn AL5 2TP (01582) 769358
A "consistent", if "expensive", high street Chinese, which is one of the few places to attract any volume of commentary in this thinly-served area. / **Sample dishes:** satay chicken; chicken in black bean sauce; ice cream. **Details:** just off the High Rd; 10.45 pm; no smoking area.

Bettys £ 24 Ⓐ
1 Parliament St HG1 2QU (01423) 502746
A reputation as "the best café in England, bar none" and "a Yorkshire institution" precedes these wonderfully retro premises; "it's pricey but lovely as a tea shop – but, as a restaurant, only acceptable". / **Sample dishes:** Yorkshire rarebit; sausages & mash; fresh fruit tart. **Details:** www.bettysandtaylors.com; opp Cenotaph; 9 pm; no Mastercard or Amex; no smoking area; no booking.

Drum & Monkey £ 27 ★★
5 Montpellier Gardens HG1 2TF (01423) 502650
"Outstanding fresh fish" at "excellent value" prices has created a huge reputation for this "thoroughly unpretentious" and "cramped" Victorian bar, whose "very loyal clientèle" creates a "lively", "clubby" feel – book ahead, or you'll have to queue. / **Sample dishes:** prawn & spinach delice; steamed whole lobster; crème brûlée. **Details:** 10.15 pm; closed Sun; no Amex; booking: max 8.

Rajput £ 18 ★★
11 Cheltenham Pde HG1 1DD (01423) 562113
"It's ordinary in appearance", but thanks to the "freshly cooked and beautifully spiced" Indian dishes from an "innovative" menu (with an "excellent choice of veggie options"), Perveen Khan's "friendly" subcontinental receives nothing but a hymn of praise. / **Sample dishes:** chicken tikka; lamb Karahi; ice cream. **Details:** midnight; D only, closed Mon; no Amex.

Villu Toots
Balmoral Hotel £ 27
Franklin Mount HG1 5EJ (01423) 705805
Opinions continue to differ somewhat regarding this "stylish and different" venue; the majority laud its "unusual" ambience and "creative" cooking, but there are sceptics who find that the service is "variable" and that the food "tries to be adventurous, but just succeeds in being too complicated". / **Sample dishes:** crisp tiger prawns & Thai sauce; guinea fowl with wild mushroom fricassée; chocolate & cherry clafoutis. **Details:** www.villutoots.co.uk; off King's Rd; 10 pm; closed Sat L. **Accommodation:** 20 rooms, from £84.

The Mermaid Café £ 13 ★
2 Rock-a-Nore Rd TN34 3DW (01424) 438100
The best "fish 'n' chippy" on the South Coast, say fans of this small fixture, which has a "superb" location on the beach. / **Sample dishes:** potted shrimps; cod & chips with salad; spotted dick & custard. **Details:** 7.30 pm; no credit cards; no booking, except D in winter.

Sea Pebbles £ 20 ★
348-352 Uxbridge Rd HA5 4HR (020) 8428 0203
The "fresh fish" is if anything "underpriced" at Sabbas Andreou's "clean and bright" fixture – "the best chippy" for miles around, and a good option in this thin area. / **Sample dishes:** Arbroath smokies; haddock & chips; bread & butter pudding. **Details:** 9.45 pm; closed Mon L & Sun; no credit cards; need 10+ to book.

Blue Strawberry £ 34 A ★
The Street CM3 2DW (01245) 381333
"Steady quality of food and service" makes it "worth the journey"
to this "fashionable French bistro", whose modern style seems at
odds with its beamed, rural cottage location; tables are "close",
and the place can feel "too busy" for some tastes. / **Sample
dishes:** smoked venison; chicken in lobster sauce; lemon & lime parfait with
pecan shortcake. **Details:** 3m E of Chelmsford; 10 pm; closed Mon L, Sat L &
Sun D.

Weavers £ 28 A ★
15 West Ln BD22 8DU (01535) 643822
"They maintain high standards" – both in the restaurant and wine
bar – at Colin & Jane Rushworth's "very obliging" establishment,
housed in former weavers' cottages in the heart of the village.
/ **Sample dishes:** monkfish, scallops & prawns; seared pork with wilted
greens; sticky toffee pudding. **Details:** www.weaverssmallhotel.co.uk; 1.5m W
on B6142 from A629 close to Parsonage; 9.15 pm; D only, closed Mon & Sun;
no smoking. **Accommodation:** 3 rooms, from £75.

Dining Room 2 £ 34
65 The Broadway RH16 3AS (01444) 417755
TV-chef Tony Tobin's year-old second operation is a "well
appointed" and "well run" place offering "reliable" and "tasty"
modern British fare; some do fear it's a mite "overpriced", however.
/ **Sample dishes:** scallop & coconut crab cakes; baked brill with herb crust;
white chocolate mousse. **Details:** 10 pm; closed Mon D, Sat L & Sun;
no smoking area.

Jeremys at Bordehill £ 34 A ★
Balcombe Rd RH16 1XP (01444) 441102
"Imaginative international food" from a "frequently-changing
menu" makes Jeremy Ashpool's "cheerful" and "beautifully-located"
country house restaurant an almost unanimous recommendation,
despite the odd doubter who finds it a touch "pretentious".
/ **Sample dishes:** leek & Parmesan tart; saddle of venison with beetroot &
mint salad; rum baba with caramelised apples.
Details: www.homeofgoodfood.co.uk; 15m S of M23, J10a; 9.30 pm; closed
Mon & Sun D; no smoking.

1086
Hazlewood Castle Hotel £ 47 X
Paradise Ln LS24 9NJ (01937) 535354
"Stateliness" and "grandeur" it may have in abundance, but both
the cooking and the service (not to mention the excruciating menu
descriptions) at this ancient dining room (of a castle listed in the
Domesday Book) "leave a lot to be desired"; (some tip the
brasserie as being "a lot better"). / **Sample dishes:** hot smoked salmon
with dried fruit chutney; salmon with oriental greens; 'predictable' cheese &
biscuits. **Value tip:** set 3-crs Sun L £19.50.
Details: www.hazlewood-castle.co.uk; signposted off A64; 9.30 pm; closed
Mon, Tue–Sat D only, closed Sun D; no smoking; children: before 7 pm only.
Accommodation: 21 rooms, from £125.

HELMSLEY, NORTH YORKSHIRE
Black Swan   **£ 46**   ★   8–4C

Market Pl YO62 5BJ   (01439) 770466
This "small country hotel" (occupying an historic building in a "gorgeous market town") may be "an old-fashioned sort of place", but its "lovely" cooking makes it "a favourite with tourists and locals alike". / **Sample dishes:** poached egg & smoked salmon with caviar hollandaise; duck breast & confit leg with raspberry jus; vodka & lime parfait. **Details:** 9 pm; no smoking. **Accommodation:** 44 rooms, from £150.

HEREFORD, HEREFORDSHIRE
Café at All Saints   **£ 14**   A★   2–1B

All Saints Church, High St HR4 9AA   (01432) 370415
This "modern café built within a beautiful functioning medieval church" serves "probably the best vegetarian food in the vicinity" and is also praised for its "kind and cheerful" service. / **Sample dishes:** broccoli & Stilton soup; courgette, sun-dried tomato & feta quiche; pear & raspberry torte. **Details:** nr Cathedral; L only; closed Sun; no smoking; no booking; children: 6+ upstairs.

La Rive at Castle House
Left Bank Village   **£ 51**

Castle St HR1 2NW   (01432) 356321
This hotel restaurant (recently merged with nearby La Rive) generally wins praise for its "well-spaced" tables, "pleasant" staff and "well-presented" food; a few say it's "overpriced and oversmart for the area". / **Sample dishes:** Thai risotto with tempura frogs legs; salmon & crab brandade with lobster won tons; Pimm's jelly with cucumber ice. **Details:** www.castlehse.co.uk; 10 pm. **Accommodation:** 15 rooms, from £155.

HERSHAM, SURREY
Dining Room   **£ 27**   ★   3–3A

10 Queens Rd KT12 5LS   (01932) 231686
For "good, old-fashioned" English cooking in a "domestic" setting, you're unlikely to do much better than this quirky and "intimate" spot. / **Sample dishes:** salt & pepper squid; lemon-baked bream with leek risotto; white chocolate mousse with raspberries. **Details:** www.the-dining-room.co.uk; just off A3, by village green; 10.30 pm; closed Sat L & Sun D.

HETTON, NORTH YORKSHIRE
The Angel   **£ 37**   ★★   5–1B

BD23 6LT   (01756) 730263
"So exceptional we travel over 100 miles just for the eating experience"; with its remote but "beautiful" Dales location, the country's best known dining pub has a lot to live up to, and "continuously high standards" in both the bar and the restaurant mean few leave disappointed; "excellent fish specialities" and a "very good wine list" are amongst the highlights. / **Sample dishes:** grilled goat's cheese; pan-fried sea bass; sticky toffee pudding. **Value tip:** set 3-crs pre-th £16.50. **Details:** www.angelhetton.co.uk; 5m N of Skipton off B6265 at Rylstone; 9.30 pm; D only, except Sun when L only; no smoking area.

HEYDON, CAMBRIDGESHIRE
King William IV   **£ 25**   A★   3–2B

Chishill Rd SG8 8PN   (01763) 838773
The vegetarian menu "is always extremely good, well presented and inventive" at this friendly and sometimes "very crowded" boozer, tucked up a steep lane. / **Sample dishes:** potted salmon with julienne cucumber; chicken stuffed with asparagus mousse; lemon tart with kumquat compote. **Details:** 4m from M11, J10 on A505; 10 pm; no Amex; no smoking area.

HINDON, WILTSHIRE

Grosvenor Arms £ 37 ★

High St SP3 6DJ (01747) 820696

This place is "more expensive than local rivals", but reporters reckon it's worth the premium for the "good" and "imaginative" cooking at this "real" pub – "a great find in an area without much in the way of choice". / **Sample dishes:** scallop & cep risotto; chicken & lobster with rosti potatoes; lemon tart with blueberry coulis. **Details:** 9 pm; closed Sun D; no Amex; no smoking. **Accommodation:** 7 rooms, from £75.

HINTLESHAM, SUFFOLK

Hintlesham Hall £ 46

IP8 3NS (01473) 652334

For some, it's "always a pleasure" to dine at this "beautiful", country house, still best remembered for its past association with Robert Carrier; however, even some who say the cooking's "good" say it "could be so much better", or that its "quality is obscured" by the place's "self-conscious grandiosity". / **Sample dishes:** guinea fowl & peppercorn sausage; char-grilled lamb with roasted vegetables; chilled rhubarb soup. **Details:** www.hintleshamhall.com; 4m W of Ipswich on A1071; 9.30 pm; closed Sat L; jacket & tie required; no smoking; no booking; children: 12+. **Accommodation:** 33 rooms, from £120.

HINTON CHARTERHOUSE, BATH & NE SOMERSET 2–3B

Homewood Park £ 54

BA2 7TB (01225) 723731

"Fantastic" cooking and "excellent" service make this dining room in a part-Georgian country-house hotel a "lovely" and "relaxing" venue for most reporters; some, however, remain resolutely unmoved by its charms. / **Sample dishes:** smoked salmon with beetroot & sour cream; roast duck with lentil mousse & jasmine jus; chocolate fondant with basil ice cream. **Details:** www.homewoodpark.com; 6m from Bath on A36 to Warminster; 9.30 pm; no smoking. **Accommodation:** 19 rooms, from £139.

HISTON, CAMBRIDGESHIRE

Phoenix £ 24 ★

20 The Green CB4 4JA (01223) 233766

"Booking is essential" at this Chinese restaurant near the village green, whose "well cooked" dishes are consistently applauded. / **Sample dishes:** pepper & salt squid; smoked chicken salad; ice cream. **Details:** 10.30 pm; no Amex or Switch; no smoking area.

HOGNASTON, DERBYSHIRE

Red Lion £ 28 ★

Main St DE6 1PR (01335) 370396

Handily-located en route to the Peak District, this "warm" and "friendly" pub serves "good home-cooked food", from a "wide-ranging blackboard menu". / **Sample dishes:** New Zealand green-lipped mussels; warm smoked chicken salad; whisky bread & butter pudding. **Details:** www.lionrouge.com; 9 pm; closed Mon & Sun D; no Amex; no smoking area; no booking, Sun L; children: 7+. **Accommodation:** 3 rooms, from £75.

HOLT, NORFOLK

Yetman's £ 44 🅰 ★

37 Norwich Rd NR25 6SA (01263) 713320

For "a posh meal in a small market town", Alison & Peter Yetmans' establishment is hard to beat; it's a "friendly" and "helpful" place, offering an "interesting" choice of "exceptional" dishes, and "good wines" too. / **Sample dishes:** deep-fried sardines in Parmesan; Longshore cod with anchovy butter; toasted apricot pancakes. **Details:** www.yetmans.net; on A148, 20m N of Norwich; 9.30 pm; D only, except Sun when L only (open Sun D Jul & Aug); no smoking area.

Mustard & Punch   £ 29
6 Westgate HD7 2AA   (01484) 662066
*For a "great night out", this cheerful restaurant is a popular
destination, though its "realistically priced" cooking is a less reliable
attraction than its fun atmosphere. / Sample dishes: veal sweetbread
ravioli with langoustine consommé; venison with oxtail macaroni & chanterelles;
white chocolate tart. Details: 10 pm; closed Mon, Sat L & Sun; no Amex.*

The Bell Inn   £ 27   ★
High Rd SS17 8LD   (01375) 642463
*It can seem "almost impossible to get a table" at this "olde
worlde" spot, thanks to the "very good" food from the "small,
but interesting menu", and its "friendly village pub atmosphere".
/ Sample dishes: duck & foie gras ravioli; dorade with seared scallops; peach
tarte Tatin. Details: www.bell-inn.co.uk; signposted off B1007, off A13; 10 pm;
no smoking. Accommodation: 15 rooms, from £40.*

Knife & Cleaver   £ 32
The Grove MK45 3LA   (01234) 740387
*This country restaurant-with-rooms (a converted pub next to the
village church) achieves very consistent reports, not least for its
"good all round" menu, including some "first-class fish dishes".
/ Sample dishes: ham & caper rillettes; char-grilled aubergine & buffalo
Mozzarella crepes; chocolate marquise with raspberry coulis. Value tip: set
2-crs L £12.95. Details: www.knifeandcleaver.com; off A6, 5m S of Bedford;
9.30 pm; closed Sat L & Sun D; no smoking. Accommodation: 9 rooms,
from £49.*

Linos   £ 28   𝔸 ★
122 Market St CH47 3BH   (0151) 632 1408
*"The best place to eat on the Wirral" – the Galantini family's
"small" venture has a hugely enthusiastic local following, on account
of its personal service and its "consistently good" French cooking
(with "heavenly" puds singled out for particular attention). / Sample
dishes: three cheese & onion tartlet; roast duck with bitter sweet orange
sauce; coffee ice cream. Details: www.linos-restaurant.co.uk; 3m from M53,
J2; 10 pm; closed Mon & Sun; no Amex.*

Bradley's   £ 23
84 Fitzwilliam St HD1 5BB   (01484) 516773
*"Terrific-value set lunches", "good-value earlybird menus" and
"jazz evenings" are the sorts of attractions that make it worth
knowing about this "unpretentious but generally reliable spot",
in the centre of the town. / Sample dishes: chicken fritters with peanut &
lime dip; roast lamb with cherry tomato couscous; mango tart with caramel ice
cream. Value tip: set 3-crs L £6.95. Details: www.bradleysrestaurant.co.uk;
in town centre above the railway arches; 10 pm; closed Sat L & Sun; no Amex;
no smoking area.*

Nawaab   £ 20   ★
35 Westgate HD1 1NY   (01484) 422775
*This "smart", quite "stylish" curry house (part of a mini-chain)
"consistently maintains a high culinary standard". / Sample
dishes: mixed tandoori; Nerali special; kulfi. Details: www.nawaab.com;
between bus & railway stations; 11 pm, Fri & Sat midnight; D only.*

Hitchcocks £ 13 ★

I Bishop Ln HUI IPA (01482) 320233

"Everything is home-made and fresh" at this "studenty" vegetarian buffet, known for its "value for money"; they only open if someone has booked – if you're first for that night, you can determine the culinary theme; BYO. / **Sample dishes:** guacamole & bean dip; artichoke & Mozzarella pizza; pecan pie. **Details:** follow signs to Old Town; 8.30 pm; D only; no credit cards; booking essential.

Pheasant £ 35 ★

PE28 0RE (01832) 710241

"Similar in style to The Three Horseshoes at Madingley" (to which it is related), this popular thatched tavern received (almost) nothing but praise from reporters for its "varied" and "innovative" cuisine and for its "good service and atmosphere" too. / **Sample dishes:** spinach soup with nutmeg cream; crab & mussel tagliatelle with Parmesan; moist chocolate cake with cherries. **Value tip:** set 2-crs L £9.90. **Details:** 1m S of A14 between Huntingdon & Kettering; 10 pm; no smoking area.

The Box Tree £ 42 ✕

35-37 Church St LS29 9DR (01943) 608484

New chef Toby Hill took over the stoves of this famously "chintzy" establishment too recently for our survey; what's clear from reporters, however, is that it's the "stuffy" atmosphere engendered by the front-of-house – which strikes some as "snooty", "intimidating", or even "contemptuous" – which is most in need of reform. / **Sample dishes:** brill in red wine; lamb cutlet with shallot purée; hot chocolate soufflé. **Details:** www.theboxtree.co.uk; on A65 near town centre; 9.30 pm; closed Mon & Sun D; closed 2 weeks in Jan; no smoking in dining room.

Far Syde Café £ 27 ★

back of The Grove LS29 9EE (01943) 602030

"Reliably hearty" food – that's "well presented" and "imaginative" too – and "a good choice of wines" make this "relaxed" and "lively" spot a very popular destination; with its "low ceiling and wood floors", however, it's a bit "noisy" for some tastes. / **Sample dishes:** chicken & prawn risotto; lamb wrapped in Mozzarella & aubergine; cappuccino cup. **Details:** 10 pm; closed Mon & Sun (open Sun brunch Oct-May); no smoking area.

Baipo £ 23

63 Upper Orwell St IP4 1HP (01473) 218402

"It could do with a facelift", but aficionados say this town-centre Thai's cooking is "hot enough to blow your socks off". / **Sample dishes:** garlic prawns; spicy chicken in spinach leaves; pineapple ice cream. **Details:** www.baipo.co.uk; 10.45 pm; closed Mon L & Sun.

The Galley £ 32

25 St Nicholas St IP1 1TW (01473) 281131

A *"small restaurant under Turkish ownership",* providing an "interesting mix" of English and Middle Eastern dishes; "fresh and tasty fish" is especially commended. / **Sample dishes:** crispy feta & parsley filo pastry; Norfolk smoked trout; Belgian chocolate delice. **Value tip:** set 2-crs L £10.95. **Details:** www.galley.uk.com; 10 pm; closed Sun; no smoking area.

Mortimer's on the Quay £ 30 ★

3 Wherry Quay IP4 1A5 (01473) 230225

An *"amazing variety of fish"* helps Ken Ambler's well-established riverside spot to continue living up to the promise of its name, and its *"good, plain cooking"* is almost universally praised; service, however, *"could be better"*. / **Sample dishes:** black tiger prawns; monkfish tandoori with rice; Mortimer's ice cream. **Details:** 9.15 pm; closed Sat L & Sun; no smoking area.

IRON BRIDGE, SHROPSHIRE 5–4B

Malthouse £ 27 𝔸

The Wharfage TF8 7NH (01952) 433712

"Live music" (most nights) creates a *"great"* atmosphere at this revamped inn on the banks of the Severn; a *"varied"* and *"tasty"* menu provides a worthy accompaniment. / **Sample dishes:** confit chicken with pineapple salsa; roast lamb with bubble & squeak polenta; lemon pudding with ginger fudge sauce. **Details:** www.malthousepubs.co.uk; 500 metres from the Iron Bridge; 9.45 pm; no smoking area. **Accommodation:** 9 rooms, from £59.

IVINGHOE, BEDFORDSHIRE 3–2A

Kings Head £ 49

Station Rd LU7 9EB (01296) 668388

"Still the best", says one reporter who for over 30 years now has been visiting this *"French restaurant in a very well-restored old English pub"*; fans particularly laud the *"splendid duck"* and *"superb maître d'"* but doubters say the place is just *"expensively average"* and a *"relic from the '70s"*. / **Sample dishes:** goat's cheese & spiced pepper salad; roast duck with sage & onion stuffing; caramel soufflé. **Value tip:** set 3-crs L £14.95. **Details:** 3m N of Tring on B489 to Dunstable; 9.45 pm; closed Sun D; jacket & tie required at D; no smoking in dining room.

JERSEY, CHANNEL ISLANDS

Jersey Pottery Restaurant £ 35 𝔸★

Jersey Pottery JE3 9EP (01534) 851119

"Pity it's only open for lunch" – this *"airy"* and *"attractive"* conservatory restaurant is a *"very popular"* destination, where *"plateaux de fruits de mer"* (locally caught of course) are a speciality. / **Sample dishes:** pan-fried scallops in lemon & lime sauce; grilled fish platter; cassata ice cream. **Details:** www.jerseypottery.com; signposted from St Helier; L only; closed Mon; no smoking area.

Longueville Manor £ 63

Longueville Rd, St Saviour JE2 7WF (01534) 725501

With its *"quaint, château ambience"* – *"formal, but not stuffy"* – this is the Channel Islands' grandest dining experience; it's certainly *"not cheap"*, but it is *"consistently good"*. / **Sample dishes:** lobster risotto with asparagus & scallops; roast lamb with potato gratin & roasted vegetables; chocolate & pistachio soufflé. **Value tip:** set 3-crs L £22.50. **Details:** www.longuevillemanor.com; 10.30 pm; no smoking area. **Accommodation:** 31 rooms, from £160.

Suma's £ 39 𝔸★

Gorey Hill, Gorey JE3 6ET (01534) 853291

"A fantastic location overlooking the harbour" distinguishes this *"classically elegant"* Mediterranean-style establishment, whose *"wonderful"* cooking is universally approved; if there is a criticism, it is that some find the approach a touch *"precious"*. / **Sample dishes:** sweet onion quiche with tuna sushi; lobster & crab salad; selection of mini desserts. **Details:** underneath castle in Gorey Harbour; 9.45 pm; booking: max 12.

Hungry Monk £ 33   Ⓐ
BN26 5QF (01323) 482178
This "well-established and very English countryside restaurant" occupies a "beautiful, old cottage" – "all open fires and snugs" – and claims to have invented banoffi pie; fans report a "perfect blend of atmosphere, style and culinary substance", but for others the place is "overpriced", and "trading on its past reputation". / **Sample dishes:** crab & avocado tian; lamb with Moroccan spiced crust & butternut squash; baked chocolate & raspberry Alaska. **Details:** www.hungrymonk.co.uk; 5m W of Eastbourne; 9.30 pm; D only, except Sun open L & D; no smoking in dining room; children: 5+.

Bosquet £ 41   ★★
97a Warwick Rd CV8 1HP (01926) 852463
This is "a real restaurant, not an assembly line" and Monsieur et Madame Lignier's cooking "never fails in terms of quality"; if the "quiet" setting were a touch more atmospheric, this could be an establishment of even more considerable note. / **Sample dishes:** artichoke soup with truffles; Scottish beef with red wine sauce; blueberry & almond tart. **Details:** 10 pm; closed Mon, Sat L & Sun; closed Aug.

Simpsons £ 47   ★
101-103 Warwick Rd CV8 1HL (01926) 864567
A recent makeover has brought a more contemporary 'look' to this town-centre restaurant, providing a much more suitable setting for cooking which is generally (but not unanimously) proclaimed "wonderful". / **Sample dishes:** Salcombe crab torte with smoked salmon & guacamole; roast brill with baby spring vegetables; turron parfait with marinated pineapple. **Value tip:** set 2-crs L £20. **Details:** www.simpsons-restaurant.co.uk; 10 pm; closed Sat L & Sun; no smoking area.

King's Cliffe House Restaurant £ 36   ★
31 West St PE8 6XB (01780) 470172
Most agree that the food is "excellent" at this small restaurant in the centre of the village – unfortunately, they also tend to think that the atmosphere is "cold" and "stilted". / **Sample dishes:** scallops with lentils & wild fennel; lamb with oyster mushrooms & Marsala wine; oranges in rosemary syrup. **Details:** 4m W of A1, close to A47; 9.15 pm; D only, open Wed-Sat only; no credit cards; no smoking in dining room; booking: max 8.

The Cross £ 48   ★
Tweed Mill Brae, Ardbroilach Rd PH21 1TC (01540) 661166
"Absolutely nothing is too much trouble for the staff" at Ruth & Tony Hadley's "most enjoyable" restaurant with rooms in a former mill; the "modern"-style cooking achieves enthusiastic reports, with the cheeseboard "a highlight". / **Sample dishes:** spiced crab cakes; roast Ayrshire guinea fowl; polenta & lemon cake. **Details:** www.thecross.co.uk; head uphill on Ardbroilach Rd, turn left into private drive after traffic lights; 8.30 pm; D only, closed Tue; no Amex; no smoking; children: 8+. **Accommodation:** 9 rooms, from £115.

KIRKBY LONSDALE, CUMBRIA
7–4D

Snooty Fox Hotel　£ 23　✗

Main St LA6 2AH (01524) 271308

"The charismatic ex-owner is much missed" at this elegant town-centre hostelry; now part of the Mortal Man group – 'a collection of Traditional Country Inns' – the place seems to be becoming an object-lesson in the "mediocre" standards multiple ownership so often entails. / **Sample dishes:** goat's cheese in filo pastry; roast pheasant with spring vegetables; iced chocolate parfait. **Details:** www.mortal-man-inns.co.uk; off A65, 6m from M6, J36; 10 pm; no smoking area. **Accommodation:** 9 rooms, from £56.

KNIGHTWICK, WORCESTERSHIRE
2–1B

Talbot　£ 28　★

WR6 5PH (01886) 821235

"Home-cooked, often home-grown food", "beer brewed on the premises" and "lovely surroundings" by the River Teme make this "relaxed" country inn a "classic" for some reporters; there were some this year, though, who thought the place "overhyped". / **Sample dishes:** warm game liver salad; roast sea bass with pesto; sticky toffee pudding. **Details:** www.the-talbot.co.uk; 9m from Worcester on A44; 9 pm.

KNUTSFORD, CHESHIRE
5–2B

Belle Epoque　£ 29

King St WA16 6DT (01565) 633060

This "impressive" Art Nouveau building once (under the same family's ownership) housed a restaurant of some repute, but its bistro style of the last few years never seems to have struck quite the right note; still, it's a "friendly", "bustling" and "cheerful" sort of place, serving cooking which, even if it's "plain", is generally of a "good" standard. / **Sample dishes:** Tuscan spring salad; sea bass with red onion salsa; apricot fritters with Cointreau mousse. **Details:** 1.5m from M6, J19; 10.30 pm; closed Sat L; no smoking area. **Accommodation:** 6 rooms, from £60.

LACOCK, WILTSHIRE
2–2C

At the Sign of the Angel　£ 31　Ⓐ★

6 Church St SN15 2LB (01249) 730230

This "intimate" dining room of a 14th-century house in a "fantastic" National Trust village has obvious advantages on the atmosphere front; the odd gripe is recorded, but most feedback speaks of "excellent local produce that's beautifully prepared". / **Sample dishes:** smoked chicken & avocado salad; seared pink trout; crème brûlée. **Details:** www.lacock.co.uk; close to M4, J17; 9 pm; closed Mon L. **Accommodation:** 10 rooms, from £99.

LANCASTER, LANCASHIRE
5–1A

Bay Horse　£ 29　★

Bay Horse Ln LA2 0HR (01524) 791204

"A country pub boasting a chef with style" – "exceptional presentation" is a particular strength of this "small village boozer" off the M6, which "makes a serious effort to offer a good eating experience". / **Sample dishes:** seared scallops & smoked salmon; pan-fried sea bass & lobster risotto; lemon tart & lemon sorbet. **Value tip:** set 3-crs Sun L £14. **Details:** www.bayhorseinn.com; 0.75m S of A6, J33; 9.30 pm; closed Mon & Sun D; no smoking.

Simply French　£ 21

27a St Georges Quay LA1 1RD (01524) 843199

"Very consistent" standards of Gallic cooking and a "pleasant" atmosphere make this quayside restaurant a "good-value" choice. / **Sample dishes:** smoked scallops & streaky bacon salad; pan-fried beef & mushrooms; apricot tart. **Details:** 9.30 pm; closed Mon, Tue & Wed L; no Amex.

Son Siam Thai   £ 24   ★
11-15 Meeting House Ln LA1 1TJ   (01524) 848049
It may have a setting which is "cramped" and "uninspiring", but "by far the best oriental eating experience in this area" is to be had at this "friendly" central spot. / **Sample dishes:** vegetable spring rolls; pad Thai with chicken & pork; Thai ice cream. **Details:** 11 pm; D only; no smoking area; children: any age welcome (up to 8 pm at weekends).

Sultan of Lancaster   £ 15   Ⓐ★
Old Church, Brock St LA1 1UU   (01524) 61188
An "amazing setting" and "top-notch Indian/Gujerati cooking" have made quite a name for this curry house in a converted church, and it's "extremely affordable" too – even more so as there's no prospect of wasting your hard-earned money on alcohol. / **Sample dishes:** seafood samosas; tikka masala; coconut supreme. **Details:** 11 pm; D only; no Amex; no smoking area.

LANGAR, NOTTINGHAMSHIRE   5–3D
Langar Hall   £ 34   Ⓐ
NG13 9HG   (01949) 860559
"The owner makes all feel welcome" in the "atmospheric" dining room of this "lovely", slightly "eccentric" Georgian country house, where the overall verdict is that the fairly traditional cooking is "good, without being fantastic". / **Sample dishes:** smoked chicken & quail's egg in tomato aspic; John Dory with saffron & tomato dressing; raspberry & almond gratin. **Value tip:** set 2-crs L £10. **Details:** off A52 between Nottingham & Grantham; 9.30 pm, Sat 10 pm; no smoking area. **Accommodation:** 10 rooms, from £130.

LANGHO, LANCASHIRE   5–1B
Northcote Manor   £ 54   ★★
Northcote Rd BB6 8BE   (01254) 240555
"Nigel Haworth stays in his kitchen, and it shows" – "wonderful", "imaginative" cooking "using local produce" and with "excellent attention to detail" is the theme of almost all reports on the "gracious" dining room of this Ribble Valley country house hotel; "lunchtime value" is especially commended. / **Sample dishes:** black pudding & trout with nettle sauce; thyme-crusted lamb with leeks & chive mash; Bakewell tart soufflé. **Value tip:** set 3-crs Sun L £16. **Details:** www.northcotemanor.com; M6, J31 then A59; 9.30 pm; closed Sat L; no jeans or trainers; no smoking. **Accommodation:** 14 rooms, from £130.

LAPWORTH, WARWICKSHIRE   5–4C
The Boot   £ 35   ★
Old Warwick Rd B94 6JU   (01564) 782464
"Imaginative", "high-class" pub food served in a "modern, but still cosy" setting is a formula which wins almost unanimous support for this canalside fixture; with its "pleasant" garden and its "lovely" location, it makes a "great summer destination". / **Sample dishes:** rustic bread with olive oil; chicken with goat's cheese & saffron; Bailey's cheesecake. **Details:** off A34; 10 pm.

LAVENHAM, SUFFOLK   3–1C
Great House   £ 34   Ⓐ
Market Pl CO10 9QZ   (01787) 247431
A "medieval house on the market square" provides a great setting for this "very French" establishment, and is generally applauded for its "very good" food – "from snacks to full meals" – but some reporters have found the place "pleasant enough, but not as good as expected". / **Sample dishes:** lobster ravioli in courgette broth; fillet of beef with béarnaise sauce; lemon tart with red fruit coulis. **Value tip:** set 2-crs L £12.95. **Details:** www.greathouse.co.uk; follow directions to Guildhall; 9.30 pm; closed Mon & Sun D; closed Jan & part of Aug; no smoking in dining room. **Accommodation:** 5 rooms, from £70.

Swan Hotel £ 40

High St C010 9QA (01787) 247477

*Given its riot-of-Tudor architecture, it's no surprise that this town-centre spot is "full of tourists, except on weekdays"; standards – including of the "well presented", quite contemporary dishes – are thought "surprisingly good, for Forte", and "very attentive" service wins much praise. / **Sample dishes:** scallops & Parma ham with green bean salad; sea bass with salt crust & lemon sauce; peach & thyme ice cream. **Value tip:** set 2-crs L £13.95. **Details:** www.heritage-hotels.com; 9 pm; no smoking. **Accommodation:** 51 rooms, from £145.*

LEEDS, WEST YORKSHIRE 5–1C

The Leeds restaurant scene has its highlights, but it's seriously patchy. On the positive side, the city centre boasts a couple of restaurants of undoubtedly high culinary standards – *Pool Court at 42* and *Gueller* – but neither of these offers particular charm. On the negative side, many of the most mentioned places – *Brasserie Forty Four*, *Rascasse*, *Leodis* – inspire very mixed feelings. The only true all-rounders are the long-established Indian *Darbar* and the newish Italian *Brio*.

Italian restaurants provide much of the interest away from the city centre. In Chapel Allerton, *Casa Mia Grande* is making itself a real destination, emulating (and indeed eclipsing) Headingley's long-established *Salvo's*. Roundhay's *Flying Pizza* remains the local poseurs' paradise.

With the exception of the establishments mentioned above, and some relatively small Indians and Japaneses, the city offers relatively few places where the cooking is of real quality, and there are some whose standards are below what could reasonably be expected.

Aagrah £ 21 ★

Aberford Rd LS25 1BA (0113) 287 6606

*The food is "consistently good in all Aagrah restaurants", and this "smart" branch of that eminent subcontinental chain is particularly roundly praised for its "extensive" and "tasty" menu, and its "welcoming" and "attentive" service. / **Sample dishes:** mushroom pakora; king prawn biryani; mango kulfi. **Details:** www.aagrahgroupofrestaurants.co.uk; from A1 take A642 Aberford Rd to Garforth; 11.30 pm; D only; no smoking area.*

Art's Bar (Café) £ 23 A

42 Call Ln LS1 6DT (0113) 243 8243

*"Bohemian", "friendly" and "relaxed" – the good atmosphere of this artified Exchange Quarter hang-out is its particular strength, though the "down-to-earth", "efficient" staff and "moreish", "home-cooked" fare also come in for praise. / **Sample dishes:** Mozzarella & tomato salad; char-grilled lamb with garlic mash; lemon tart. **Value tip:** 1-crs set L £5. **Details:** www.artscafe.co.uk; nr Corn Exchange; 11 pm; no Amex.*

Bibis £ 35 A

Minerva Hs, 16 Greek St LS1 5RU (0113) 243 0905

*The "noisy" and "flashy" '70s-survivor may offer a vision of "organised chaos", but it still has many fans who think it offers "the best Italian meal in the city-centre", thanks in no small part to its "happy" and "bustling" atmosphere. / **Sample dishes:** beef tomatoes with basil oil dressing; pigeon & foie gras terrine; chocolate & Amaretto cake. **Details:** off Park Row ; 11.15 pm; no booking, Sat.*

Brasserie Forty Four £ 33
44 The Calls LS2 7EW (0113) 234 3232
"Ask for a canalside seat" if you pay a visit to this "reliable" modern brasserie; it has many supporters who praise its "well-presented" fare and "lively" style, but portions are "on the nouvelle cuisine side", and a pronounced minority snipe at "unexciting" cooking, "indifferent" service and a lacklustre ambience. / **Sample dishes:** *summer leaf & herb salad; seared yellowfin tuna; burnt passion fruit ice cream.* **Value tip:** *set 2-crs L £9.75.* **Details:** *www.dine-services.com; 10.30 pm, Fri & Sat 11 pm; closed Sat L & Sun.*

Brio £ 27 𝔸★
40 Great George St LS1 3DL (0113) 246 5225
"Reasonable prices" and "genuine Italian staff" contribute to the success of this "smart" and "sophisticated" two-year old (which has a younger sibling in Harrogate, 44 Commercial St, tel 01423 529933); it's an "extremely well run" place generally, and numbers "very flavourful" cooking as not the least of its attractions. / **Sample dishes:** *haricot beans in chilli & wine sauce; seared tuna niçoise; pannacotta.* **Details:** *www.brios.co.uk; 10.30 pm; closed Sun.*

Bryan's £ 24
9 Weetwood Ln LS16 5LT (0113) 278 5679
This famous Headingley chippy increasingly gets a resounding thumbs-down from reporters – some still acclaim it's "superb", but the consensus is that it's become "grossly overpriced and overrated". / **Sample dishes:** *Thai fishcakes; lemon sole; hot chocolate fudge cake.* **Details:** *nr Headingley cricket ground; 10 pm; no Amex; no smoking; need 8+ to book.*

The Calls Grill £ 29
Calls Landing, 38 The Calls LS2 7EW (0113) 245 3870
A "civilised", if "standard" brasserie setting and "nice view" continues to help win quite a following for this canalside fixture; for the most part there is also praise for the "simple" fare ("excellent steaks" in particular), though iffy service lets the side down. / **Sample dishes:** *smoked tuna with Spanish omelette; Dover sole with citrus butter; rice pudding bavarois.* **Value tip:** *set 3-crs L £11.95.* **Details:** *opp Tetleys brewery on waterfront; 10.30 pm; closed Mon L & Sun; booking: max 6, Sat.*

Casa Mia Grande £ 19 𝔸★★
33 Harrogate Rd LS7 3PD (0113) 2392555
"A heaving family-run Italian duo that's special" – reporters comment as much on this "tastefully decorated" Chapel Allerton restaurant as they do on the original café/deli (a stone's throw away at 10-12 Stainbeck Ln, tel 0113 266 1269) – both provide "cheerful and thoughtful" service and a "bustling" and "atmospheric" setting; the speciality here is "fish to die for", while down the road they serve "a wide range of pizza, pasta, salads and so forth". / **Sample dishes:** *smoked chicken salad with mango vinaigrette; honey-roasted salmon with spinach & lemon sauce; Bailey's crème brûlée.* **Details:** *www.casa-mia.co.uk; 10.30 pm; no Amex; no smoking area.*

Clockhouse Café £ 19 𝔸
16a Headingley Ln LS6 2AS (0113) 294 5464
"Good-value food" – on an East-meets-West theme – attracts a "young" clientèle to this "really nice", studenty venture – a café by day, bistro by night. / **Sample dishes:** *moules marinière; Malaysian chicken; fruit crepes.* **Details:** *10 pm, Fri & Sat 10.30 pm; no Amex.*

Darbar £ 29   Ⓐ★

16-17 Kirkgate LS1 6BY   (0113) 246 0381

It looks nothing from the outside, but this city-centre subcontinental is a "sumptuously" decorated restaurant whose "beautiful" (if "kitsch") interior really is "unique"; the "flavourful" cooking is consistently "good value" too. / **Sample dishes:** onion bhaji; chicken balti with peshwari naan; gulab jaman (Indian sweets). **Details:** 11.30 pm; closed Sun.

Flying Pizza £ 27

60a Street Ln LS8 2DQ   (0113) 266 6501

"If mingling with the footballers and soap celebrities is what you want", this "vibrant", long-established Roundhay institution is "the place to be seen in Leeds"; to lesser mortals, however, it can seem like a "bog-standard Italian", with "disinterested" and "slow" service. / **Sample dishes:** Caprese salad; chicken in cream sauce; tiramisu. **Details:** www.theflyingpizza.co.uk; just off A61, 3m N of city centre; 11.30 pm; no smoking area; no booking at D.

Fourth Floor Café
Harvey Nichols £ 34   ✗

107-111 Briggate LS1 6AZ   (0113) 204 8000

Standards are slipping wholesale at Harvey Nics's northern flagship – the cooking is "standard", the setting "bleak", the menu "overpriced" and the service "mixed"-going-on-"unacceptable". / **Sample dishes:** smoked chicken with pears & Roquefort; rib-eye steak with sweet potato mash; passion fruit mousse. **Value tip:** set 2-crs L & Sun L £13. **Details:** 10.30 pm; L only, except Thu-Sat when L&D; no smoking area; no booking, Sat L.

Fuji Hiro £ 15   ★

45 Wade Ln LS2 8NJ   (0113) 243 9184

For "a healthy, hearty and cheap meal", this "clinical-looking", but "relaxed" Japanese diner is a top budget destination, serving "beautifully-cooked noodles" and other "consistently good" oriental fare. / **Sample dishes:** chicken dumplings; pan-fried noodles with baby corn; no puddings. **Details:** 10 pm, Fri & Sat 11 pm; no credit cards; no smoking; need 5+ to book.

Gueller £ 31   ★

3 York Pl LS1 2DR   (0113) 245 9922

Simon Gueller made a big name for himself at Rascasse, and his "very, very good" Gallic cooking has won quite a following for his year-old townhouse venture in the city's business district; "delusions of grandeur" was the gist of a number of complaints, however, and the place was briefly closed shortly before we went to press, due to financial problems. / **Sample dishes:** roasted scallops with celeriac purée; braised turbot with crab tortellini; passion fruit sorbet. **Value tip:** set 2-crs L & pre-th £12.50. **Details:** www.guellers.com; 10 pm; closed Mon & Sun; children: 5+.

Hansa £ 17   ★

72-74 North St LS2 7PN   (0113) 244 4408

"You go for a meal, not at the end of a boozy night", to this "perennial favourite"; Hansa and her husband Kish are "charming" hosts, and their "freshly-made" Gujerati cuisine – all vegetarian, and "wheat and dairy-free if you want" – is of a "consistently high standard". / **Sample dishes:** banana bhaji; rice pancakes with spiced mixed vegetables; seero (Indian semolina). **Details:** www.hansas.co.uk; 200 yds from Grand Theatre; 10.30 pm; closed Sun D; no smoking area; children: under 5s eat free.

Leodis   £ 39   ✗
Victoria Mill, Sovereign St LS1 4BJ   (0113) 242 1010
*Service which is too often "slapdash" or "arrogant" is helping erode
reporters' esteem for this well-known canalside brasserie; some still
"love the place" and its "constantly inventive fare", but those
damning "very ordinary food at extraordinary prices" are getting
ever more numerous. / **Sample dishes:** warm bacon & poached egg salad;
confit duck with peas & bacon; chocolate nut brownie.*
Details: www.leodis.co.uk; 10 pm, Sat 11 pm; closed Sat L & Sun.

Lucky Dragon   £ 23
Templar Ln LS2 7LP   (0113) 245 0520
*"If this is supposed to be the best Chinese in Leeds, I'd have to
question whether there is a good Chinese in Leeds" – this "old-
established" city-centre spot may be "reliable" and "much
frequented by orientals", but it's as the best of an indifferent bunch
that it earns its popularity. / **Sample dishes:** prawns wrapped in rice
paper; pork with cashew nuts; lychees. Details: www.luckydragon.co.uk;
11.30 pm.*

Malmaison   £ 33
Sovereign Quay LS1 1DQ   (0113) 398 1000
*This brasserie at this design-hotel is praised in some quarters as an
"enjoyable" and "intimate" place that suits a "cool clientèle"; for
too many, though, the food is "expensive" and "very disappointing".
/ **Sample dishes:** char-grilled asparagus & new potatoes; honey-roasted cod &
chorizo salad; crème brûlée. **Value tip:** set 2-crs L £9.95.*
Details: www.malmaison.com; 11.45 pm. **Accommodation:** 100 rooms,
from £115.

Maxi's   £ 24
6 Bingley St LS3 1LX   (0113) 244 0552
*"Grandiose" and rather "cavernous", this Chinese warehouse-
conversion on the city-centre's western fringe offers a "huge" choice
of dishes, which fans say are "pricey, but generally of a high
standard"; service varies from "fast and furious" to "too slow",
however, and some dismiss the place as a "conveyor belt"
experience. / **Sample dishes:** spare ribs in Peking sauce; sizzling steak with
ginger & spring onions; toffee bananas. Details: www.maxi-s.co.uk; 11.30 pm;
no smoking area.*

New Jumbos   £ 21
120-122 Vicar Ln LS2 7NL   (0113) 245 8547
*"Brisk", "well-established" Chinese fixture, which most still find a
"dependable" choice. / **Sample dishes:** deep-fried chicken wings; sweet &
sour pork; ice cream. Details: 11.45 pm; no Amex; no smoking area.*

Olive Tree   £ 26
55 Rodley Ln LS13 1NG   (0113) 256 9283
*"Good Greek food in gently decaying surroundings" continues to
please most (but not all) visitors to this family-run establishment on
the city's main ring road. / **Sample dishes:** kalamata olives; moussaka;
custard tart. Value tip: set 2-crs L & Sun L £6.95. Details: at junction of
A6120 & A657; 11 pm.*

Pool Court at 42   £ 53   ★
42 The Calls LS2 7EW   (0113) 244 4242
*The décor may seem "rather '80s" – in fact it's 1994 – but this
"tiny" restaurant attached to a canalside design-hotel is
undoubtedly the "top" place in town, thanks to its "very good-
quality" cooking and its "professional" service. / **Sample
dishes:** smoked salmon with blinis & caviar; beef with foie gras & truffles in
Madeira sauce; apricot & almond frangipane. **Value tip:** set 3-crs Sun L £19.
Details: 10 pm; closed Sat L & Sun; no smoking; children: no babies.*

regular updates at www.hardens.com

Rajas £ 18
186 Roundhay Rd LS8 5PL (0113) 248 0411
"The setting is downmarket, but that's part of the fun" at this
dependable budget Indian, near Roundhay Park. / *Sample
dishes: onion bhaji; chicken balti; mango kulfi.* **Details:** *close to Roundhay
Park; 10.30 pm; no Amex.*

Rascasse £ 39 X
Canal Whf, Water Ln LS11 5BB (0113) 244 6611
*"A let-down for what is supposed to be one of the best restaurants
in the city"* – despite some praise for new chef John Lyons's
"contemporary" cuisine, this canal-side conversion is decidedly
"not as good as it thinks it is"; complaints include *"ordinary"*
cooking, *"abysmal"* service and a *"clinical"* ambience. / *Sample
dishes: sea bass fishcake with fennel purée; yellowfin tuna niçoise; rum baba
with coconut risotto.* **Value tip:** *set 2-crs L & pre-th £14.*
Details: *www.rascasse-leeds.co.uk; off M621, J3, behind Granary Wharf;
10 pm, Fri & Sat 10.30 pm; closed Sat L & Sun.*

Sala Thai £ 23
13-17 Shaw Ln LS6 4DH (0113) 278 8400
With its *"almost majestic"* décor and its *"beautifully-presented"*
dishes, this Headingley Thai – in a *"fabulous old building"* – is
the most popular oriental in town; neither cooking nor ambience
convince everyone, however. / *Sample dishes: fishcakes with sweet chilli;
green pork Thai curry; Thai custard.* **Details:** *just off Otley Rd, nr Arndale
Centre; 10.30 pm; closed Sat L & Sun; no smoking area.*

Salvo's £ 24
115 Otley Rd LS6 3PX (0113) 275 5017
This highly popular, *"noisy"* Headingley Italian has quite a name for
its *"authentic"*, *"good-value"* cooking, with the *"main drawback"*
being that there's no booking for dinner; however, gently declining
ratings are grist to the mill for those who say it's *"been nothing
special recently"*. / *Sample dishes: creamy garlic mushrooms; roast ham
with basil mash; ginger pudding & custard.* **Details:** *www.salvos.co.uk; 2m N of
University on A660; 10.45 pm, Fri & Sat 11 pm, Sun 9 pm; no smoking area;
no booking at D.*

Sheesh Mahal £ 16 ★
346-348 Kirkstall Rd LS4 2DS (0113) 230 4161
"Azram is an excellent host", and his *"traditional"* Indian restaurant
– with its *"great"* curries, its *"personal"* service and its *"good-
value"* prices – is arguably the best in town and *"worth the trek"*
to these outlying premises, *"opposite the Warner Village"*. / *Sample
dishes: lamb balti tikka; shish kebab with vegetables; home-made ice cream.*
Details: *www.sheeshmahal.co.uk; next to Yorkshire TV centre; midnight;
D only; no smoking.*

Shogun Teppanyaki £ 30 𝔸★
Unit V-W, Granary Whf LS1 4BN (0113) 245 1856
"Combining food with theatre", this unusual Japanese
establishment offers teppanyaki (*"watching everything being cooked
right in front of you"*), with conveyor-belt sushi and noodle options;
"for this type of cuisine, it's good, basic stuff at a fair price".
/ *Sample dishes: king prawn tempura; beef teppanyaki with mushrooms; fruit
salad.* **Details:** *www.shogunteppanyaki@btconnect.com; in arches under
railway station; 11 pm; closed Mon D & Sun; no smoking.*

Sous le Nez en Ville £ 34
Quebec House, Quebec St LS1 2HA (0113) 244 0108
"Great for the early-evening menu" – the food at this long-
established, well-known central basement wine bar may be no more
than *"perfectly pleasant"*, but pre-7.30pm it's special three-course
deal represents *"excellent value"*. / *Sample dishes: deep-fried Brie with
pepper & mango sauce; rib of beef with béarnaise sauce; white chocolate pâté.*
Value tip: *set 3-crs 'early bird' menu £16.95 (6 pm-7.30 pm; includes bottle
of wine).* **Details:** *10 pm, Fri & Sat 10.30 pm; closed Sun.*

Tasca £ 22
4 Russell St LS1 5PT (0113) 244 2205
"OK, but I've had better" is the verdict on most aspects of this
"buzzy" branch of a national tapas chain (whose dash for growth
of late has knocked its fairly unambitious standards across the
board and across the country). / *Sample dishes:* garlic bread with
cheese; meatballs in spicy tomato sauce; strawberry cheesecake.
Details: www.latasca.co.uk; 11 pm; need 8+ to book.

Thai Siam £ 24
68 New Briggate LS1 6NU (0113) 245 1608
"Consistently good-value" fodder still wins majority support for this
central oriental, but a recent change of chef seems to have
provoked the odd unsettled report. / *Sample dishes:* fishcakes with
sweet chilli; roast duck in Thai red curry sauce; jasmine cake.
Details: www.thai-siam.co.uk; 11 pm; closed Mon & Sun L.

Whitelocks Luncheonette £ 18   𝔸
Turk's Head Yd, off Briggate LS2 6HB (0113) 245 3950
"The most characterful bar in Leeds" has a wonderful location just
off Briggate; the period (Victorian) charms of its cosy dining room
are a rather greater attraction than its basic grub. / *Sample
dishes:* crispy haddock fingers; steak & Stilton pie; jam roly-poly with custard.
Details: 8.30 pm; children: 18+.

LEICESTER, LEICESTER CITY   5–4D

Bobby's £ 15   ★
154-156 Belgrave Rd LE4 5AT (0116) 266 0106
"Fresh", *"wonderful"* and *"inexpensive"* south Indian vegetarian
fare makes this *"café-style"* spot one of the highlights of the Golden
Mile; some think its décor *"abysmal"*, however, and service can be
"slow". / *Sample dishes:* deep-fried potato baskets; aubergine stuffed with
peanut & potato; caramelised ice cream. *Details:* www.bobbys.co.uk; 10 pm;
closed Mon; no Amex; no smoking.

Case £ 30
4-6 Hotel St LE1 5AW (0116) 251 7675
"It's even better with the new champagne bar!", proclaims one of
the many local fans who tout this attractive modern brasserie by
St Martins, with its *"tasty"*, *"well-presented"* cooking, as *"the best
of the city-centre restaurants (of a non-Indian nature, anyhow)"*.
/ *Sample dishes:* warm salad of chicken livers & bacon; spinach & ricotta
pancakes with tomato sauce; caramelised lemon tart.
Details: www.thecase.co.uk; nr the Cathedral; 10.30 pm; closed Sun;
no smoking area.

Curry Fever £ 16   ★
139 Belgrave Rd LE4 6AS (0116) 266 2941
"An interesting menu choice" helps distinguish this small and lively
subcontinental café (of over 20 years' standing) in this curry-mad
city. / *Sample dishes:* vegetable samosa; masala lamb; kulfi. *Details:* 0.5m
from city centre; 11 pm; closed Mon.

Friends Tandoori £ 15   ★
41-43 Belgrave Rd LE4 6AR (0116) 266 8809
*"Among the dozens of curry houses in the Belgrave area, this has
stood out over many years for its excellent and distinctive north
Indian (and particularly Punjabi) food…"* – this smarter-than-
average fixture is *"as good as it gets on Leicester's Golden Mile"*.
/ *Sample dishes:* lamb tikka; tandoori chicken; kulfi. *Details:* 11.30 pm;
closed Sun; no Amex; no smoking in dining room.

Opera House £ 39 Ⓐ
10 Guildhall Lane LE1 5FQ (0116) 223 6666
"A quaint old building and cellar" (originally part of St George's Hall) provide the "romantic" setting for this two-year old town-centre spot; fans say it "deserves to be very successful" – even one who thought the cooking "disappointing" says "I still recommend the place, as the choice in Leicester is awful". / Sample dishes: avocado mousse; roast brill; apple soufflé. Value tip: set 2-crs L £9.75. Details: 10 pm; closed Sun D; no smoking.

Shimla Pinks £ 25
69 London Rd LE2 0PE (0116) 247 1471
"I was pleasantly surprised by the food, and I don't like trendy Indian restaurants!" – this "chic" branch of the national subcontinental chain may not hit the heights, but the reports it attracts are generally favourable. / Sample dishes: spiced potato cakes; chicken tikka masala; rasmalai (cream cheese dessert). Value tip: set 2-crs L £6.95. Details: opp railway station; 11 pm; closed Sat L & Sun; no smoking area.

Stones £ 27
29 Millstone Ln LE1 5JY (0116) 291 0004
With its central location, "lively" atmosphere, and reasonable "world-influenced" cuisine, this "trendy" establishment – in a converted Victorian hosiery mill – is an OK destination for those who don't want a curry in this still relatively underserved city. / Sample dishes: sausages with honey & mustard; lamb chops with green beans; chocolate pudding. Details: 11 pm; closed Sun; smoking discouraged.

The Tiffin £ 26
1 De Montfort St LE1 7GE (0116) 247 0420
A "comprehensive" and "unusual" menu helps distinguish this family-run subcontinental, near the station, which provides a much more comfortable option than a trip to the Belgrave Road; popularity can have its drawbacks, though, such as "overbooking" and "long waits". / Sample dishes: chilli-fried chicken; aubergine & tamarind curry; kulfi. Details: www.the-tiffin.co.uk; nr railway station; 10.45 pm; closed Sat L & Sun; no smoking area.

Watsons £ 26 ★
5-9 Upper Brown St LE1 5TE (0116) 222 7770
"It's quite a change to see this sort of thing in Leicester", and this "minimally styled" factory-conversion, with its "tasty and well-cooked" modern British cooking, is welcomed as "a really enjoyable experience" by almost all who comment on it. / Sample dishes: fish soup with rouille & Gruyère; salmon with wok-fried greens; strawberry millefeuille. Value tip: set 2-crs L £8.50. Details: next to Phoenix Art Theatre; 10.30 pm; closed Sun.

LEIGH ON SEA, ESSEX 3–3C

Boat Yard £ 37 Ⓐ
8-13 High St SS9 2EN (01702) 475588
"They've spent a fortune on the building" at this "fascinating" new bar/restaurant on the seafront, so it's a shame that – initially at least – the "very poor food and service" just don't measure up. / Sample dishes: mussels in aromatic green curry; teriyaki beef with crispy noodle salad; white chocolate pannacotta with biscotti. Details: www.theboatyardrestaurant.co.uk; nr railway station; 10.30 pm; closed Mon & Sun D; no Amex.

Auberge du Lac
Brocket Hall £ 56
AL8 7XG (01707) 368888
With its "superb situation" – in a lodge by the lake of the Brocket Hall estate – this ambitious venture still pleases most with its "good all-round quality", in particular the "excellent" Gallic cuisine; it is "very expensive", however, and there were more gripes this year about "aloof" service, and a "flat" atmosphere.
/ **Sample dishes:** warm boudin blanc; lobster & squid with sautéed asparagus & parsnips; mini rum baba. **Value tip:** set 3-crs L £25.
Details: www.brocket-hall.co.uk; on B653 towards Harpenden; 10 pm; closed Mon & Sun D; no jeans. **Accommodation:** 16 rooms, from £150.

Lewtrenchard Manor £ 42   𝔸
EX20 4PN (01566) 783256
"Elaborate" and "imaginative" cooking helps make this "classic, old manor house" on the fringe of Dartmoor – "with much panelling and many antiques" – a "delightful" destination for most reporters; support is undercut by those who just find the whole approach "fussy" – perhaps its new, cheaper bistro will address such concerns. / **Sample dishes:** langoustine cappuccino with truffled leeks; sautéed liver with garlic mash & crispy bacon; apricot bread & butter pudding.
Details: www.lewtrenchard.co.uk; off A30 between Okehampton & Launceston; 9 pm; jacket required; no smoking in dining room; children: 8+.
Accommodation: 9 rooms, from £120.

Lickfold Inn £ 32   𝔸★
GU28 9EY (01798) 861285
"The food is always consistently good, and attractively served" at this "beautiful old inn" in the heart of the South Downs, and staff are "friendly" and "helpful" too. / **Sample dishes:** speck & Mozzarella salad; char-grilled marlin with mango salsa; peaches with lemongrass syrup.
Details: 3m N of A272 between Midhurst & Petworth; 9.30 pm.

Star Inn £ 31   ★
The Street CBY 9PP (01638) 500275
"A big menu with a Spanish flavour" is the culinary attraction at this "quaint" and "out-of-the-way" pub/restaurant – it's "well worth the trip", and gets "very busy". / **Sample dishes:** baby squid crèole; venison in port sauce; treacle tart. **Details:** on B1063 6m SE of Newmarket; 10 pm; closed Sun D; no smoking.

Arundell Arms £ 36   ★
Fore St PL16 0AA (01566) 784666
"Reliably high standards" of straightforward food make the "relaxing" dining room of this "small country hotel" on the river Tamar ("renowned for its fishing breaks") an all-too-rare find; "even if you are full, do not refuse the coffee and homemade truffles". / **Sample dishes:** baked goat's cheese salad; monkfish, brill, sea bass & lobster casserole; peach melba. **Details:** 0.5m off A30, Lifton Down exit; 9.30 pm; no smoking. **Accommodation:** 28 rooms, from £110.

Browns Pie Shop £ 26 ★

33 Steep Hill LN2 1LU (01522) 527330

"Excellent pies" (in *"enormous portions"*) and other *"mouthwatering"* traditional fare at *"very good value-for-money"* prices ensure that this popular local institution, near the Cathedral, *"can get very crowded"* (perhaps explaining why service is occasionally *"distracted"*). / **Sample dishes:** queen scallops; Lincoln red beef; Bailey's cheesecake. **Value tip:** set 2-crs pre-th £5.95. **Details:** nr the Cathedral; 10 pm; no smoking area.

Jew's House £ 42

15 The Strait LN2 1JD (01522) 524851

This well-known establishment, occupying one of the oldest buildings in the city, changed hands in May '01 – too late for a rating from the survey – and has been refurbished by new owner Rowan Bainbridge. / **Sample dishes:** wild mushroom vol-au-vents; braised monkfish with spinach; white chocolate cheesecake. **Details:** halfway down Steep Hill from Cathedral; 9.30 pm; closed Sun D; no smoking.

The Wig & Mitre £ 35

30-32 Steep Hill LN2 1TL (01522) 535190

"It seems to have lost something since it changed premises" a couple of years ago – this *"old-favourite"* pub, *"overshadowed by the cathedral"*, is still praised for its *"reliable"* cooking, but a number of reporters think it *"slightly overpriced"* nowadays. / **Sample dishes:** cheese soufflé with spinach & mushrooms; salmon & herb fishcakes; banoffi pie. **Value tip:** set 3-crs L £12. **Details:** between Cathedral & Castle; 11 pm; no smoking.

Champany Inn £ 52

EH49 7LU (01506) 834532

For *"outstanding food"* (including *"stunningly good steak and lobster"*) and *"wonderful wines"* (over 1000 bins) served amidst *"majestic"* scenery, this *"dressed up"* old inn not that far from Edinburgh has long had legendary status; the experience *"doesn't come cheap"*, though, and some wonder if the standards are quite up to the prices – the adjoining Chop & Ale house can be sampled at more modest cost. / **Sample dishes:** marinated herring fillets; rib-eye steak with olive mash; fruit waffles. **Value tip:** set 2-crs L £16.75. **Details:** www.champany.com; 2m NE of Linlithgow on junction of A904 & A803; 10 pm; closed Sat L & Sun; jacket & tie required; children: 8+. **Accommodation:** 16 rooms, from £95.

Sycamore House £ 33 ★

1 Church St CB2 5HG (01223) 843396

"Reliably good food" and *"sound and courteous service"* make Michael and Susan Sharpe's *"homely"* establishment a consistently popular destination. / **Sample dishes:** spicy tomato, aubergine & apricot soup; calves liver with charred onions & bacon; jam roly-poly with vanilla sauce. **Details:** 1.5m from M11, J11 on A10 to Royston; 9 pm; D only, closed Mon & Sun; no Amex; no smoking; children: 12+.

It's appropriate that the best all-rounder in Liverpool is a restaurant called *60 Hope Street* – a name which perhaps hints at better times ahead in a city which has long had a pretty much moribund restaurant scene. That's not to say that there has not been a certain amount of apparent activity in recent years, but that's led to the creation of little of note.

Atmosphere at modest cost is the general theme of most of the city's more satisfactory places, including two good all-rounders – *Everyman Bistro* and *Pod* – as well as *L'Alouette*, *Jalons Wine Bar* and *Keith's Wine Bar*.

For a city with a long-established Chinatown, there are remarkably few orientals of note – only *Tai Pan* stands out (and then only modestly). Visitors from any other major English city may be struck by the almost complete absence of good curry houses.

L'Alouette £ 36   A
2 Lark Ln L17 8US   (0151) 727 2142
"Fine French food" makes this *"crowded"* and *"friendly"* restaurant a popular destination; the city-centre offshoot, never as successful, closed in July '01. / **Sample dishes:** snails & frogs legs in garlic; steak with Roquefort; lemon tart. **Details:** 10 pm; closed Mon.

Becher's Brook £ 44
29a Hope St L1 9BQ   (0151) 707 0005
Some report "superb" cooking at this "small establishment in a Georgian house" – Merseyside's most established modern restaurant of any aspiration; *"at these prices the food should be more consistent"*, however, and *"sometimes the service just doesn't happen"*; a Birkenhead sibling was short-lived, and closed in April. / **Sample dishes:** king scallops with Waldorf salad; turbot with caramelised onions; coconut & banana parfait. **Value tip:** set 3-crs L & pre-th £14.95. **Details:** between the Cathedrals; 10 pm; closed Sat L & Sun; no smoking; children: 7+.

Casa Italia £ 21
40 Stanley St L1 6AL   (0151) 227 5774
This *"busy"* and *"brisk"* old-style Italian can seem *"a bit of a conveyor-belt experience"*, but its *"basic pizzas and pastas and decent house plonk"* make it a reasonable *"cheap and cheerful"* stand-by. / **Sample dishes:** antipasti & herb focaccia; baked tortellini with spinach & ricotta; cassata ice cream. **Details:** off Victoria St; 10 pm; closed Sun; no Amex; need 8+ to book.

Everyman Bistro £ 17   A★
5-9 Hope St L1 9BH   (0151) 708 9545
"The old favourite" – this 30 year-old self-service bistro under the Everyman Theatre remains a touchstone in this still under-served city; the *"amazing choice"* of *"cheap, cheerful and appetising"* dishes offered includes *"excellent"* salads, a *"fabulous"* veggie selection and *"great"* puddings. / **Sample dishes:** aubergine & sweet pepper pâté; lemon & ginger fried chicken; dark chocolate truffles. **Details:** www.everyman.co.uk; midnight, Fri & Sat 2 am; closed Sun; no Amex; no smoking area.

Far East £ 23
27-35 Berry St L1 9DF   (0151) 709 3141
"A Chinese favourite for bargain banquets" where *"traditional dishes are solidly done"*; perched atop an oriental cash & carry, it's a large venue that some find a mite *"grotty"*. / **Sample dishes:** spare ribs; chicken in black bean sauce; ice cream. **Details:** by church on Berry St; 11.15 pm; no smoking area.

Gulshan £ 23
544-548 Aigburth Rd L19 3QG   (0151) 427 2273
"A carnation for the ladies" sets the rather kitsch tone at this popular local destination – *"the best of a very average bunch of Liverpool Indians"*. / **Sample dishes:** battered prawns; lamb passanda; ice cream. **Details:** www.gulshan-liverpool.com; 10.45 pm; D only.

Jalons Wine Bar £ 27   A

473-475 Smithdown Rd L15 5AE   (0151) 734 3984

"Great entertainment from the piano" helps make this *"friendly"* wine bar a *"popular"* destination; the menu is quite *"interesting"* too, though the odd misfire is not unknown, and *"poor"* service can be a problem. / **Sample dishes:** chicken liver pâté; pot-roasted lamb in red wine & port; apple pie. **Details:** 10 pm; D only, closed Mon.

Keiths Wine Bar £ 15   A

107 Lark Ln L17 8UR   (0151) 728 7688

"In the cosmopolitan student quarter", near Sefton Park, this *"cheap and cheerful"* spot stands out, especially for its *"relaxed"* and *"sociable"* atmosphere; the dishes are *"simple"* and *"good value"*. / **Sample dishes:** grilled halloumi with pitta bread; Spanish-style chicken with rice; sticky toffee pudding. **Details:** 11 pm; no Amex.

Left Bank £ 29

1 Church Rd L15 9EA   (0151) 734 5040

This *"bistro-type"* restaurant *"looks the part"*, and it's been something of a local foodie champion in recent years; there were more *"bad days"*, this year, though – even fans found service that was *"disappointing"*, and some thought the cooking plain *"mediocre"*. / **Sample dishes:** prawns in garlic butter; beef in red wine & cream sauce; crème brûlée. **Value tip:** set 3-crs L £7.95. **Details:** www.leftbankfrenchrestaurant.co.uk; off Penny Lane; 10 pm; closed Sat L.

Number 7 Café £ 21

7-11 Falkner St L8 7PU   (0151) 709 9633

"Light and airy" (some feel slightly *"cold"*) café/deli/gallery with a *"relaxing and informal"* atmosphere, which is known for serving *"enormous portions of wholesome food"*. / **Sample dishes:** tuna & olive salad; lemon & chilli chicken ragoût; chocolate mousse. **Details:** between the Cathedrals; 9 pm; closed Sun D; no credit cards; no smoking area; need 6+ to book.

Pod £ 18   A★

137-139 Allerton Rd L18 2DD   (0151) 724 2255

"The best range of tapas in town" helps make this *"popular wine bar-style café"* a key destination for *"the more mature local sophisticates"*; *"superb Sunday breakfasts"* are a highlight. / **Sample dishes:** chicken satay kebabs; steak with Dolcelatte & red onions; sticky toffee pudding. **Details:** 9.30 pm; no Amex; booking: max 6 at weekends.

Siam Garden £ 24

607 Smithdown Rd L15 5AG   (0151) 734 1471

"It always hits the spot", say local supporters of this *"authentic"* Thai restaurant in Sefton Park, which offers an *"extensive"* menu and *"charming"* service. / **Sample dishes:** Chiang Mai sausage with sweet sauce; Penang chicken with coconut cream; apple pie & ice cream. **Details:** 11.45 pm; closed Sun L.

60 Hope Street £ 38   ★

60 Hope St L1 9BZ   (0151) 707 6060

With its *"first-class restaurant upstairs and a very good café/bar downstairs"*, this is *"rapidly becoming the best place on Merseyside"*, say the many supporters of this *"minimalist"* yearling between the Cathedrals, with its *"friendly and professional"* service. / **Sample dishes:** stir-fried squid with chorizo & rocket; venison with red cabbage & red wine jus; Italian trifle. **Value tip:** set 3-crs L £13.95. **Details:** www.60hopestreet.com; between the Cathedrals; 10.30 pm; closed Sat L & Sun; no Amex; no smoking area.

Tai Pan £ 20 ★
WH Lung Building, Gt Howard St L5 9TZ (0151) 207 3888
On Sundays "the local Chinese flock for dim sum" to this "huge",
"lavishly-furnished" restaurant above an oriental supermarket; at
that and at other meal times its "sumptuous" choice of dishes win
consistent recommendations from reporters. / *Sample dishes:* chicken
satay; pork & green peppers in black bean sauce; ice cream.
Details: 11.30 pm.

Yuet Ben £ 20
1 Upper Duke St L1 9DU (0151) 709 5772
It's been in business for over thirty years, but this "friendly"
Chinatown "fixture" still offers "a really pleasant night out" and
one that "doesn't leave a hole in your wallet"; "a good range of
vegetarian fare" is among the culinary attractions. / *Sample
dishes:* Peking aromatic duck; chilli shredded beef; glazed Chinese toffee
apples. *Details:* 11 pm; D only, closed Sun.

Ziba £ 27
15-19 Berry St L1 9DF (0151) 708 8870
This "brash" and "noisy" city-centre spot has a strong local
reputation for its "well crafted", "continuously evolving" food; it took
more flak this year, though, for being "on the trendy, pretentious
and disappointing side". / *Sample dishes:* seared tuna with aubergine
chutney; suckling pig with dauphinoise potatoes; white chocolate & mango
terrine. *Details:* 10 pm; closed Sat L & Sun; no smoking area.

LLANDDEINIOLEN, GWYNEDD 4–1C

Ty'n Rhos £ 31 ★
LL55 3AE (01248) 670489
"Delicious home-cooked fare", with "flair", contributes much to the
pleasure of a stay at this converted farmhouse, now an "excellent
small hotel". / *Sample dishes:* crab tart with crab bisque dressing;
lamb with bean & rosemary casserole; gooseberry & elderflower tart. *Value tip:* set
2-crs L £10.50. *Details:* www.tynrhos.co.uk; 8.30 pm; closed Mon L;
no smoking; children: 6+. *Accommodation:* 14 rooms, from £80.

LLANDEGLA, DENBIGHSHIRE 5–3A

Bodidris Hall Hotel £ 45 𝔸★★
LL11 3AL (01978) 790434
This medieval manor house (it was good enough for Elizabeth I
apparently) is as highly lauded as ever for its "imaginative" and
"well-presented" cooking – including "superb local venison and
beef" and "irresistible" puds; "warm" service is also praised, as
is the "delightful" setting, with its wonderful hill and lake views.
/ *Sample dishes:* warm pigeon & bacon salad; spicy prawn & smoked salmon
parcels; roast pear & almond tart. *Value tip:* set 3-crs L £18.50. *Details:* on
A5105 from Wrexham; 9 pm; no jeans; no smoking; children: 18+ on Sat.
Accommodation: 9 rooms, from £105.

LLANDEILO, CARMARTHENSHIRE 4–4C

Cawdor Arms £ 30 ★
Rhosmaen St SA19 6EN (01558) 823500
A "restful old hotel in a pretty market town" where it's "always
a pleasure to dine and stay"; the cooking is "rich" but "beautifully
presented", and the "interesting" wine list is "comprehensibly
explained by the proprietor". / *Sample dishes:* salmon & gravadlax
terrine with salsa; steamed salmon with fennel & tomato; white chocolate
brûlée. *Details:* www.cawdor-arms.co.uk; NE of Carmarthen, off A40; 9 pm;
no smoking. *Accommodation:* 17 rooms, from £60.

Bodysgallen Hall £ 51 𝔸★

Pentywyn Rd LL30 IRS (01492) 584466

"Excellent surroundings, food and service" leave little to fault at this impressive country house hotel, just outside the town; it makes a particularly *"great setting for lunch"*, when the *"superb"* gardens – with some 17th-century features – can best be enjoyed. / **Sample dishes:** roast tomato soup with pesto tortellini; cutlets of Welsh lamb with bacon potato cake and mint jus; grape and grenadine jelly with mixed fruit. **Value tip:** set 3-crs L £18. **Details:** www.bodysgallen.com; 2m off A55 on A470; 9.30 pm; jacket & tie required at D; no smoking; children: 8+. **Accommodation:** 36 rooms, from £160.

Richards £ 33 ★

7 Church Walks LL30 2HD (01492) 877924

A *"consistently high"* standard of cooking, a *"good wine list"* and *"amiable"* staff ensure continuing success for Richard Hendey's *"excellent bistro-restaurant"* in this charming, old-fashioned seaside town. / **Sample dishes:** salmon, crab, avocado & prawns; medallions of steak with whisky & Stilton; orange & caramel trifle. **Details:** 11 pm; D only, closed Mon & Sun.

St Tudno Hotel £ 43 ★

Promenade LL30 2LP (01492) 874411

"Superb" cooking, *"featuring local fish and meat"*, an *"extensive wine list"* and *"very good staff"* are among the features which make Martin and Janette Bland's small, slightly chintzy seaside hotel near the pier an (almost) unanimously acclaimed culinary destination. / **Sample dishes:** fishcakes with caper sauce; chicken & leeks in whisky sauce; lemongrass water ice. **Value tip:** set 2-crs L £10. **Details:** www.st-tudno.co.uk; 9.30 pm; no smoking; children: no babies or toddlers at D. **Accommodation:** 19 rooms, from £90.

Lake Country House £ 46 ★

LD4 4BS (01591) 620202

That it's *"in the middle of nowhere"* seems to explain why the sizeable dining room of this Edwardian country house attracts so little commentary; what there is continues to proclaim it as *"a wonderful find"* with *"exceptional"* cuisine. / **Sample dishes:** roast Mediterranean vegetable soup; confit duck & foie gras terrine; rum & mango crème brûlée. **Value tip:** set 3-crs L £17.50. **Details:** off A483 at Garth, follow signs; 9 pm; jacket & tie required; no smoking; children: 7+. **Accommodation:** 19 rooms, from £130.

Bryn Howel Hotel £ 27

LL20 7UW (01978) 860331

"Lovely mountain views" make this hotel dining room just outside the town a long-standing local destination; reports on the food and service at this once reliable fixture, however, remain rather mixed. / **Sample dishes:** char-grilled aubergine; roast supreme of chicken; peach & frangipane tart. **Details:** on A539 towards Ruabon; 9 pm; no smoking. **Accommodation:** 36 rooms, from £95.

Corn Mill £ 24 𝔸

Dee Ln LL20 8PN (01978) 869555

An *"amazing restoration of an old mill"* provides the setting for this *"fantastically-located"* new pub, perched above the river in this charming town; the food is satisfying rather than spectacular. / **Sample dishes:** melon, feta & pine kernel salad; aubergine & goat's cheese stack with red pepper dressing; bara brith bread & butter pudding. **Details:** 9.30 pm; no smoking area; children: before 5.30 pm only.

Jonkers £ 23

9 Chapel St LL20 8NN (01978) 861158

An "eccentric", "front-room type" licensed coffee shop, offering diverse "home cooking" – from "vegetarian pâtés to pheasant stew". / **Sample dishes:** avocado & Mozzarella salad; pork chops with cheese & herb crust; meringues with strawberries & cream. **Details:** 9.30 pm; D only, closed Mon & Sun; no smoking; booking: max 10. **Accommodation:** 3 rooms, from £40.

LLANWDDYN, POWYS 4–2D

Lake Vyrnwy Hotel £ 37 𝔸 ★

Lake Vyrnwy SY10 0LY (01691) 870692

"There can't be many settings better" than this Victorian hotel dining room, which offers "breathtaking" views over the equally impressive Victorian reservoir – an ideal vantage point from which to enjoy cooking of "high quality for the price", using "imaginative 'local' recipes". / **Sample dishes:** lobster, pickled cucumber & mango; monkfish & scallops; chocolate tart with pistachio ice cream. **Details:** www.lakevyrnwy.com; on B4393 at SE end of Lake Vyrnwy; 9.15 pm; no jeans or trainers; no smoking. **Accommodation:** 35 rooms, from £110.

LLYSWEN, POWYS 2–1A

Griffin Inn £ 26 𝔸 ★

LD3 0UR (01874) 754241

"Sound and tasty pub cuisine", using "good local produce", makes this "lovely, ivy-clad old inn near the River Wye" a uniformly popular destination. / **Sample dishes:** hot smoked salmon salad; braised lamb shank with roasted garlic; treacle tart. **Details:** www.griffin-inn.co.uk; on A470; 9 pm; no Amex; no smoking area. **Accommodation:** 9 rooms, from £70.

Llangoed Hall £ 52

LD3 0YP (01874) 754525

As usual, reports on this country house hotel, sited on the River Wye and owned by the family of the late Laura Ashley, are rather a curate's egg – some say it offers a "magnificent setting for a sumptuous meal", whereas others find the whole experience "pretentious" and "disappointing". / **Sample dishes:** butternut squash velouté with smoked chicken; herb-crusted lamb with pea purée; seared pineapple with tarragon sorbet. **Value tip:** set 3-crs L £16.50. **Details:** www.llangoedhall.com; 11m NW of Brecon on A470; 9.30 pm; jacket & tie required; no smoking; children: 8+. **Accommodation:** 23 rooms, from £145.

LOCKINGTON, EAST RIDING OF YORKSHIRE 6–1A

Rockingham Arms £ 41 ★

52 Front St YO25 9SH (01430) 810607

"Fantastic quality cooking, attentive service and a cosy atmosphere" – we had nothing but good reports this year on this family-run pub conversion. / **Sample dishes:** spiced crab cakes; roast Gressingham duck; glazed cherry sabayon. **Details:** between Beverly & Gt Driffield on A164; 9.30 pm; D only, closed Mon & Sun; no Amex; children: 10+. **Accommodation:** 3 rooms, from £110.

LOCKSBOTTOM, KENT 3–3B

Chapter One £ 37 ★

Farnborough Common BR6 8NF (01689) 854848

"Modern European food in suburbia" – this "London-style" venture is "one of the very few decent brasseries in the area", and its popularity is such that "you always need to book well in advance". / **Sample dishes:** smoked goose, walnut & raspberry salad; roast pigeon with pearl barley risotto; hot chocolate fondant. **Details:** www.chapter-1.co.uk; 2m E of Bromley on A21; 10.30 pm.

LONG CRENDON, BUCKINGHAMSHIRE 2–2D
Angel **£ 39**
Bicester Rd HP18 9EE (01844) 208268
It may style itself as a restaurant nowadays, but this ancient former inn still exerts a "very traditional" appeal; it offers "unusually good fish" from "an extensive blackboard menu" and there's "an absence of crush, even when the place is full". / **Sample dishes:** smoked goose & rocket salad; leek & smoked cheddar risotto; black cherry cheesecake. **Value tip:** set 3-crs Sun L £17.95. **Details:** 2m NW of Thame, off B4011; 10 pm; closed Sun D; no Amex; no smoking area. **Accommodation:** 3 rooms, from £65.

LONGRIDGE, LANCASHIRE 5–1B
Heathcote's **£ 54**
104-106 Higher Rd PR3 3SY (01772) 784969
"When it's on form", entrepreneurial chef Paul Heathcote's rural "flagship" restaurant is a "class act", whose "excellent" native cooking is "a rare treat in Lancashire"; a very large proportion of reports, however, continue to speak in terms of disappointment – of "uninspiring" food, "fussy" service or a "stilted" atmosphere. / **Sample dishes:** smoked chicken & celeriac soup; deep-fried hake with creamed peas & tomato butter; mulled pear tart & yoghurt ice cream. **Value tip:** set 3-crs L £16.50. **Details:** www.heathcotes.co.uk; follow signs for Jeffrey Hill; 9.30 pm; closed Mon & Tue; no smoking.

LONGSTOCK, HAMPSHIRE 2–3D
Peat Spade Inn **£ 28** ★
SO20 6DR (01264) 810612
"Bernie is a great cook, and the welcome is always warm" at this "comfortable" and "unassuming" pub-conversion in the Test Valley, which offers a selection of "traditional or more modern choices". / **Sample dishes:** pork & pistachio terrine; red bream & croutons with rosemary fish sauce; toffee & banana crumble. **Details:** 1.25m from Stockbridge; 9 pm; closed Mon & Sun D; no credit cards; no smoking area. **Accommodation:** 2 rooms, from £58.75.

LOUGHBOROUGH, LEICESTERSHIRE 5–3D
Thai House **£ 25**
5a High St LE11 2PY (01509) 260030
"Reasonable food in a culinary desert" – this "reliable" high street spot is a consistently popular local recommendation. / **Sample dishes:** spare ribs; Thai green curry; coconut roll. **Details:** 10.45 pm.

LOUGHTON, ESSEX 3–2B
Ne'als Brasserie **£ 32**
241 High Rd IG10 1AD (020) 8508 3443
Though some report "average" experiences, this "modern brasserie" in "a local high street setting" mostly wins praise for its "interesting", "well-presented" cooking. / **Sample dishes:** Scottish smoked salmon salad; calves liver & bacon with mash & fried onions; dark chocolate pudding with a liquid centre. **Value tip:** set 2-crs L £9.95. **Details:** off M25, J26; 10 pm; closed Mon & Sun D; no Amex.

LOW FELL, TYNE & WEAR 8–2B
Eslington Villa Hotel **£ 31** Ⓐ
8 Station Rd NE9 6DR (0191) 487 6017
"Well worth knowing about in a gastronomic desert", this hidden-away country house has a "relaxed and intimate atmosphere", and wins praise for its "good" modern food and dependable service. / **Sample dishes:** toasted muffin with mushrooms & bacon; seared yellow fin tuna; chocolate cherry mousse. **Value tip:** set 2-crs L £11.50. **Details:** A1 exit for Team Valley Retail World, then left off Eastern Avenue; 9 pm, Fri & Sat 9.30 pm; closed Sat L & Sun D; no smoking. **Accommodation:** 18 rooms, from £50.

LOWER ODDINGTON, GLOUCESTERSHIRE 2–1C
The Fox Inn £ 25 A★
GL56 OUR (01451) 870555
The "great food, wine and ambience" at this agreeable Cotswold
inn – which, despite some gentrification, is "still a real pub" – win a
wholehearted thumbs up from reporters; "you can't book, so get
there early". / Sample dishes: chicken liver, oyster mushroom & bacon
salad; crab & haddock fishcakes with chive cream; berry & hazelnut meringue.
Details: www.foxinn.net; on A436 nr Stow on the Wold; 10 pm; no Amex.
Accommodation: 3 rooms, from £58.

LOWER PEOVER, CHESHIRE 5–2B
Bells of Peover £ 22
The Cobbles WA16 9PZ (01565) 722269
With its "great setting" by a church in an attractive village, this pub
continues to win praise as a good venue for a "relaxing" meal;
some, though, say it's "lost its previous excellence". / Sample
dishes: pâté & toast; steak & Theakstons pie; plum & apple crumble.
Details: opp St Oswald's church, off B5081; 9 pm; no booking; children: 14+.

LOWER SLAUGHTER, GLOUCESTERSHIRE 2–1C
Lower Slaughter Manor £ 63
GL54 2HP (01451) 820456
This "lovely old manor house" has as "pretty" a village setting as
the nearby Lords of the Manor at Upper Slaughter, but it attracts
only a fifth as much commentary; fans say it delivers "terrific" food
and a "wonderful" atmosphere, but it's more expensive than down
the road, and some think it "unmemorable" given the price.
/ Sample dishes: foie gras with black pudding & mushy peas; chicken with
belly bacon & artichoke risotto; hot chocolate soufflé with orange custard.
Value tip: set 3-crs L £15. Details: www.lowerslaughter.co.uk; 2m from
Burton-on-the-Water on A429; 9.30 pm; no smoking; children: 12+.
Accommodation: 16 rooms, from £150.

LOWER WOLVERCOTE, OXFORDSHIRE 2–2D
Trout Inn £ 22 A
195 Godstow Rd OX2 8PN (01865) 302071
A "wonderful riverside location" is both the making and ruination of
this "traditional weir-side pub", near Oxford, whose most famous
regular is Inspector Morse; the food may now have deteriorated to
"bad pub grub level", but "you still won't get a seat after 11.30 am
at the weekends". / Sample dishes: salmon & broccoli fishcakes;
Mediterranean chicken with new potatoes; toffee apple bread & butter pudding
with ice cream & whipped cream. Details: www.the-trout-inn.co.uk; 2m from
junction of A40 & A44; 9 pm, Fri & Sat 9.30 pm; no smoking area; no booking.

LUDLOW, SHROPSHIRE 5–4A
Ego Café Bar £ 26
Quality Square SY8 1AR (01584) 878000
For those bored by the pursuit of culinary nirvana, this unfoodie
wine bar is a top choice; its food "displays many influences but is
always of good quality". / Sample dishes: pork kebabs with satay sauce;
baked trout with rhubarb mayonnaise; pan-fried bananas in rum. Details: off
Castle Square, through timber arches; 9 pm; closed Sun D; no Amex;
no smoking area.

Hibiscus £ 46
17 Corve St SY8 1DA (01584) 872325
It may have achieved instant recognition from Michelin, but Claude
Bosi's year-old venture, occupying the panelled dining room of a
17th-century inn, got short shrift from reporters, who find it
"pretentious" and "overpriced". / Sample dishes: white onion & lime
ravioli with broad beans; roast turbot with tarragon & orange; chocolate tart
with star anise. Details: 9.30 pm; closed Mon L, Tue L & Sun; no Amex;
no smoking.

Koo £ 22 ★

127 Old St SY8 1NU (01584) 878462

"Artfully prepared" and "exquisitely flavoured" Japanese food has created an instant following for this new establishment, which is "small, intimate and very friendly". / **Sample dishes:** hot prawn salad; spicy beef with noodles; green tea ice cream. **Details:** 10 pm; closed Mon & Sun; no Amex.

Merchant House £ 40 ★★

Lower Corve St SY8 1DU (01584) 875438

"Shaun Hill's cooking created Ludlow as a foodie destination, and it's still superb", say fans of his "small" and "relaxed" venture – in one of the town's historic houses – an "unassuming" showcase for his "simple, but highly accomplished" cuisine; surprisingly "frosty" service is a recurrent gripe. / **Sample dishes:** grilled John Dory with aubergine; lamb with haricots in bacon & red wine sauce; apricot tart with Amaretto ice cream. **Details:** 9 pm; closed Mon & Sun; no Amex or Switch; no smoking in dining room.

Mr Underhill's £ 40 ★

Dinham Wier SY8 1EH (01584) 874431

"Considering it's a Hobson's Choice deal, it's damn good", says one of the many fans of the "fantastic" no-choice menu at Chris and Judy Bradley's riverside restaurant, whose "outstanding" service receives particular praise; perhaps the 'Ludlow effect' is raising hopes excessively, though, as a voluble minority of visitors found their experience "nothing special at all". / **Sample dishes:** asparagus & broad bean risotto pancake; Barbary duck with parsley cream; prune & armagnac tart. **Details:** www.mr-underhills.co.uk; 8.30 pm; closed Tue; no Amex; no smoking. **Accommodation:** 6 rooms, from £75.

Overton Grange £ 42

Hereford Rd SY8 4AD (01584) 873500

Even those who discern "real magic" in the cooking on offer at this established foodie destination can rail against the dull, "rather Edwardian" setting; for the doubters – who make up a good proportion of reporters – it's plain "oppressive", and the fare simply "showy". / **Sample dishes:** roast scallops & langoustines with truffles; seared turbot with salsify & roast shallots; chocolate cup with pistachio ice cream. **Details:** www.overtongrangehotel.co.uk; 9.30 pm; closed Mon L; no smoking area. **Accommodation:** 14 rooms, from £95.

LYDGATE, GREATER MANCHESTER 5–2B

White Hart £ 30 Ⓐ★★

51 Stockport Rd OL4 4JJ (01457) 872566

"Superb quality", "home-made" sausages (this is also the HQ of a sausage company) and "deliciously different mash" are the stock-in-trade of this "brilliant" pub/brasserie/restaurant, set high in the moors near Oldham. / **Sample dishes:** crab bavarois with crab fritters; chicken & black pudding sausage with horseradish mash; chocolate & cherry fondant tart. **Details:** 2m E of Oldham on A669, then A6050; 9.30 pm; no smoking area. **Accommodation:** 12 rooms, from £90.

MADINGLEY, CAMBRIDGESHIRE 3–1B

Three Horseshoes £ 34

CB3 8AB (01954) 210221

A reputation for "the best food for miles" has long made this "traditional" pub, with its "pleasant" conservatory, a major destination around Cambridge; many continue to praise the "scrummy and inventive" cooking, but even some fans feel that they "overdo the mixing up of ingredients" rather, and others sense that the place is a bit "full of its own importance" nowadays. / **Sample dishes:** leek & morel tortellini with leek mousse; venison with star anise noodles & pak choy; lemon tart with cherry vodka sorbet. **Details:** 2m W of Cambridge, off A14 or M11, J13; 9.30 pm, Fri & Sat 10 pm; closed Sun D; no smoking area.

Five Horseshoes £ 27 Ⓐ

RG9 6EX (01491) 641282

"Out of the way, but worth finding" – this extremely popular inn provides a *"scenic setting in the Chiltern Hills"* and a *"genuine traditional pub atmosphere"*; the food is *"not cheap"*, but it is reliable (and there's an array of options from bar snacks to full meals, with the summer BBQ the top attraction). / **Sample dishes:** prawn & crab mornay; seafood plate; Oreo cookie cheesecake. **Value tip:** set 2-crs meal £10. **Details:** on B481 between Nettlebed & Watlington; 10 pm; no Amex.

Old Bell £ 35

Abbey Rw SN16 0AG (01666) 822344

Reputedly England's oldest hotel, this attractive Cotswold building still has plenty of appeal for modern travellers (especially those "with kids"), including "good-value" cooking and "charming" service. / **Sample dishes:** chicken liver crostini; Cotswold lamb shepherds pie; chocolate fondant with pistachio ice cream. **Details:** www.oldbellhotel.com; next to Abbey; 9.30 pm; no smoking. **Accommodation:** 31 rooms, from £100.

Croque en Bouche £ 41 ★★

221 Wells Rd WR14 4HF (01684) 565612

For a "memorable one-off meal", you won't do much better than Marion Jones's "simple" but "superb" cooking, which is admirably complemented by husband Robin's "excellent" list of over 1000 wines at their converted bakery premises; the service – generally "entertaining" going on "eccentric" – can occasionally seem a touch "severe" (don't be late!). / **Sample dishes:** crab & lobster croustade; roast Gressingham duck; pineapple & coconut tart. **Details:** www.croque-en-bouche.co.uk; 2m S of Gt Malvern on A449; 9.30 pm; open only Thu, Fri & Sat for D; no Amex; no smoking; booking: max 6.

MANCHESTER, GREATER MANCHESTER 5–2B

Manchester has lots of restaurants. Few of the non-ethnic restaurants are of any great quality however, and the city's culinary champion is as ever the *Yang Sing*, arguably the best Chinese in the country.

When it comes to European cooking, the city still lacks anything truly notable in the way, say, Leeds or Bristol has. Its only seriously ambitious non-ethnic restaurants are some way south west of the city centre, near the Airport (the antediluvian *Moss Nook*) or in suburban Altrincham (see *Juniper*).

In the city centre, the idiosyncratic *Market* is the top choice, but its opening times are very limited. The only other central destinations where reporters find European food of any note are *El Rincon* and the *New Bouchon*, while for atmosphere rather than cooking, *Croma* and *Dimitri's* are worth considering. Those in search of a good-quality, atmospheric brasserie must make the journey to West Didsbury's *Lime Tree*.

Central Manchester has a burgeoning host of pretenders which don't really measure up – *Simply Heathcote's*, *The Lincoln*, *The Reform* and *Stock*. To these may be added a ballooning rogue's gallery of (generally mediocre or worse) national chain outlets: *Chez Gérard*, *Hard Rock Café*, *Livebait*, *Nico Central*, *Le Petit Blanc*, *Rhodes & Co* and *Zinc*. The story is in many respects similar to Birmingham – so much apparent activity, so little real quality. Hopefully this is all just a necessary preliminary to the creation of a 'real' restaurant scene.

When it comes to ethnic restaurants, the position is very much more positive. For top-notch oriental fare, the Yang Sing is supported by *Little Yang Sing*, and also by *Pacific*, *Pearl City*, *Tai Pan* and *Wong Chu*. There are some good Thais, such as *Lemongrass* and *Royal Orchid* (but sadly no longer Chaing Rai, which closed shortly before we went to press). Fans of the subcontinent are well catered for – but only at the cheaper end of the market – not only with Rusholme's curry strip (*Tandoori Kitchen*, *Lal Haweli* and the *Punjab Tandoori*), but also with the likes of West Didsbury's *Great Kathmandu*, or *Gurkha Grill*.

Manchester's huge number of students help support a growing number of gastropubs with food of some note (*Mark Addy*, *The Ox*) as well as some good veggies (most notably *Green's*). The instutionalised alternative lifestyle of the Gay Village sustains what is perhaps the UK's best gay bar/restaurant, *Velvet*.

The Bridgewater Hall £ 28
Lower Mosley St M2 3WS (0161) 950 0000
The café/bar at the Hallé Orchestra's "beautiful" home provides "interesting" sandwiches and other light snacks throughout the day (and also early evenings on concert days); the limited feedback on the grander Charles Hallé restaurant (open pre-concert only) praises "reliably good" cooking. / **Sample dishes:** shredded chicken salad; roast cod with pesto gnocchi; chocolate marquise with poached apricots. **Details:** www.bridgewater-hall.co.uk; 10.30 pm; openings affected by concert times; no smoking.

Cachumba £ 15
220 Burton Rd M20 2LW (0161) 445 2479
"Reliably tasty food with varying Asian influences" wins unanimous support for this "cheap" and "chilled out" BYO café in West Didsbury, in spite of service that can be "abrupt". / **Sample dishes:** red coconut chicken curry; swordfish steak with garlic; mango & berry crumble. **Details:** 9 pm; closed Sun D; no credit cards.

Chez Gérard £ 29
43a Brown St M2 2JJ (0161) 214 1120
This chain beloved of London businessmen – best known for its steak/frites – now has a branch in a comfortable-enough basement in the commercial heart of Manchester; some attack it as a "dull" and "derivative" place – that's chains for you – but the "simple" prix-fixe menus (available all day) are "well cooked" and "reasonable value". / **Sample dishes:** toasted goat's cheese salad; corn-fed chicken with chips; chocolate cake. **Details:** www.santeonline.co.uk; 11 pm; closed Sun.

Croma £ 19 A
1 Clarence St M2 4DE (0161) 237 9799
This "bright" and "shiny" new city-centre pizza-and-more
restaurant is the creation of the original franchisees of the
Deansgate PizzaExpress (by repute, the most successful in the
country); they've brought much "pizzazz" to their immediately
popular venture, which is "like the famous chain, but better".
/ *Sample dishes:* buffalo mozzarella; chicken Caesar pizza; blueberry &
almond pie. *Details:* off Albert Square; 11 pm; no smoking area; need 6+ to
book.

Darbar £ 19
65-67 Wilmslow Rd M14 5TB (0161) 224 4392
As ever, opinions differ on this Rusholme subcontinental stalwart;
some say it offers "consistently good food", whereas for others it's
an establishment that's just "shabby" and "lazy".
/ *Details:* 11.30 pm; no Amex; no smoking area.

Didsbury Brasserie £ 28
747 Wilmslow Rd M20 2RQ (0161) 438 0064
"Recently refurbished", this long-established Gallic fixture receives
a mixed press – fans say it "always offers good food and a nice
atmosphere", but the feeling that "it's not what it used to be"
remains. / *Sample dishes:* Cajun prawn salad; Louisiana chicken; strawberry
shortcake. *Details:* 10 pm; children: before 9 pm only.

Dimitri's £ 25 A
1 Campfield Avenue Arc M3 4FN (0161) 839 3319
With its "interesting" location and "vibrant", "laid-back"
atmosphere, this favourite taverna, handily located just off
Deansgate, provides "ample portions" of "fairly well cooked"
Greek and Mediterranean fare at a "great price". / *Sample
dishes:* chorizo salad; ribs with vegetable couscous; baklava.
Details: www.dimitris.co.uk; nr Museum of Science & Industry; 11.30 pm.

Dukes 92 £ 17 A
19-25 Castle St M3 4LZ (0161) 839 8646
"A canalside pub which specialises in cheese ploughmans" – a
"very simple" formula, but a highly popular one (especially amongst
trendy twentysomethings) on account of the "exceptional choice"
and "generous portions"; service can be "dodgy". / *Sample
dishes:* roast tomato soup; ciabatta with bacon & pesto; hot fudge cake.
Details: off Deansgate; 9 pm; no Amex.

Eighth Day Café £ 9
111 Oxford Rd M1 7DU (0161) 273 4878
"Bargain grub for students and academics" wins praise for this
"cheap and cheerful veggie" – a café/shop run as a co-op on the
university campus; their building is being demolished as we go to
press (they're temporarily just round the corner on Sidney Street),
but re-opening on the same site with a bold new look is promised
in April '02. / *Sample dishes:* Armenian lentil soup; vegan pâté with pitta
bread & salad; vegan chocolate cake. *Details:* www.eighth-day.co.uk; 7 pm;
closed Sat D & Sun; no smoking.

El Rincon £ 25 A★
Longworth St, off St John's St M3 4BQ (0161) 839 8819
This "very traditional Spanish restaurant" and tapas bar near
Deansgate is "always booked weeks in advance", thanks to its
"top notch", "authentic" cooking, its "friendly" service and its
"great", "bustling" atmosphere. / *Sample dishes:* prawns 'pil-pil'; grilled
sea bass with lemon; cheesecake. *Details:* off Deansgate; 11.30 pm.

Est Est Est £ 24 ✗
5 Ridgefield M2 6EG (0161) 833 9400
*"Uninspiring food in an uninspiring environment" – the "vibrant"
Mancunian branch of this now-national Italian chain used to be
especially popular; like its peers, however, it seems to be going from
bad to worse, with "rude" or "rushed" service the weakest link.
/ **Sample dishes:** carpaccio of beef; chicken with pasta & spring vegetables;
dark chocolate mousse cake. **Details:** 11 pm; no smoking area; need 8+ to
book, Fri & Sat.*

Great Kathmandu £ 22 ★
140 Burton Rd M20 1JQ (0161) 434 6413
*This "cult Nepalese cuzza" in West Didsbury has fans who claim
it's "much better than anywhere on the Curry Mile" (though as-
good-as-the-best, is probably a fairer assessment); the setting is
"not what you'd call classy", and service can seem "confused",
but the place is always "packed" nonetheless. / **Sample dishes:** mixed
tandoori kebabs; Nepalese mixed masala; rosmalai (Indian rice pudding). **Value
tip:** set 3-crs L & Sun L £5.95. **Details:** near Withington hospital; midnight.*

Green's £ 27 ★
43 Lapwing Ln M20 2NT (0161) 434 4259
*That "half the customers are carnivores" is perhaps the most telling
fact about this "excellent" and highly popular West Didsbury
venture, whose "consistently imaginative" cooking makes it the
"best vegetarian restaurant in Manchester"; the "café-like" setting
is quite intimate but can be "noisy" (and "try to avoid the draughty
seats near the door"); BYO. / **Sample dishes:** feta & sun-dried tomato
parcels; sweet potato & fried corn tortillas; coconut & strawberry sherry trifle.
Details: 4m S of city centre; 10.30 pm; closed Mon L & Sat L; no Amex.*

The Greenhouse £ 14
331 Great Western St M14 4AN (0161) 224 0730
*This "end-of-terrace vegetarian café" in Rusholme wins praise for
its "very wide menu" of "simple" but satisfying fare, and its "great
selection of wines and beers including organic options"; having
looked a little worn in recent times, it has recently been somewhat
spruced up. / **Sample dishes:** houmous & pitta bread; peppers stuffed with
cashews & pilau rice; knickerbocker glory.
Details: www.greenhouserest.freeuk.com; at junction of Great Western St &
Heald Grove; 9.30 pm; no smoking.*

The Grinch £ 22 Ⓐ
5-7 Chapel Walks, off Cross St M2 1HN (0161) 907 3210
*"Unusual and original" – this "trendy" and "lively" city-centre
café/bar offers decent cocktails, "good snack food" and "good
value". / **Sample dishes:** crispy duck wrap; grilled chicken Caesar salad; hot
cheesecake. **Details:** www.grinch.co.uk; 10.30 pm; no smoking area.*

Gurkha Grill £ 17 ★★
198 Burton Rd M20 1LH (0161) 445 3461
*"Far better than anywhere in Rusholme" – this "'70s time-warp"
in Didsbury maintains quite a reputation for "the best curry in
Manchester"; it's pretty "shabby", though, and "service can be
erratic". / **Sample dishes:** shish kebab; chicken tikka masala; ice cream.
Details: 11.30 pm, Fri & Sat 12.30 am; D only; no Amex.*

Hard Rock Café £ 27 ✗
Corporation St M4 2BS (0161) 831 6700
*"Rubbish!" – reporters are not shy in their criticisms of this "loud",
"arrogant" and "seriously overpriced" new theme diner in the
Printworks Development, where (quite remarkably) even "children
are not catered for properly". / **Sample dishes:** nachos & dips; roast
pork sandwich & fries; hot fudge brownie. **Details:** www.hardrock.com; 11 pm;
no smoking area; no booking.*

Lal Haweli   £ 18   ★

68-72 Wilmslow Rd M14   (0161) 248 9700
There are many better-known local competitors, but this Rusholme
curry house is cited as a "favourite" by its loyal fan club, who say
its "varied" menu (including Pakistani and Nepalese dishes) is
"regularly very good". / *Sample dishes:* king prawn kebabs; chilli chicken;
'funky pie'. *Details:* 1.30 am; no smoking area.

Lead Station   £ 24

99 Beech Rd M21 9EQ   (0161) 881 5559
"One of the first café/bars and still one of the best", this converted
police station is a "fun" and "trendy" destination; considering its
slightly off-the-beaten-track Chorlton location, it generates an
impressive amount of feedback. / *Sample dishes:* Mozzarella, tomato &
basil salad; salmon fishcakes; sticky toffee pudding. *Details:* 9.30 pm, Thu-Sat
10 pm ; no booking.

Lemongrass   £ 25   ★

19 Copson St M20 3HE   (0161) 434 2345
This "small" (but "lively") oriental, in an "unassuming" Withington
street, is "full of character" and has a disproportionately large fan
club on account of its "extensive" range of "fresh" and "exciting"
Thai dishes; BYO. / *Sample dishes:* fishcakes; Thai green chicken curry;
ice cream. *Details:* midnight; closed Mon L & Sun L; no Amex.

The Lime Tree   £ 31   𝔸 ★

8 Lapwing Ln M20 2WS   (0161) 445 1217
"A most agreeable" and "lively" setting, "friendly and
knowledgeable" service, and "consistently good" cooking continue
to make a visit to this "justifiably popular" West Didsbury brasserie
a "memorable" all-round experience for most reporters (and it
remains "better than virtually anywhere in the city-centre"); this
year, however, there were one or two more reports along the lines
of "generally a favourite, but recently proved poor". / *Sample
dishes:* roast langoustines & piri piri prawns; Thai monkfish; roasted peaches.
Value tip: set 2-crs L & pre-th £10.95. *Details:* www.thelimetree.com; near
Withington hospital; 10.30 pm; closed Mon L & Sat L; no smoking area.

The Lincoln   £ 40

1 Lincoln Sq M2 5LN   (0161) 834 9000
With its "classily-presented" food and "interesting interior design",
this ambitious city-centre venue certainly "looks the part" and its
popularity means that it is regularly "crowded"; the atmosphere
can be "flat", however, the menu is "not cheap", and for a vocal
minority the whole experience is "reliably uninspiring". / *Sample
dishes:* wild mushroom & chicken ravioli; mustard & pepper crusted sirloin;
spotted dick with custard ice cream. *Value tip:* set 2-crs L & pre-th £14.50.
Details: opp Manchester Evening News building; 10.30 pm, Fri & Sat 11 pm;
closed Sat L & Sun D.

Little Yang Sing   £ 25   ★★

17 George St M1 4HE   (0161) 228 7722
"It's better than its big brother" claim many fans of this "small,
basement eatery" (the original site of the famous oriental); with its
"top quality Cantonese fare" it makes a "very dependable" choice.
/ *Sample dishes:* mushroom fritters with satay sauce; mange tout & straw
mushrooms in oyster sauce; toffee apples. *Details:* 11.30 pm.

Livebait £ 29

22 Lloyd St M2 5WA (0161) 817 4110

"At last, a fish restaurant for the city" with "diverse", "modern" dishes – that's the optimistic view on this newly-installed export from the capital; to many, it's a "very formulaic chain set-up", however, that seems "pretentious", "expensive", "unfriendly" and "lacking in atmosphere". / **Sample dishes:** Mediterranean fish soup; lobster with new potato salad; pannacotta & strawberries. **Value tip:** set 2-crs meal £9.95. **Details:** www.santeonline.co.uk; by town hall; 11 pm; closed Sun; no smoking area.

The Lowry £ 28

Pier B, Salford Quays M5 2AZ (0161) 876 2121

It enjoys "wonderful views", "overlooking the Manchester ship canal", but this café in the foyer of Salford's new arts centre was "very disappointing" under TV chef Steven Saunders; his active involvement recently ended and there was a refurb' as we went to press. / **Sample dishes:** sea bass & salmon millefeuille; venison sausages with herb mash; praline crème brûlée. **Value tip:** set 2-crs L £10.95. **Details:** www.thelowry.com; 10 pm; closed Mon D & Sun D; no smoking.

Malmaison £ 33

Piccadilly M1 3AQ (0161) 278 1000

Like its siblings in other cities, this "stylish" city-centre design-hotel used to be a top local recommendation; these days, though, "the bar is more fun than the restaurant", given the latter's "cheap brasserie food at high prices" and "slow service". / **Sample dishes:** smoked salmon with lemon; roast spring lamb with Dijon crust; bitter chocolate tart. **Details:** www.malmaison.com; nr Piccadilly Station; 10.45 pm; no smoking area. **Accommodation:** 167 rooms, from £115.

The Mark Addy £ 10 ★

Stanley St M3 5EJ (0161) 832 4080

"Hidden-away below street level, with views of the river" – the formula may be simple at this subterranean spot ("just cheese and pâtés", complemented by "delicious" bread), but "interesting" selections and "generous" portions make it a unanimously popular recommendation. / **Sample dishes:** chive & onion cheese with bread; duck pâté & salad; no puddings. **Details:** 11 pm; no Amex.

The Market £ 34 Ⓐ★

104 High St M4 1HQ (0161) 834 3743

The "best of the bunch" in the town centre – "a nice welcome is guaranteed" at this "quirky", long-established fixture, whose cosy interior helps create an "unusual and chilled" atmosphere; the "interesting" British dishes (served on antique crockery) come in "healthy-sized portions" and are complemented by a "fabulous wine and beer list". / **Sample dishes:** potato ravioli with mint; Parmesan turkey with red pepper confit; banana & passion fruit pavlova. **Details:** www.market-restaurant.com; on corner of Edge St & High St; 9.30 pm; open only Wed-Sat for D; closed first week in Aug.

Metropolitan £ 24

2 Lapwing Ln M20 2WS (0161) 374 9559

"Huge" and "splendidly revamped", this Withington gastropub draws a "trendy", "lively" crowd with its "good and varied pub food" and "wide range of beers"; "big open fires" are a feature in winter. / **Sample dishes:** buffalo mozzarella & beef tomatoes; Tay salmon with vegetable couscous; sticky toffee pudding & toffee sauce. **Details:** near Withington hospital; 9.30 pm; no smoking area.

Metz   £ 23
2 Canal St M1 3PW   (0161) 237 9852
*"It gets a little loud, but it's certainly lively and friendly" at this
popular 'gay space' by the canal; the food's quite "good" too,
and it's "nice to sit on the barge on a sunny day". / **Sample
dishes:** chicken liver terrine with apricot chutney; lamb & herb casserole with
new potatoes; chocolate fudge cake. **Details:** www.metz.co.uk; nr coach
station; 10 pm; children: before 7 pm only.*

Moss Nook   £ 45
Ringway Rd M22 5WD   (0161) 437 4778
*"Some may think the décor OTT, but the food is of a high quality"
say fans of this old-fashioned-plush Gallic establishment near
Manchester Airport, which has been a top "dressy" local
destination since 1973. / **Sample dishes:** lobster salad with smoked
salmon parcels; grilled duckling with glazed pears; crème brûlée. **Details:** on
B5166, 1m from Manchester airport; 9.30 pm; closed Mon, Sat L & Sun;
no jeans; children: 11+.*

Mr Thomas's Chop House   £ 30   𝔸
52 Cross St M2 7AR   (0161) 832 2245
*"Good" traditional British lunchtime food – "lamb chops" and
"mustard dumplings", for example – and "well-kept real ale" help
make this "characterful" and unspoilt Victorian bar-cum-restaurant
the city-centre's "business venue par excellence". / **Sample
dishes:** potted duck with spiced pear chutney; chicken & mushroom pie;
spotted dick & custard. **Details:** www.mrthomas-chophouse.co.uk; L only;
closed Sun.*

New Bouchon   £ 29   ★
63 Bridge St M3 3BQ   (0161) 832 9393
*"As near a French provincial restaurant as you will find", this
"small" and "traditional" central spot – a sibling to Lymm's
La Bohème – wins impressively consistent support for its "genuine"
cooking; set menus, in particular, offer "excellent value". / **Sample
dishes:** Burgundy snails with garlic confit; beef with Applewood dauphinoise;
profiteroles. **Details:** 10 pm; closed Mon & Sun; no smoking.*

Nico Central
Crowne Plaza   £ 33   ✗
Mount St M60 2DS   (0161) 236 6488
*"Appalling and third-rate" – many reporters "would never return"
to this "overpriced" and "pompous" city-centre Gallic brasserie,
where "nobody seems to care". / **Sample dishes:** spiced apple & crab
salad; red snapper with garlic pasta & basil oil; raspberry crème brûlée.
Details: www.trpplc.com; opp St Peter's Square; 10.30 pm, Fri & Sat 11 pm;
closed Sat L & Sun L; no smoking area.*

The Nose   £ 21
6 Lapwing Ln M20 8WS   (0161) 445 3653
*"An unfussy and cosy" atmosphere, together with "cheap and
sensible food" from a blackboard menu makes this "consistent"
West Didsbury bar/restaurant a hugely "popular meeting place"
for a wide-ranging clientèle; it's "particularly good in warm weather,
when you can sit on the front terrace". / **Sample dishes:** guacamole,
tuna & olive dip; mixed fish kebabs; sticky toffee pudding. **Details:** between
Pallatine Road & Woodington hospital; 9.30 pm; no smoking area.*

The Ox   £ 24   ★
71 Liverpool Rd M3 4NQ   (0161) 839 7740
*"Relatively recently converted into a gastropub", this "revamped",
but "unpretentious" Castlefield boozer consistently pleases the
punters with its "delicious", "well thought-out" modern cooking,
not to mention its "simple, but varied" wines and "good beer".
/ **Sample dishes:** teriyaki beef; roast rack of lamb; toffee & pecan
cheesecake. **Details:** www.theox.co.uk; 9.45 pm; closed Sun D; no Amex;
no smoking area. **Accommodation:** 9 rooms, from £44.95.*

Pacific £ 29 ★
58-60 George St M1 4HF (0161) 228 6668
"Trendy", *"light and airy"* Chinatown yearling, with two floors –
Thai and Chinese; *"very tasty"* dishes at *"good-value"* prices are
roundly praised throughout, and the place has quickly become one
of the most popular destinations in town. / **Sample dishes:** steamed
scallops in garlic sauce; sizzling beef in black pepper sauce; toffee banana &
ice cream. **Details:** www.pacific-restaurant-manchester.co.uk; 10.45 pm;
no smoking area; children: 3+.

Palmiro £ 25
197 Upper Chorlton Rd M16 0BH (0161) 860 7330
"Very authentic, rustic fare" quickly earned quite a reputation for
this year-old Whalley Range Italian; early success seems to have
gone to its head, though – the food is now often found *"good, not
great"* (and in quite a few cases *"overpriced"* and *"pretentious"*),
and the ambience can be *"chilly"*. / **Sample dishes:** char-grilled
calamari with salsa; roast lamb with artichokes; chocolate tart with vanilla
sauce. **Details:** www.palmiro.net; 10.30 pm; D only, closed Mon; no Amex.

Pearl City £ 21 ★
33 George St M1 4PH (0161) 228 7683
Even its supporters don't claim that this vast Chinatown institution
is Manchester's best Cantonese, but they do say that its
"reasonable prices" and *"consistently good"* performance make
it *"the best for everyday eating"*. / **Sample dishes:** dim sum; chicken in
black bean sauce; coconut pudding. **Details:** 3 am, Fri & Sat 4 am, Sun
midnight.

Le Petit Blanc £ 34
55 King St M2 4LQ (0161) 832 1000
Mancunians rightly had *"high expectations"* of Raymond Blanc's
new city-centre brasserie, and for many it is, indeed, a *"good all-
rounder"*, serving *"the best non-oriental food in town"*; it's hard to
ignore the sizeable minority of disappointed reporters, though, who
found the place *"lacking in individuality"*, and the cooking *"rather
average"* – that was certainly our experience. / **Sample
dishes:** guacamole & crab tian; roast pork tenderloin with mousseline potatoes;
'floating islands'. **Value tip:** set 2-crs L & pre-th £12.50.
Details: www.petitblanc.com; Chapel Walk side of the former NatWest
building; 10 pm; no smoking area.

Punjab Tandoori £ 16 ★
177 Wilmslow Rd M14 5AP (0161) 225 2960
"Really good dosas" are a menu highlight at this leading Rusholme
subcontinental, whose *"most interesting"* south Indian (ie non meat
eating) cooking makes it *"a good destination for veggies and
vegans"*. / **Sample dishes:** fish tandoori; chicken & mango with rice;
rosmalai (Indian rice pudding). **Details:** midnight; no Amex.

The Reform £ 47 ✗
Spring Gdns, King St M2 4ST (0161) 839 9966
Even some who've *"never met Posh 'n' Becks there"* say that the
"very grand", *"high camp/kitsch"* surroundings of the former
Liberal Club provide an *"opulent and extravagant"* setting for
this city-centre spot – *"expensive, but worth it"* (*"at least once"*);
roughly a quarter of reports, however, say the place is *"all style
and no content"* – offering *"unimaginative"* food and *"unattentive"*
service, and all at *"extortionate"* prices. / **Sample dishes:** pan-fried
quail with barley risotto; smoked haddock with Welsh rarebit & colcannon;
bread & butter pudding. **Value tip:** set 3-crs pre-th £16.95. **Details:** 11 pm;
closed Sat L & Sun.

The Restaurant Bar & Grill £ 29
14 John Dalton St M2 5JR (0161) 839 1999
*This hard-edged city-centre newcomer opened in the spring of
2001 – too late, it seems, to attract much survey commentary
(or perhaps the name is just too elusive for our system); it has high
ambitions, and as the latest venture from the founders of Est Est
Est, should be one to watch. / **Sample dishes:** spicy shrimp risotto;
crispy duck with pear & watercress salad; bread & butter pudding.
Details: 10.45 pm; no smoking area; booking: max 8 at weekends.*

Rhodes & Co £ 34
Waters Reach M17 1WS (0161) 868 1900
*"A decent meal next to a football ground" is not to be sneezed at,
but many feel that "something is missing" from Gary R's English
brasserie, near Old Trafford – the "typical Rhodes school-dinners"
cooking is "good, but just not special" and the atmosphere strikes
many as "impersonal". / **Sample dishes:** stuffed Piedmont red peppers;
salmon fishcakes with lemon butter sauce; lemon rice pudding. **Value tip:** set
2-crs L £12.50. **Details:** next to Golden Tulip Hotel at Old Trafford; 9.45 pm;
closed Sat L & Sun L.*

Royal Orchid £ 31   ★
36 Charlotte St M1 4FD (0161) 236 5183
*It's not particularly well known, but this "friendly" city-centre
oriental wins high praise from its small fan club for "top-quality"
Thai cooking. / **Sample dishes:** Thai wontons; fish with sweet & sour sauce;
ice cream. **Value tip:** set 3-crs L £7.50. **Details:** nr Piccadilly Gardens;
11.30 pm.*

Sangam £ 14
13-15 Wilmslow Rd M14 5TB (0161) 257 3922
*"Expect to wait for a table" at this "popular" Rusholme curry
house, whose decent value and "efficient service" ensures it's
"always busy". / **Sample dishes:** fish tikka; lamb masala; kulfi.
Details: www.sangam.co.uk; 2m from city centre; midnight; no smoking area.*

Shere Khan £ 16
52 Wilmslow Rd M14 5TQ (0161) 256 2624
*"It looks like a petrol station", but this "large" and "lively" Curry
Mile landmark is "packed every night", and, though some find the
cooking rather "identikit" it's about "as good as any in Rusholme";
(shopaholics will now also find a branch in the Trafford Centre,
tel 0161 749 9900). / **Sample dishes:** chicken tikka; lamb jalfrezi; kulfi.
Details: www.skrestaurant.com; midnight.*

Shezan £ 23
119 Wilmslow Rd M14 5AN (0161) 224 3116
*A "good variety" of "reliable" fare makes this glitzy cuzza one of
the better known on the Curry Mile. / **Sample dishes:** chicken in spiced
yoghurt; sizzling lamb with ginger & coriander; rasmalai (cream cheese
dessert). **Details:** midnight, Fri & Sat 3.30 am; no smoking area.*

Shimla Pinks £ 30
Dolefield, Crown Sq M3 3EN (0161) 831 7099
*"Traditional Indian food in a cool restaurant setting" is a potentially
winning formula, but this year-old city-centre venture is drifting like
others in this troubled national chain, and increasingly the place is
seen as "pretentious and unconvincing". / **Sample dishes:** paneer
cheese with mango & herbs; king prawns with peppers & tomatoes; sweet
dumplings in rose syrup. **Value tip:** set 2-crs L £8.95. **Details:** opp Crown
Courts; 10.45 pm, Sat & Sun 11.30 pm; closed Sat L & Sun L.*

Siam Orchid £ 26
54 Portland St M1 4QU (0161) 236 1388
*"Always good", say fans of this small, relatively unknown Thai,
behind Piccadilly station. / **Sample dishes:** chicken satay; Thai fried
noodles & prawns; pistachio ice cream. **Details:** 11.30 pm;
closed Sat L & Sun L.*

Simply Heathcote's £ 28 ✗

Jackson Row, Deansgate M2 5WD (0161) 835 3536

The "cold" and "cavernous" interior of this well-known, city-centre outpost of the North West's most prominent chef was having a much needed revamp as we were going to press; while they're at it, let's hope they sort out the "bland" cooking and the "lifeless" service. / Sample dishes: artichoke & leek tart; confit pork with roast tomatoes; creamed rice pudding. Details: nr Opera House; 10 pm, Sat 11 pm.

Stock £ 39

4 Norfolk St M2 1DW (0161) 839 6644

With its "magnificent", if somewhat "daunting" location in the old stock exchange, this airy Italian provides "smart" surroundings, particularly suited to business, and is "rather pricey"; it serves "possibly the best Italian food in Manchester" — that is to say it's "perfectly good, without setting the world on fire". / Sample dishes: linguine with crayfish tails; calves liver in balsamic vinegar sauce; caramelised peach tartlet. Details: www.stockrestaurant.co.uk; 10.30 pm; closed Sun.

Tai Pan £ 24 ★

81-97 Upper Brook St M13 9TX (0161) 273 2798

"Go for the dim sum on Sunday lunch time, and go early" is the top recommendation if you want to enjoy some "superb" cooking at this enormous Chinese restaurant; on the practical front, its location a little way from the city-centre "makes parking easier". / Sample dishes: dim sum; king prawns in black bean sauce; mango pudding. Details: 2m from city centre; 11 pm.

Tampopo £ 23

16 Albert Sq M2 5PF (0161) 819 1966

"Interesting eastern-fusion food" has made this "popular", "canteen"-style noodle bar a key city-centre budget destination; there were, however, this year a few reports of "uninspiring" results. / Sample dishes: honey-marinated ribs; prawns in coconut & basil sauce; ginger crème brûlée. Details: 11 pm; no Amex; no smoking; need 7+ to book; children: 7+.

Tandoori Kitchen £ 15 ★

131-133 Wilmslow Rd M14 5AW (0161) 224 2329

"One of Rusholme's oldest and best" — "you don't get the homogenised gloop of today's Curry Mile" at this long-established, "friendly" and "unpretentious" Indian — reporters' favourite in the area — whose "very consistent" cooking includes some Persian options; BYO. / Sample dishes: paneer pakora; balti cod with coconut; kulfi. Details: midnight; no smoking area.

La Tasca £ 24

76 Deansgate M3 2FW (0161) 834 8234

"Expansion of the chain has diluted quality" is a perceptive view on this national tapas group, whose ratings have nose-dived; this long-standing, "incredibly popular" branch remains "busy and bustling", but the service can seem "non-existent" and cooking that was never cutting edge now seems "very poor". / Sample dishes: langoustines; seafood paella; chocolate truffle. Details: www.latasca.co.uk; 10.30 pm; need 8+ to book.

That Café £ 32 ★

1031-1033 Stockport Rd M19 2TB (0161) 432 4672

"You'd drive straight past if you didn't know it was there" — this "quirky" Levenshulme fixture wins continued praise for its "changing, good quality" menu, its friendly welcome, and its "laid-back" ambience. / Sample dishes: avocado, fennel & haricot gateaux; salt & pepper duck with quince gravy; coconut mousse in a chocolate cup. Value tip: set 2-crs pre-th & Sun L £9.95. Details: www.thatcafe.co.uk; on A6 between Manchester & Stockport; 10.30 pm; closed Mon, Tue-Sat D only, closed Sun D; no Amex; no smoking area.

This & That £ 5 ★

3 Soap St M4 1EW   (0161) 832 4971
"Worth every penny of £2.30 for the rice-plus-three" – the "fabulous" budget cooking at this "lunchtime-only curry canteen", near Victoria Station, has won it something of a cult following. / **Sample dishes:** *shish kebabs; chicken with vegetables; no puddings.* **Details:** *5 pm; closed Sat & Sun; no credit cards.*

Velvet £ 25   Ⓐ★

2 Canal St M1 3HE   (0161) 236 9003
An "interesting" menu helps make this "trendy", "buzzy" and "so friendly" spot a very popular Gay Village destination – "you'd think trimmings like goldfish in the floor would detract from the food, but this is not the case". / **Sample dishes:** *soup of the day; steak with pepper sauce & chips; chocolate fudge cake.* **Details:** *10 pm, Fri & Sat midnight.*

Wong Chu £ 21 ★

63 Faulkner St M1 4FF   (0161) 236 2346
If you're looking for "the fewest concessions to western tastes", this "basic noodle and duck house" in Chinatown offers "good value", and "great choice too – especially if you're hungry". / **Sample dishes:** *chicken & sweetcorn soup; roast pork with fried rice; coconut ice cream.* **Details:** *midnight; no Amex.*

Woodstock Tavern £ 23

139 Barlow Moor Rd M20 2DY   (0161) 448 7951
"A wide variety of unusual dishes" (including exotic meats) add interest to a visit to this popular Chorlton-cum-Hardy boozer; praise tends to be a touch equivocal, though, and even a former worker there (who confirms that "everything is freshly prepared on the spot") says that to get "great" results you need to be "selective". / **Sample dishes:** *salt & pepper chicken wings; kangaroo steak with port & mushroom sauce; strawberry daquiri cheesecake.* **Details:** *0.5m from junction for Princess Parkway on M56; 7.30 pm; no Amex; no smoking area; no booking; children: weekends only (until 8 pm).*

Yang Sing £ 28 ★★

34 Princess St M1 4JY   (0161) 236 2200
"Simply the best Chinese restaurant in the UK!" – this "flash" institution in Chinatown has a lot to live up to, and the chorus of praise for Harry Yeung's "wonderful" cooking (including "incredible" dim sum) remains almost as great as ever; for a slightly greater minority this year, however, results were good rather than great. / **Sample dishes:** *crispy spring rolls; pan-fried squid with vegetables; sweet dim sum.* **Details:** *www.yang-sing.com; 11.45 pm, Fri & Sat 12.15 am.*

Zinc Bar & Grill £ 29 ✗

The Triangle, Hanging Ditch M4 3ES   (0870) 333 4333
At Conran Restaurants' first UK venture outside London, its good to see there's no discrimination against the provinces – locals hail this Triangle Mall newcomer as just as "mediocre" and "overpriced" as the dismal Mayfair original. / **Sample dishes:** *fried squid in chilli; lamb kebabs with bulgar wheat salad; lemon tart.* **Value tip:** *set 2-crs L £10.* **Details:** *www.conran.com; 10 pm.*

MANNINGTREE, ESSEX 3–2C

Stour Bay Café £ 28 ★

39-43 High St CO11 1AH   (01206) 396687
The "unusual" food is "always perfect, imaginative and beautifully presented" say fans of this consistently popular bistro, "at the centre of the high street". / **Sample dishes:** *red mullet, thyme & lemon risotto; sea bass with clam stew & chorizo oil; Devon toffee ice cream.* **Details:** *www.allaboutessex.co.uk; 9.30 pm; closed Mon & Tue; no Amex; no smoking in dining room.*

Travellers Rest   £ 26

Mapperley Plains, Plains Rd   NG3 5RT   (0115) 926 4412

An "extensive menu" – which supporters say offers "excellent choice and value" – contributes to the popularity of this "friendly" and "homely" boozer, near Nottingham. / **Sample dishes:** black pudding tower; lamb en croûte; chocolate muffin sundae. **Details:** off B684 between Nottingham & Woodborough; 10 pm; no smoking area; no booking.

MARKET HARBOROUGH, LEICESTERSHIRE   5–4D

Han's   £ 28   ★

29 St Mary's Rd   LE16 7DS   (01858) 462288

A popular town-centre Chinese, "known locally for its excellent food and service". / **Sample dishes:** seafood & lettuce wraps; sizzling beef & black pepper; toffee apples & banana. **Value tip:** set 3-crs L £6.50. **Details:** 11 pm; closed Sat L & Sun.

MARLBOROUGH, WILTSHIRE   2–2C

Harrow Inn   £ 48   ★

Little Bedwyn   3JP   (01672) 870871

It's worth seeking out this "lovely", "cosy" small restaurant, "in a converted pub in the middle of the countryside", which provides "great" food, "enthusiastic" service, and an "excellent" wine list. / **Sample dishes:** foie gras with ham & apple sauce; Welsh Black beef with Indian spices; chocolate platter. **Details:** www.harrowinn.co.uk; 9 pm; closed Mon & Sun D; no smoking area.

MARLOW, BUCKINGHAMSHIRE   3–3A

Compleat Angler   £ 55   ✗

Marlow Bridge   SL7 1RG   (01628) 484444

"Views of the Thames as good as you'll find" are scant compensation for the "appalling" food and "snooty" service too often endured at this famous – but "dreadful", "pretentious" and "self-satisfied" – hotel. / **Sample dishes:** deep-fried courgette flowers; pork with slow-roasted tomatoes; rhubarb parfait with strawberries. **Value tip:** set 3-crs L £23. **Details:** 10.30 pm; no jeans; no smoking area. **Accommodation:** 64 rooms, from £225.

Danesfield House   £ 60   𝔸

Henley Rd   SL7 2EY   (01628) 891010

It's the "wood panelling and pictures" charm and "great view" at this "old-fashioned country house hotel" (occupying a large Victorian mansion overlooking the Thames) which make it of most note – its gastronomic attractions receive a somewhat mixed reception. / **Sample dishes:** seared scallops & caramelised apples; chicken in truffles & champagne with noodles; apple parfait & baby toffee apple. **Value tip:** set 2-crs L £18.50. **Details:** www.danesfieldhouse.co.uk; 3m outside Marlow on the A4155; 10 pm; no jeans or trainers; no smoking. **Accommodation:** 87 rooms, from £205.

MASHAM, NORTH YORKSHIRE   8–4B

Floodlite   £ 27   ★

7 Silver St   HG4 4DX   (01765) 689000

It "looks like a café", but it's "very nice" – if you like the "pink boudoir look" – inside Charles Flood's popular Dales town eatery where "superb game" is a particular attraction. / **Sample dishes:** king prawn & squid salad; fillet steak with mushroom purée; blackberry & apple bread & butter pudding. **Details:** 9 pm; closed Mon, Tue L-Thu L & Sun; no Switch; no smoking area; booking essential, Sun.

Bay Tree £ 35 ★

4 Potter St DE73 1DW (01332) 863358

This "very personal" restaurant, in a former 17th-century town-centre coaching inn has "benefited much from a new, less complicated menu and improved décor", and all reports sing the praises of Rex Howell's "superb and imaginative" cooking. / **Sample dishes:** game consommé; haddock & salmon fishcake with tomato salad; sticky toffee pudding. **Value tip:** set 4-crs Sun L £17.50. **Details:** www.baytreerestaurant.co.uk; 10 pm; closed Mon & Sun D; no smoking area.

Ruskins £ 34 Ⓐ★

2 Blanchcroft DE73 1GG (01332) 864170

"Bring your own wine, and book six months ahead!" – our reporter may exaggerate, but this "homely" and "intimate" spot, which offers "simple but well cooked" fare, is "hugely popular". / **Sample dishes:** crab thermidor; crispy duck in plum & ginger sauce; summer pudding. **Details:** 9.30 pm; closed Mon, Tue, Wed, Thu L & Sun; no credit cards; booking essential.

Pink Geranium £ 53 Ⓐ★

25 Station Rd SG8 6DX (01763) 260215

Mark Jordan is still settling in at this "lovely", "cottagey" thatched restaurant (which he took over last year from TV chef Steven Saunders), but his "fresh" and "well presented" cooking is already making the place a "cracking" destination for many reporters. / **Sample dishes:** niçoise vegetable terrine with tapenade dressing; boudin of lobster with new potatoes; crème brûlée with raspberry coulis. **Details:** off A10, 2nd exit (opp church); 10 pm; closed Mon; jacket required; no smoking.

Sheene Mill £ 41

Station Rd SG8 6DX (01763) 261393

TV-chef Steven Saunders (who used to own the more famous Pink Geranium) has now turned his attention to this less ambitious venture in a converted riverside mill; the cooking pleases most (but not all) reporters, and while some find the style "charming", others say it's "pretentious". / **Sample dishes:** prawn tempura; braised lamb with garlic mash & onion gravy; banana soufflé with toffee sauce. **Value tip:** set 2-crs L £10. **Details:** www.stevensaunders.co.uk; off A10, 10m S of Cambridge; 10 pm; closed Sun D; no smoking before 9.30 pm. **Accommodation:** 9 rooms, from £70.

Oddfellows Arms £ 24 ★

73 Moor End Rd SK6 5PT (0161) 449 7826

"Very good cooking" (with fish a speciality) in a "traditional pub setting" is a formula which attracts limited, but all positive, reports on this 18th-century village boozer. / **Sample dishes:** Thai-spiced prawns in filo pastry; monkfish & crayfish tails; bread & butter pudding. **Details:** 7m S of Stockport; 9.30 pm; closed Mon D & Sun D; no smoking in dining room; book for D & Sun L only.

Shepherd's Inn £ 19 ★

CA10 1HF (0870) 7453383

"Puddings to die for" ("and what a choice") seem especially to linger in the minds of reporters who have visited this "warm" and "friendly" pub; it also offers an "excellent" range of more savoury dishes. / **Sample dishes:** dill-marinated herrings; breaded wholetail scampi; lemon cheesecake. **Details:** www.shepherdsinn.net; on village green; 9.45 pm; no smoking area; no booking.

Village Bakery £ 18 ★

CA10 1HE (01768) 881515

The fare – based around "all-organic home baking of the highest standard" – may be a touch "limited" in scope, but reporters speak only well of this "delightful country tea room"; it has friends in high places, too, the new dining facilities having been inaugurated by no less an organicist than HRH The Prince of Wales. / **Sample dishes:** vegetable soup; grilled trout with herb butter; upside down pear & ginger pudding. **Details:** www.village-bakery.com; 10m NE of Penrith on A686; 5 pm; L only; no Amex; no smoking.

MERTHYR TYDFIL, MERTHYR TYDFIL 4–4D

Nant Ddu Lodge £ 29 ★

Brecon Rd CF48 2HY (01685) 379111

This "old mountain hunting lodge" by a river strikes some as "cramped", but it offers "good food, and value for money"; "booking is advisable" if you want to eat in the restaurant rather than the bar. / **Sample dishes:** chicken liver, port & hazelnut pâté; black bream with herb sauce; plum crumble. **Details:** www.nant-ddu-lodge.co.uk; 6m N of Merthyr on A470; 9.30 pm; closed Sun D; no smoking; booking: max 8. **Accommodation:** 28 rooms, from £69.50.

MICKLEHAM, SURREY 3–3A

King William IV £ 24 ★

Byttom Hl RH5 6EL (01372) 372590

"Well-cooked pub fayre" makes this "small, rural ale house", in "attractive gardens", a "reliable" destination. / **Sample dishes:** garlic bread with Mozzarella; steak & kidney pie; treacle tart. **Details:** off A24; 9.30 pm; no Amex; no booking in summer; children: 12+.

MIDDLESBROUGH, MIDDLESBROUGH 8–3C

Purple Onion £ 33 Ⓐ

80 Corporation Rd TS1 2RF (01642) 222250

It may be "unique" – at least in this part of the world – but this "lively" and "eclectic" bistro gets mixed reports, and there's a strong minority feeling that it's just rather "overpriced" and "average". / **Sample dishes:** seared king scallop & crab fritters; honey-glazed pork with courgettes; char-grilled peaches in Cointreau. **Details:** by law courts; 10.30 pm; closed Sun D; no Amex.

MILTON KEYNES, MILTON KEYNES 3–2A

Jaipur £ 25

502 Eldergate MK9 1LR (01908) 669796

It may seem "an unlikely place for an excellent Indian" – next to Milton Keynes BR – but "better-than-average cooking", "interesting spicing" and "old-fashioned courtesy" have combined to make this such a popular destination that it's moving to a new purpose-built home in October '01. / **Sample dishes:** prawn puri; chicken tikka makhani; kulfi. **Details:** www.jaipur.co.uk; next to railway station; 11.30 pm; no smoking area.

MOLD, FLINTSHIRE 5–2A

Glasfryn £ 28

Raikes Ln CH7 6LR (01352) 750500

"A huge dining area with panoramic views" lends interest to a visit to this popular gastropub; the food is "beautifully cooked" too, so it's no great surprise that the place is "very busy". / **Sample dishes:** prawn, grape & watermelon salad; Chinese duck with coconut rice; summer pudding. **Details:** 9.30 pm; children: 16+ after 6 pm.

MORETON-IN-MARSH, GLOUCESTERSHIRE

Marsh Goose £ 40

High St GL56 0AX (01608) 653500

*The modern cooking is often "beautifully prepared and presented" at this well-known, "airy" rustic dining room, near the centre of the village, which is perennially "booked up"; some feel the food is "over-rated", however, and "a good meal can be let down by incompetent service". / **Sample dishes:** mushroom ravioli with chicken & leek velouté; sea trout with shellfish bisque, fennel & chorizo; sticky toffee pudding. **Details:** www.marshgoose.com; 9.30 pm; closed Mon, Tue L & Sun D; no smoking area.*

MORSTON, NORFOLK

Morston Hall £ 41 A★★

Main Coast Rd NR27 7AA (01263) 741041

*"Brilliant each and every time", say fans of this "charming" coastal hotel (set in a 17th century building amidst "lovely" gardens), where "attentive" staff deliver "consistently good" cooking from "two superb chefs". / **Sample dishes:** roast lamb & lamb's kidneys with angel hair pasta; roast duck with baby carrots & turnips; baked Alaska. **Details:** www.morstonhall.com; between Blakeney & Wells on A149; 8 pm; D only, except Sun open L & D; no smoking at D. **Accommodation:** 6 rooms, from £200, incl D.*

MOULSFORD, OXFORDSHIRE

Beetle & Wedge £ 43 A

Ferry Ln OX10 9JF (01491) 651381

*"One of the most tranquil settings on a sunny day" makes this picturebook house by the Thames a "perfect getaway" (especially for romantics); the charcoal grill in the less expensive and "livelier" boathouse is a better-known attraction than the rather "rich", traditional fare served in the main house; service is "knowledgeable and enthusiastic", while the cooking is somewhere between "delicious" and "pleasant, but overpriced". / **Sample dishes:** artichoke hearts with wild mushrooms; Dover sole with shellfish; fresh fruit pavlova. **Details:** on A329 between Streatley & Wallingford, take Ferry Lane at crossroads; 9.45 pm; closed Mon & Sun D; no smoking area. **Accommodation:** 10 rooms, from £165.*

MOULTON, NORTH YORKSHIRE

Black Bull £ 37 A★

DL10 6QJ (01325) 377289

*A "delightful" dining room in a former Pullman railway carriage (whose "sexy" two-by-two seating is ideal for "adulterous couples") is the most distinctive feature at this well-known, attractively converted pub, off the A1; this is not just an atmosphere place, though – the cooking can be "excellent", with "very good seafood" the speciality. / **Sample dishes:** shellfish bisque; lemon sole in prawn, leek & cheese sauce; pancakes with lemon sauce. **Value tip:** set 3-crs L £15.50. **Details:** 1m S of Scotch Corner; 10.15 pm; closed Sun; children: 7+.*

MYLOR BRIDGE, CORNWALL

Pandora Inn £ 27 A

Restronguet Creek TR11 5ST (01326) 372678

*With its "wonderful", remote waterside setting, this well-known thatched pub makes a "marvellous" destination, and "there's a good atmosphere either in the restaurant or sitting out by the creek"; service is generally "warm" and the seafood in particular can be "excellent". / **Sample dishes:** avocado, mango & smoked salmon salad; turbot with fresh greens; lemon ricotta cheesecake. **Details:** signposted off A390, between Truro & Falmouth; 9 pm; no Amex; no smoking; children: 12+.*

NAILSWORTH, GLOUCESTERSHIRE 2–2B

Calcot Manor £ 38 ★
GL8 8YJ (01666) 890391
There's a choice of restaurants – the Conservatory and the
Gumstool Inn – at this "smart" hotel in a converted Cotswold
farmhouse; together they offer an "enormous selection" of dishes,
"always realised to a high standard", and are both "very popular,
especially at weekends". / *Sample dishes*: oak-smoked salmon with
potato pancakes; braised lamb shank & spring onion mash; pannacotta &
strawberries. *Details*: www.calcotmanor.co.uk; junction of A46 & A4135;
9.30 pm; no smoking area; booking essential; children: no children at D.
Accommodation: 28 rooms, from £125.

NAYLAND, SUFFOLK 3–2C

White Hart £ 32
11 High St C06 4JF (01206) 263382
Opinions remain divided on Michel Roux's makeover of this well-
known coaching inn; critics still ask "why did they change it?"
deriding the new incarnation as "expensive", "pretentious" and
"too fussy", but there were reports this year of an "all-round
winner", where "classic French cooking meets country bistro in
a rural setting". / *Sample dishes*: shellfish ravioli; wood pigeon in puff
pastry; mint & bitter chocolate soufflé. *Value tip*: set 3-crs L £13.
Details: www.whitehart-nayland.co.uk; off A12, between Colchester &
Sudbury; 9.30 pm. *Accommodation*: 6 rooms, from £71.50.

NETHER ALDERLEY, CHESHIRE 5–2B

Wizard £ 38 🅐
Macclesfield Rd SK10 4UB (01625) 584000
It's "difficult to find on a wet winter's night", but this old coaching
inn "right on the edge of Cheshire" is pretty "swish" nowadays, and
its "good" ("but not inexpensive") cooking is generally praised.
/ *Sample dishes*: baked goat's cheese with chorizo; sirloin with salad & chips;
apple tarte Tatin with honey ice cream. *Value tip*: set 3-crs L £13.50.
Details: from A34, take B5087; 9.30 pm; closed Mon & Sun D; no smoking
area.

NEW BARNET, GREATER LONDON 3–2B

Mims £ 25
63 East Barnet Rd EN5 8RN (020) 8449 2974
Fans of this odd Barnet foodie Mecca still find the singular cooking
"quite amazing for the price"; service can be "terrible", though,
and the old hand who says "this place was great in the early '90s,
but the decline continues" probably has it about right. / *Sample
dishes*: deep-fried tomato & onion salad; roast duck with roast vegetables;
banana crepes. *Details*: between Cockfosters & High Barnet; 11 pm, Sat
10.30 pm; closed Mon; no Amex or Switch; no smoking area.

NEW MILTON, HAMPSHIRE 2–4C

Chewton Glen £ 54 🅐
Christchurch Rd BH25 6QS (01425) 275341
"Grand" and "gracious", this New Forest-fringe country house has
many admirers for its "beautiful" and "luxurious" setting and for its
"classic" French cuisine; even a reporter who lauds "one of the
world's great hotels", however, admits that the restaurant "is not
the ultimate in culinary delights", and a vociferous minority finds it
"predictable", "stuffy" and "overpriced". / *Sample dishes*: cheese
soufflé; stuffed pork cheeks & lobster; chocolate fondant.
Details: www.chewtonglen.com; on A337 between New Milton & Highcliffe;
9.30 pm; jacket required at D; no smoking; children: 7+.
Accommodation: 63 rooms, from £275.

Newbury Manor   £ 53   ★

London Rd RG14 2BY   (01635) 528838

Nick Evans's "brilliant" cooking is beginning to make quite a name for the dining room of this mid-sized country house hotel, located in woodland; despite its tranquil location, however, it scores very indifferently for ambience – perhaps its bold restoration a couple of years back was just a touch too much. / **Sample dishes:** salmon with creamed leeks & trompette mushrooms; roast beef with rosti potatoes & red wine sauce; blackberry & apple soufflé. **Value tip:** children under 12 eat half-price. **Details:** www.newbury-manor-hotel.co.uk; on A4 towards Thatcham; 9.30 pm; closed Sat L & Sun D; no smoking.

NEWCASTLE UPON TYNE, TYNE & WEAR   8–2B

Newcastle is famously a going-out sort of place, and, though the quality restaurant scene is not huge, the city sustains a fair number of eating places of interest.

Most of the action is round the Quayside – an area utterly transformed over the past few years. Culinarily, *Café 21*, one of the best big-city restaurants outside London, is the undoubted star. There are also a couple of notable Indians (*Leela's*, *Vujon*).

In the centre of town, *Barn Again Bistro* is a great favourite as an informal venue. A short taxi-ride from town, and leafily located in Jesmond Dene, the city's grandest restaurant, *Fisherman's Lodge*, enjoys a particularly picturesque situation.

For diners on a budget, such Italians as *Francesca's*, *Pani's* and *Paradiso* offer a number of options with character.

Barn Again Bistro   £ 34   𝔸 ★

21a Leazes Park Rd NE1 4PF   (0191) 230 3338

"The food is adventurous and eclectic, but very good" and "consistently so" at this "kitsch" and "quirky" city-centre favourite, which does, indeed, occupy a converted barn. / **Sample dishes:** crab & salmon cakes with Szechuan cucumbers; monkfish, red lentil & coconut milk curry; fallen chocolate soufflé. **Details:** nr St James's Park football ground; 10 pm; closed Sun.

Café 21   £ 26   ★★

21 Queen St, Princes Whf NE1 3UG   (0191) 222 0755

"Standards have barely changed since the change of status" at Terry Laybourne's 'dumbed down' Quayside establishment (formerly a temple of gastronomy called 21 Queen Street) which many still cite as "the best restaurant in the North East" on account of its "lovingly prepared", "beautifully-presented" French cooking. / **Sample dishes:** duck & green peppercorn pâté; sirloin with parsley butter & chips; crème brûlée. **Value tip:** set 3-crs D £13. **Details:** 10.30 pm; closed Sun; no smoking area.

Dragon House   £ 23

30-32 Stowell St NE1 4XQ   (0191) 232 0868

For most reporters, this remains a "reliable" oriental that "stands out from the others in Newcastle's Chinatown"; it does have detractors, though, who find it a "depressing", "bog-standard" experience, especially where the "humdrum" cooking is concerned. / **Sample dishes:** chicken & sweetcorn soup; chicken in black bean sauce; orange sorbet. **Details:** 11 pm; no Amex.

Fisherman's Lodge £ 49
Jesmond Dene NE7 7BQ (0191) 281 3281
This "old house in a wooded valley" a short way out of town has long been a classic local "special occasion" destination, and many laud it for its "good-quality seafood" (the speciality) and "excellent staff"; some find it "stuffy and middle-aged", though, and on occasions both food and service have "failed to deliver". / **Sample dishes:** assiette of crab; trio of salmon with langoustine sauce; chocolate ganache tart. **Details:** www.fishermanslodge.co.uk; 2m from city centre on A1058, follow signposts to Jesmond Dene; 10.45 pm; closed Sat L & Sun; no smoking in dining room; children: 8+.

Francesca's £ 18   Ⓐ
Manor House Rd NE2 2NE (0191) 281 6586
"You just can't beat it for atmosphere, friendliness and a good nosh up", says fans of this "ever-popular Italian" – "it gets ever-shabbier and rougher", but still "the queues stretch outside the door by 7pm". / **Sample dishes:** garlic king prawns; mixed fish grill; tiramisu. **Details:** 9 pm; closed Sun; no Amex; no booking.

King Neptune £ 27   ★
34-36 Stowell St NE1 4XQ (0191) 261 6657
There's "consistently good food" to be had at this "very welcoming" and "busy" spot, located "in the middle of Chinatown". / **Sample dishes:** crispy duck pancakes; chicken with Szechuan sauce; lemon sorbet. **Details:** in Chinatown; 10.45 pm.

Leela's £ 28   ★★
20 Dean St NE1 1PG (0191) 230 1261
"Personal service and advice" from Leela the proprietress and her family contribute to a "friendly" atmosphere at her hugely popular city-centre South Indian; the vegetarian dishes, in particular, are "wonderfully different" and "light", and many declare them "exceptional". / **Sample dishes:** spiced prawn & cashew nut salad; pork marinated in herbs; roast vermicelli in coconut milk. **Value tip:** set 3-crs L £9.95. **Details:** 11.30 pm; closed Sun; no Switch; no smoking area.

Pani's £ 21   Ⓐ★
61-65 High Bridge NE1 6BX (0191) 232 4366
Is this "the most authentic Italian café in the UK"? – this "friendly", extremely popular institution is certainly "an excellent spot for a snack or for a more substantial meal", and it's certainly "very lively". / **Sample dishes:** bruschetta; chicken stuffed with Dolcelatte; tiramisu. **Details:** www.pani.net; off Gray Street; 10 pm; closed Sun; no Amex; no booking at L.

Paradiso £ 25   Ⓐ
1 Market Ln NE1 6QQ (0191) 221 1240
As "a very nice place to hang out", this "lovely Italian café-bar in the city centre" with its "great buzz" comes highly recommended; fans say the light dishes it offers are "reliably good" too, but there are sceptics who "question its value for money" and who think its most suited to "rich teenagers". / **Sample dishes:** fresh mussels; scallops with monkfish & mash; egg custard tart. **Details:** www.paradiso.co.uk; opp fire station; 10.45 pm; closed Sun; no smoking area.

Sachins £ 25
Forth Banks NE1 3SG (0191) 261 9035
"Huge" naans ("one between four is ample") set a generous tone at this ever-popular Indian, which offers a "good" range of "reliable" dishes at "reasonable prices". / **Sample dishes:** tandoori platter; chicken rogan josh; kulfi. **Details:** behind Central Station; 11.15 pm; closed Sun.

Tasca £ 24

106 Quayside NE4 3DX (0191) 230 4006

"Great views across the quayside" and a *"good"* atmosphere remain the key attractions at this *"noisy, bustly"* tapas bar; as at branches in other cities, the feeling grew this year that culinary standards were *"not very impressive"*. / **Sample dishes:** *patatas bravas; chicken & sausage paella; apricot tart.* **Details:** www.latasca.co.uk; beside Gateshead Millennium Bridge; 10.30 pm; need 8+ to book.

Valley Junction 397 £ 21 ★

Old Jesmond Station, Archbold Ter NE2 1DB
(0191) 281 6397

"Wonderful" food, *"delightful"* décor, *"friendly"* staff – reporters find little to criticise at this *"unusual"* Indian, which inhabits a converted signal box and railway carriage. / **Sample dishes:** *onion bhaji; lamb with pepper & coriander; gulab jaman (Indian sweets).* **Details:** nr Civic Centre, off Sandyford Rd; 11.15 pm; closed Mon; no smoking area.

Vujon £ 29 ★

29 Queen St NE1 3UG (0191) 221 0601

"Exceptional quality and diversity" characterise the menu of this *"top-notch"* Indian – a *"quiet and sophisticated"* place on the Quayside that's *"good for business or pleasure"*. / **Details:** 11 pm; closed Sun L.

NEWENT, GLOUCESTERSHIRE 2–1B

Three Choirs Vineyards £ 35 A★★

GL18 1LS (01531) 890223

"You could be in the South of France" or *"Tuscany"* – *"excellent food and wine from the surrounding fields, in a superb setting"* is a combination pretty rare in England, and reports, though modest in number, are a hymn of praise to the *"beautiful"* cooking, the *"friendly"* service and the *"interesting"* surroundings of the dining room at this leading English vineyard. / **Sample dishes:** *marinated goat's cheese with roast peppers; sea bass with minted potatoes; passion fruit pannacotta.* **Details:** www.three-choirs-vineyards.co.uk; 9 pm; closed Mon & Sun D; no Amex; no smoking. **Accommodation:** 8 rooms, from £85.

NEWPORT, NEWPORT 2–2A

Junction 28 £ 28

Station Approach NP10 8LD (01633) 891891

This converted railway station has quite a reputation for transcending its unpromising name and *"slightly lacking"*, *"'80s"* setting; not all were impressed, this year, but most still plugged its *"reasonably priced"* food and *"attentive"* service. / **Sample dishes:** *warm scallop, bacon & mange tout salad; roast duck & goat's cheese salad; Grand Marnier mousse with candied oranges.* **Details:** www.junction-28.co.uk; off M4, J28 towards Caerphilly; 9.30 pm; closed Sun D; no Amex; smoking discouraged.

NEWTON LONGVILLE, BUCKINGHAMSHIRE 3–2A

Crooked Billet £ 30 ★★

2 Westbrook End MK17 0DF (01908) 373936

"Wonderful", *"gutsy"* cooking and an *"exceptional"* wine list (with 250 bins, any of which can be served by the glass) have helped this seemingly *"simple"* pub/restaurant to *"take the area by storm"* – be prepared to book well ahead. / **Sample dishes:** *lobster & courgette flower fritters; pork & black pudding with apple & celeriac mash; apricot rice pudding brûlée.* **Details:** www.the-crooked-billet-pub.co.uk; 10 pm; closed Mon & Sun D; no smoking; no booking at L.

Cook & Barker   £ 23   ★

LA65 9JY   (01665) 575234

With its "plain food, cooked well, in portions to satisfy hearty eaters", this "out of the way", "characterful, rural pub" is "very popular", and remains "the best gastropub in the area". / **Sample dishes:** seafood tapas; supreme of chicken with lobster sauce; crème brûlée. **Details:** 12m N of Morpeth, just off A1; 9 pm; no smoking area. **Accommodation:** 4 rooms, from £70.

NEWTON, CAMBRIDGESHIRE   3–1B

Queens Head   £ 12   ★

Fowlmere Rd CB2 5PG   (01223) 870436

"Small, but perfectly formed", this hidden-away boozer offers only a restricted range of food (and mainly cold at that), but the landlord of four decades' standing does what he does very well. / **Sample dishes:** brown soup; charcuterie platter with pickles; no puddings. **Details:** off A10; 9.30 pm; no credit cards; no booking.

NOMANSLAND, WILTSHIRE   2–3C

Les Mirabelles   £ 31   ★

Forest Edge Rd SP5 2BN   (01794) 390205

There's a decidedly Gallic approach at this "treat" of a restaurant, whose "interesting" and "reasonably priced" dishes win unanimous praise; there's an "excellent wine list" too. / **Sample dishes:** hot foie gras with Mirabelle plums; chicken in prawn & saffron sauce; cherry soufflé. **Details:** off A36 between Southampton & Salisbury; 9.30 pm; closed Mon & Sun D; no smoking at D.

NORTON, SHROPSHIRE   5–4B

Hundred House   £ 42

Bridgnorth Rd TF11 9EE   (01952) 730353

Characterful, family-run inn with attractive gardens; reporters note the odd misfire, but its "wide-ranging" menu – particularly the "good steak and kidney pie" – is an attraction worth remembering in this not over-provided bit of the world. / **Sample dishes:** confit duck with rocket & chorizo salad; roast cod & champ with parsley ice cream; raspberry & meringue ice cream. **Value tip:** set 3-crs Sun L £17.95. **Details:** www.hundredhouse.co.uk; on A442 between Bridgnorth & Telford; 9.30 pm; no smoking. **Accommodation:** 10 rooms, from £95.

NORWICH, NORFOLK   6–4C

Adlards   £ 44

79 Upper Giles St NR2 1AB   (01603) 633522

David Adlard's eminent fixture, charmingly located on the fringe of the city, continues to put in a curate's egg of a performance; fans do vaunt his Anglo-French cuisine as "reliable" and "meticulously presented", but many leave disappointed by "remote" and "inattentive" service, or by cooking they judge "over-rated" and "overpriced". / **Sample dishes:** foie gras in cumin with toasted brioche; veal with mash & roast parsnips; banana tarte Tatin. **Details:** nr the Roman Catholic Cathedral; 10.30 pm; closed Mon L & Sun; no smoking at D.

By Appointment   £ 36   𝔸★

25-29 St George's St NR3 1AB   (01603) 630730

"Unusual" and "eclectic" surroundings help make this former merchant's house an "amazing", "totally romantic" destination for all who report on it, though that's not to detract from the cooking, which is "very good" too. / **Sample dishes:** marinated salmon; medallions of beef wrapped in bacon; apricot & pistachio baked cheesecake. **Details:** in a courtyard off Colegate; 9 pm; D only, closed Mon & Sun; no Amex; no smoking in dining room; children: 12+.

Delia's City Brasserie   £ 30   ✕

Norwich City Football Ground, Carrow Rd NR1 1JE
(01603) 218705

*It may be associated with England's leading domestic cookery writer
(also a Norwich City director), but reporters judge this football-
themed dining room "top of the league for poor value" —
complaints include "incompetent service", a "total lack of
atmosphere" and — most surprisingly — "mean" portions of
"bland" fare.* / **Sample dishes:** Thai fishcakes with sesame & lime sauce;
roast salmon with Pecorino & pesto topping; chocolate crème brûlée.
Details: www.canaries.co.uk; 9.30 pm; open Sat D only; no Amex; no smoking
area; booking: max 12.

Garden House   £ 27

Salhouse Rd NR13 6AA   (01603) 720007

*"Very good" grub is to be had at this popular pub — well worth
knowing about in a city without a plethora of competing mid-range
attractions.* / **Sample dishes:** hot bacon & avocado salad; beef stroganoff &
rice; butterscotch ice cream. **Value tip:** set 3-crs L £6.95. **Details:** 5m from
city centre; 8.45 pm; closed Mon & Sun D; no smoking in dining room.
Accommodation: 6 rooms, from £50.

Siam Bangkok   £ 28   ★

8 Orford Hill NR1 3QD   (01603) 617817

*"Once tried, never bettered", insist supporters of this "friendly",
"efficient" and "intimate" city-centre Thai.* / **Sample dishes:** chicken
satay; sizzling mixed seafood; ice cream. **Details:** nr Timber Hill; 10.30 pm;
closed Mon L & Sun L; children: 5+.

Tatlers   £ 32   𝔸★

21 Tombland NR3 1RF   (01603) 766670

*"The ambience is good" and there's an "interesting" menu of
"fresh" and "well presented" dishes at this "reliable" restaurant,
handily located near the Cathedral.* / **Sample dishes:** deep-fried crab
puffs with tomato salsa; goat's cheese ravioli with wild garlic pesto; chocolate
fondant with orange sorbet. **Details:** www.tatlers.com; nr Cathedral, next to
Erpingham Gate; 10 pm.

The Tree House   £ 18   ★

14-16 Dove St NR2 1DE   (01603) 763258

*"Varied" and "reasonably priced" veggie and vegan fare makes this
"cramped" but "friendly" workers co-operative "a jewel", so far as
many local reporters are concerned.* / **Sample dishes:** spicy vegetable
soup; pasta with tomatoes, courgettes & olives; blackcurrant tofu cheesecake.
Details: 9 pm; closed Mon D, Tue D, Wed D & Sun; no credit cards;
no smoking; no booking at L.

NOTTINGHAM, CITY OF NOTTINGHAM   5–3D

For a city without any great reputation as a restaurant
destination, Nottingham in fact has a fair amount to offer.
Hart's is the undoubted city-centre star (having now eclipsed
its chief rival the longer-established *Sonny's*), with *French Living*
and *La Toque* also of some note among non-ethnic restaurants.
The city also boasts good examples of Thai (*Royal Thai, Siam
Thani*) and Indian (*Beeston Tandoori, Laguna Tandoori, Saagar*)
establishments.

Bees Make Honey   £ 30

12 Alfreton Rd NG7 3NG   (0115) 978 0109

*"The plastic tablecloths belie the above-average quality of the
cooking", say fans of this small BYO spot.* / **Sample dishes:** cuttlefish
tagliatelle; sea bass with ackee & okra; white chocolate cheesecake.
Details: 5 mins from Playhouse & Theatre Royal; 10.15 pm; D only,
closed Mon & Sun; no credit cards.

Beeston Tandoori   £ 12   ★
150-152 High Rd NG9 2LN (0115) 922 3330
A "favourite local curry house", that makes an inexpensive and reliable destination. / **Details:** *11.45 pm; no Amex or Switch; no smoking area.*

La Boheme   £ 29
Barker Gt, Lace Mkt NG1 1JU (0115) 912 7771
Now re-opened (in March '01) under the ownership of existing chef Peter Smith and his wife Susan, this city-centre brasserie is winning renewed praise for its cooking, now in the modern British mould. / **Sample dishes:** *chorizo & red onion risotto; chicken stuffed with black pudding; chocolate & pear tart.* **Details:** *11 pm; closed Sun; mainly nonsmoking.*

French Living   £ 21   ★
27 King St NG1 2AY (0115) 958 5885
"Consistently good", "down-to-earth" Gallic cooking "at extremely low prices" ensures nothing but praise for this "unpretentious", "relaxed" and highly popular bistro, overseen by the "ever-present owner and his henchmen". / **Sample dishes:** *Burgundy snails with garlic & parsley butter; pheasant & red wine casserole; pear & walnut mousse.* **Value tip:** *set 2-crs L £5.90.* **Details:** *www.frenchliving.co.uk; nr Market Square; 10 pm; closed Sun; booking: max 10, Sat pm.*

Hart's   £ 34   𝔸★
Standard Ct, Park Row NG1 6GN (0115) 911 0666
Tim Hart's "very modern" and "chic" establishment – in a "great location near the Castle" – is one of the UK's very best city-centre brasseries; it attracts a huge volume of praise for its "gorgeous" and "imaginative" cooking, its "attentive" and "discreet" service and its "buzzing" atmosphere. / **Sample dishes:** *pan-fried squid with chorizo; veal with spinach & Parmesan risotto; banana & dark chocolate parfait.* **Value tip:** *set 2-crs L £11.* **Details:** *www.hartsnottingham.co.uk; nr Nottingham Castle; 10.30 pm.*

Laguna Tandoori   £ 27   ★
43 Mount St NG1 6HE (0115) 941 1632
It doesn't please everyone, but "surprisingly good food" is the general theme of commentary on this "ordinary"-looking Indian. / **Sample dishes:** *chicken shashlik; lamb bhuna; kulfi.* **Details:** *nr Nottingham Castle; 11 pm; closed Sat L & Sun L; no smoking area.*

Mem Saab   £ 30
12-14 Maid Marian Way NG1 6HS (0115) 957 0009
"Minimalist", yet "welcoming" – this "business-like" Indian is praised by all reporters for its across-the-board consistency. / **Sample dishes:** *vegetable pakora; honey & mustard salmon; kulfi.* **Details:** *nr Nottingham Castle; 11 pm, Fri & Sat 11.30 pm; D only, closed Sun; no smoking area; children: 5+.*

Merchants
Lace Market Hotel   £ 34   ✕
29-31 High Pavement NG1 1HE (0115) 852 3232
It's very rare for a place to inspire such a volume of negative commentary as this city-centre brasserie (part of a boutique hotel) – it seems "more focussed on trendiness than quality", and attracted complaints of a "limited" menu, "poor" food, "wrong" orders, "squabbling" staff and "cramped" seating. / **Sample dishes:** *crab & rocket croquettes; grilled kangaroo salad; chocolate marquise.* **Value tip:** *set 3-crs L £9.90.* **Details:** *www.lacemarkethotel.co.uk; 10.30 pm; closed Sat L & Sun D.* **Accommodation:** *29 rooms, from £89.*

Pretty Orchid £ 29
12 Pepper Street NG1 2GH (0115) 958 8344
"Good all round" – this city-centre, ten-year-old Thai remains one of the most popular orientals in town. / **Sample dishes:** chicken yakitori; stir-fried seafood with Thai chilli oil; sticky rice & mango. **Details:** 11 pm; no Amex.

Royal Thai £ 20 ★
189 Mansfield Rd NG1 3FS (0115) 948 3001
The cooking is "excellent", even if the atmosphere can be rather "uninspiring", at this popular oriental. / **Sample dishes:** tom yum soup with prawns; green chicken curry; banana fritter. **Details:** 11 pm; closed Sun L; no Amex; no smoking area.

Saagar £ 25 ★
473 Mansfield Rd NG5 2DR (0115) 962 2014
"Who cares about the décor" – the "living room" setting "may not be to all tastes", but "authentic cooking" that's "always fresh and well prepared" makes this long-established fixture, some way from the city-centre, "still the best Indian in town". / **Sample dishes:** prawn kebabs; tikka chicken; banana split. **Details:** 1.5m from city centre; midnight; closed Sun L; no smoking area; children: 5+.

Shimla Pinks £ 29
38-46 Goosegate NG1 1FF (0115) 958 9899
This "trendy" curry house scored a little better than its siblings in other major cities, winning praise for its "varied" menu and "original" presentation; it didn't get off scot-free, however, from mixed reports and allegations that it is rather "overpriced". / **Sample dishes:** onion bhajis; chicken in spicy tomato sauce; Indian rice pudding. **Details:** www.shimlapinks.bite2enjoy.com; off Mansfield Road; 11 pm; closed Sat L & Sun L; no smoking area.

Siam Thani £ 23 ★
16-20a Carlton St NG1 1NN (0115) 958 2222
An "airy" Thai restaurant with a "modern" feel, whose "well presented" dishes, "friendly" service and "reasonable" prices make it reporters' top oriental choice in town. / **Sample dishes:** hot & sour chicken soup; Thai sweet & sour pork with pineapple; banana fritters. **Details:** www.siamthani.co.uk; 10.30 pm; closed Sun L; no Amex; no smoking area.

Sonny's £ 33
3 Carlton St NG1 1NL (0115) 947 3041
"Modern cooking, carefully done and well presented" has created quite a name for this "trendy" city-centre brasserie (est 1989) as something of a 'veteran' (by the standards of the 'modern British' movement); the perception that it is becoming "jaded" is deepening, however, with more complaints this year of "quite ordinary" food. / **Sample dishes:** tomato linguine with roasted peppers; rump of lamb with Daphne potatoes; blueberry & almond tart. **Value tip:** set 2-crs L £10 (Sun L £15). **Details:** nr Victoria Centre; 10.30 pm, Fri & Sat 11 pm.

La Toque £ 39 ★
61 Wollaton Rd NG9 2NG (0115) 922 2268
It may look like a "very average bistro", but Swede Mathias Karlsson's establishment offers "fine" Gallic cooking – "it's not cheap, but it is value for money". / **Sample dishes:** quail consommé & toasted brioche; lemon sole with green bean fricassée; baked prune soufflé. **Details:** off A52 towards Beeston; 10.30 pm; closed Sun; no Amex; no smoking area; children: 6+.

Victoria Hotel £ 22

Dovecote Ln NG9 IJG   (0115) 925 4049

"It outdoes most of the restaurants round here", says one of the supporters of this *"popular"* railway-side pub, which is generally praised for *"cooking that's very good for a boozer"*, not to mention *"excellent beer"*. / **Sample dishes:** spinach & apple soup; rack of lamb with herb crust; Mars bar cheesecake. **Details:** by Beeston railway station; 8.45 pm; no Amex; no smoking; children: before 8 pm only.

World Service £ 35

Newdigate Hs, Castle Gate NG1 6AF   (0115) 847 5587

Over its first year, this lavishly-designed 'fine dining restaurant and lounge bar' has quickly established itself as "one of the best in Nottingham"; for most (but not all) reporters, the trendy food "lives up to the imposing surroundings". / **Sample dishes:** seared tuna with oriental dressing; roast halibut with warm cucumber salad; pear & cinnamon tarte Tatin. **Details:** www.worldservicerestaurant.com; 10.30 pm; no smoking.

OAKHAM, RUTLAND 5–4D

Nicks
Lord Nelson's House £ 36 ★

11 Marketplace LE15 6DT   (01572) 723199

Tucked away in a medieval timber-framed building in the corner of the marketplace, this "spacious" restaurant (part of a small hotel) attracts nothing but praise – presumably that's why it's "not always easy to get a table". / **Sample dishes:** roast goat's cheese with poached pears; steak with rosti & caramelised onions; walnut & ginger steamed pudding. **Details:** www.nelsons-house.com; 9.30 pm; closed Mon & Sun; no Amex; no smoking. **Accommodation:** 4 rooms, from £80.

OCKLEY, SURREY 3–4A

Bryce's at the Old School House £ 29 ★

RH5 5TH   (01306) 627430

This "good-value fish restaurant in a pub" is "as great as ever", say fans who compliment its *"very friendly and personal"* service. / **Sample dishes:** minced lamb kofte; chilli & salt skate fillets; butterscotch & honeycomb cheesecake. **Details:** 8m S of Dorking on A29; 9 pm; closed Sun D in Nov, Jan & Feb; no Amex; no smoking in dining room.

ODIHAM, HAMPSHIRE 2–3D

The Grapevine £ 25 🅰★

121 High St RG29 1LA   (01256) 701122

This sweet little village bistro is a "friendly" and "welcoming" place, and its "imaginative" cooking is consistently of "high quality". / **Sample dishes:** smoked pigeon & asparagus salad; tandoori monkfish with cucumber ribbons; strawberry & passion fruit crème brûlée. **Value tip:** set 2-crs L £8.95. **Details:** www.grapevine-gourmet.com; follow signs from M3, J5; 10 pm; closed Sat L & Sun.

OLD BURGHCLERE, BERKSHIRE 2–2D

Dew Pond £ 37 ★

RG20 9LH   (01635) 278408

The Marshall family's "small country restaurant" only attracts a limited following amongst reporters, but it's a "friendly" place, serving "very good" Gallic cooking. / **Sample dishes:** chicken & Parma ham salad; roe deer with wild mushrooms, apple & port; chocolate cake. **Details:** 6m S of Newbury, off A34; 10 pm; D only, closed Mon & Sun; no Amex; no smoking area; children: 5+.

OLD DALBY, LEICESTERSHIRE   5–3D

Crown Inn   £ 32
7 Debdale Hill LE14 3LF (01664) 823134
Some think it a little "overpriced", but this "upmarket village pub"
is worth knowing about in this under-served area. / **Sample
dishes:** asparagus, spinach & poached egg salad; slow-roasted rib-eye beef;
oranges in Cointreau cream. **Details:** 5m N of Melton Mowbray; 9.30 pm;
closed Sun D; no Amex; no smoking area; children: 5+ at L, 10+ at D.

OLDHAM, GREATER MANCHESTER   5–2B

Ho Ho's   £ 34   ★
57-59 High St OL4 3BN (0161) 620 9500
It may seem slightly odd that "the second best Chinese restaurant
in Greater Manchester" (in a stone built building, in Lees) is
decorated in Mediterranean style, but it offers "an excellent range
of dishes" and, say its supporters, "a great all-round experience".
/ **Sample dishes:** seafood spring rolls; hot & spicy chicken casserole;
deep-fried coconut balls. **Value tip:** set 2-crs L £7.95.
Details: www.hohos.co.uk; follow signs from M62, J20; 11 pm; closed
Mon L-Wed L.

OMBERSLEY, WORCESTERSHIRE   2–1B

Kings Arms   £ 27   Ⓐ
Main Rd WR9 0EW (01905) 620142
"Buzzing", "olde-worlde-style" pub-restaurant that offers "a good
variety of fresh fish as well as more traditional pub food". / **Sample
dishes:** black pudding, bacon & quails egg salad; calves liver & bacon with
mash; chocolate praline brûlée. **Details:** www.kingsarmsombersley.co.uk;
10.15 pm; no smoking area.

ONGAR, ESSEX   3–2B

Smiths Brasserie   £ 35
Fyfield Rd CM5 0AL (01277) 365578
"The 'in' place" hereabouts – "tasty fish" is the menu highlight
at this "always bustling and busy" town-centre spot. / **Sample
dishes:** smoked Scottish salmon; crab & prawn salad with avocado;
strawberry & ice cream tart. **Details:** left off A414 towards Fyfield; 10.30 pm;
closed Mon; no Amex; children: 12+.

ORFORD, SUFFOLK   3–1D

Butley Orford Oysterage   £ 28
Market Hill IP12 2LH (01394) 450277
For "delicious fresh and smoked fish", many are prepared to brave
the basic '50s-café conditions of this "no-nonsense, no-ambience
eating experience"; some find the place "tackily touristy" nowadays,
however, and "surly" or "grudging" service colours many reports.
/ **Sample dishes:** smoked salmon pâté; hot smoked mackerel with mustard
sauce; rum baba. **Details:** 8.45 pm; closed Mon L-Thu L in winter; no Amex;
no smoking.

The Crown & Castle   £ 29   ★
IP12 2LJ (01394) 450205
"An old hotel that has been given a major shock by new owners" –
"the cooking is much more imaginative that it was previously"; the
overall approach is "informal and pleasant" – just occasionally it
teeters into being "shambolic". / **Sample dishes:** grilled asparagus in
Parma ham; Asian squid & pork belly salad; banana custard with nutty biscuits.
Details: 9 pm; no Amex; mainly nonsmoking. **Accommodation:** 18 rooms,
from £80.

regular updates at www.hardens.com   219

ORKNEY ISLANDS

The Creel £ 37 A★
Front Rd, St Margaret's Hope, South Ronaldsay KW17 2SL
(01856) 831311
Allan Craigie's "superb family-run restaurant with rooms" continues to win nothing but praise, albeit from the rather limited number of reporters who make the pilgrimage. / Sample dishes: shore crab bisque; supreme of cod; Drambuie pannacotta.
Details: www.orknet.co.uk/creel/; off A961 S of town, across Churchill barriers; 9 pm; D only; no Amex or Switch; no smoking. **Accommodation:** 3 rooms, from £65.

ORPINGTON, KENT 3–3B

Xian £ 22 ★
324 High St BR6 0NG (01689) 871881
"The best restaurant in the area", this "reliably good" Chinese is "usually noisy" and "always full" – "book well in advance". / Sample dishes: sesame prawn toast; chicken with cashew nuts; toffee apples. **Details:** 11.15 pm, Fri & Sat 11.45 pm; closed Sun L

OSMOTHERLEY, NORTH YORKSHIRE 8–4C

Golden Lion £ 28 A
6 West End DL6 3AA (01609) 883526
There's a "calming upstairs dining room" at this favourite village boozer, but the "lively" atmosphere of the "cosy bar with its open fire" perhaps makes the more attractive venue in which to sample the place's "above-average" (if "slightly hit and miss") pub grub. / Sample dishes: spaghetti with clams; pork & Parma ham with sage mash; lemon & passion fruit pavlova. **Details:** 10.30 pm; no Amex; no smoking area.

Three Tuns £ 34 A
9 South End DL6 3BN (01609) 883301
It's only been going for a couple of years, but this little "converted brewery (which still brews its own beer)" in the heart of a moorland village is already "very popular and busy"; the "superb modern interior", however, tends to attract slightly more consistent support than its cooking. / Sample dishes: crab & salmon fishcakes; Dover sole with lemon & chive butter; mini croque-em-bouche.
Details: www.lifeandstyle.co.uk; 6m NE of Northallerton; 9.30 pm; no Amex.
Accommodation: 7 rooms, from £65.

OSWESTRY, SHROPSHIRE 5–3A

Sebastians £ 36 ★
45 Willow St SY11 1AQ (01691) 655444
"There's not much to do in Oswestry, but this is a gem", say supporters of this cramped-looking spot, where fans say the Fishers' careful Gallic cooking is "just as good as ever". / Sample dishes: prawn & fish soup; turbot tagliatelle with asparagus; banana tarte Tatin. **Details:** www.sebastians-hotel.co.uk; nr town centre, follow signs towards Selattyn; 9.45 pm; closed Mon & Sun; no smoking. **Accommodation:** 8 rooms, from £55.

OTFORD, KENT 3–3B

Bull £ 22 A★
High St TN14 5PG (01959) 523198
A "large" and atmospheric pub whose "wide" variety of "surprisingly good" food helps make it a "very popular" choice. / Sample dishes: garlic mushrooms; lemon sole; passion fruit parfait.
Details: 10 pm; children: before 5 pm only.

Korks £ 28 🄰

40 Bondgate LS21 1AD (01943) 462020

A "cosy", "buzzing" and "unpretentious" atmosphere is the special attraction of this "lovely" brasserie and wine bar (not to forget the disco some nights, too) – with its "very good-value fixed-price menus" it's something of a local institution. / **Sample dishes:** tandoori chicken with coriander noodles; pork with cauliflower & turmeric jus; summer berry pavlova. **Value tip:** set 3-crs pre-th £10.95 (Mon-Thu). **Details:** www.korks.com; 10 pm, Fri & Sat 11 pm; closed Sat L & Sun.

Falcon Inn £ 33

Fotheringay PE8 5HZ (01832) 226254

A "friendly", "family" atmosphere pervades this "charming" (but, some find, rather "cramped") village pub/restaurant, and it's a "reliable" place whose fare is "above-average". / **Sample dishes:** chicken liver pâté with brioche; char-grilled chicken & spinach mash; sticky toffee pudding with rum & raisin ice cream. **Value tip:** set 2-crs L £11. **Details:** just off A605; 9 pm; no smoking.

Dog Inn £ 27

Well Bank Ln WA16 8UP (01625) 861421

"Generous portions of home-cooked food" in a "gorgeous" location make this friendly country boozer one worth seeking out. / **Sample dishes:** smoked chicken with melon & orange salad; spinach & mushroom lasagne; sticky toffee pudding. **Details:** www.thedoginncheshire.co.uk; off A50; 9.30 pm; no Amex; no smoking. **Accommodation:** 6 rooms, from £75.

The Bush Inn £ 31 🄰

SO24 0RE (01962) 732764

A "delightful" setting is the special strength of this popular, rural riverside boozer; it wins praise for its "good-quality, pub-restaurant food", though some find it rather on the "pricey" side for what it is. / **Sample dishes:** spinach & Roquefort salad; venison casserole; sticky toffee pudding. **Details:** just off A31 between Winchester & Alresford; 9.30 pm; closed Sun D; no smoking area.

OXFORD, OXFORDSHIRE 2–2D

This beautiful city offers a number of attractive European restaurants, almost all of which – Cherwell Boathouse, Gees, The Old Parsonage and Quod – offer pretty unremarkable food. In its early days, the same can also be said of the newest kid on the block, the seriously aspiring Gousse d'Ail.

Some of the city's restaurants, despite being very well known, do not even achieve an acceptable level of reporter satisfaction. The most egregious of these is Le Petit Blanc. Monsieur Blanc – based only eight miles away at the Manoir aux Quat' Saisons in Great Milton – should keep a closer eye on his 'offspring'.

Given the scope the city might be thought to offer, it is remarkable that the only restaurant to offer food of notable quality in a particularly pleasant environment is Chaing Mai – a Thai establishment which occupies a building of historical interest in the heart of the city.

Al Shami £ 23 ★

25 Walton Cr OX1 2JG (01865) 310066

"Consistently tasty Lebanese dishes" at prices that represent "good value for money" continue to make this Spartan, but "very friendly" Jericho fixture a huge local favourite; regulars tip the mezze as "more exciting than the main courses". / **Sample dishes:** falafel; mixed grill; Lebanese sweets. **Details:** www.al-shami.co.uk; 10 mins from A40; 11.45 pm; no Amex; no smoking area. **Accommodation:** 12 rooms, from £35.

Aziz £ 27

228-230 Cowley Rd OX4 1UH (01865) 794945

"More expensive than most Indians, but well worth it" is still the overwhelming local view on this "classy" curry house ("devoid of naff wallpaper") to the south east of the city, and it's "always busy"; ratings slipped across the board this year, however. / **Sample dishes:** lentil cakes with yoghurt & tamarind; lamb tikka with onions; gulab jaman (Indian sweets). **Value tip:** 3-crs Sun buffet £8.50. **Details:** www.oxfordpages.co.uk/aziz; 10.45 pm; closed Fri L; no smoking area.

Bangkok House £ 23 ★

42a High Bridge St OX1 2EP (01865) 200705

"An oasis in central Oxford" – the "yummy" Thai fare is consistently praised at this "charming" oriental, where "lovely wooden décor" contributes to an "interesting" setting. / **Sample dishes:** spring rolls; chicken curry; Thai pudding. **Value tip:** set 3-crs L £9.50. **Details:** between BR & bus stations; 10.45 pm; closed Mon & Sun L.

Bombay £ 18 ★

82 Walton St OX2 6EA (01865) 511188

The chef at this Jericho Indian has twice won the Oxfordshire Curry Chef of the Year award, or so we are told; its "excellent" range of dishes and "lovely" service certainly win the approval of reporters, with the BYO policy contributing to a "great-value" overall impression. / **Sample dishes:** chick pea dahl & chapatis; duck curry; pistachio kulfi. **Details:** 11.45 pm; closed Fri L; no Amex.

Browns £ 28 ✗

5-11 Woodstock Rd OX2 6HA (01865) 319655

"How have the mighty have fallen, this used to be a chic and fun place"; it's particularly sad that this famous brasserie – the best-known of the national group – seems "very much like a chain" nowadays, where "disinterested" staff serve food that is "increasingly inauthentic and formulaic" – "since it was taken over by Bass (now known as Six Continents), standards have dropped like a stone". / **Sample dishes:** grilled goats cheese salad; confit duck with plum relish; bread & butter pudding. **Details:** www.browns-restaurants.com; 11.30 pm; no smoking area; no booking at D.

Chaing Mai £ 28 𝔸★★

130a High St OX1 4DH (01865) 202233

"A Thai restaurant in a fourteenth-century building" seems a "curious" concept, but this very central, "panelled" fixture (just off the High Street) is hugely popular, and almost all reports laud its "gorgeous and authentic" cooking and "characterful" (if "crowded") setting; the service, however, "is not always great". / **Sample dishes:** tofu satay; stir-fried pork with curry paste; green tea ice cream. **Details:** 10.30 pm, Fri & Sat 10.45 pm; no smoking area.

Cherwell Boathouse £ 28 𝔸

Bardwell Rd OX2 6ST (01865) 552746

"It's cramped inside, but pleasant being by the river" at this "small", "friendly" and "romantic" destination; the "simple" cooking is not the key attraction, but generally gets the thumbs-up, and there is an "exceptional" wine list. / **Sample dishes:** tomato & Mozzarella salad; vegetable Wellington with sorrel sauce; lemon posset. **Details:** www.cherwellboathouse.co.uk; 10 pm; no smoking.

Chutney's £ 20
36 St Michael St OX1 2EB (01865) 724241
With its "bright" setting, this "smarter than average" central subcontinental is of some "renown" locally as "the most innovative in town"; it's "best for vegetarian and south Indian dishes".
/ **Sample dishes:** *lamb kebab; chicken Karahi; mango delight.*
Details: *www.chutneys.co.uk; off George St; 11 pm; closed Mon.*

Edamame £ 14 ★
15 Holywell St OX1 3SA (01865) 246916
"Long queues at lunchtime" speak for the popularity of this "tiny", "friendly" and "relaxed" venture, serving "cheap but excellent" Japanese "home cooking". / **Sample dishes:** *salted edamame beans; white fishcake with Japanese dressing; oolong tea.*
Details: *www.edamame.co.uk; opp New College; 8.30 pm; L only, except Fri & Sat when L&D, closed Mon; no Amex; no cards at L; no smoking; no booking.*

Elizabeth's £ 41
82 St Aldates OX1 1RA (01865) 242230
Flying the flag since 1966, this is "one of Oxford's top French restaurants" and traditionalists still proclaim the virtues of its "exceptional" cooking and its "superb location" (by Christ Church); for doubters, though, it's simply "lost the plot", offering a "dull" experience all round. / **Sample dishes:** *seafood mousse; roast wood pigeon; champagne sorbet.* **Value tip:** *set 3-crs L £17.*
Details: *www.restaurant-elizabeth.com; 11 pm; closed Mon.*

Fishers £ 33
36-37 St Clements OX4 1AB (01865) 243003
"Booking can be very difficult" at this "busy", "cramped" and "cluttered" bistro, which has quite a name for its "no-nonsense" fish cooking; "given its sometimes mediocre standards, it's a tad overpriced, but on a good day…"; (devotees will wish to note that there is now a branch in Bristol, tel 0117 974 7044). / **Sample dishes:** *king prawns with garlic mayonnaise; sea bass with aubergine salsa & orange essence; iced mango parfait.* **Details:** *www.fishers-oxford.co.uk; by Magdalen Bridge; 10.30 pm; closed Mon L; no Amex; no smoking area.*

Gees £ 35 Ⓐ
61 Banbury Rd OX2 6PE (01865) 553540
A "charming and romantic" setting in a Victorian conservatory is the undoubted strength of this well-known, long-established fixture, just north of the city-centre; service is "variable", though, and the food is "good, but doesn't really justify the high prices". / **Sample dishes:** *king scallops with leeks; roast lamb with borlotti beans & tapenade; chocolate soufflé with pistachio sauce.* **Details:** *11 pm; no smoking.*

La Gousse d'Ail £ 58
268 Woodstock Rd OX2 7NW (01865) 311936
"Very trendy" new occupant of the 1930s villa that used to house the Lemon Tree (RIP), which has had a "modern and chic" makeover; service can be "curt" and "off-hand", and opinions on the food are mixed – what is "sublime" Gallic cuisine to some is "OK, but very expensive" to others. / **Sample dishes:** *warm salad of skate with oyster beignets; roast Angus beef; prune & armagnac soufflé.*
Value tip: *set 3-crs L £21.50.* **Details:** *www.lagoussedail.com; 10.30 pm; closed Mon & Sun D; no Amex; no smoking in dining room.*

Kazbah £ 20 Ⓐ
25-27 Cowley Rd OX4 1HP (01865) 202920
For "a 'holiday' feel, without the hassle of airport queues", head to this "novel", successful "Spanish/Moroccan-themed tapas bar" ten minutes walk from the city-centre, which serves some "lovely snacky food" at "not unreasonable" prices. / **Sample dishes:** *anchovies cured in vinegar; chicken & olive tajine with preserved lemon; baklava.* **Details:** *11 pm; no Amex; no booking.*

The Old Parsonage £ 33   A

1 Banbury Rd OX2 6NN (01865) 310210

With its "log fires and panelling", this medieval townhouse makes a very "soothing" retreat, just a few minutes' walk from the city-centre; the "simple" food is "well cooked and presented" – as it should be, for the price. / **Sample dishes:** seared smoked salmon; rare marinated beef & salad; New York style cheesecake. **Details:** www.oxford-hotels-restaurants.co.uk; 0.5m N of city centre; 11 pm. **Accommodation:** 30 rooms, from £130.

Le Petit Blanc £ 30   X

71-72 Walton St OX2 6AG (01865) 510999

"A pity Monsieur Blanc doesn't seem to care any more" – for a (diminishing) number of fans this star chef's Jericho brasserie remains a "relaxed but stylish" venture with a "bustling" if "noisy" ambience, but the volume of reports of "boring" food and "careless" service lead many to conclude that the place is "very overrated and disappointing". / **Sample dishes:** foie gras & chicken liver pâté; confit of guinea fowl with wild mushrooms; 'floating island' dessert. **Value tip:** set 2-crs L & pre-th £12.50. **Details:** www.petitblanc.co.uk; 11 pm; no smoking except D Fri & Sat.

Quod
Old Bank Hotel £ 31   A

92-94 High St OX1 4BN (01865) 202505

A year or so after opening, there's still "much potential" waiting to be realised at this "relaxed" city-centre Italian (the latest venture from the creator of Browns); it has a "great", "fun" and "buzzy" atmosphere, but though the food is "much improved" since the place opened, many still say it "never quite reaches expectations". / **Sample dishes:** grilled smoked ricotta; frittata with courgettes; pannacotta with raspberries. **Details:** opp All Souls College; 11 pm; no smoking area; no booking at L, Fri-Sun. **Accommodation:** 44 rooms, from £155.

Radcliffe Arms £ 11

67 Cranham St OX2 6ED (01865) 514762

"Very, very cheap" prices are the draw to this "cheerful" student boozer near the Phoenix cinema, where Sunday lunch is something of an institution. / **Sample dishes:** tomato soup; lasagne & salad; chocolate fudge cake. **Details:** 9 pm; no Amex.

Randolph £ 31   X

Beaumont St OX1 2LN (01865) 203100

"A step back to the '70s, when the Trust House empire had hit rock bottom" – the standards in the dining room at "the best hotel in Oxford" are variously described as "sloppy", "provincial" and "atrocious"; avoid. / **Sample dishes:** clam chowder; spiced duck with red cabbage; walnut tart with maple syrup ice cream. **Value tip:** 3-crs L & pre-th £9. **Details:** www.heritage-hotels.com; opp Ashmolean Museum; 10 pm. **Accommodation:** 119 rooms, from £99.

White House £ 30

2 Botley Rd OX2 0AB (01865) 242823

Its location is "inconvenient" – unless you happen to be catching a train from Oxford Station, that is – but there's some warm praise for this inn's "quality" cooking. / **Sample dishes:** sizzling red mullet & spring onions; beef medallions with sweet chilli sauce; tarte Tatin. **Details:** W of Oxford, past railway station; 9.30 pm; no Amex.

Xian £ 23

197 Banbury Rd OX2 7AR (01865) 554239

A "reliable standard" of cooking and "attentive" service maintain the loyal fan club of this "old-favourite" Summertown Chinese; try to nab a spot in the attractive conservatory. / **Sample dishes:** sweet & sour soup; chicken chow mein; ice cream. **Details:** in Summertown, next to bank; 11.15 pm; closed Sun L.

Margot's   £ 33   ★

11 Duke St PL28 8AB   (01841) 533441
"Small but wonderful" – Adrian and Julie Oliver's bistro serves up
some "superb" dishes, and they extend a "very friendly" welcome.
/ **Sample dishes:** salmon & spinach tartlet; turbot with leeks & chive butter
sauce; saffron poached pears. **Details:** www.margots.co.uk; 9.30 pm; closed
Mon & Tue; no smoking.

No 6 Café   £ 37   ★

6 Middle St PL28 8AP   (01841) 532093
For "simple, good-quality fish" (in "good portions", and with
"excellent presentation"), this "minimalist" but "pleasant" spot
is preferred by some to the town's more famous establishments.
/ **Sample dishes:** Cornish scallops with sweet chilli sauce; sea bass with
lemongrass risotto; chocolate pot with Tia Maria cream. **Details:** 10.30 pm
(9.30 pm in winter); closed Mon L, Tue, Wed L, Thu L, Fri L, Sat L & Sun L;
no Amex; no smoking; children: 12+. **Accommodation:** 2 rooms, from £65.

Seafood Restaurant   £ 51

Riverside PL28 8BY   (01841) 532700
TV-chef Rick Stein's "passion" for "glorious seafood, simply cooked"
has made this Cornish town a place of culinary pilgrimage, and for
many devotees a visit to his large, harbourside HQ is a "fishtastic",
"feel good" experience; there remain many heretics, however, for
whom the place is "overpriced" and "resting on its laurels", with
particular flak reserved for the "unwelcoming", "blunt", and "slow"
service. / **Sample dishes:** cuttlefish salad; shark & Dover sole vindaloo;
pannacotta & stewed rhubarb. **Details:** www.rickstein.com; 10 pm; no Amex;
no smoking in dining room; children: 3+. **Accommodation:** 19 rooms,
from £95.

St Petroc's House Bistro   £ 37

4 New St PL28 8BY   (01841) 532700
Fans discover "all the magic of Rick Stein's food" at his more
"relaxed" establishment, a few paces from his famous Seafood
Restaurant; it's "surprisingly small and cramped", though, and
a number find the cooking rather "bland". / **Sample dishes:** poached
egg, bacon & crouton salad; lemon sole with sea salt & lemon; Gorgonzola with
honey & walnuts. **Details:** www.rickstein.com; 9.30 pm; closed Mon; no Amex;
no smoking. **Accommodation:** 13 rooms, from £95.

Kam's Palace   £ 32   ★

1 Bridge Rd SO31 7GD   (01489) 583328
"Built like a Chinese pagoda", this oriental establishment is praised
not only for its "outrageous" surroundings, but also for food that's
"a cut above the average". / **Sample dishes:** Chinese hors d'oeuvres;
crispy duck & pancakes; toffee bananas. **Details:** 10.30 pm, Fri & Sat 11 pm.

Marsh Cat   £ 24   ★

1 Mostyn Sq CH64 6SL   (0151) 336 1963
Set menus which offer "amazing value for money" are making
quite a name for this "Creole-influenced" bistro on the Wirral, and
"the sunset views across the marshes of the estuary are stunning".
/ **Sample dishes:** crab claws & monkfish in Thai coconut sauce;
Cajun-blackened swordfish & cat fish; nutty torte with raspberries.
Details: www.marshcat.com; 10 pm; smoking discouraged.

PAULERSPURY, NORTHANTS 2–1D

Vine House £ 41 ★

100 High St NN12 7NA (01327) 811267

Supporters say there's "fabulous" results to be had from the "very imaginative" menus at this "tiny, family-run place" in an old country house, which doubters find a touch "pricey" for what it is. / **Sample dishes:** *prawn & leek risotto; baked sea bass; coconut & Malibu pannacotta.* **Details:** *2m S of Towcester just off A5; 9.15 pm; closed Mon L-Wed L, Sat L & Sun; no Amex or Switch; no smoking in dining room.* **Accommodation:** *6 rooms, from £69.*

PAXFORD, GLOUCESTERSHIRE 2–1C

Churchill Arms £ 30 ★

GL55 6XH (01386) 594000

Thanks to the "reliably interesting cooking" from the "ever-changing menu", it can be "difficult to get a table" at this well-known, "gourmet" Cotswolds pub (part of a well-reputed local mini-group); though it has a "beautiful rural location", service is "patchy", and some find it "very annoying that you can't book". / **Sample dishes:** *duck with grapefruit & fennel salad; guinea fowl in Madeira & mushroom cream sauce; sticky toffee pudding.* **Details:** *off Fosse Way; 9 pm; no Amex; no booking.* **Accommodation:** *4 rooms, from £70.*

PENARTH, VALE OF GLAMORGAN 2–2A

Tomlins £ 25 A★★

46 Plassey St CF64 1EL (029) 2070 6644

With its "excellent" and "imaginative" cooking, its "informative" staff and its "really bright and cheerful décor", it's hard to find fault with David and Lorraine Tomlinson's "fantastic" vegetarian, near Cardiff, which offers "a delightful experience every time". / **Sample dishes:** *won-tons with black bean sauce; black olive polenta with grilled vegetables; steamed syrup pudding.* **Details:** *www.tomlinsvegetarianrestaurant.co.uk; 10 pm; closed Mon, Tue L-Thu L & Sun D; no smoking.*

PERTH, PERTH & KINROSS 9–3C

63 Tay Street £ 36 A★

63 Tay St PH2 8NN (01738) 441451

Does Jeremy and Shona Ware's "fresh and simple" spring 2001 newcomer offer "the best-value fine quality food in Scotland"? – early reports are necessarily few in number, but they are unanimous that this place is "one to watch". / **Sample dishes:** *Skye scallops with sweet onion risotto; rump of lamb with Mediterranean vegetables; chocolate mocha tart & chocolate ice cream.* **Details:** *city-side of River Tay, 1m from Dundee Rd; 9 pm; closed Mon & Sun; no smoking; children: 10+ at D.*

Let's Eat £ 32 A★

77-79 Kinnoull St PH1 5EZ (01738) 643377

"As good as anything in London, but cheaper", say proponents of the "fine modern food with a Scottish twist" served at this "consistently good" bistro, whose "unobtrusive" service contributes to a "relaxed" atmosphere. / **Sample dishes:** *moules marinière; Dunkeld smoked salmon with lemon; orange & Mascarpone cheesecake.* **Details:** *opp North Inch Park; 9.45 pm; closed Mon & Sun; no smoking area.*

PETERSFIELD, HAMPSHIRE 2–3D

River Kwai £ 27 ★

16-18 Dragon Hs GU13 4JJ (01730) 267077

"Delicious" and "well presented" Thai dishes make this "consistently good" restaurant "the best of its type in the area". / **Sample dishes:** *chicken satay; Thai green curry; sticky rice & mango.* **Details:** *10.30 pm; closed Sun; no smoking area.*

Roseland Inn   £ 24   Ⓐ

TR2 5NB   (01872) 580254

This "picturesque" pub – "best enjoyed on a sunny day, under the rose canopies" – offers "good, healthy portions of tasty food" (including, at dinner, some quite eclectic fare); "local seafood" gets a particular thumbs-up. / **Sample dishes:** duck liver pâté; rump steak with potatoes & salad; chocolate bread & butter pudding. **Details:** nr King Harry ferry; 9 pm; no Amex.

PICKERING, NORTH YORKSHIRE   8–4C

White Swan   £ 32   Ⓐ★

Market Pl YO18 7AA   (01751) 472288

"Welcoming" town-centre coaching inn, to which most reporters accord "the highest praise" on account of its "extremely hospitable staff", "reliably good food" and decent wines. / **Sample dishes:** foie gras with potato pancakes; braised veal shin with parsley mash; dark chocolate cake. **Details:** www.white-swan.co.uk; 9 pm; no smoking. **Accommodation:** 12 rooms, from £90.

PINNER, GREATER LONDON   3–3A

La Giralda   £ 18

66-68 Pinner Grn HA5 2AB   (020) 8868 3429

The "varied" menu at this long-established suburban Spaniard may offer no more than "standard fayre", but this is a modestly-priced, "good family outing venue", and one that's always "very busy". / **Sample dishes:** deep-fried whitebait with paprika; peppered turkey in cream sauce; poached pears with syrup. **Details:** A404 to Cuckoo Hill Junction; 10 pm; closed Mon & Sun D.

PLUMTREE, NOTTINGHAMSHIRE   5–3D

Perkins   £ 28

Old Railway Station NG12 5NA   (0115) 937 3695

Even a reporter who accuses Tony and Wendy Perkins' "small" bistro (occupying a converted station) of being "dated" in its appeal concedes that the cooking is realised "quite well", and more enthusiastic fans say it's a "reliable" place that "gets busy and crowded". / **Sample dishes:** wild mushroom omelette; Cornish red mullet with crab risotto; lime torte with dark chocolate pastry. **Value tip:** set 2-crs L £9.75. **Details:** off A606 between Nottingham & Melton Mowbray; 9.30 pm; closed Mon & Sun D; no smoking area.

PLYMOUTH, DEVON   1–3C

Chez Nous   £ 43   ★

13 Frankfort Gate PL1 1QA   (01752) 266793

Suzanne & Jacques Marchal's "really good French cooking" presents a "stark contrast" to the urban hell, "downtown" location and simple shop-conversion premises of this "long-time favourite" – "the top prices reflect the food, not the surroundings". / **Sample dishes:** pigeon salad with pine nuts; roast ducking with lentils; tarte Tatin. **Details:** www.business.thisisplymouth.co.uk/cheznous; nr Theatre Royal; 10.30 pm; closed Mon, Sat L & Sun.

Thai Palace   £ 23   ★

3 Elliot St, The Hoe PL1 2PP   (01752) 255770

An "interesting" menu delivering "very fresh" tastes, and "pleasant" décor combine to make this "efficient" oriental a place worth remembering in this under-provided town. / **Sample dishes:** chicken satay; green beef curry; raspberry pavlova. **Details:** 11 pm; D only, closed Sun.

---

regular updates at www.hardens.com   227

Café 21 £ 28 ★

35 The Broadway, Darras Hall NA20 9PW (01661) 820357

It "doesn't have the best location" – a housing estate, near Newcastle Airport – and the tables are "too close together", but the "delicious" cooking and "friendly and efficient" service "help you forget" at this "reliable" shop-conversion offshoot of the celebrated Quayside establishment. / **Sample dishes:** artichokes stuffed with mushrooms; smoked haddock with bubble & squeak; rhubarb & Sauternes trifle. **Value tip:** set 3-crs D £13. **Details:** 1m past Newcastle Airport, off A1; 10 pm; D only, closed Sun.

Mansion House £ 37 A★

Thames St BH15 1JN (01202) 685666

"Hidden away in the backstreets", this "splendid" panelled hotel dining room "has it all" – "a good mix of modern and traditional dishes", "efficiently" served in an impressive Georgian building whose atmosphere is reminiscent of a "gentlemen's club" (well, in fact it is in part a club, but non-members can eat in the Dining Room, if not the bistro). / **Sample dishes:** mackerel terrine; scallops with lentils & Indian spices; bread & butter pudding.
Details: www.themansionhouse.co.uk; follow signs for Ferry, turn left onto quayside; 9 pm; closed Sat L & Sun D; no smoking in dining room; children: 5+. **Accommodation:** 32 rooms, from £100.

Airds Hotel £ 62 A★

PA38 4DF (01631) 730236

We don't get as much commentary as we would like on the Allen family's luxury hotel on the Loch Linnhe shoreside, but such as it is – "best I've come across outside London" – affirms its continuing "excellence". / **Sample dishes:** seared scallops with slow-cooked fennel; salmon with deep-fried capers & bean salad; caramel parfait with toasted almonds. **Details:** www.airds-hotel.com; 20m N of Oban; 8.30 pm; no Amex; no smoking; children: 8+. **Accommodation:** 12 rooms, from £141.

Pier House Hotel £ 34 A★

PA38 4DE (01631) 730302

"A beautiful lochside location" with "super views", and "excellent, fresh and generous seafood platters" make this dependable spot by the Lismore Island ferry a consistently popular recommendation. / **Sample dishes:** scallops with rice; beef stroganoff; death by chocolate. **Details:** www.pierhousehotel.co.uk; just off A828 by pier; 9.30 pm; no Amex; no smoking. **Accommodation:** 12 rooms, from £70.

The Narrows £ 33 ★

8 Shore Rd BT22 1JY (028) 42728148

Some find the ambience a touch lacking at this restaurant with rooms, overlooking Strangford Loch, but the "lovely" cooking uses "top-class local produce" to good effect. / **Sample dishes:** lobster & marinated tomato salad; grilled turbot with tarragon cream; strawberries with hazelnut meringue. **Details:** www.narrows.co.uk; opposite the marina; 9 pm; no smoking area. **Accommodation:** 13 rooms, from £85.

Portaferry Hotel £ 34 A★

10 The Strand BT22 1PE (028) 4272 8231

"Great oysters" and other "plain and consistently very good seafood" are served at this ferry-side hotel, overlooking Strangford Lough – an "excellent place for a quiet and relaxing weekend". / **Sample dishes:** scallops with bacon & garlic; turbot & spinach with glazed apples; sticky toffee pudding. **Details:** www.portaferryhotel.com; on shore front, opposite ferry slipway; 9 pm. **Accommodation:** 14 rooms, from £90.

Portmeirion Hotel £ 40 A ★
LL48 6ER (01766) 770000

A couple of reporters found it a "let down", but the real surprise is the impressive all-round satisfaction achieved by this "spectacularly located" hotel dining room, where a view of Sir Clough Williams-Ellis's fantasy-Mediterranean village contributes to an "unrivalled" setting; both "very" attentive service and "fantastic, good quality Welsh cooking" were roundly praised. / **Sample dishes:** Galia melon with caramelised strawberries; braised lamb shank with creamed white onions; plum & almond tart. **Value tip:** set 2-crs L £11. **Details:** off A487 at Minffordd; 9 pm; closed Mon L; no smoking. **Accommodation:** 51 rooms, from £115.

Crown Hotel £ 28
9 North Cr DG9 8SX (01776) 810261

"A beautiful view over the harbour" is an undoubted attraction of this "comfortable" hotel dining room, where most (but not quite all) reporters praise "good-value" fish and other fare. / **Sample dishes:** herring & prawn platter; venison in pepper & brandy sauce; strawberry shortcake. **Details:** 10 pm; no smoking area. **Accommodation:** 12 rooms, from £72.

Tabb's £ 31 ★
Tregea Ter TR16 4LD (01209) 842488

"Trying hard in a culinary wasteland", Nigel Tabb – whose establishment is housed in a former granite forge – attracts nothing but praise for his "super" food; service is "efficient" and "friendly" too. / **Sample dishes:** mussel & pepper fricassée; turbot & fennel in dry sherry sauce; dark chocolate marquise. **Details:** 9 pm; closed Mon L, Tue, Wed L, Thu L, Fri L & Sat L; no Amex; no smoking.

Ramore Wine Bar £ 24 ★
The Harbour BT56 8D3 (028) 7082 4313

"It can't be true that they are making it a pizza parlour – yet it is true!!!" – there's no longer a 'proper' restaurant adjoining this popular, stylish wine bar, but rather a new Mediterranean "canteen"; reports of the food in both locations are positive, though not quite as glowing as they were under the previous set-up. / **Sample dishes:** tortilla chips with guacamole; pizza with spicy meatballs & peppers; tiramisu. **Details:** 10 pm; no Amex; need 10+ to book; children: 12+.

White House £ 37 A
New Rd SK10 4DG (01625) 829376

"Smart", "busy" and "efficient" – there's nothing but praise for this "posh" village restaurant, where (for once) a recent "modern makeover" has actually "improved" the atmosphere. / **Sample dishes:** Caesar salad with sautéed tiger prawns; Dover sole with sea salt & lime; strawberry brûlée with roast rhubarb. **Details:** 2m N of Macclesfield on A538; 10 pm; closed Mon L & Sun D. **Accommodation:** 11 rooms, from £70.

PRESTEIGNE, POWYS 5–4A

Hat Shop £ 24

7 High St LD8 2BA (01544) 260017

Its menu can seem a touch "limited", but this "small, warm" high-street restaurant is worth knowing about for "dependable and tasty" food that's "well prepared from local ingredients". / **Sample dishes:** watercress roulade; chicken stuffed with apricots & mint; chocolate charlotte. **Value tip:** set 2-crs L £4.50. **Details:** 9 pm; closed Sun; no credit cards; no smoking area.

PRESTON BAGOT, WARWICKSHIRE 5–4C

The Crabmill £ 36 🅰★

B95 5DR (01926) 843342

For most reporters (if not quite all), "relaxed surroundings create the ideal moods for eating" at this "upmarket pub plus restaurant", which serves an "imaginative" Mediterranean menu. / **Sample dishes:** roast veal with tuna confit & lemon mayonnaise; char-grilled pork with sage & lemon polenta; pannacotta with honeycomb biscuits. **Details:** on main road between Warwick & Henley; 9.30 pm; closed Sun D; booking: max 11.

PRESTON, LANCASHIRE 5–1A

Simply Heathcote's £ 27

23 Winckley Sq PR1 3JJ (01772) 252732

"Well-prepared food at prices lower than at Longridge" is the general verdict on Paul Heathcote's modern, town-centre brasserie spin-off, a few miles from his rural HQ; that it is "expensive" is a recurrent complaint, however, and the "stark" setting is too "chilly" and "noisy" for some tastes. / **Sample dishes:** wild mushroom terrine; roast chump of lamb; chocolate & honeycomb parfait. **Details:** www.heathcotes.co.uk; 10 pm, Sat 10.30 pm.

PRESTWOOD, BUCKINGHAMSHIRE 3–2A

Polecat £ 25

170 Wycombe Rd HB16 0HJ (01494) 862253

The food is "not ambitious but plentiful" at this "nice" roadside pub; it's "always packed" and some complain that there's a hint of "production line" about the place. / **Sample dishes:** baked field mushrooms with melted cheese; beef Wellington; steamed syrup sponge. **Details:** on A4128 between Great Missenden & High Wycombe; 9 pm; closed Sun D; no credit cards; no smoking area; children: not permitted in dining room.

PRIORS HARDWICK, WARWICKSHIRE 2–1D

Butchers Arms £ 41

Church End CV47 7SN (01327) 260504

It has a "lovely garden" and most reporters say the cooking is "consistently good and enjoyable" at this "pub-turned-upmarket-restaurant"; there are some fears, though, that the place risks becoming "a victim of its own success". / **Sample dishes:** grilled sardines; steak with mustard & chips; parfait roll. **Details:** www.thebutchersarms.com; 9.30 pm; closed Sat L & Sun D; no smoking.

PURTON, WILTSHIRE 2–2C

Pear Tree at Purton £ 41 ★

SN5 4ED (01793) 772100

If you're looking for "a posh place to eat" hereabouts, this lavishly-extended former rectory (with a large conservatory) fits the bill nicely; its "beautifully presented" cooking and "attentive" service win general (if not universal) approval. / **Sample dishes:** smoked haddock & vegetable broth; roast lamb; white chocolate & orange mousse. **Details:** www.peartreepurton.co.uk; 9.15 pm; closed Sat L; no jeans or trainers. **Accommodation:** 18 rooms, from £105.

PWLLHELI, GWYNEDD

Plas Bodegroes   £ 42   🅐★★

Nefyn Rd LL53 5TH   (01758) 612363

The "fantastic" setting of this manor house restaurant with rooms
(which is set in wonderful grounds) is not the least of the place's
attractions – Chris Chown's "perfectly balanced" cooking is
"of rare quality", and it's "excellent value for money" too. / **Sample
dishes:** foie gras with ham & spiced pears; pork with black pudding & bacon;
chocolate tart with white chocolate ice cream. **Details:** www.bodegroes.co.uk;
on A499 1m W of Pwllheli; 9.30 pm; closed Mon, Tue–Sat D only, Sun open
L & D; no Amex; no smoking. **Accommodation:** 11 rooms, from £70.

RAMSGILL-IN-NIDDERDALE, NORTH YORKSHIRE   8–4B

Yorke Arms   £ 40   🅐★★

HG3 5RL   (01423) 755243

It's "worth the long and winding drive" to this well-known, small
country hotel, "picturesquely located" on a village green in the
Dales; Frances Atkins's "exciting", "beautifully-presented" cooking
is just part of the formula which makes this "excellent"
establishment a "perfect bolt hole". / **Sample dishes:** pavé of leek &
foie gras; beef with celeriac purée; millefeuille of banana & caramel mousse.
Details: www.yorke-arms.co.uk; 4m W of Pateley Bridge; 9.15 pm;
closed Sun D; no smoking; booking: max 6; children: 12+.
Accommodation: 14 rooms, from £105.

RAWTENSTALL, LANCASHIRE   5–1B

Samrat   £ 35

13 Bacup Rd BB4 7NG   (01706) 216183

Mr Alkas, the "award-winning" owner-chef sets the tone at this
mid-sized subcontinental, which a tiny band of loyal locals proclaim
"the best in the region". / **Sample dishes:** lamb kebab; chicken tikka
masala; chocolate bombe. **Details:** midnight, Sat & Sun 1 am; D only;
no Amex.

READING, BERKSHIRE   2–2D

Bens Thai   £ 24

Royal Ct, Kings Rd RG1 4AE   (0118) 959 6169

"There are none of the usual ethnic trappings" at this "basic" Thai
wine bar, by the river, which benefits from "very polite and friendly
service" and where "wonderfully-spiced curries are cooked in front
of you". / **Sample dishes:** spring rolls & sweet chilli sauce; pad Thai with
prawns; egg custard. **Details:** 10 pm; closed Sun.

London Street Brasserie   £ 38

2-4 London St RG1 4SE   (0118) 950 5036

"The only decent place to eat in Reading" (of a non-ethnic nature,
anyhow), this "modern brasserie" (which opened in spring 2000),
is undoubtedly a "welcome addition to the town"; even so, some
find this sibling to Stoke Row's Crooked Billet "slightly pricey" for
what it is. / **Sample dishes:** seared tuna with oriental pickled vegetables;
roast lamb with spinach & niçoise sauce; summer pudding & clotted cream.
Details: www.londonstbrasserie.co.uk; 10.30 pm.

Old Siam   £ 26   ★

Kings Wk, Kings St RG1 2HG   (0118) 951 2600

It has an "unattractive setting in a shopping mall", but this
"accommodating" town-centre Thai continues to draw a strong
local following on account of its "charming" service, "attractive"
interior and "reasonable" prices. / **Sample dishes:** Thai dim sum;
stir-fried beef in oyster sauce; mango & sticky rice.
Details: www.oldsiam.co.uk; in shopping complex; 10 pm; closed Sun;
no smoking in dining room.

Standard Nepalese Tandoori £ 19

141-143 Caversham Rd RG1 8AU   (0118) 959 0093

"Reading's most established and popular Indian" – it's over twenty years old – is "simply the best", say fans, and it's "always reliable". / **Sample dishes:** *king prawn delight; chicken jalfrezi with pilau rice; mango kulfi.* **Details:** *11 pm; no smoking area.*

REDMILE, LEICESTERSHIRE   5–3D

The Peacock Inn £ 30   A★

Church Corner NG13 0GA   (01949) 842554

"Not to be confused with the Peacock (Hotel), in the same village", this "great" pub near Belvoir Castle wins wholehearted praise for its "brasserie-style" cooking. / **Sample dishes:** *ham hock & smoked cheese terrine; pork stuffed with black pudding; white & dark chocolate parfait.* **Details:** *Grantham exit from A52; 9.30 pm; no smoking.* **Accommodation:** *10 rooms, from £75.*

REIGATE, SURREY   3–3B

La Barbe £ 40

71 Bell St RH2 7AN   (01737) 241966

"Good French cooking and service" ensure that this "intimate" and "very reliable" bistro is often "busy". / **Sample dishes:** *tiger prawns in chilli & garlic; pan-fried beef with tarragon & shallot sauce; pears poached in red wine.* **Details:** *www.labarbe.co.uk; 9.45 pm; closed Sat L & Sun; no smoking area.*

Dining Room £ 47   ★

59a High St RH2 9AE   (01737) 226650

It's no thanks to the "non-ambience" of TV chef Toby Tobin's "cramped" town-centre dining room or its "indifferent" service that the place is "impossible to book", so it must be down to his "creative" Mediterranean-influenced cooking, incorporating lots of fish and seafood. / **Sample dishes:** *crispy squid with fried green tomatoes; crispy duck with melted onions; banana tart with vanilla ice cream.* **Value tip:** *set 2-crs weekday L £13.* **Details:** *10 pm; closed Sat L & Sun D; no smoking.*

REYNOLDSTON, SWANSEA   1–1C

Fairyhill £ 41   A★★

SA3 1BS   (01792) 390139

With its "beautiful and tranquil setting" – in the wilds of the Gower Peninsula – this "wonderful", homely and relaxing country house hotel is among the UK's best, certainly in culinary terms; it offers some "great" cooking ("using the finest Welsh ingredients") and an "outstanding wine list". / **Sample dishes:** *crispy cockle cakes & bacon with tomato chutney; Welsh lamb with mash & laver gravy; praline glacé with mocha sauce.* **Details:** *www.fairyhill.net; 20 mins from M4, J47 off B4295; 9 pm; no smoking; children: 8+.* **Accommodation:** *8 rooms, from £125.*

RHOS-ON-SEA, CONWY   4–1D

La Dolce Vita £ 25

25 Penrhyn Ave LL28 4PS   (01492) 541145

Worth knowing about in a thin area – this small, "comfy" and "welcoming" family-run Italian offers some "good" cooking and is often "very busy". / **Sample dishes:** *baby squid with garlic mayonnaise; fillet steak with Madeira sauce; tiramisu.* **Details:** *10.30 pm; D only; no Amex.*

Burnt Chair   **£ 39**
5 Duke St TW9 1HP   (020) 8940 9488
*An "interesting menu" and an "accommodating" owner – who
dispenses "very good" advice on the impressive wine list – win
a disproportionate local following for this small restaurant, off
Richmond Green. / **Sample dishes:** pineapple gazpacho; lime-marinated
snapper with banana & lentil salad; orange & honey nougat glace.
Details: www.burntchair.com; 11 pm; D only, closed Mon & Sun; no Amex;
no smoking.*

Canyon   **£ 34**   X
Riverside TW10 6UJ   (020) 8948 2944
*For an "American-style brunch in a lovely setting near the river",
this well-designed Richmond two-year-old still has its advocates;
prices are "high" though, especially given the number of reports
of "dreadful" food and "disgraceful" service. / **Sample dishes:** spicy
tomato soup; tuna with spinach & butternut squash; crème caramel.
Details: www.canyonfood.co.uk; 11 pm; no smoking area.*

Old Vicarage   **£ 45**   X
Ridgeway Moor S12 3XW   (0114) 247 5814
*Something has gone very wrong or our reporters have been
incredibly unlucky at Tessa Bramley's well-renowned restaurant that
occupies a restored Victorian vicarage in the Lakes – practically all
reports this year were to the effect that it's "overpriced" and "very
over-rated". / **Sample dishes:** sea bass & mussels with saffron mash; beef,
pineapple & lime salad with roast cauliflower; chocolate brownie & pistachio ice
cream. **Details:** www.theoldvicarage.co.uk; 10 mins SE of city centre; 10 pm;
closed Mon & Sun D; no smoking in dining room.*

The Boar's Head   **£ 27**   𝔸
Ripley Castle Estate HG3 3AY   (01423) 771888
*This grand hotel (whose owners also own most of the surrounding
village) provides a "great setting"; it's a place which "tries hard,
and usually succeeds", thanks to the "tasty" and "honest" cooking
which is served both in the "crowded" bistro and in the restaurant.
/ **Sample dishes:** rabbit with caramelised apples; duck with summer vegetable
risotto; hot strawberry soufflé. **Value tip:** set 2-crs L £10. **Details:** off A61
between Ripon & Harrogate; 9 pm; no smoking. **Accommodation:** 25 rooms,
from £115.*

Michels   **£ 43**
High St GU23 6AQ   (01483) 224777
*As usual, feelings are rather mixed regarding this grandly housed
restaurant on a cobbled high-street; most acknowledge that Erik
Michel is a "dedicated" chef, whose "innovative" approach can
yield some "great" results; "awful", "brusque" service, however,
helps a number to the conclusion that it is just a "very boring"
place. / **Sample dishes:** potato pancake with smoked salmon & caviar; roast
sea bass with artichoke hearts; rhubarb & strawberry terrine. **Details:** 9 pm;
closed Mon, Sat L & Sun D.*

ROCKBEARE, DEVON   1–3D
Jack in the Green Inn   £ 27   ★
London Rd EX5 2EE   (01404) 822240
"A real find for very good pub grub" – all agree this "very popular"
establishment makes a worthwhile deviation from the A30.
/ *Sample dishes:* duck liver pâté; braised faggots with mash & onion gravy;
rice pudding with pralines. *Value tip:* set 3-crs Sun L £14.95.
Details: www.jackinthegreen.uk.com; 9.30 pm; no Amex; no smoking in dining
room; children: Sun L only.

ROMALDKIRK, COUNTY DURHAM   8–3B
The Rose & Crown   £ 34   Ⓐ★
DL12 9EB   (01833) 650213
Nothing but good is spoken of this beautiful village green "coaching
inn" in walking country, which offers "fantastic" food – making
"ingenious" use of "excellent local produce" – and "friendly"
service. / *Sample dishes:* scallop, mushroom & bacon gratin; char-grilled
entrecôte with garlic mushrooms; dark chocolate terrine.
Details: www.rose-and-crown.co.uk; 6m NW of Barnard Castle on B6277;
9 pm; D only, except Sun when L only; no Amex; no smoking; children: 6+.
Accommodation: 12 rooms, from £86.

ROMSEY, HAMPSHIRE   2–3D
Old Manor House   £ 39
21 Palmerston St SO51 8GF   (01794) 517353
The Bregolis' tiny restaurant of over two decades' standing offers
"traditional Italian food of high quality" (with game a speciality);
it's a shame it continues to strike some "non-regulars" as "smug"
and "arrogant". / *Sample dishes:* carpaccio of foie gras; chicken with wild
mushrooms; ice cream. *Details:* 9.30 pm; closed Mon & Sun D.

ROTHWELL, NORTHANTS   5–4D
The Thai Garden   £ 25
3 Market Hl NN14 6EP   (01536) 712345
The place looks pretty "standard", but locals says you get "great"
("if fairly expensive") Thai cooking at this "busy", family-owned
oriental. / *Sample dishes:* Thai fishcakes; coriander chicken with egg fried
rice; Thai pancakes. *Details:* off A14 nr Kettering; 11 pm; no smoking area.

ROWDE, WILTSHIRE   2–2C
George & Dragon   £ 34   ★
High St SN10 2PN   (01380) 723053
"Delicious and gutsy" cooking ("superb fish" is the speciality) is the
reason to seek out this "tiny and cramped" pub, in the back roads
of the West Country, with its "traditional and relaxed" ambience.
/ *Sample dishes:* leek & mussel soup; fried squid with lemon, garlic & parsley;
clementines in brandy. *Value tip:* set 2-crs L £10. *Details:* on A342 between
Devizes & Chippenham; 10 pm; closed Mon & Sun; no Amex; no smoking.

ROYAL LEAMINGTON SPA, WARWICKSHIRE   5–4C
Emperors   £ 26   ★
Bath Pl CV31 3BP   (01926) 313666
"Authentic" Chinese food served "with simple grace" makes this
upmarket oriental a notable destination hereabouts. / *Sample
dishes:* spring rolls; Cantonese style beef; toffee apples. *Details:* 10.45 pm,
Fri & Sat 11.15 pm; closed Sun.

Thai Elephant   £ 29
20 Regent St CV32 5HQ   (01926) 886882
"Tasty" and "beautifully presented" food and an "unusual"
basement setting – with "wonderful low ceilings and huge round
tables" – help to make this "lively" oriental a popular local
destination. / *Sample dishes:* duck pancakes; Thai chicken curry; ice cream.
Details: 10.30 pm; closed Sat L.

Biskra Beach £ 35 🄰
17 St Thomas St PO33 2DL (01983) 567913
"Right on the beach" (and with "outdoor dining in summer"), this boutique hotel offers "stunning views across the Solent", and is praised for its "inexpensive lunch menu" and its "elegant evening fare". / **Sample dishes:** Isle of Wight potted crab with tomato bread; roast chicken & boudin noir with dried tomatoes; pear tart with calvados sauce. **Details:** www.biskra-hotel.com; close to Ryde station; 10 pm; no smoking. **Accommodation:** 14 rooms, from £75.

Landgate Bistro £ 25 ★
5-6 Landgate TN31 7LH (01797) 222829
"Never a bad meal in over 20 years" – loyal fans still applaud the "splendid" English cooking at this "pleasant" bistro, although service tends to be "indifferent". / **Sample dishes:** onion & feta cheese tart; Gressingham duck with lime sauce; crème caramel. **Details:** www.landgatebistro.co.uk; 9.30 pm, Sat 10 pm; D only, closed Mon & Sun; no smoking in dining room.

Mermaid £ 50 🄰
Mermaid St TN31 7EY (01797) 223065
Rebuilt in 1492, this is as "historic" an inn as you could hope to find, and it has a "wonderful" panelled dining room; inevitably, perhaps, the "unpretentious", traditional fare can't quite keep up, but still generally wins praise. / **Sample dishes:** pan-fried scallops & langoustines; lobster thermidor; crème brûlée. **Value tip:** set 3-crs L £17.50. **Details:** 9.15 pm. **Accommodation:** 31 rooms, from £140.

Clare's £ 32 ★
55 Fore St TQ8 (01548) 842646
The "characterful" former proprietor has moved on, but the chef and staff of this popular fish restaurant are unchanged, as are its "reliable" culinary standards. / **Sample dishes:** sticky stir-fried crab claws; sea bass with rock salt crust; rhubarb crème brûlée. **Details:** 9.45 pm; D only; no Amex; no smoking before 9 pm; children: before 7 pm only.

Galley £ 28
5 Fore St TQ8 8BY (01548) 842828
A "good selection" of "fresh local fish", "imaginatively cooked" has earned popularity for this waterside establishment, though the setting's spick-and-span charms are slightly lacking in atmosphere for some tastes. / **Sample dishes:** smoked haddock fishcakes with sweet chilli; roast sea bass in lemon & chervil butter; syrup sponge & custard. **Details:** 10 pm; D only, closed Sun; no smoking; children: 5+.

Jade £ 28 ★
109a Exeter St SP1 2SF (01722) 333355
"Very good seafood specialities" – "the lobster is especially nice" – puts this well established spot near the Cathedral in a different league from your typical provincial Cantonese; "people come all the way from Southampton to eat here". / **Sample dishes:** spare ribs; lobster with ginger & spring onion; banana split. **Details:** near the Cathedral; 11.30 pm; closed Sun; no Amex.

LXIX £ 37 ★

69 New St SP1 2PH (01722) 340000

"The only good restaurant in Salisbury" (of an indigenous variety at
least) is a *"sophisticated"* spot, whose success has led to expansion
(and since July '01 there has also been a neighbouring bar and
bistro); even some supporters, though, wonder if it's not *"trying
too hard"*, and there are reservations about what some see as a
"clinical" ambience. / **Sample dishes:** blue fin tuna with chilli salsa; roast
cod with lime oil & noisette butter; chocolate marquise. **Details:** adjacent to
Cathedral Close; 10 pm; closed Sat L & Sun; no smoking; children: 12+.

SALTAIRE, WEST YORKSHIRE 5–1C

Salts Diner £ 21 Ⓐ

Salts Mill, Victoria Rd BD18 3LB (01274) 530533

"Always fun for lunch", this *"huge warehouse space"* in a former
mill is a *"bustling"* and *"casual"* destination – it offers *"a wide
variety of tasty food"*, and you can *"look at Hockneys while you
eat"* (the building incorporates a gallery, and the late owner was
a friend of the artist). / **Sample dishes:** garlic bread; confit duck leg; sticky
toffee pudding. **Details:** 2m from Bradford on A650; 5 pm; L only; no Amex;
no smoking area.

SANDGATE, KENT 3–4D

La Terrasse
Sandgate Hotel £ 46 ★★

CT20 3DY (01303) 220444

You'll have to cross the Channel (which it overlooks), to find a more
"genuinely French" dining experience than that at the Gicqueau
family's *"brilliantly-run"* seaside restaurant with rooms, where
the *"spectacular cooking"* is *"tremendous value"*. / **Sample
dishes:** warmed duck foie gras; fricassée of eels with crushed potatoes;
pineapple & mango brochette with coconut rice pudding.
Details: www.sandgatehotel.com; on A259 (main coastal road); 9.30 pm;
closed Mon, Tue L & Sun D; closed Jan; no smoking in dining room; booking:
max 8. **Accommodation:** 14 rooms, from £58.

SANDIWAY, CHESHIRE 5–2B

Nunsmere Hall £ 56

Tarporley Rd CW8 2ES (01606) 889100

It's *"luxurious, but not pretentious"* (a rarity for Cheshire), say fans
of this *"superb country house hotel, set on a sort of island"*, on the
fringe of Delamere Forest; as ever, though, there are some who find
it falls short of their culinary expectations. / **Sample
dishes:** langoustine & lobster broth; roast lamb with woodland mushroom
ragoût; chocolate truffle cake with pears. **Details:** www.nunsmere.co.uk; off
A49, 4m SW of Northwich; 10 pm; no jeans or trainers; no smoking; children:
12+. **Accommodation:** 36 rooms, from £160.

SAWLEY, LANCASHIRE 5–1B

Spread Eagle £ 23 ★

BB7 4NH (01200) 441202

A *"superb"* setting on the River Ribble is not the least of the
attractions of this *"pleasant"* old hostelry (under the same
ownership as the Punch Bowl at Crosthwaite) – it also provides
"courteous" service, *"imaginative"* cooking and an *"excellent"*
wine list. / **Sample dishes:** fish hors-d'oeuvres; braised lamb with root
vegetable sauce; tarte Tatin. **Value tip:** set 2-crs L £8 (Sun L £10.95).
Details: www.the-spreadeagle.co.uk; NE of Clitheroe off A59; 9 pm;
closed Mon & Sun D; no smoking.

Plough Inn   **£ 30**

Headwell Ln LS24 9BP   (01937) 557242

This "cosy" pub in a "lovely village" is unanimously praised for its
"good" and "interesting" cooking, but – as last year – some tip that
the popular Sunday lunchtime is "to be avoided". / **Sample
dishes:** stuffed peppers with toasted goat's cheese; sea bass with Milanese
risotto; lemon tart & raspberry coulis. **Value tip:** set 3-crs Sun L £13.95.
Details: off A162 between Tadcaster & Sherburn in Elmet; 9.15 pm; closed
Mon & Sun D; no Amex; no smoking in dining room.

Hare Inn   **£ 27**   𝔸★

YO7 2HG   (01845) 597289

This little, "family-run" country inn is "the best pub/restaurant for
miles around" – it has a "great atmosphere" and serves "excellent-
value" grub. / **Sample dishes:** warm smoked duck & bacon salad; rack of
lamb with rosemary sauce; strawberry pavlova. **Details:** off A170; 9.30 pm;
closed Mon L; no Amex; no smoking area.

Seaview Hotel   **£ 31**   𝔸★

High St PO34 5EX   (01983) 612711

"High quality" cooking continues to earn a good rep for the
"quaint" dining room of this "lovely" seaside hotel, where "great"
seafood is unsurprisingly the menu highlight. / **Sample dishes:** hot
crab ramekin; seared scallops with fennel; meringue & coconut with strawberry
coulis. **Details:** www.seaviewhotel.co.uk; 9.30 pm; closed Sun D; no smoking
area; children: 5+. **Accommodation:** 16 rooms, from £95.

Dun Cow   **£ 26**   ★

43 Front St TS21 3AT   (01740) 620894

An "excellent changing menu, with fresh ingredients" helps make
this "thriving" boozer near the village green a unanimously popular
destination. / **Sample dishes:** freshwater prawns with lime dressing;
medallions of pork with apple sauce; cheesecake. **Details:** 9.30 pm.
Accommodation: 6 rooms, from £65.

Thai Kitchen
The Lady in Grey Hotel   **£ 19**

3 Wilne Ln DE72 2HA   (01332) 793311

"Reasonably priced" Thai cooking is a "good" setting makes this
an oriental worth seeking out in an area offering little in the way
of competition. / **Sample dishes:** shrimps in pastry with piquant sauce;
steamed fish with chilli & lime; banana fritters.
Details: www.thethaikitchen.co.uk; 11 pm; closed Mon L; no smoking area.

Bahn Nah   **£ 23**   ★

19-21 Nile St S10 2PN   (0114) 268 4900

"Small", "intimate" and "reasonably priced" – Mrs Low's well-
established Thai is a popular local destination, and even if some
question whether the food is good enough to make up for the
"cramped" surroundings, most reporters proclaim it the "genuine"
article. / **Sample dishes:** chicken satay; spicy beef curry & jasmine rice; fresh
fruit. **Details:** 11 pm; D only, closed Sun; no smoking.

Everest £ 25

59-61 Chesterfield Rd S8 ORL (0114) 258 2975

"Really nice and friendly" service helps distinguish this *"enjoyable"* and *"well-priced"* Indian. / **Sample dishes:** vegetable pakora; north Indian garlic chicken; gulab jaman (Indian sweets). **Details:** www.everest-restaurant.co.uk; close to Newbridge; 12.45 am, Thu 1.45 am, Fri & Sat 2.45 am; D only.

Kashmir Curry Centre £ 12 ★

123 Spital Hill S4 7LD (0114) 272 6253

"Don't expect tablecloths", but this self-explanatory spot is a reliably *"cheap and cheerful"* destination; *"it's unlicensed, but you can BYO"*. / **Sample dishes:** masala lamb chops; chicken tikka jalfrezi; mango kulfi. **Details:** midnight; D only; no credit cards; no smoking area.

Marco @ Milano £ 33

Archer Rd S8 OLA (0114) 235 3080

It's a *"top class Italian"* say fans of this quite stylish two-year-old some of whom think the place bears a passing resemblance to a PizzaExpress; a minority finds it a *"disappointment"*. / **Sample dishes:** mussel, prawn & fennel risotto; venison in Gorgonzola sauce with white grapes; chocolate velvet pudding. **Details:** 11.30 pm; closed Sat L & Sun; no Amex.

Nirmals £ 21

189-193 Glossop Rd S10 2GW (0114) 272 4054

"It remains Sheffield's firm-favourite Indian", say the many ardent fans of Mrs Gupta's well-reputed fixture, known for her *"delight in welcoming people"* and for *"yummy and original"* cooking; a disgruntled minority emerged this year, however, who reported *"rude"* service and thought the place an *"expensive bog-standard curry house"*. / **Sample dishes:** lamb kebab; king prawn curry; gulab jaman. **Details:** nr West St; midnight, Fri & Sat 1 am; closed Sun L; no smoking area.

Nonnas £ 17

539-541 Ecclesall Rd S11 8PR (0114) 268 6166

"Good Italian food is quite a rarity in the North", so it's sad that recent expansion has dented the performance of this *"ever-popular"* deli and espresso bar; it still wins praise for *"the best antipasti"* and *"great coffee and desserts"*, but more this year registered *"disappointment"* with the cooking and *"uninterested"* service. / **Sample dishes:** Mozzarella with roasted vine tomatoes; rosemary-skewered chicken with garlic oil; grappa pannacotta. **Details:** www.nonnas.co.uk; M1, J33 towards Bakewell; 9.45 pm; no Amex.

Richard Smith at Thyme £ 28

32-34 Sandygate Rd S10 5RY (0114) 266 6096

Formerly Smiths of Sheffield, but still under the same ownership, this popular local destination is now an all-day operation; fans say it's *"trying even harder"* in its new guise, but reports remain very mixed, and the atmosphere, in particular, seems *"a problem"*. / **Sample dishes:** smoked salmon & haddock with cucumber gazpacho; Tuscan veal casserole with polenta mash; sticky toffee pudding & toffee sauce. **Details:** 10 pm; closed Sun D; smoking in bar only.

Zing Vaa £ 21

55 The Moor S1 4PF (0114) 275 6633

"Reliable food and service" make this *"cavernous"* spot the best Chinese restaurant hereabouts – in default, it must be said, of much local competition. / **Sample dishes:** tomato & sweetcorn soup; Chinese chicken & straw mushrooms; ice cream. **Details:** 11.30 pm; no smoking area.

Three Acres   £ 35   A ★
Roydhouse HD8 8LR   (01484) 602606
"An amazing success-story", this "superb", "cosy" pub "on a
windswept moor beneath a TV mast" is "great at any time of year,
but especially in winter"; its "varied" menu (which includes some
"excellent seafood") is complemented by "a good choice of wines,
real ale and whisky"; "book well ahead to avoid disappointment".
/ **Sample dishes:** chicken piri piri with lime salad; braised ox tails with
horseradish mash; trio of rhubarb desserts. **Details:** nr Emley Moor TV
transmitter; 9.45 pm; closed Sat L. **Accommodation:** 20 rooms, from £70.

Edwinns   £ 33
Church Rd TW17 9JT   (01932) 223543
"Consistently good" service and "generally good" cooking makes
this "smart but informal" fixture (one of a small chain) a popular
destination in an area without a huge number of competing
attractions. / **Sample dishes:** warm duck salad; beef Wellington; sticky
toffee pudding. **Details:** www.edwinns.co.uk; opp church & Anchor Hotel;
10.15 pm, Fri & Sat 10.45 pm; no smoking area.

Charlton House   £ 55   A ★
Charlton Rd BA4 4PR   (01749) 342008
"Wonderful", "traditional" cooking is twinned with "attentive" and
"knowledgeable" service at this "beautiful" small hotel; it's owned
by the founders of the Mulberry fancy goods company, and dressed
accordingly. / **Sample dishes:** linguini with sevruga caviar; stuffed rabbit with
sweetbreads; pear mousse with ricotta cheesecake. **Value tip:** set 2-crs L
£12.50. **Details:** www.charltonhouse.com; on A361 towards Frome; 9 pm;
no smoking. **Accommodation:** 16 rooms, from £155.

Kinghams   £ 35   A ★
Gomshall Ln GU5 9HB   (01483) 202168
Even those who gripe of a "tea shoppe" ambience at this "lovely
thatched cottage" in a pretty village say the modern cooking is
"good", and more reports say this is a "warm" and "cosy" (if rather
"crowded") spot, where everything is "always of a high standard".
/ **Sample dishes:** oxtail broth; guinea fowl with Puy lentils; butterscotch tart.
Details: www.kinghams-restaurant.co.uk; off A25 between Dorking &
Guildford; 9.30 pm; closed Mon & Sun D; no smoking.

Seven Stars   £ 29
High St DH1 2NU   (0191) 384 8454
This spacious inn – decorated with antiques – offers a "large"
range of "good pub food", and it's a popular destination from the
under-served City of Durham. / **Sample dishes:** king prawns & bean
sprouts; oriental spiced pork & pak choy stir fry; sticky toffee pudding &
butterscotch sauce. **Details:** off A177; 9.30 pm; no Amex; no smoking.
Accommodation: 8 rooms, from £50.

Aagrah £ 23 ★

27 Westgate BD18 3QX (01274) 530880
"Very good and imaginative" Indian cooking has been the bedrock
for the growth of Yorkshire's "pre-eminent subcontinental chain",
which numbers a "wide choice for veggies" among its attractions;
the "cheerful", original Shipley branch is closed as we go to press,
however, shortly to re-open in the nearby Polar Ford building.
/ **Sample dishes:** deep-fried masala fish; balti lamb paneer; mango kulfi.
Details: www.aagrah.com; off Saltaire Rd; midnight, Fri & Sat 1 am; D only;
no smoking area.

Chavignol at The Old Mill
Old Mill Hotel £ 52 ★★

Mill St CV36 4AW (01608) 663888
In mid-2001, Marcus Ashenford turned his old tea-shop premises
into a brasserie (see Chipping Norton) and moved to this new
home in a converted mill; it sounds like a more fitting venue for his
excellent venture, which combined "superb", "creative" cooking,
"attentive" service and an "excellent" wine list – our ratings
assume more of the same here. / **Sample dishes:** wood pigeon with
apple salad; braised pigs cheek with parsley mash; chocolate delice & raspberry
jelly. **Details:** www.chavignol.co.uk; off A34; 9.45 pm; no smoking area.
Accommodation: 5 rooms, from £100.

Cromwells Hotel £ 30 ★

11 Dogpole SY1 1EN (01743) 361440
A "wide range" of dishes of "a consistently high standard" – "from
the inexpensive bar menu or the pricier restaurant" – makes this a
useful destination in a thinly served area. / **Sample dishes:** baked
aubergine & goat's cheese; Cajun seafood sausages; rhubarb tart with ginger
custard. **Details:** opp Guildhall; 10 pm; no smoking in dining room.
Accommodation: 7 rooms, from £45.

Floating Thai Restaurant £ 22

Welsh Bridge SY3 8JQ (01743) 243123
This Thai restaurant floating on the Severn is certainly "really
unusual", and some proclaim a visit here a "lovely" experience.
/ **Sample dishes:** satay Thai fishcakes; sea bass & sweet chilli sauce; coconut
ice cream. **Details:** www.floatingthairestaurant.co.uk; 10.30 pm; D only.

Sol £ 41 ★

82 Wyle Cop SY1 1UT (01743) 340560
"Great food, great value", say fans of this "informal and
welcoming" outfit, which is beginning to make quite a name for
its bright, Mediterranean-influenced cooking. / **Sample dishes:** roast
pigeon with foie gras; beef galette with wild mushroom sauce; passion fruit
parfait with blackcurrant jelly. **Details:** www.solrestaurant.co.uk; 9.30 pm;
closed Mon & Sun; no smoking; children: 8+ at D.

The Crown Inn £ 29 A

Bridge Rd IP17 1SL (01728) 688324
This "attractive country restaurant", near the Maltings, is "rustic in
an upper-crust way" and serves "good beer, good wine and good
home-made food". / **Sample dishes:** tempura king prawns; pan-fried sea
bass; banana parfait. **Details:** off A12 towards Aldeburgh; 9 pm; no Amex;
no smoking in dining room; children: 14+. **Accommodation:** 3 rooms,
from £65.

Beau Thai £ 31 ★

761 Olde Lode Ln B92 8JE (0121) 743 5355

*For "a real taste of Thailand", many have "never had a bad meal"
at this small, but well-known family-run Solihull fixture. / Sample
dishes: spare ribs in garlic & butter; beef with chilli & spring onions; fruit & ice
cream. Details: www.beauthai.co.uk; 10 pm; closed Mon L, Sat L & Sun;
no smoking area.*

Chez Julien £ 28

1036-1044 Stratford Rd B90 4EE (0121) 744 7232

*This "small" and traditionally-French establishment is handy for the
NEC; it offers "good value at lunchtimes, less so in the evening".
/ Sample dishes: courgette & tomato flan; steak with fine herb sauce & chips;
crème brûlée. Value tip: set 3-crs L £10.90. Details: www.chezjulien.co.uk; nr
M42, J4; 10 pm; closed Sat L & Sun.*

Bull Inn £ 28

High St RG4 6UP (0118) 969 3901

*A "wonderfully picturesque", "quaint beamed pub, near the
Thames", offering "enjoyable" traditional grub. / Sample
dishes: tricolore salad; Peking pork; cheese cake. Details: off A4, J10
between Oxford & Windsor; 9 pm; no smoking area; no booking.
Accommodation: 7 rooms, from £60.*

The French Horn £ 46 🅐

RG4 6TN (0118) 969 2204

*"Still delighting after all these years" – "there are very few
restaurants with great food, super service and a setting to die for"
and for its fans, this "old school" fixture ("overlooking the Thames
with weeping willows draped on grassy banks") is one of them;
it's "very expensive", though, and not everyone is seduced by its
"middle England" charms. / Sample dishes: warm goat's cheese salad;
roast halibut with mushrooms & herbs; bread & butter pudding.
Details: www.thefrenchhorn.com; M4, J8 or J9, then A4; 9.30 pm.
Accommodation: 20 rooms, from £110.*

Madhu's Brilliant £ 22 ★

39 South Rd UB1 1SW (020) 8574 1897

*"Indian doesn't get better than this", says a South Kensington fan
justifying his schlep all the way to this Southall "classic"; our own
view would be that it's a good place, but not worth quite such a
journey. / Sample dishes: butter chicken; lamb chops in spicy sauce; almond
kulfi. Details: nr railway station; midnight; closed Tue, Sat L & Sun L.*

Kuti's £ 25

37-39 Oxford St SO14 3DP (023) 8022 1585

*"Well known in Southampton" as the only half-decent place in the
vicinity, this relatively "welcoming" Indian provides "consistently
good" cooking in quite a "stylish" setting, and all at "reasonable
prices". / Sample dishes: tandoori quail; chicken korma; vanilla ice cream.
Details: www.kutis.co.uk; nr Ocean Village; midnight.*

Pipe of Port £ 24 🅐

84 High St SS1 1JN (01702) 614606

*"Still the best in the area", say fans of this unpretentious, long-
established English bistro. / Sample dishes: avocado & prawn salad;
seared marinated tuna; lemon meringue pie. Details: 10.30 pm; closed Sun;
children: 16.*

L'Auberge Bistro £ 31

1b Seabank Rd PR9 0EW (01704) 530671

"Quality French cuisine" helps make this "small" and "friendly" bistro a popular local option. / **Sample dishes:** wild mushroom & asparagus fricassée; duck in kirsch with black cherries; chocolate & basil marquise. **Value tip:** set 3-crs Sun L £6.95. **Details:** 10.30 pm.

Hesketh Arms £ 19

Botanic Rd PR9 7NA (01704) 509548

A popular boozer where "pleasant" staff serve "delicious home-cooked food" in "large portions". / **Sample dishes:** potted shrimps; steak & kidney pie; bread & butter pudding. **Details:** nr Botanical gardens; 8 pm; closed Mon D & Sun D; no smoking area.

Warehouse Brasserie £ 26 ★

30 West St PR8 0DP (01704) 544662

This "busy, bustling and chic" brasserie comes as something of "a surprise, in a town full of senior citizens" – all reports agree, however, that the "modern" cooking here is "very good". / **Sample dishes:** goat's cheese & spinach wontons; roast duck with spring onion mash; milk chocolate & orange tiramisu. **Details:** 10.15 pm; closed Sun.

The Crown £ 26 𝔸★

High St IP18 6DP (01502) 722275

"It's a real bunfight to get a seat" in the "buzzy" bar of this famous inn (which also has a quieter, less atmospheric restaurant), but most say it's "worth" it on account of the "great food", "wonderful" surroundings, "superb and affordable" wine and "excellent beers from the Adnams' brewery nearby"; however, the voices of those who say the place is becoming "a victim of its own success" are getting louder. / **Sample dishes:** Norfolk crab with potato salad; cod tempura with sweet potato chips; apple & cinnamon tart. **Details:** 9.30 pm; no smoking. **Accommodation:** 14 rooms, from £57.

The Swan £ 35

The Market Pl IP18 6EG (01502) 722186

"Posher and more formal than the Crown", Adnams' "wonderfully old-fashioned" hotel on the market square has a "pleasant" dining room, known for its "well-prepared and presented" British cooking; there's a feeling, though, that "it's definitely not as good as it was". / **Sample dishes:** roasted quail with honey-glazed gammon; braised brill with new potato chowder; warm chocolate fondant. **Details:** 9 pm; no jeans; no smoking; children: 5+ at D. **Accommodation:** 43 rooms, from £105.

Gimbals £ 28 𝔸★

Wharf St HX6 2AF (01422) 839329

An "excellent out-of-the-way venue" – this "busy" wine bar/restaurant, with its "modern, artistic interior" and "accommodating" service provides "a range of food for everyone" that "cannot be faulted". / **Sample dishes:** marinated pork tempura; smoked fish & parsley pie; strawberry crème brûlée. **Details:** 9.15 pm; D only, closed Tue; no Amex; no smoking at D.

Java £ 17 ★

75 Wharf St HX6 2AF (01422) 831654

"Lovely" Indonesian cooking makes this a unanimously popular recommendation – "I was pleasantly surprised at how close to the real thing the food here is", says one reporter freshly back from SE Asia. / **Sample dishes:** king prawns in filo pastry; chicken in spicy tomato sauce; coconut & chocolate crepes. **Details:** 11 pm; D only; no Amex; no smoking.

The Millbank £ 29
Millbank HX6 3DY (01422) 825588
*This was formerly a "dying" pub, but Stephen Smith, who took it over in July 2000, has "brought it back to life", and it's already attracting plaudits for its "good" cooking and pleasant outside eating area. / **Sample dishes:** gratinated queen scallops; pork & leek sausage with mash; mango mousse with mango sauce. **Details:** 9.30 pm; closed Mon & Tue L; no Amex; no smoking in dining room; book only at weekends.*

SPARSHOLT, HAMPSHIRE 2–3D

Plough Inn £ 30
SO21 2NW (01962) 776353
*"A good average place with decent cooking" – even supporters don't claim this pub/restaurant is anything exceptional, but it is consistently recommended. / **Sample dishes:** grilled goat's cheese with herb croutons; roast pork in smoked bacon, apricot & ginger sauce; pear Condé with chocolate sauce. **Details:** 8.30 pm, Fri & Sat 9.30 pm; no Amex; no smoking area.*

SPEEN, BUCKINGHAMSHIRE 3–2A

Old Plow £ 42
HP27 OPZ (01494) 488300
*This "attractive" Chilterns pub-conversion (incorporating bar and restaurant) offers "reliable", "French-style" cooking and achieves a fair degree of support; it's "rather expensive", though, and "not quite as good as it thinks it is". / **Sample dishes:** Parma ham with fresh figs; skate with prawns & herb butter sauce; French apple tart. **Details:** 20 mins from M40, J4 towards Princes Risborough; 8.45 pm; closed Mon, Sat L & Sun D; smoking in bar only.*

ST ALBANS, HERTFORDSHIRE 3–2A

La Cosa Nostra £ 22
62 Lattimore Rd AL1 3XR (01727) 832658
*Critics say it's "more about quantity than quality", but this "frantic" ("wine-bar-like") pizza and pasta joint is worth knowing about in this under-served town. / **Sample dishes:** grilled aubergine salad; spaghetti with garlic & parsley; tiramisu. **Details:** nr railway station; 11 pm; closed Sat L & Sun.*

Thai Rack £ 26
13 George St AL3 4ER (01727) 850055
*"The décor could be better" and the cooking is "not amazing", but if you insist on eating in downtown St Albans, this "crowded" oriental – the most popular place in town – is your "best bet". / **Sample dishes:** king prawn tempura with dipping sauce; chilli beef; ice cream. **Details:** 10.30 pm; no Amex.*

The Waffle House
Kingsbury Water Mill £ 19 𝔸
Kingsbury Water Mill, St Michael's St AL3 4SJ
(01727) 853502
*This "lovely", "olde-worlde" water mill (still functioning) only serves waffles, "but they are absolutely gorgeous" – "all sorts come here" and "there's always a queue". / **Sample dishes:** chunky vegetable soup; ham, cheese & mushroom waffle; banana & butterscotch waffle. **Details:** nr Roman Museum; 6 pm (5 pm in winter); L only; no Amex; no smoking; no booking.*

Vine Leaf Garden   £ 33   ★

131 South St KY16 9UN   (01334) 477497

*Reporters have few complaints regarding this "small" and "friendly" venture, where Mrs Hamilton cooks some "superior", "eclectic" dishes and her husband does the front-of-house. / **Sample dishes:** scallops & tiger prawns with noodles; pigeon, venison & wild boar with mushrooms; lemon pavlova. **Details:** 9.30 pm; D only, closed Mon & Sun; no smoking.*

ST IVES, CORNWALL   1–4A

Al Fresco   £ 32   𝔸★

Harbourside Wharf Rd TR26 ILF   (01736) 793737

*It's not just a "scenic location" that makes this harbourside spot a consistent success; it offers "vibrant" and "imaginative" cooking – with "lots of fish dishes, and other alternatives" – complemented by a "well-chosen wine list". / **Sample dishes:** steamed crab dumplings; red mullet tart with basil; strawberry pavlova with raspberry coulis. **Details:** www.stivesharbour.com; on harbour front; 9.30 pm; no Amex.*

Blue Fish   £ 30   ★

Norway Ln TR26 ILZ   (01736) 794204

*Over a couple of years, this "unpretentious" restaurant/tapas bar above a craft centre has become a "popular" destination; "excellent" fish dishes are a highlight, and they are complemented by "fine views from the balcony across the bay". / **Sample dishes:** shrimps in garlic; chicken & goat's cheese salad; chocolate ganache. **Details:** behind the Sloop Inn; 10.30 pm (9 pm in winter).*

Garrack Hotel   £ 33

Burthallan Ln TR26 3AA   (01736) 796199

*"Consistently good food" from a "frequently-changing menu" makes this "friendly" hotel dining room universally popular with reporters; "ask for a table in the conservatory for stunning coastal views". / **Sample dishes:** tomato & goat's cheese tart; pan-fried scallops with roast pepper dressing; rum baba with cardamom ice cream. **Details:** www.garrack.com; 9 pm; D only; no smoking. **Accommodation:** 18 rooms, from £106.*

Porthminster Beach Café   £ 30   𝔸★

Porthminster Beach TR26 2EB   (01736) 795352

*"Don't be fooled by the name, this is near perfection"; with its "wonderful views" and "the stunning quality of the light", this "colourful" and "unpretentious" beachside fixture is "a delight even on a dull day"; chefs change regularly – this year they produced some "inventive and flavoursome" Mediterranean/fusion fare, though as we go to press a simpler, more modern British style is on the cards. / **Sample dishes:** grilled scallops & goat's cheese; turbot with braised leeks; chocolate pudding with orange ice cream. **Details:** nr railway station; 10 pm; no smoking in dining room.*

Walletts Court   £ 47   ★

Westcliffe CT15 6EW   (01304) 852424

*Reports on the Oakley family's country house hotel, scenically located at the top of a cliff, are less copious than we would like – such as they are confirm that it's a "relaxed" place, serving "generous" and "imaginative" Gallic cooking. / **Sample dishes:** grilled squid & blackened green peppers; roast partridge stuffed with game parfait; crème brûlée with raspberries. **Details:** www.wallettscourt.com; on B2058 towards Deal, 3m NE of Dover; 9 pm; closed Sat; no smoking. **Accommodation:** 16 rooms, from £90.*

Hotel Tresanton   **£ 46**   Ⓐ
Lower Castle Rd TR2 5DR   (01326) 270055
"The stunning view across St Mawes harbour", together with its "delightful" decor help make the dining room at Forte scion Olga Polizzi's rural design-hotel a "special place" for many reporters; though some would be more exaggerated in their praise, the consensus is that the food is "reasonably good" too. / Sample dishes: tuna carpaccio; roast rib of beef with vegetables; chocolate nemesis with pistachio sauce. Value tip: set 2-crs L £25. Details: www.tresanton.com; nr St Mawes Castle; 9.30 pm; D only; no smoking at D. Accommodation: 26 rooms, from £195.

McCoys at the Tontine   **£ 42**   ★
DL6 3JB   (01609) 882671
Fans say this "buzzy" and "slightly quirky" bistro and restaurant is "still worth an hour's drive" to the fringe of the North York Moors, as both offer "food and wine of the highest quality"; satisfaction slipped across the board this year, though, with prime complaints being of "squashed" seating and "disappointing" service. / Sample dishes: king scallops with potato crepes & caviar; roast duck with duck confit ravioli & cider sauce; baked Alaska. Value tip: set 2-crs L £9.95. Details: www.mccoysatthetontine.co.uk; junction of A19 & A172; 10 pm; bistro L&D all week; restaurant Sat D only. Accommodation: 6 rooms, from £95.

Crazy Bear   **£ 43**
Bear Ln OX44 7UR,   (01865) 890714
This aptly-named oddity, set in "picturesque" gardens is "really two restaurants, in a converted pub" (the – stuffed – bear is in the bar); most reporters prefer the cheaper oriental section downstairs (where the Thai food is "full of flavour") to the more expensive Anglo/French section. / Sample dishes: Roquefort soufflé with pears & walnuts; roast duck with cider braised potatoes; warm chocolate cake. Value tip: set 2-crs L £10 (Tue-Thu only). Details: www.crazybearhotel.co.uk; 10 pm; closed Mon & Sun D. Accommodation: 13 rooms, from £80.

Julians   **£ 31**
21 High St ST21 6BW   (01785) 851200
This "small, bistro-style restaurant" is worth knowing about in the wilds of Staffordshire; disappointments are not unknown, but most reports speak of "good-quality cooking", "friendly" service and a high level of overall value. / Sample dishes: leek Tatin with scallops; lamb with fine beans & white truffle sauce; trio of lemon desserts. Details: 9.30 pm; closed Sun D; no smoking; children: 8+ at D.

Endeavour   **£ 32**   ★
1 High St TS13 5BH   (01947) 840825
This well-established "seaside village restaurant" is unanimously hailed for its "exceptionally good" food – "fabulous" fruits de mer are the menu highlight, but all the dishes are of solid quality. / Sample dishes: Staithes octopus with avocado; skate wing with red peppercorn & lemon sauce; crème brûlée with raspberries. Details: 10m N of Whitby, off A174; 9 pm; closed Mon & Sun (& mostly closed Nov-Mar); no credit cards; no smoking area; booking essential. Accommodation: 3 rooms, from £42.

The George Hotel   £ 43   Ⓐ
71 St Martins PE9 2LB (01780) 750750
*This impressive building at the heart of a fine Georgian town is
perhaps England's most famous coaching inn, and for many
reporters it remains an "admirable" destination on account of its
"wonderful" ambience; the "traditional" cooking in the "beautiful",
"formal" dining doesn't set the world alight, but is "reliable";
(as to the cheaper, rather "tacky" brasserie, "don't bother").*
/ **Sample dishes:** *rabbit & apple terrine with mustard cream; roast pork
with goats cheese & cider sauce; Stilton with celery & grapes.*
Details: *www.georgehotelofstamford.com; off A1, 14m N of Peterborough,
onto B1081; 10.30 pm; jacket & tie required; no smoking before 10 pm.*
Accommodation: *47 rooms, from £105.*

Leaping Hare Vineyard   £ 25   Ⓐ★
Wyken Vineyards IP31 2DW (01359) 250287
*A "fabulous countryside setting" and "sensible food served with
care and attention" ensure nothing but favourable commentary on
this "imaginative addition to a vineyard"; the indigenous vino is
"surprisingly palatable" too.* / **Sample dishes:** *gravadlax with dill crème
fraîche; sea bass with rocket noodles & Mediterranean vegetables; kiwi & mint
sorbet.* **Details:** *9m NE of Bury St Edmunds; follow tourist signs off A143;
9 pm; closed Mon D, Tue D, Wed D, Thu D & Sun D; no Amex; no smoking.*

Stapleford Park   £ 50   Ⓐ
LE14 2EF (01572) 787522
*All agree that this impressive country house hotel is a "beautiful"
place to eat; it has also in recent years often been a "particularly
disappointing" one – let's hope its new owners will buck up
standards.* **Sample dishes:** *tomato tarte Tatin; fillet steak with foie gras
sauce; soufflé.* **Details:** *4m from Melton Mowbray on B676; 9.30 pm, Fri &
Sat 10.30 pm; jacket and/or tie required; no smoking; children: 9+.*
Accommodation: *51 rooms, from £175.*

Fox & Hounds   £ 20   Ⓐ★
BD23 5HY (01756) 760269
*"Great beers and a welcoming open fire – bliss!", say fans of this
"cosy", "down-to-earth" Dales pub whose culinary attractions
include "super" sandwiches and "veggie dishes that are tasty
and a bit different".* / **Sample dishes:** *blue cheese soufflé; Whitby
scampi & chips; sticky toffee pudding.* **Details:** *on B6160 N of Kettlewell;
9 pm; closed Mon; no Amex; no smoking area; no booking.*

Bell Inn   £ 30
Great North Rd PE7 3RA (01733) 241066
*A "lovely old inn" whose "pleasant surroundings and atmosphere"
and good "English-with-a-twist" cooking commend it to most
visitors; some find the antique-filled style rather "mumsy" though,
and others say the food is "OK, but too ordinary".* / **Sample
dishes:** *parfait of chicken livers; ricotta & spinach samosas; dark chocolate
torte.* **Value tip:** *set 3-crs L £12.95.* **Details:** *www.thebellstilton.co.uk; follow
signs from A1(M), J16; 9.30 pm; no smoking area; children: 12+.*
Accommodation: *19 rooms, from £89.50.*

Vineyard at Stockcross £ 61
RG20 8JU (01635) 528770
This rather "overdone" California-style country restaurant (with a huge wine list to match) was launched three years ago with the highest ambitions, but it's never quite taken off – "indifferent" service and the somewhat "austere" atmosphere are among the factors limiting enthusiasm. / **Sample dishes:** crab & pink grapefruit tian; sea bass with chow mein & spicy seaweed; cherry Bakewell tart. **Value tip:** set 3-crs L £22. **Details:** www.the-vineyard.co.uk; from M4, J13 take A34 towards Hungerford; 9 pm; no smoking. **Accommodation:** 31 rooms, from £209.

Bruerne's Lock £ 34
5 The Canalside NN12 7SB (01604) 863654
On a good day, this "intimate" canalside restaurant offers "superb" food in a "beautiful" location; recent reports, however, have expressed a number of doubts about "unimaginative" and "overpriced" cooking. / **Sample dishes:** shin & leek terrine; pork tenderloin in marsala & thyme cream; sticky toffee pudding. **Details:** www.bruerneslock.co.uk; 0.5m off A508 between Northampton & Milton Keynes; 9.45 pm; closed Mon, Sat L & Sun D; no smoking in dining room.

Angel Inn £ 26
Polstead St CO6 4SA (01206) 263245
"Diners travel from all over East Anglia" to enjoy the "consistent" delights of this "elegant" but still "rustic" inn, which numbers fish and puddings among its special strengths; the strain can show, though, in "cramped" tables and "pressured" service and some feel the cooking "over-rated". / **Sample dishes:** marinated herrings; medallions of beef in red wine sauce; steamed syrup pudding. **Details:** 5m W of A12, on B1068; 9 pm; no Amex; no smoking area; children: 14+. **Accommodation:** 6 rooms, from £65.

Wildebeest £ 34
Norwich Rd NR14 8QJ (01508) 492497
It's certainly "relaxed" – too much so for some tastes – but this idiosyncratic pub-conversion has a small, but loyal fan club who proclaim the virtues of its "very good" food. / **Sample dishes:** crab & avocado tian; pesto chicken with goats cheese mash; champagne & raspberry jelly. **Value tip:** set 2-crs L £9.95 (Sun L £11.95). **Details:** from A140, turn left at Dunston Hall, left at T-junction; 10 pm; no smoking area.

The Crooked Billet £ 35 𝔸★
Newlands Ln RG9 5PU (01491) 681048
This "hard to find", "unspoilt country pub in deepest Oxfordshire" achieves unanimously favourable commentary, not just on account of its "charming surroundings", but also due to its "good value", enjoyable grub. / **Sample dishes:** wild mushroom salad; Thai marinated chicken; banana & toffee cheesecake. **Value tip:** set 2-crs L £11.95. **Details:** www.thecrookedbillet.co.uk; on A4130; 10 pm; no Amex or Switch.

Chapters   £ 34   ★
27 High St TS9 5AD   (01642) 711888
*The "constantly developing" modern menu at Alan and Catherine
Thompson's town-centre hotel wins nothing but praise (not least for
"the best steaks"). / **Sample dishes:** cured meats with artichokes &
Parmesan; confit duck leg with carrot purée & foie gras; sticky toffee pudding &
caramel sauce. **Details:** by town hall; 9.30 pm; closed Sun; no smoking area.
Accommodation: 13 rooms, from £60.*

Y-Thai   £ 28
4 High St TS9 5DQ   (01642) 710165
*"Don't be put off by the exterior" – for "a good introduction to Thai
food", this town-centre spot is unusually good for a rural ethnic
restaurant. / **Sample dishes:** won-ton prawns with sweet chilli sauce; spicy
fried chicken with basil leaves; sticky rice pudding with coconut.
Details: 10 pm; no smoking.*

Lairhillock Inn   £ 26   A★
Netherley AB39 3QS   (01569) 730001
*Especially if you stick to the bar – some think "the restaurant is
probably not worth the extra cash" – this "relaxed" pub provides
some "superb", "traditional" grub and makes a "rewarding"
destination for Aberdeen city-dwellers. / **Sample dishes:** chunky
seafood chowder; lamb shank with roast parsnips; sticky toffee pudding.
Details: www.lairhillock.co.uk; 7m S of Aberdeen; 9.30 pm; no smoking area.*

Tolbooth   £ 35
Old Pier Rd AB39 2JU   (01569) 762287
*"Good seafood" and a "civilised" (and ancient) setting in a
"picturesque" harbour have made quite a name for Chris
McCarrey's establishment – to the extent, sadly, that there are
those who find prices "too high". / **Sample dishes:** smoked salmon with
Parma ham & pesto; wolf fish with champagne & watercress sauce; sticky
toffee pudding. **Details:** www.tolboothrestaurant; 9.30 pm; D only, closed
Mon & Sun; no Amex; children: 8+.*

Peking   £ 27
117 High St MK11 1AT   (01908) 563120
*"Good, basic Chinese cooking, nicely presented" makes this a useful
destination in a thin area. / **Sample dishes:** crispy aromatic duck; chicken
with cashew nuts & egg noodles; ice cream. **Details:** off A5; 11.30 pm;
no smoking area.*

Fleur de Sel   £ 47   A★★
Manley's Hill RH20 4BT   (01903) 742331
*"Best overall in West Sussex", says one reporter whose view on
this "immaculate and stylish" French country restaurant (once
called Manleys) is shared by many – "very good food is beautifully
prepared from exceptional ingredients and nicely served". / **Sample
dishes:** smoked quail stuffed with foie gras; Gressingham duck with honey &
ginger sauce; orange & Grand Marnier soufflé. **Value tip:** set 2-crs L £14.50.
Details: W of Storrington on A283; 9.30 pm; closed Mon, Sat L & Sun D;
no smoking.*

French Connection   £ 31   ★
3 Coventry St DY8 1EP   (01384) 390940
*A "small", "family-run" French restaurant that's "cosy", "well run"
and "authentic", where "huge portions" contribute to its "value-for-
money" reputation. / **Sample dishes:** chicken liver, brandy & garlic pâté;
salmon, prawn, cod & Gruyère crepe; brioche bread & butter pudding.
Details: 9.30 pm; closed Mon, Tue D, Thu D & Sun; no smoking area.*

Tot Hill House   £ 38   𝔸★
Tot Hill IP14 3QH   (01449) 673375
*"A jewel in Suffolk's crown", this "friendly family restaurant" –
whose "interesting" menus include "especially good puds" – is
consistently proclaimed "delightful in every way". / **Sample
dishes:** chive rosti with smoked salmon & horseradish; lamb with garlic &
rosemary mash; iced nougat glace & peaches. **Details:** 8.30 pm; Sat 9 pm;
closed Mon, Tue, Sat L & Sun D; no smoking.*

Desports   £ 38
13-14 Meer St CV37 6QB   (01789) 269304
*Above a ground-floor deli/café, this half-timbered house has a
"welcoming" and "warmly decorated" dining room housing the
most ambitious place in town; some reporters continue to proclaim
its good quality, "fresh"-tasting cooking, while others complain that
"earlier high standards are not being maintained". / **Sample
dishes:** cashew & herb risotto; Dover sole with curry sauce & big chips; cherry
custard tart with cherry ice cream. **Details:** www.desports.co.uk; 9.30 pm;
closed Mon & Sun; no smoking area.*

Hussains   £ 20
6a Chapel St CV37 6EP   (01789) 205804
*"Nice food and friendly staff" win praise for this "crowded" Indian;
it's also a useful post-theatre option. / **Sample dishes:** mixed tandoori
kebabs; lamb korma; coconut supreme. **Details:** 11.30 pm.*

Lambs   £ 27
12 Sheep St CV37 6EF   (01789) 292554
*"Cosy" and "efficient", and serving "good food at a reasonable
price", this reliable fixture remains the most popular place in town
for "a tasty meal before the theatre". / **Sample dishes:** crispy duck &
watercress salad; roast chicken & mango in lime butter; banoffi pie.
Details: nr Royal Shakespeare Theatre; 10 pm.*

Opposition   £ 27
13 Sheep St CV37 6EF   (01789) 269980
*The "bistro food" is "reliable" and the staff are "efficient, even
during the pre-RST rush", at this well-known "casual" wine bar.
/ **Sample dishes:** salmon fishcake; spinach & feta filo pie; brioche & butter
pudding. **Details:** nr Royal Shakespeare Theatre; no Amex; booking: max 12.*

Russons   £ 29   ★
8 Church St CV37 6HB   (01789) 268822
*"Very friendly" and "very reliable" – this "family-run", town-centre
bistro enjoys a solid following, and not just as "a very good place
for pre-theatre meals". / **Sample dishes:** peaches with Mozzarella &
Parma ham; stuffed fish with oyster sauce; blackberry & apple crepes.
Details: 9.45 pm; closed Mon & Sun; no smoking area; booking: max 8;
children: 8+ after 7pm.*

Thai Boathouse £ 28 A★

Swans Nest Ln CV37 7LS (01789) 297733

"Authentic" (and "reasonably priced") Thai cooking, "attentive" service and a "lovely" setting make a compelling combination at this popular riverside spot. / *Sample dishes:* crispy duck; steak with oyster sauce; assorted Thai sweets. *Details:* www.thai-boathouse.co.uk; 10.30 pm; closed Sat L.

Thai Kingdom £ 27 ★

11 Warwick Rd CV37 6YW (01789) 261103

"If it's good enough for the Crown Prince of Thailand…" – this small town-centre spot, briefly Under Royal Patronage, attracts strong support for its "very good" cooking and its "fast" but "caring" service. / *Sample dishes:* prawn cakes & mixed satay; crispy fried bream in Thai spices; mango mousse. *Details:* 10.45 pm; closed Sun; no smoking area.

STUCKTON, HAMPSHIRE 2–3C

Three Lions £ 43 ★★

Stuckton Rd SP6 2HF (01425) 652489

"Terrific" cooking ("especially fish") and "charming" service – "we finished lunch at 4.30 pm, and didn't feel under any pressure" – come together to make Michael and Jayne Womersley's New Forest-fringe pub-conversion a model destination. / *Sample dishes:* shrimps in crab bisque; roasted roe buck with ceps; hot chocolate pudding. *Value tip:* set 2-crs L £14.50. *Details:* 1m E of Fordingbridge off B3078; 9.30 pm; closed Mon & Sun D; no Amex; no smoking. *Accommodation:* 3 rooms, from £65.

STURMINSTER NEWTON, DORSET 2–3B

Plumber Manor £ 30 A

DT10 2AF (01258) 472507

"Proper-size" portions of "perfect country house food" help make this "homely" (family-run) hotel "an excellent choice for dinner with a stop overnight". / *Sample dishes:* linguine with wild mushrooms; chicken with Thai curry sauce; lemon meringue pie. *Details:* off A357 towards Hazelbury Bryan; 9.30 pm; D only, except Sun open L & D; booking essential. *Accommodation:* 16 rooms, from £100.

SUDBURY, SUFFOLK 3–1C

Red Onion Bistro £ 23

57 Ballingdon St CO10 2DA (01787) 376777

An uncomplicated formula – "good basic grub, well cooked" and served in "simple but agreeable surroundings" – has made this "fun" place a well-known local success story; even fans concede that "some days are better than others", however; a Colchester sibling opened in March '00 (19 Head St, tel 01206 366319). / *Sample dishes:* mushrooms stuffed with goat's cheese; char-grilled rump steak with mushrooms; white & dark chocolate mousse. *Value tip:* set 2-crs L £7.50. *Details:* on A131; 9.30 pm; closed Sun D.

SUNDERLAND, TYNE & WEAR 8–2C

throwingstones
National Glass Centre £ 20 A★

Liberty Way SR6 0GL (0191) 565 3939

"Consistently good and imaginative cooking", "very reasonable prices", a "beautiful river location" … – why can't more tourist attractions have good restaurants like this one at the National Glass Centre, which makes use of the material it celebrates to create an interesting dining environment. / *Sample dishes:* roast pepper & Mozzarella salad; salmon with rocket & orange salad; brandy snap with toffee ice cream. *Details:* A19 to Sunderland, follow signs for National Glass Centre; 9.30 pm; L only, except Fri & Sat when L&D; no Amex.

New Hall £ 57   🅰

Walmley Rd B76 IQX (0121) 378 2442

The oldest manor house in England is certainly "a wonderful place" – especially as "a refuge from Brum, only eight miles distant" – but the cooking is "pretty ordinary", and prices "astronomical". / **Sample dishes:** saffron risotto with confit tomatoes; canon of lamb with cucumber noodles; cinnamon & apple parfait. **Details:** www.newhallhotel.net; from A452, right onto B4148, past Walmley; 10 pm; closed Sat L; no smoking; booking essential; children: 8+. **Accommodation:** 60 rooms, from £160.

La Braseria £ 32   🅰

28 Wind St SA1 IDZ (01792) 469683

It's all quite basic and no-nonsense, but there's "an excellent choice of fresh fish" and meats (you choose what you want grilled and how) and some "favourably priced wine" at this "large", "atmospheric" Spanish institution (no longer connected with the similar Cardiff venture); there's no booking so "queue early to get a table". / **Sample dishes:** calamari; char-grilled fillet steak; crème caramel. **Value tip:** set 2-crs L £6.95. **Details:** 11.30 pm; closed Sun; need 6+ to book; children: 6+.

Dermotts
Morgans Hotel £ 37   ★

219 High St SA1 INN (01792) 459050

"A proper treat" is to be had at this city-centre restaurant; it was established in 1998 (stepping into the shoes of 'Number One'), and its "exceptional" cooking is helping to maintain it as a top local destination. / **Sample dishes:** seared scallops with butternut squash; roast goose with sweet onion couscous; citrus tart with gin & tonic sorbet. **Details:** www.dermotts.org.uk; 9.30 pm; D only, closed Mon & Sun; no Amex; no smoking area.

Moghul Brasserie £ 25

81 St Helen's Rd SA1 4BQ (01792) 475131

"Always achieving a satisfying standard at reasonable prices" is the unanimous verdict on this "consistent" Indian. / **Sample dishes:** onion bhaji; chicken tikka masala; coconut surprise. **Details:** follow the King's Way; midnight, Fri & Sat 2 am; no Amex.

Opium Den £ 18

20 Castle St SA1 IJF (01792) 456160

There's "always a pleasant evening" to be had at this useful central oriental. / **Sample dishes:** crispy spring rolls; Cantonese style chicken; ice cream. **Details:** 11.30 pm; closed Sun L.

Patricks £ 28   ★

638 Mumbles Rd SA3 4EA (01792) 360199

"Pleasant", "friendly" and "reliable", this "lively" family-run bistro – overlooking Swansea bay from the Mumbles – is "always popular". / **Sample dishes:** bacon salad with Stilton dressing; Barbary duck with strawberry sauce; peanut butter & chocolate sandwich. **Details:** www.patricks-restaurant.co.uk; in Mumbles, 1m before pier; 9.50 pm; closed Sun D; no Amex. **Accommodation:** 2 rooms, from £85.

Wheatsheaf Inn £ 30   ★

Main St TD11 3JJ (01890) 860257

"Consistently good over the years" – this "pleasant" pub in the Borders serves "lovely" food in "relaxing" surroundings. / **Sample dishes:** avocado & prawn timbale; roast venison with spiced poached pears; iced Drambuie parfait. **Details:** between Kelso & Berwick-upon-Tweed, by village green; 9.15 pm; closed Mon & Sun D (to non-residents); no Amex; no smoking. **Accommodation:** 7 rooms, from £80.

Aagrah   £ 23   ★

York Rd LS24 8EG   (01937) 530888

There's "something to please everyone" at this branch of the eminent chain of Yorkshire Indians, where the food is "always good". / *Sample dishes:* chick pea samosas; tandoori chicken stuffed with lamb & coriander; mango kulfi. *Details:* www.aggrah.com; 7m from York on A64; 11.30 pm; D only; no smoking area.

Maes y Neuadd   £ 28   𝔸★

LL47 6YA   (01766) 780200

"They grow their own vegetables, and cook local ingredients to an international standard", say fans of this family-run country hotel, which occupies a part-14th-century manor house, with views of Snowdonia. / *Sample dishes:* ham & melon salad with a poached egg; pot-roasted chicken with cream & mushroom sauce; apple & cinnamon strudel. *Details:* www.neuadd.com; 3m N of Harlech off B4573; 9 pm; no smoking. *Accommodation:* 16 rooms, from £141, incl D.

Waldo's at Cliveden   £ 74   ✗

Berry HI SL6 0JF   (01628) 668561

"The food is secondary" at the "hugely expensive" subterranean gourmet dining room of this famous, "very grand", country house hotel – that's just as well as, for far too many reporters, the cooking is just "too rich, elaborate and lacking flavour". / *Sample dishes:* sea bass poached in champagne; roast partridge with blackcurrant vinegar; fig tartlet with honey ice cream. *Details:* www.clivedenhouse.co.uk; M4, J7 then follow National Trust signs; 9.30 pm; D only, closed Mon & Sun; jacket & tie required; no smoking; booking: max 6; children: 12+. *Accommodation:* 38 rooms, from £385.

Brazz   £ 27

Castle Bow TA1 3NF   (01823) 252000

"How things begin to date…" and how quickly sentiment has started to shift against this smart brasserie two-year old, an offshoot of the famous Castle; even fans of the "fabulous" décor say the cooking is "competent, but not thrilling" and many are scathing about "stressed" and "hamfisted" service. / *Sample dishes:* duck terrine with carrot marmalade; steak & kidney pudding; rhubarb Bakewell tart. *Details:* 10 pm.

The Castle Hotel   £ 41

Castle Grn TA1 1NF   (01823) 272671

The "pleasant" dining room of this landmark hotel was once a culinary destination of real note, and some continue to praise its "superb" English cooking; since Phil Vickery left a couple of years ago, however, there have continued to be too many reports of "disappointing recent visits". / *Sample dishes:* scrambled duck eggs with smoked eel; Brixham scallops with celeriac; chocolate dessert platter. *Value tip:* set 2-crs L £14.95. *Details:* www.the-castle-hotel.com; follow tourist information signs; 9 pm; no smoking. *Accommodation:* 44 rooms, from £150.

Trouble House Inn £ 29

Cirencester Rd GL8 8SG (01666) 502206

An ex-City Rhodes chef puts a quality spin on the cooking at this "roadside pub" near Highgrove; the menu is "limited", though, and some felt that "the ambience could be improved" – perhaps a July 2001 expansion will change things for the better. / **Sample dishes:** *asparagus & smoked haddock salad; duck with white beans & lentils; lemon tart.* **Details:** *1.5m from Tetbury on A433 towards Cirencester; 9.30 pm; closed Mon; need 10+ to book; children: 14+ in bar.*

Old Trout £ 38

29-30 Lower High St OX9 2AA (01844) 212146

It's "not always consistent", but this "olde worlde rustic" restaurant can offer some "surprisingly interesting" dishes, with fish the speciality; it is "always busy", and service sometimes suffers accordingly. / **Sample dishes:** *prawn & clam fritter with tomato fondue; roast hake with olive & chorizo stew; chocolate brownie with caramel sauce.* **Details:** *www.theoldtrouthotel.co.uk; 10 pm; closed Sun; no Amex; no smoking area.* **Accommodation:** *7 rooms, from £75.*

Thornbury Castle £ 57

Castle St BS35 1HH (01454) 281182

"A real castle!" provides an imposing backdrop for a meal at this Tudor landmark; even fans say its modern British cooking is "expensive", however, and for others there is a sense that its approach is rather "lost in time". / **Sample dishes:** *mushroom tortellini with celeriac; sea bass with parsley mash; lemon tart with rosemary sorbet.* **Details:** *www.thornburycastle.com; nr intersection of M4 & M5; 9.30 pm, Sat 10 pm; jacket & tie required; no smoking in dining room.* **Accommodation:** *24 rooms, from £130.*

Lifeboat Inn £ 29

PE36 6LT (01485) 512236

"Once a fab place to eat, now complacent and overpriced"; some still find "great" food at this "packed" pub, which attracts much commentary, but it "has suffered with its increased popularity" and too many experience "indifferent fare served slowly". / **Sample dishes:** *Thai crab cakes with capsicum chutney; lemon sole with crisp capers & prawns; fruit crumble.* **Details:** *www.lifeboatinn.co.uk; 20m from Kings Lynn on A149 coast road; 9.30 pm; no Amex.* **Accommodation:** *12 rooms, from £64.*

Bakers Arms £ 30   Ⓐ

Main St LE16 7TS (01858) 545201

"A very relaxed and friendly atmosphere" helps make this "village pub/restaurant", with its "profusion of beams", a consistently popular destination; the menu is "constantly changing" but "always reliable". / **Sample dishes:** *fresh mussels; sea bass with sweet potato mash; chocolate tart with caramelised bananas.* **Details:** *nr Market Harborough off the A6; 9.30 pm; open only Tue-Fri for D, all day Sat & Sun L; no smoking area; children: 12+.*

Horse & Farrier £ 26
CA12 4SQ (01768) 779688

The "good variety and quality" of its "predictable but honest pub food" ("in Cumbrian quantities of course") make this "busy" and "welcoming" walkers' inn quite "a surprise" find for some reporters; the local (Jennings) ale is also warmly applauded. / **Sample dishes:** scallops & black pudding with orange oil; smoked haddock with chive mash & mustard; raspberry pavlova. **Details:** 9.30 pm; no Switch; no smoking. **Accommodation:** 9 rooms, from £30.

TILE HILL, WEST MIDLANDS 5–4C

Rupali £ 26 ★
337 Tile Hill Ln CV4 9DU (024) 7642 2500

"The owners and staff always make you feel welcome" at this "high-class" Indian, which offers "well-cooked" dishes, often to refugees from nearby Coventry; it recently doubled in size, and the "ornate" new fit-out is "very flash". / **Sample dishes:** chicken tikka kebabs; lamb jalfrezi; blue coral ice cream. **Details:** 10.30 pm; no smoking area.

TITLEY, HEREFORDSHIRE 2–1A

Stagg Inn £ 30 ★
HR5 3RL (01544) 230221

Steven Reynolds's "crowded", "rural pub turned restaurant" offers "a high level of cooking" – "like a proper French restaurant" – at very "fair" prices; we're not questioning the place's "excellent" standards, but why it has been singled out as the one and only pub the Michelin men deem worthy of a star is a total mystery. / **Sample dishes:** stuffed quail with thyme juice; herbed chicken with potato fondant; hazelnut pavlova with butterscotch sauce. **Details:** www.thestagg.co.uk; on B4355, NE of Kington; 9.30 pm; closed Mon; no Amex; no smoking area. **Accommodation:** 2 rooms, from £60.

TODMORDEN, WEST YORKSHIRE 5–1B

The Old Hall Restaurant £ 34 A★
Hall St OL14 7AD (01706) 815998

"Very friendly service" helps to put this "beautifully restored" 17th-century hall on "the informal side of formal", and – with its "imaginative" cooking and "charming" atmosphere – it makes an impressive all-rounder. / **Sample dishes:** grilled mackerel with potato cakes; crispy duck & watercress salad; winter berry pavlova. **Value tip:** set 2-crs L £7.50 (Sun L £9.95). **Details:** 15 mins from M62; 9 pm, Sat 9.45 pm; closed Mon & Sun D; no Amex; no smoking in dining room.

TONBRIDGE, KENT 3–3B

Bottle House £ 26
Coldharbour Rd TN11 8ET (01892) 870306

It's the "pleasant surroundings" which make this picturesque pub of most note – its grub is "good value", but rather "average". / **Sample dishes:** breaded lemon & pepper scallops; spicy Cajun chicken with salsa; banoffi pie. **Details:** SW of Penshurst on B2188; 10 pm; no Amex; no smoking area.

The Galley £ 42 ★
41 Fore St EX3 0HU (01392) 876078
"Superb fish" and *"very fresh seafood"* make this wittingly-whimsical 'restaurant with cabins' (rooms, to you and us), overlooking the estuary, a unanimously popular recommendation.
/ **Sample dishes:** lobster, prawn & melon salad; turbot with parsnip mash & scallop sauce; warm oozing chocolate sponge.
Details: www.galleyrestaurant.co.uk; 11 pm; closed Mon L, Tue L & Wed L; no smoking; booking essential; children: 12+. **Accommodation:** 4 rooms, from £75.

Springer Spaniel £ 28
PL15 9NS (01579) 370424
"Gone downhill under new ownership" or *"much improved"?* – early reports on the new regime at this *"traditional and friendly pub with restaurant"* are rather mixed, but those who say the food is *"good and at a reasonable price"* still have the upper hand.
/ **Sample dishes:** soused Orkney herrings; lamb forestière with potatoes; fresh lemon mousse. **Details:** 4m S of Launceston on A388; 9 pm; no Amex; no smoking before 10 pm.

Gurnards Head £ 28
TR26 3DE (01736) 795313
In *"an area not well served"* (near the famous Minack Theatre) this pub-cum-hotel is worth knowing about for its *"good grub"* – fish in particular. / **Sample dishes:** mug of prawns with brown bread; trio of Cornish fish; bread & butter pudding. **Details:** on coastal road between Land's End & St Ives, near Zennor; 9.15 pm; no smoking.
Accommodation: 6 rooms, from £50.

Lochgreen House £ 40 Ⓐ★
Lochgreen Hs, Monktonhill Rd KA10 7EN (01292) 313343
"High standards are always maintained" – not least of the Franco-Gallic cooking – at this *"chintzy and luxurious"* Edwardian hotel, near the links; some complain, however, that *"popularity with American golf enthusiasts leads them to overdo the tartan"*.
/ **Sample dishes:** scallop mousseline with champagne; Scottish beef Bourguignonne with celeriac purée; glazed lemon tart.
Details: www.lochgreenhouse.co.uk; 9.30 pm; no smoking.
Accommodation: 15 rooms, from £195.

The Oyster Bar £ 32 ★
The Harbour, Harbour Rd KA10 6DH (01292) 319339
"Can fish be fresher?" – it may be *"simply cooked"* but the raw materials are of *"unbeatable"* quality at this no-nonsense mill-conversion, overlooking the harbour. / **Sample dishes:** roast scallops & tomatoes with prosciutto; baked turbot with mushrooms, leeks & truffles; lemon Mascarpone with blueberry coulis. **Details:** follow signs for Sea Cat Ferry Terminal, past shipyard; 9.30 pm; closed Mon & Sun D; no Amex.

TROUTBECK, CUMBRIA

Queen's Head
£ 27

Townhead LA23 1PW (01539) 432174

"A fun place to go in the middle of a walk" – this "quaint" 17th-century coaching inn is set amidst spectacular Lakeland scenery; it provides "above-average pub food", "very reliably". / **Sample dishes:** wild mushroom, Stilton & black olive terrine; supreme of chicken with mash; bread & butter pudding. **Details:** www.queensheadhotel.com; A592, on Kirkstone Pass; 9 pm; D only; no Amex; no smoking area. **Accommodation:** 15 rooms, from £70.

TRURO, CORNWALL

Numberten
£ 28 ★

10 Kenwyn St TR1 3DU (01872) 272363

This "Aussie-style restaurant/bistro/coffee shop" is a bit of a rarity in the West Country, and its "fabulous fusion fare" (and the fact that you can BYO if you want to) help make it a "fun" and "good-value" destination. / **Sample dishes:** Thai beef salad; scallops & monkfish with fennel salsa; peaches with Mascarpone. **Details:** 9.30 pm; closed Sun L (& Sun D in winter); no smoking in dining room.

TUNBRIDGE WELLS, KENT

Hotel du Vin et Bistro
£ 39

Crescent Rd TN1 2LY (01892) 526455

The second member of this well-regarded chain of "informal" and attractive boutique hotels is very much the weakest link – the cooking is "overhyped" and "overpriced", and "slow", "overstretched" service is a particular bugbear. / **Sample dishes:** crab & baby spinach salad; char-grilled marlin with niçoise potatoes; pineapple crème brûlée. **Details:** www.hotelduvin.com; opp police station; 9.30 pm; booking: max 10. **Accommodation:** 32 rooms, from £80.

Signor Franco
£ 40

5a High St TN1 1UL (01892) 549199

"Cramped but fun", this "upmarket" Italian is a good, if not inexpensive, option in this surprisingly under-served town. / **Sample dishes:** smoked sturgeon; pasta filled with white truffles; pancakes with crème pâtissière. **Details:** opp railway station; 11 pm; closed Sun; no Amex.

TURNBERRY, SOUTH AYRSHIRE

Turnberry Hotel
£ 65 𝔸★

KA26 9LT (01655) 331000

"Wonderful" surroundings… "exemplary food"… "absolutely superb all-round" – the impressive dining room of this famous golfing hotel (which boasts two world-class courses, and a great sea view) may be no bargain but it wins consistent praise. / **Sample dishes:** oak-smoked Scottish salmon; seared monkfish with basil polenta; fresh raspberries & mango. **Details:** www.turnberry.co.uk; A77, 2m after Kirkswald turn right, then right again after 0.5m; 9.30 pm; closed Sun L. **Accommodation:** 221 rooms, from £170.

TUTBURY, STAFFORDSHIRE

Olde Dog & Partridge
£ 28

High St DE13 9LS (01283) 813030

Carvery establishments don't figure large in this guide, but this particular example is "very well organised", and many (if not quite all) reporters think it offers "outstanding value"; it's housed in a half-timbered coaching inn – dating back to the Tudors – which also has a brasserie. / **Sample dishes:** cheese soufflé; chicken stuffed with herbs & lemon; pear tarte Tatin. **Value tip:** set 2-crs L & Sun L £9.50. **Details:** www.dogandpartridge.net; 9.45 pm; no smoking in dining room. **Accommodation:** 20 rooms, from £70.

Sidney's £ 23 A★

3-5 Percy Park Rd NE30 4LZ (0191) 257 8500

"A brilliant find", this "small", "superb neighbourhood bistro near the sea" is universally praised for its "intimate" atmosphere, for its "consistently good" and "always interesting", "modern" cuisine and for its "staff who care". / Sample dishes: crispy Parma ham & roast fig salad; turkey saltimbocca with roast root vegetables; star anise pannacotta. Value tip: set 3-crs meal £9.95. Details: www.sidneys.co.uk; 10 pm; closed Sun D; no smoking before 9 pm.

Altnaharrie Inn £ 88 A★★

IV26 2SS (01854) 633230

"An experience worth saving for", say fans of Gunn Eriksen and Fred Brown's "ultimate in unique dining experiences", where the "magic" of a visit is completed by the fact that its only accessible by boat – you must stay in order to eat – and where "absolutely wonderful local produce" is cooked to "superb effect"; NB – the restaurant did not open for the 2001 season, but is apparently to re-open in 2002. / Sample dishes: crab & lobster soup; chicken liver & mushroom cake with truffle mash; roast pineapple with cloudberry ice cream. Details: 8 pm; D only; no smoking; children: 8+. Accommodation: 8 rooms, from £165, incl D.

Sharrow Bay £ 60 A★★

CA10 2LZ (01768) 486301

It's "a real experience" to eat at England's original country house hotel, with its "spectacular" views and its staff "for whom nothing is too much trouble"; on the food front, a few quibble over "a lack of excitement" or a tendency to "over-elaboration" (and "the five-course menu is a killer, given portions of Cumbrian dimensions"), but nothing should obscure the "consistent excellence" of the end result. / Sample dishes: crab & scallop pancake with crayfish oil; lamb with herb brioche crust & thyme jus; Old English Regency syllabub. Details: www.sharrow-bay.com; on Pooley Bridge Rd towards Howtown; 8 pm; no Amex; jacket & tie required; no smoking; children: 13+. Accommodation: 26 rooms, from £300, incl D.

Bay Horse £ 43

Canal Foot LA12 9EL (01229) 583972

"Brilliant views across the estuary" are an unchanging attraction of this well-known pub by Morecambe Bay; most say the food is "still very good", but others think the cooking may be "losing its surprise and innovative style". / Sample dishes: crab & smoked haddock croquette; rack of Cumbrian lamb; brown sugar meringue with mango. Value tip: set 3-crs L £17.75. Details: www.thebayhorsehotel.co.uk; after Canal Foot sign, turn left & pass Glaxo factory; 7.30 pm; closed Mon L & Sun L; no Amex; no smoking; children: 12+. Accommodation: 9 rooms, from £75, incl D.

Lords of the Manor £ 59 A★

GL54 2JD (01451) 820243

"A real treat in every way" – the "thoughtful" cooking is "top class" at this luxurious country house hotel, which provides a "stylish" and "romantic" Cotswolds setting. / Sample dishes: roast squab with bean stew; tournedos of rabbit with mustard tortellini; pear tarte Tatin with Roquefort ice cream. Value tip: set 2-crs L £16.95. Details: www.lordsofthe manor.com; 2m W of Stow on the Wold; 9.30 pm; no jeans; no smoking; children: 7+. Accommodation: 27 rooms, from £145.

Lake Isle   **£ 29**
16 High Street East LE15 9PZ   (01572) 822951
*With its "simple tables and fresh flowers", the dining room of
this small hotel (off the marketplace of a charming small town) is
something of a rarity in the countryside – a good "neighbourhood
restaurant"; it provides fairly traditional fare of dependable quality
and quite a serious wine list. / **Sample dishes:*** smoked haddock & prawn
fishcakes; chicken stuffed with ham & apricots; chocolate & nut pudding. **Value
tip:** set 3-crs Sun L £13.50. **Details:** 9.30 pm; closed Mon L; no smoking;
children: 8+. **Accommodation:** 12 rooms, from £69.

Five Arrows   **£ 34**
High St HP18 0JE   (01296) 651727
*There were surprisingly few reports this year, but all were very
positive on this "unexpected find" – an "ornate" Rothschild-owned
pub/restaurant, near Waddesdon Manor. / **Sample dishes:*** salmon
fishcakes with coriander jam; fillet steak with red shallot butter; honeycomb ice
cream. **Details:** www.waddesdon.org.uk; on A41; 9.30 pm; no Amex;
no smoking area; children: special area for children under 10.
Accommodation: 11 rooms, from £80.

Aagrah   **£ 21**   ★
Barnsley Rd WF1 5NX   (01924) 242222
*"Deservedly busy and versatile" – an outpost of this Yorkshire chain
of upmarket Indians where "quality-control is ever-present".
/ **Sample dishes:*** king prawn pakoras; chick pea & potato biryani; mango
kulfi. **Details:** www.aagrah.com; from M1, J39 follow Denby Dale Rd to A61;
11.30 pm; D only; no smoking area. **Accommodation:** 13 rooms, from £35.

The Manor House   **£ 41**
Northlands HU17 8RU   (01482) 881645
*"The best in the area" – this "traditional Victorian manor house"
peacefully situated in the Wolds offers "good classic food" in a
"lovely" setting; few, however, can avoid noting that it comes "at
a cost" that some find "OTT". / **Sample dishes:*** Chinese crispy lamb &
poached egg salad; roast guinea fowl with bramble sauce; chocolate tart with
white & dark chocolate ice cream. **Value tip:** 3-crs set weekday D £15.
Details: www.the-manor-house.co.uk; between Walkington & Bishop Burton;
9.15 pm; D only, closed Sun; no smoking; children: 6+. **Accommodation:** 7
rooms, from £80.

Priory   **£ 47**   Ⓐ
Church Grn BH20 4ND   (01929) 551666
*An "idyllic" location helps create a "wonderful" atmosphere at
this long-established restaurant on the banks of the River Frome,
whether you dine in the grounds or in the basement room; most –
but not all – reports are of "consistently good" cooking. / **Sample
dishes:*** creamy mussel bisque; duck with lentils & caramelised apples;
Amaretto bread & butter pudding. **Details:** 10 pm; no smoking area; children:
8+. **Accommodation:** 19 rooms, from £110.

WARHAM ALL SAINTS, NORFOLK

Three Horseshoes   £ 18   𝔸 ★

Bridge St NR23 1NL   (01328) 710547

*"An excellent range of high-quality food" ("rabbit, game pies, and so on") helps make this "lovely", "atmospheric" country pub a "simply wonderful" destination for all who comment on it. / **Sample dishes:** soused herrings; game & wine pie; cheese platter.* **Details:** *1m off A148; 8.30 pm; no credit cards; no smoking area; no booking.* **Accommodation:** *6 rooms, from £24.*

WARMINSTER, WILTSHIRE

Bishopstrow House   £ 40

BA12 9HH   (01985) 212312

*Opinions split this year on the performance of the "peaceful" conservatory dining room of this Georgian country-house hotel – fans found the cooking "as tempting as ever", but others said it "didn't match its promise". / **Sample dishes:** carpaccio of tuna with herb salad; roast rabbit wrapped in Parma ham; raspberry & orange gratin.* **Details:** *www.slh.com/bishopst; 9 pm; no smoking.* **Accommodation:** *32 rooms, from £190.*

WATERHOUSES, STAFFORDSHIRE

Old Beams   £ 53   ★

Leek Rd ST10 3HW   (01538) 308254

*There "a lack of competition" round here, certainly at these sorts of prices, and most reporters find this long-established fixture a "superb" establishment, which offers a "great welcome"; as usual, though, feedback was not 100% consistent. / **Sample dishes:** ham hock & foie gras terrine; lamb with calf's sweetbreads & truffle mash; coffee & rum soufflé with espresso sorbet.* **Details:** *on A523 between Leek & Ashbourne; 9.30 pm; closed Mon, Tue L, Wed L, Thu L, Sat L & Sun D; no smoking.* **Accommodation:** *5 rooms, from £75.*

WATH-IN-NIDDERDALE, NORTH YORKSHIRE

Sportsman's Arms   £ 32

HG3 5PP   (01423) 711306

*"Nicely located in the Dales", this "always friendly and welcoming" pub "reliably" offers a "wide variety of well cooked food". / **Sample dishes:** goat's cheese with caramelised red onions; duckling with rosti, prunes & oranges; summer pudding.* **Details:** *take Wath Road from Pateley Bridge; 9 pm; D only, closed Sun; no Amex; no smoking.* **Accommodation:** *13 rooms, from £70.*

WATTON AT STONE, HERTFORDSHIRE

George & Dragon   £ 26

82 High St SG14 3TA   (01920) 830285

*"A more ambitious menu than a typical pub" helps make this "pleasant", traditional boozer a well-known choice in an area without a huge number of competing attractions. / **Sample dishes:** potted crab with ginger; fillet steak stuffed with oysters; lemon & passion fruit tart.* **Details:** *www.georgeanddragon-watton.co.uk; A602 from Stevenage; 10 pm; no smoking; children: 5+.*

WELLS-NEXT-THE-SEA, NORFOLK

Rococo at The Crown
The Crown Hotel   £ 39   𝔸 ★

The Buttlands NR23 1EX   (01553) 771483

*Newcomers may think this an "unexpected find", but regulars know it's "always a joy" to visit Nick and Anne Anderson's "eye-catchingly" converted cottage, where the modern cooking is "wonderful", and "good value" too. / **Sample dishes:** black pudding with foie gras & apple salad; roast squab with smoked vegetables & thyme jus; caramelised strawberry tart.* **Details:** *www.rococoatthecrown.co.uk; 9 pm, Fri & Sun 10 pm; D only, except Sun open L & D; no smoking at D.* **Accommodation:** *11 rooms, from £55.*

New Oriental Pearl   **£ 26**
42-44 Bridgford Rd NG2 6AP   (0115) 945 5048
*"Friendly staff, who remember you" is one of the features that
makes this "old-fashioned Chinese restaurant" stand out in
reporters' recollections, as is the cooking which offers "good value
for money". / Sample dishes: crispy aromatic duck; chicken in black bean
sauce; chocolate ice cream. Details: 11 pm; no smoking area.*

Chu Chin Chow   **£ 28**
63 Old Woking Rd KT14 6LF   (01932) 349581
*"The best Chinese around" (not that demanding hereabouts,
it must be admitted) – "friendly" and "unobtrusive" service
contributes to the good level of satisfaction with this long-standing
oriental. / Sample dishes: sesame chicken; chicken in black bean sauce;
toffee bananas & apples. Details: 11 pm.*

Tulsi   **£ 26**
20 London Rd TN16 1BD   (01959) 563397
*"Consistently fresh ingredients", "skilled" cooking and
"knowledgeable" service combine to make this "the best non-
greasy Indian" hereabouts. / Sample dishes: mixed Karahi kebabs;
chicken tikka; melon sorbet. Details: 11.30 pm.*

The Gun Room
Linton Springs Hotel   **£ 25**   𝔸 ★
Sicklinghall Rd LS22 4AF   (01937) 585353
*It may be "run by a Continental", but this former shooting lodge
"retains its English country atmosphere", and has a strong following
for its "authentic" cooking ("wonderful fish, especially") and its
"helpful" and "friendly" service. / Sample dishes: salmon & herb
fishcake with endive salad; roast chicken with onion risotto & pancetta; pear
tarte Tatin with honey ice cream. Details: www.lintonsprings.co.uk; 9.30 pm;
D only, closed Sun. Accommodation: 12 rooms, from £95.*

Colony   **£ 33**
3 Balfour Rd KT13 8HE   (01932) 842766
*It may be "slightly expensive, compared to its competitors", but this
well-established oriental is widely regarded as "the best Chinese in
the area". / Sample dishes: spare ribs, spring rolls & crispy seaweed;
sizzling beef; toffee apples. Details: on A317; 10.30 pm; D only.*

Perry's   **£ 33**   ★
4 Trinity Rd, The Old Harbour DT4 8TJ   (01305) 785799
*"Great fish dishes" have long made this "cosy" harbourside spot a
popular destination – "on high days and holidays, it gets very busy".
/ Sample dishes: baked scallops; sea bass; strawberry sorbet.
Details: www.perrysrestaurant.co.uk; 9.30 pm; closed Mon L & Sat L;
no smoking area; children: 5+.*

Magpie Café £ 22 ★★

14 Pier Rd YO21 3PU (01947) 602058

"Brilliant traditional fish and chips" in "gargantuan" portions at "unbelievable" prices makes this "cosy" and "unpretentious" harbour-side café (with its "true seaside feel") one of the better-known places in the country; unsurprisingly, it can get a touch "crowded", and "you do have to queue". / **Sample dishes:** smoked salmon; cod & prawn mornay; spotted dick. **Details:** www.magpiecafe.co.uk; opp Fish Market; 9 pm; open L&D all week; closed part of Jan & Feb; no Amex; no smoking.

The White Horse & Griffin £ 30

Church St YO22 4AE (01947) 604857

This "old and unspoilt" town-centre tavern is still praised in many quarters for its "lovely" atmosphere and for its "interesting" food ("obviously, there are lots of fish dishes"); there were a few reports, however, of "recent poor experiences". / **Sample dishes:** seafood medley; beef with foie gras & truffles in Madeira sauce; plum & almond pizza. **Details:** centre of old town, on Abbey side of river; 9.30 pm; no Amex. **Accommodation:** 11 rooms, from £50.

Red House £ 26 ★

21 London St RG28 7LH (01256) 895558

"Excellent" and "unexpected" cooking – from a Californian chef – helps make this "pleasant" inn a "very good-value" destination for all who report on it. / **Sample dishes:** crab & Parma ham salad; chicken stuffed with crab; lemon tart & strawberry coulis. **Details:** nr silk mill; 9.30 pm; no Amex; no smoking; booking essential; children: 12+.

The Crown at Whitebrook £ 41

NP5 4TX (01600) 860254

Perhaps "it has a rather disappointing exterior", but most feel it's "worth the effort" to find this "quaint" Wye Valley restaurant with rooms – it offers quite "serious" Gallic cooking in "pleasant" surroundings. / **Sample dishes:** cheese soufflé; roast lamb & garlic with spinach stuffing; tarte Tatin with raisin ice cream. **Value tip:** set 3-crs Sun L £16.95. **Details:** www.crownatwhitebrook.co.uk; 2m W of A466, 5m S of Monmouth; 8.45 pm; closed Mon L & Sun D; no smoking; children: 12+. **Accommodation:** 10 rooms, from £85.

Zest £ 30 ★

Low Rd CA28 9HS (01946) 692848

"Quality food in a lively modern setting" is already making quite a name for this year-old brasserie on the outskirts of the town – definitely 'one to watch'. / **Sample dishes:** sticky braised pork belly; lamb with pea purée & black pudding; pear & almond tart. **Details:** 9.30 pm; D only, closed Sun-Tue; no Amex.

Crab & Winkle £ 33 ★

South Quay, Whitstable Harbour CT5 1AB (01227) 779377

"A view of the fishing boats" sets the scene for this promising two-year-old, "above the fish market" and overlooking the harbour – thanks to the attractions of its "fantastic", er, fish and its "superb" seafood, it gets "crowded" and "noisy". / **Sample dishes:** oysters; lemon sole & mixed vegetables; treacle sponge & custard. **Details:** 9.45 pm; no Amex.

Wheeler's Oyster Bar   **£ 26**   ★★

8 High St CT5 IBQ   (01227) 273311

"OK, the Oyster Fishery gets all the publicity, but try this place on the high street" – this *"small but perfectly formed"* fish restaurant gets nothing but praise for its *"totally delicious"* cooking, and *"glorious sunsets"* are sometimes thrown in; BYO. / **Sample dishes:** scallops with red pepper pasta; cod with pancetta & onion rings; date & chocolate sponge. **Details:** 7.30 pm; closed Wed; no credit cards.

Whitstable Oyster Fishery Co.   **£ 35**

Horsebridge Beach CT5 IBU   (01227) 276856

"Delicious fresh seafood" and a *"lovely atmosphere, especially in summer"* have long made this quirky seaside fixture a popular destination for a day out from London; an ever-greater proportion of reporters, however – citing *"tasteless"* cooking, *"arrogant"* (and even *"hostile"*) service and *"cramped"* seating – say it's just *"living on its trendy reputation"* nowadays. / **Sample dishes:** moules marinière; skate with black butter & capers; chocolate truffle cake with raspberries. **Details:** www.oysterfishery.co.uk; 9 pm, Sat 10 pm; closed Mon (& Sun D Sep-May). **Accommodation:** 30 rooms, from £40.

WILMSLOW, CHESHIRE   5–2B

Chili Banana
Kings Arms Hotel   **£ 27**

Alderley Rd SK9 IPZ   (01625) 539100

"Quality ingredients, reasonable prices and good service" make it well worth knowing about this *"lovely"* Thai restaurant, attached to a pub. / **Sample dishes:** chicken satay; Penang dry chicken curry; banana fritters. **Value tip:** set 3-crs L £8.45. **Details:** 11 pm; closed Mon, Tue L, Wed L & Thu L.

WINCHCOMBE, GLOUCESTERSHIRE   2–1C

Wesley House   **£ 43**   𝔸★★

High St GL54 5LJ   (01242) 602366

"The management always make you feel special" at this *"comfortable"* and *"tastefully furnished"* half-timbered house, where the British cooking – though *"conventional"* – is universally and enthusiastically hailed for its *"excellent"* quality. / **Sample dishes:** Gorgonzola & leek tart; venison with lentils & roast celeriac; chocolate soufflé. **Details:** www.wesleyhouse.com; next to Sudley Castle; 9.30 pm; closed Sun D; no smoking. **Accommodation:** 5 rooms, from £65.

WINCHESTER, HAMPSHIRE   2–3D

Hotel du Vin et Bistro   **£ 38**   𝔸

14 Southgate St SO23 9EF   (01962) 841414

The *"bistro fare"* is *"good, not excellent"*, but the *"reliable"* standards of this *"smart"* but *"relaxed"* boutique-hotel dining room, with its *"fun"* and *"buzzy"* atmosphere, continue to make it a very popular destination. / **Sample dishes:** moules marinière; salmon pavé with mussel ragoût; lime pannacotta with melon. **Details:** www.hotelduvin.com; 9.45 pm. **Accommodation:** 23 rooms, from £95.

Old Chesil Rectory   **£ 51**   ★★

1 Chesil St S023 OHU   (01962) 851555

Perhaps it's the *"stuffy"* atmosphere of this historic Tudor building which helps preserve this *"excellent"* establishment as a relatively *"well-kept secret"* – chef/patron Philip Storey's *"consistently outstanding"* modern French cooking certainly deserves a wider audience. / **Sample dishes:** wild mushroom risotto; monkfish wrapped in Parma ham; passion fruit soufflé with mango sorbet. **Value tip:** set 2-crs L £16. **Details:** 9.15 pm, Sat 9.45 pm; closed Mon & Sun; no Amex; no smoking area.

Wykeham Arms   £ 31   𝔸
75 Kingsgate St SO23 9PE   (01962) 853834
"Open fires and old school desks in the bar" set the tone at this
"superbly atmospheric" and *"pleasantly old-fashioned"* pub, next
to the college; it maintains *"high standards"* – including
"straightforward" food – and offers *"good wines"*. / **Sample
dishes:** salmon & dill terrine; roast lamb with redcurrant & thyme jus; crème
brûlée. **Details:** between Cathedral and the college; 8.45 pm; closed Sun;
no smoking area; booking: max 8; children: 14+. **Accommodation:** 13
rooms, from £79.50.

WINDERMERE, CUMBRIA   7–3D

Gilpin Lodge   £ 40   𝔸★★
Crook Rd LA23 3NE   (01539) 488818
The *"outstanding"* cooking and *"pampering"* service in the
"comfortable" dining room of this *"fabulous"* country house hotel
make it *"the best in the Lakes"* for some reporters – it *"can always
be relied upon to provide a superb meal in a convivial atmosphere"*.
/ **Sample dishes:** smoked chicken & cucumber ravioli; roast lamb with minted
pea risotto; Gilpin Lodge ice creams. **Details:** www.gilpin-lodge.co.uk; 9 pm;
no smoking; children: 7+. **Accommodation:** 14 rooms, from £150, incl D.

Holbeck Ghyll   £ 47   𝔸★
Holbeck Ln LA23 1LU   (01539) 432375
The *"beautiful setting with views of lakes and mountains"* is an
undoubted strength of this *"romantic"* country house hotel; chef
David McLaughlin is in his early days, but initial reports are *"very
good"*. / **Sample dishes:** Scottish oysters & clams; roast lamb with shallot
purée; shortbread biscuit & strawberries. **Details:** www.holbeckghyll.com; 3m
N of Windermere, towards Troutbeck; 9.30 pm; no smoking; children: 8+.
Accommodation: 20 rooms, from £170.

Jerichos   £ 35   ★
Birch St LA23 1EG   (01539) 442522
A *"small"* and *"welcoming"* town-centre restaurant, whose modern
British cooking *"maintains a very high standard"*. / **Sample
dishes:** smoked chicken, Parmesan & mushroom risotto; halibut with glazed
new potatoes; white & dark chocolate ganache. **Details:** 9.30 pm; D only,
closed Mon; no Amex; no smoking; children: 12+.

WINDSOR, WINDSOR & MAIDENHEAD   3–3A

Al Fassia   £ 26   ★
27 St Leonards Rd SL4 3BP   (01753) 855370
"It's much better than it looks" – *"the food is great and the prices
are fair"* at this un-lovely looking Moroccan, which benefits from
"extremely hospitable" service. / **Sample dishes:** chicken & almond filo
parcels; lamb stew with sweet prunes; Moroccan desserts. **Details:** 10.30 pm,
Fri & Sat 11 pm; closed Sun.

Bel & The Dragon   £ 38
Thames St SL4 1PQ   (01753) 866056
"In an area severely lacking in good places, this stands out" – not
the most ringing endorsement ever, but this *"relaxed"* year-old
boozer-conversion (one of a mini-chain) at least offers *"a wide
range of dishes"*, albeit *"slightly pricey"* ones. / **Sample dishes:** goats
cheese & red onion salad; lamb with apple & pistachio stuffing; honeycomb
cheesecake. **Details:** www.belandthedragon.co.uk; 10.30 pm, Sun 8 pm.

WINKLEIGH, DEVON

Pophams £ 32   A★

Castle St EX19 8HQ (01837) 83767

"This may be a tiny restaurant, but it offers a delightful experience", says one of the (of necessity) few supporters of this lunchtime-only 10-seater, for which *"you must book well ahead"* – the cooking is *"excellent"*, and service is *"very friendly"*. / **Sample dishes:** baked goat's cheese with spicy chutney; lamb in puff pastry with mushroom pâté; American cheesecake with fresh berries. **Details:** off A377 between Exeter & Barnstaple; L only; open only Wed-Fri for L&D; closed Feb; no credit cards; no smoking; children: 14+.

WINTERINGHAM, NORTH LINCOLNSHIRE

Winteringham Fields £ 63   A★★

DN15 9PF (01724) 733096

"Outstanding in all respects", Annie and Germain Schwab's 16th-century manor house – *"hidden away near the Humber"* – again produced reporters' top-rated cooking in the UK, invoking a hymn of praise for the *"superlative"* modern French cuisine; the *"faultless everything"* approach extends as far as the *"professional, but amiable"* service and an *"unusually genuine I'm-not-a-celebrity-chef attitude"*. / **Sample dishes:** pancake of scallops & avruga caviar; baked sea bass with salted crust; chocolate & hazelnut pavé. **Value tip:** set 2-crs L £22. **Details:** www.winteringhamfields.com; 4m SW of Humber Bridge; 9.30 pm; closed Mon & Sun; no smoking. **Accommodation:** 10 rooms, from £90.

WITHAM, ESSEX

Lian £ 31   ★

5 Newland St CM8 2AF (01376) 510684

Kim Man's cooking is well above the usual standard, and it's *"always a pleasure"* to eat at this *"formal"* (if somewhat *"crowded"*) Chinese establishment of long standing. / **Sample dishes:** tea smoked chicken; steamed sea bass with Asian greens; toffee apples. **Details:** 10 pm; closed Sun.

WITHERSLACK, CUMBRIA

Old Vicarage £ 39   A★

Church Rd LA11 6RS (01539) 552381

It may be *"isolated"*, but this *"old country house hotel"* is *"not inaccessible"* and its *"the sort of place you'll want to go back to"* – *"tender venison"* and *"expertly-cooked vegetarian dishes"* again received special praise. / **Sample dishes:** oak-roasted salmon; roast suckling pig with black pudding fritter; chocolate pannacotta with saffron syrup. **Details:** www.oldvicarage.com; from M6, J36 follow signs to Barrow on A590; 9 pm; no smoking. **Accommodation:** 14 rooms, from £65.

WOBURN, BEDFORDSHIRE

Nicholl's £ 28

13 Bedford St MK17 9QB (01525) 290896

Part of a mini-empire of bistros in the locality, this *"reliable all-rounder"* has a particularly *"friendly"* approach, that makes it *"good with the family"*. / **Sample dishes:** field mushrooms with Parma ham & Parmesan; fishcakes & salad; pannacotta with raspberries. **Details:** 10 pm; closed Sun D; no Amex; no smoking area; no booking, Sun L.

Paris House £ 61

Woburn Pk MK17 9QP (01525) 290692

"Classical cooking in the beautiful surroundings of a deer park" sounds like a compelling formula, but – as ever – there were some reporters for whom the standards achieved at this half-timbered house in the grounds of Woburn Abbey were not really up to the prices. / **Sample dishes:** prawn & crayfish with mango; roasted brill with Noilly Prat sauce; raspberry soufflé. **Details:** www.parishouse.co.uk; on A4012; 9.30 pm; closed Mon & Sun D.

Rose Street   £ 43

6 Rose St RG40 1XH   (0118) 978 8025
"Small but good", this *"quiet"*, *"front room-like"* restaurant in the
middle of the town is worth remembering in an area without a
huge number of competing attractions. / **Sample dishes:** mushroom
tart; roast Gressingham duck; crème brûlée. **Value tip:** set 2-crs pre-th
£14.95. **Details:** 9.30 pm; closed Sun; no Amex; no smoking.

Mr Man's   £ 25

Wollaton Park NG8 2AD   (0115) 928 7788
With its *"huge"* and *"flashy"* setting, this popular Chinese
restaurant can seem a bit *"overwhelming"*, but *"the food is
reliable"* (if *"fairly expensive"* of its type). / **Sample dishes:** lamb satay;
sizzling lamb with spring onion; apple fritters. **Details:** 11 pm.

Saracen's Head   £ 25

NR11 7LX   (01263) 768909
"In the middle of nowhere", Robert Dawson's *"cosy"* pub – with its
"constantly changing menu" – remains *"an unexpected treat"* for
most reporters; a few found the cooking *"over-rated"* this year,
though. / **Sample dishes:** crispy fried aubergine; venison with red fruit sauce;
treacle tart. **Value tip:** set 2-crs L £5.50. **Details:** 2m W of A140 through
Erpingham; 9 pm; smoking discouraged. **Accommodation:** 4 rooms,
from £60.

Bilash   £ 36   ★

2 Cheapside WV1 1TU   (01902) 427762
Reports are sparser than we'd like, but the few there are – *"the
best Asian food I've eaten in Britain"*, says one reporter – affirm
the continuing appeal of Sitab Khan's very personal curry house.
/ **Sample dishes:** chicken satay; spicy prawns with spinach; gulab jaman.
Value tip: set 2-crs L £7.50. **Details:** www.bilash-tandoori.co.uk; opp Civic
Centre; 11 pm; closed Sun; no smoking area.

Seckford Hall Hotel   £ 37   𝔸★

IP13 6NU   (01394) 385678
A *"wonderful, rambling Elizabethan house"* in Constable Country
whose modestly-priced dining room offers a *"high standard"* of
straightforward traditional cooking, and staff who are – in the
positive sense – *"ever-present"*. / **Sample dishes:** salmon roulade;
monkfish with pasta & wilted greens; champagne mousse with strawberries.
Details: www.seckford.co.uk; 9.30 pm; closed Mon L; no smoking; children: 6+
after 7 pm. **Accommodation:** 32 rooms, from £120.

The Feathers Hotel   £ 54

Market St OX20 1SX   (01993) 812291
This *"charming olde worlde place"* in the chi-chi village by Blenheim
Palace may still be rather *"overpriced"*, but it got a better press this
year for its *"robust"*, *"modern"* cooking and its *"polished"* service.
/ **Sample dishes:** risotto of ceps & frog's legs; roast veal with pancetta &
morel jus; peach consommé with peach sherbet. **Value tip:** set 2-crs L £17.50.
Details: www.feathers.co.uk; 8m N of Oxford on A44; 9.15 pm; no smoking.
Accommodation: 21 rooms, from £115.

Bulls Head   £ 25   ★

Stratford Rd B95 6BD   (01564) 792511
*"Interesting", "well presented" cooking is re-establishing the name
of this establishment outside Stratford as "the best pub/restaurant"
in these parts. / **Sample dishes:** pan-fried scallops with onion jam;
pan-fried chicken with cherry tomato jam; Bailey's crème brûlée. **Details:** on
A3400, N of Stratford, nr Wootton Hall; 10 pm; no smoking.*

Brown's   £ 42   Ⓐ★

24 Quay St WR1 2JJ   (01905) 26263
*Not to be confused with the ghastly chain, this "superb" spot "in a
classily-converted warehouse on the banks of the Severn", provides
"a dependable choice in a thin area" and wins uniform praise for
its "imaginative", "beautifully presented" cooking. / **Sample
dishes:** mushrooms in vermouth with a poached egg; grilled spatchcock of
quail; hot chocolate pudding. **Details:** nr the Cathedral; 9.45 pm; closed Mon,
Sat L & Sun D; no smoking area; children: 8+.*

Glass House   £ 32

Church St WR1 2RH   (01905) 611120
*A 16th-century school-house provides a rather unusual setting for
this city-centre venture; the "quality" cooking is praised by most
reporters, though there are those who find the approach a touch
"pretentious". / **Sample dishes:** crab & red mullet salad; British seafood in
tarragon cream sauce; chocolate lavender millefeuille. **Value tip:** set 2-crs L
£10.50. **Details:** 10 pm; closed Mon & Sun; no smoking.*

Lemon Tree   £ 31

12 Friar St WR1 2LZ   (01905) 27770
*With its "constantly changing" contemporary menu, this "cheerful"
and "crowded" little restaurant makes a "very welcoming"
destination. / **Sample dishes:** ham & roast vegetable antipasti; roast pork
with Stilton & walnuts; sultana bread & butter pudding.
Details: www.thelemontree.co.uk; 2 mins walk from Guildhall; 10 pm; closed
Mon, Tue D, Wed D & Sun; no Amex; no smoking.*

Pant Yr Ochan   £ 27

Old Wrexham Rd LL12 8TY   (01978) 853525
*"Is this a restaurant in a pub, or a pub in a restaurant?" – few
seem to care, and this "modern" establishment, set in an
impressive old house, has established itself as a popular local
destination for informal dining. / **Sample dishes:** mushroom ravioli; red
bream & olive potatoes with asparagus; apple tart with cider custard.
Details: 1m N of Wrexham; 9.30 pm; no smoking area; children: before 6 pm
only.*

Mulberry Tree   £ 31

9 Wrightington Bar WN6 9SE   (01257) 451400
*"Classy cooking" from "an ex-Gavroche chef, returning to his roots"
has ensured that this recently-opened gastropub in the hills is
"already established"; some feel the "bright interior" is "a let
down", though, and others find prices rather Mayfair-like, for round
here. / **Sample dishes:** duck & wood pigeon terrine; roast cod with bubble &
squeak; vanilla cheesecake with apricot coulis. **Details:** 2m along Mossy Lea
Rd, off M6, J27; 10 pm; closed Mon; no Amex; no smoking.*

Wife of Bath £ 36
4 Upper Bridge St TN25 5AF (01233) 812540
"Elaborate, but not quite right" – though fans say *"every dish pleases"* at this long-established *"olde worlde"* rural restaurant, others say the approach is just too *"fussy"*. / **Sample dishes:** smoked duck with orange couscous & rocket; baked black bream; sticky toffee pudding. **Details:** www.wifeofbath.com; off A28 between Ashford & Canterbury; 10 pm; closed Mon & Sun. **Accommodation:** 6 rooms, from £65.

George Hotel £ 37 𝔸★
Quay St PO41 0PE (01983) 760331
*This impressive waterfront hotel houses both a "slightly stuffy" restaurant and a brasserie which offers "stupendous views" over the Solent; opinions on the cooking are generally favourable throughout, but some think it "on the expensive side". / **Sample dishes:** trio of duck starters; pan-fried halibut with crab fritter; chocolate pudding. **Value tip:** set 2-crs L £13.95. **Details:** 10 pm; D only, closed Sun-Tue; no smoking area; children: 8+. **Accommodation:** 17 rooms, from £155.

D P Chadwicks £ 35 𝔸★
104b High St TS15 9AU (01642) 788558
"It just continues to get better", says one fan of this *"Continental restaurant and wine bar"*, where an *"inventive"* menu is served in a *"small but pleasant"* modern setting. / **Sample dishes:** chicken liver parfait; pork knuckle with soft polenta & spinach; baked cherry cheesecake. **Details:** www.chadwicksrestaurant.com; just after Yarm Bridge; 9.30 pm; closed Mon & Sun (open 1 Sun a month); no Amex; no smoking area; no booking.

Royal Oak Hotel £ 40 𝔸
The Square RG18 0UG (01635) 201325
*This very fine pub in a "picturesque" and "sleepy" village has settled back into a more consistent rhythm of late, with more reports this year speaking of "good" and "imaginative" cooking; there's "a wonderful garden for summer evenings". / **Sample dishes:** lobster ravioli on seasoned spinach; roast lamb with celeriac gratin; praline soufflé. **Details:** www.trpplc.com; 5m W of Pangbourne, off B4009; 9.30 pm; closed Sun D; no smoking. **Accommodation:** 5 rooms, from £120.

Bettys £ 24 𝔸
6-8 St Helen's Sq YO1 8QP (01904) 659142
"For the best cream tea" ("and more substantial meals too"), this branch of the famous Harrogate establishment has many admirers, though some do find it *"very pricey"* for what it is. / **Sample dishes:** Swiss rosti with bacon & cheese; Yorkshire rarebit with apple chutney; Yorkshire curd tart. **Details:** www.bettysandtaylors.com; down Blake St from York Minster; 9 pm; no Amex; no smoking area; no booking.

Blue Bicycle £ 36 ✗
34 Fossgate YO1 9TA (01904) 673990
"We were fans, but service was abysmal on our last visit", typifies the declining satisfaction with this *"light and airy"* bistro – once the best in town; some do still praise it as a *"relaxing venue"*, but the *"innovative"* fare is *"not as sparkling as it was"* and some feel it downright *"dull and ill-judged"*. / **Sample dishes:** chicken braised in lavender; swordfish with provençal mussels; chocolate walnut marquis. **Details:** 10 pm; no smoking; booking: max 6; children: 12+.

Café Concerto £ 27 A ★

21 High Petergate YO1 7EN (01904) 610478

"Reliable and varied" cooking – "not over-ambitious, just good" – together with "excellent", "friendly" service and an "utterly charming" atmosphere makes this "convenient", "consistent" and "lively" bistro, by the Minster, the city's top "spur-of-the-moment" recommendation. / **Sample dishes:** grilled sardines with aioli; Toulouse sausages with Puy lentils; Key lime cream pie. **Details:** by the W entrance of York Minster; 9.30 pm, Fri & Sat 10 pm; no Amex; no smoking; no booking at L.

Melton's £ 32 ★★

7 Scarcroft Rd YO23 1ND (01904) 634341

"Excellent", "imaginative" cooking and "very friendly" and professional service win very high praise for this "cosy" conversion of a Victorian shop, where restrained wine mark-ups contribute to "super" overall value; an offshoot bar/bistro opens in Walmgate in October 2001 (tel 01904 629222). / **Sample dishes:** crab & herb cannelloni; oriental glazed pork; chocolate morello Alaska. **Value tip:** set 2-crs L £13.25. **Details:** www.meltonsrestaurant.co.uk; 10 mins walk from Castle Museum; 10 pm; closed Mon L & Sun D; closed for 3 weeks in Dec; no Amex; no smoking area.

Middlethorpe Hall £ 48 A

Bishopthorpe Rd YO23 2GB (01904) 641241

"Lovely old-fashioned surroundings" are the highlight at this "beautiful" country house hotel (and spa), which though only just outside the city is set in 200 acres; even some fans concede that the cooking can be "variable", but the overall verdict remains that if you "want to make an occasion", this is "the best place in the area". / **Sample dishes:** braised pork knuckle; squab pigeon casserole; warm Black Forest pudding. **Value tip:** set 3-crs Sun L £22.
Details: www.middlethorpe.com; next to racecourse; 9.45 pm; jacket & tie required; no smoking area; children: 8+. **Accommodation:** 30 rooms, from £160.

Rish £ 34 ★

7 Fossgate YO1 9TA (01904) 622688

Already "one of the best restaurants in York", this trendy town-centre yearling attracts lots of praise for its "unusual" fusion cooking ("good-value set menus" in particular) and its "enthusiastic service"; some think it "lacks atmosphere" though. / **Sample dishes:** lobster & tiger prawn spring rolls; duck confit with cider apples & caramelised onions; tiramisu in a chocolate cup. **Value tip:** set 2-crs L & pre-th £9.95. **Details:** www.rish-york.co.uk; 10 pm, Fri & Sat 10.30 pm; no smoking area.

UK MAPS

IO

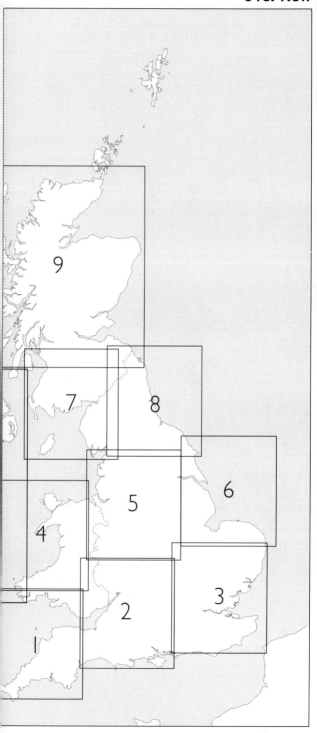

Map 1

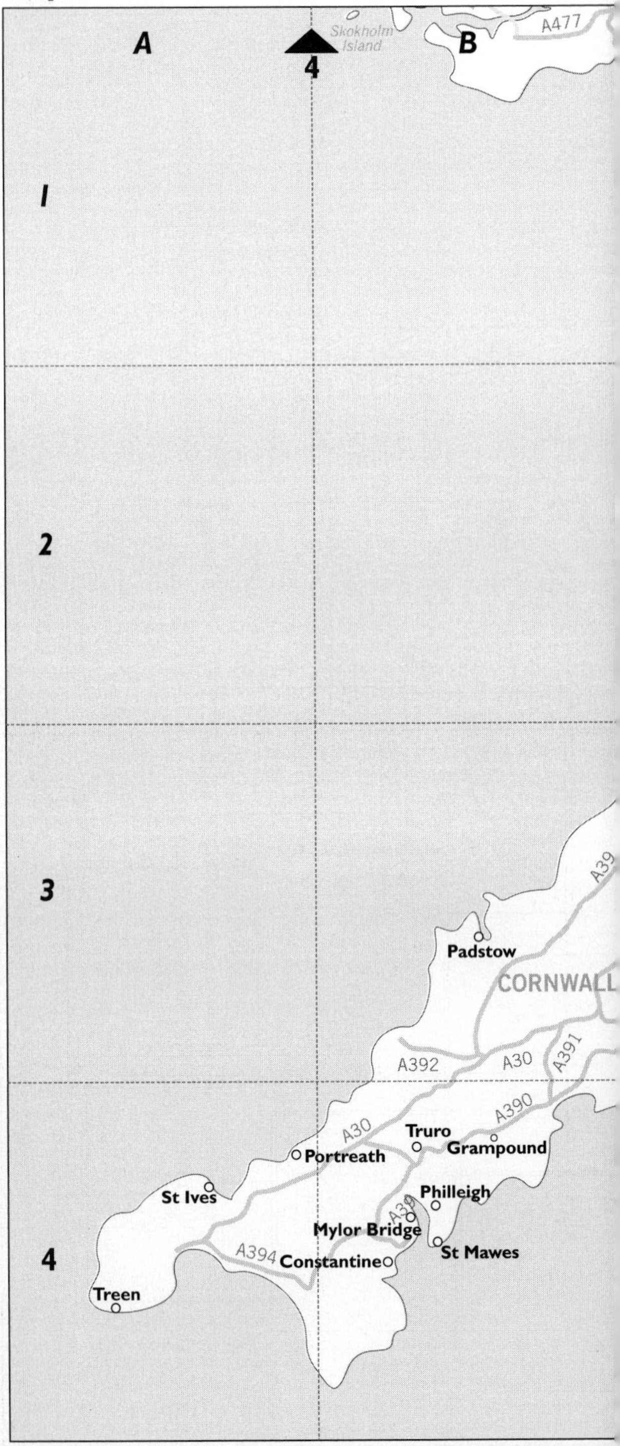

A

B

Skokholm
Island

A477

4

1

2

3

Padstow

CORNWALL

A39

A392   A30   A391

A30   A390

Truro   Grampound

Portreath

St Ives   Philleigh

Mylor Bridge

A394   Constantine   St Mawes

4   Treen

Map 1

Map 2

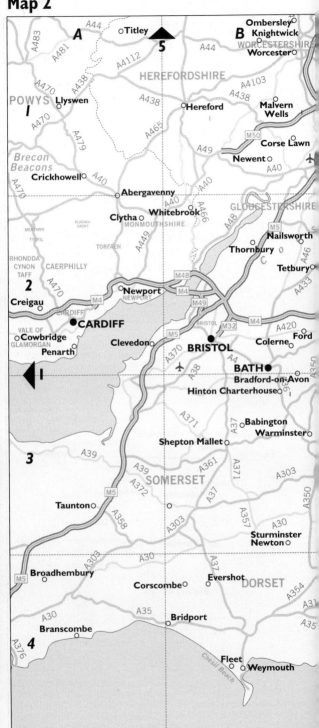

Map 2

Map 3

Map 3

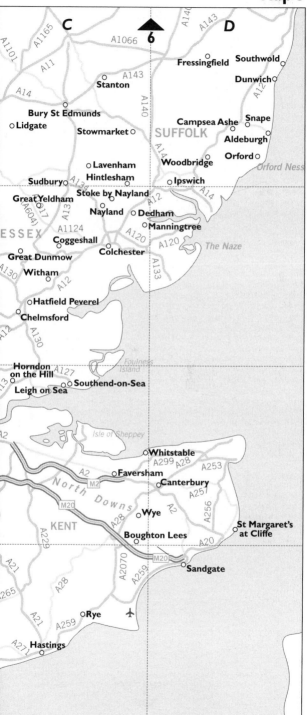

Map 4

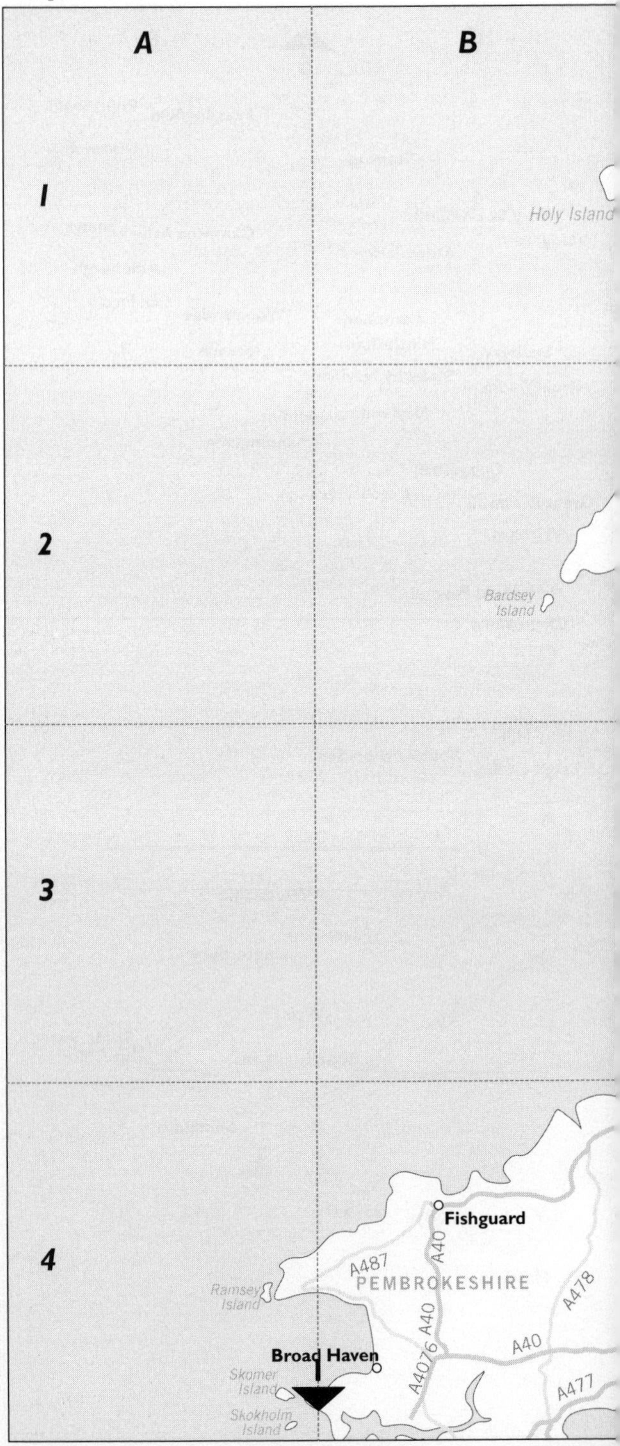

A   B

1

2

3

4

Holy Island

Bardsey Island

Fishguard

A487

A40

PEMBROKESHIRE

A478

Ramsey Island

A4076 A40

A40

Broad Haven

A477

Skomer Island

Skokholm Island

Map 4

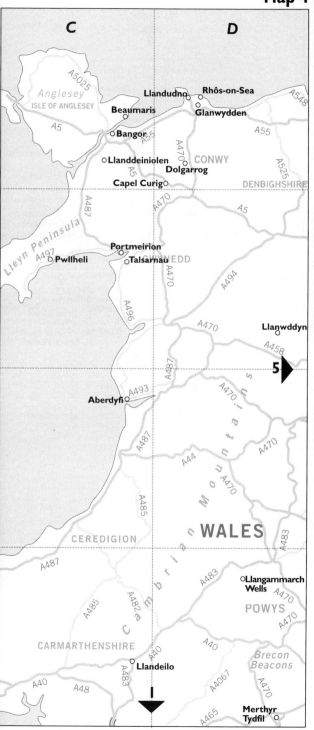

Map 5

Map 5

Map 6

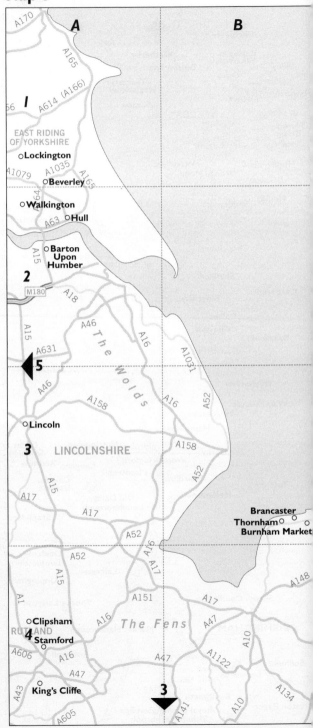

A170

A

B

A165

A614 (A166)

56

1

EAST RIDING
OF YORKSHIRE

○**Lockington**

A1079   A1035   A16

○**Beverley**

A164

○**Walkington**

A63   ○**Hull**

A15

○**Barton
Upon
Humber**

2

M180

A18

A46   A16

A15

A631   5

A46

T h e   W o l d s

A16

A1031

A52

A158

A16

○**Lincoln**

3   LINCOLNSHIRE

A158

A52

A17

A15

A17

A52

A16

Brancaster

Thornham○   ○

Burnham Market

A52

A16

A17

A148

A151

A17

A1

A47

A10

○**Clipsham**   A16   T h e   F e n s

RUTLAND

4 **Stamford**

A606   A16

A47   A1122   A10

A43

○**King's Cliffe**

3

A605   A141   A10   A134

Map 6

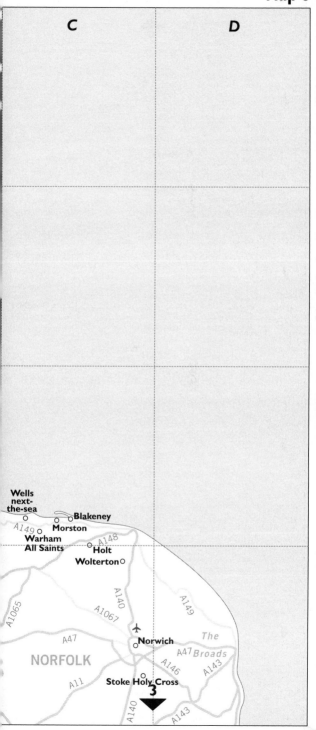

C

D

Wells next-the-sea

Blakeney

A149

Morston

Warham

All Saints

A148

Holt

Wolterton

A140

A1067

A1065

A149

A47

The

Norwich

A47 *Broads*

NORFOLK

A146

A143

A11

A140

Stoke Holy Cross

3

A143

Map 7

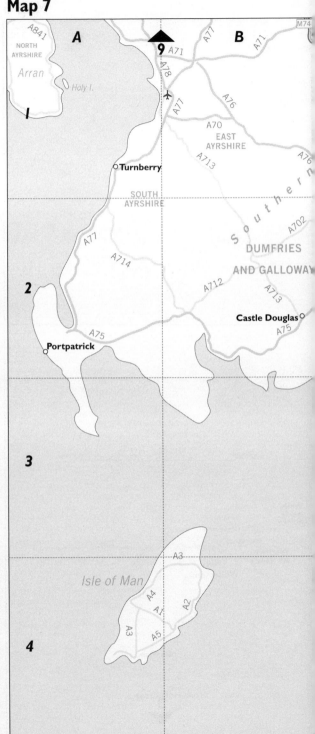

Map 7

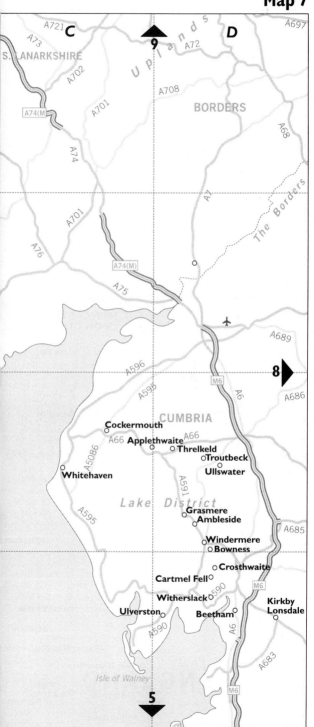

Map 8

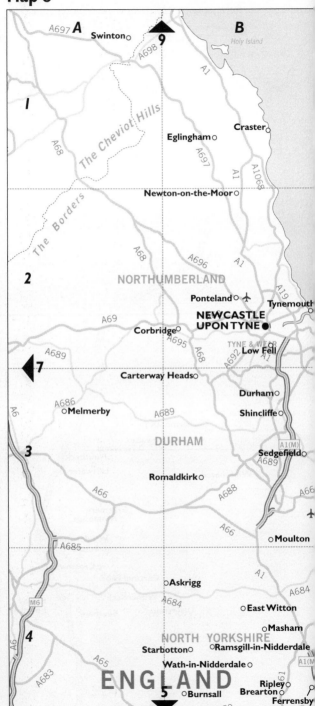

Map 8

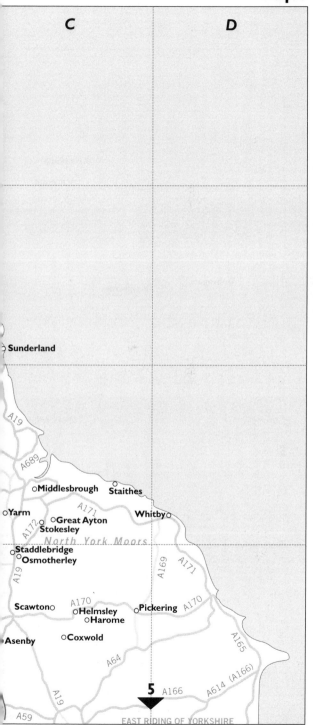

C

D

Sunderland

A19

A689

Middlesbrough Staithes

Yarm A171 Whitby
Great Ayton
A172 Stokesley
North York Moors
Staddlebridge A169 A171
Osmotherley
A19

Scawton A170 A165
Helmsley Pickering A170
Harome
Asenby Coxwold
A64

A19 5 A166 A614 (A166)
A59 EAST RIDING OF YORKSHIRE

Map 9

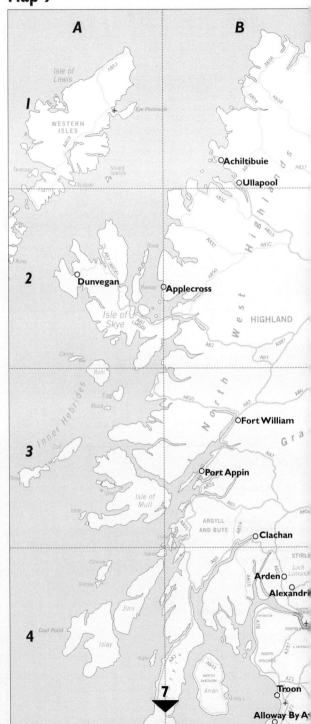

Map 9

Map 10

Map 10

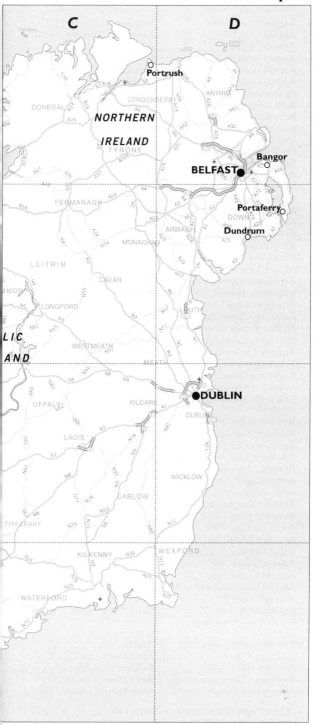

ALPHABETICAL INDEX

ALPHABETICAL INDEX

ALPHABETICAL INDEX

regular updates at www.hardens.com

ALPHABETICAL INDEX

ALPHABETICAL INDEX